The Executive Game

Richard C. Henshaw
Michigan State University

James R. Jackson
University of California at Los Angeles

Fifth Edition

IRWIN
Burr Ridge, Illinois
Boston, Massachusetts
Sydney, Australia

Sponsoring editor:	Craig Beytien/William R. Bayer
Project editor:	Jean Roberts
Production manager:	Bette K. Ittersagen
Cover photograph:	Courtesy of AT&T Archives
Production services:	Boardwork
Compositor:	Print Productions
Typeface:	11/13 Century Schoolbook
Printer:	Malloy Lithographing, Inc.

Library of Congress Cataloging-in-Publication Data

Henshaw, Richard C.
The executive game / Richard C. Henshaw, James R. Jackson. — 5th ed.
p. cm.
Includes bibliographical references.
ISBN 0-256-07360-0
1. Management games. I. Jackson, James R. (James Richard), 1924
II. Title.
HD30.26.H46 1990
658.4'0353—dc20

89–39022
CIP

Printed in the United States of America

8 9 0 ML 6

DEDICATED to all
who have contributed to
business gaming

TABLE OF CONTENTS

TABLES

CHARTS

FOREWORD

You are about to participate in an experience that has interested and educated more than 250,000 college students and business managers.

The Game is not real business. Profits and losses are not in real dollars. But it is a real business game, a lively personal experience in which you will be highly motivated and become deeply involved. You will enjoy the fruits of your good decisions and suffer from your bad ones as the results of the Game unfold in the form of business accounting reports, prepared by an impartial computer. These reports will enable you to compare your performance both with absolute standards of profitability and with the performance of your competitors.

The Game captures much of the excitement and many of the problems of top management. It enables you to take part in top management work and thus to learn by doing. It offers unique opportunities to learn from your fellow participants through both cooperative and competitive interactions, and to learn with your fellow participants about teamwork in a decision-making environment.

The possibility of investing in robotics is a major addition to the fifth edition of The Executive Game. Robotics utilization can increase production capacity, with improvements in quality, reduce costs, and make the Game even more exciting and interesting.

The Game is a superior means for preventing or correcting the parochial points of view often developed by business students, and even experienced middle managers, as a result of continuing specialized concern with one or another part of the total business problem. You will have to deal simultaneously with production, marketing, finance, competition, business cycles, inflation and so on. Practice at coping with these factors in the Game will help you understand and appreciate the need to consider the company as an integrated system even when making what may previously have seemed to be independent decisions about advertising, pricing, inventories, or whatever.

The Game emphasizes quantitative skills, but not to the exclusion of qualitative considerations. In fact, at the beginning of play you will have no choice but to depend largely on intuitive judgments grounded in your previous experience and your common sense. And throughout the Game it is important to be able to second-guess your competitors, to camouflage your own strategy, to respond decisively to the successful actions of other firms, and to take advantage of their errors. It is safe to say that those Executive Game managements who *over*emphasize quantitative analysis, as opposed to non-analytic judgment, especially in the area of competition, will show poor profit performance.

In another direction, the Game is a lively exercise in teamwork. The authoritarian boss still exits in the business world, and is often successful; but most firms, and most subdivisions of firms, except perhaps at the lowest level of organization, function best as collaborative ventures. Cooperative activities among managers who are more or less peers in the organizational hierarchy are at least as important as actions coordinated by central authority. The Executive Game is an excellent framework for team efforts, which emphasize getting the best from everyone rather than putting the most capable individual (or the loudest individual) in charge. Your team, as you learn to collaborate effectively will become more capable than any one person.

The real winners in the Executive Game are those who learn most. These fortunate persons are not necessarily the managers of the most profitable firms: as in the business world, luck may be an important factor, along with ability, knowledge, skills, and hard work. Your success as a learner will depend most crucially on your readiness to take an active role in the learning process, not just putting in time and effort, but directing your efforts toward the lessons the Game has to offer. Happily, it seems that a focus on intrinsically valuable learning is in fact also the best basis for learning to make money in the Game, so that your natural immediate wish to come out on top is in pleasant harmony with your ultimate motive of acquiring practical knowledge about management and how to be a good manager.

The Game offers varied learning opportunities, going beyond facts and techniques. For instance, many students who play the Game in introductory courses are really in these courses because they want to understand the business side of things, even though their main educational interests are technical or cultural. The Game often helps to attract such students to business careers. Conversely, a few students tentatively headed toward the managerial world redirect their career efforts as a result of taking such courses. The Executive Game can't do the work of a career counselor, but it can help players toward realistic career planning.

The Game has also proved itself to be an outstanding means for stimulating thoughtful discussions of the real significance of two years of educational effort grounded on 10 to 30 years of managerial experience, in a capstone course for experienced managers in the Advanced Management MBA program at Michigan State University.

Between these extremes — shopping in the career market, and topping off an advanced education based on an already successful career — the educational potentialities of the Executive Game are almost endless. Some of the possibilities are explored briefly in Chapter 1, below.

Outline of the text. As well as looking further into the educational uses of the Executive Game, Chapter 1 offers a general description of the Game and how it is played. The major details of the Game are explained in Chapter 2, which emphasizes the decisions you'll have to make and the reports that tell you how your choices have worked out. Chapter 3, on planning, takes a longer view toward the management process in which you'll be involved. Chapter 4 fills in many small but important details, in the framework of a step-by-step procedure that will help you to make good decisions in the Game. These first four chapters are "must" reading for all players. But you should not expect to absorb them fully the first time through, or even before you start playing the Executive Game. Like real business, the Game is sometimes complicated, and you'll have to go back and refresh your knowledge of special issues as they come to the fore.

Chapter 5, concerned with the use of formal modeling, is more technical than Chapters 1 through 4. Careful study is required to get the most out of this chapter. But even a relatively quick reading will help toward profitable management in the Game as well as having educational value, partly by clarifying the qualitative as well as the quantitative nature of certain problems that can best be handled quantitatively.

Appendix A presents the mathematical model underlying the Executive Game. This material is included mainly for students taking special courses in which the Game is used primarily to illustrate computer modeling. Other suitably prepared players may find Appendix A to be of interest — although experience shows that it is not likely to be very helpful toward profit making, except perhaps for a few advanced specialists in management science or computer analysis.

Finally, Appendices B through E provide technical material supporting Appendix A, and Appendix F supplies convenient printed forms for use in playing the Executive Game.

The examples in this manual are based on actual decisions made by players at Michigan State University.

Acknowledgments

The Executive Game is the lineal descendent of the executives games developed at the University of California, Los Angeles (UCLA) by the second of the undersigned authors, with the assistance of Tibor Fabian, James L. McKenney, and Kendall R. Wright. Those games were by far the best known and most widely played of the pioneering efforts in their field. The present Executive Game has evolved over 23 years of use at several hundred institutions of higher learning and in scores of other settings. In addition to the persons just named, we are grateful to the hundreds of teachers and the many thousands of players who have contributed directly or indirectly to the refinement of the Game. Special thanks are due to those, too numerous to list, who have suggested specific improvements. We hope that this fifth edition fully reflects the help and encouragement that we have received.

Richard C. Henshaw
East Lansing, Michigan

James R. Jackson
Los Angeles, California

December 1989

INSTRUCTIONS FOR PLAYERS

1

Introduction

This chapter describes the Executive Game and how it is played, relates it to other management learning methods, and then looks at specific kinds of learning to be sought by playing the Game. The preliminary description of the Executive Game serves both as a takeoff point for the rest of this chapter and as a start toward the more detailed information given in later chapters.

Preliminary Description

The Executive Game is a simulated business environment in which participants can practice the art and science of planning and decision making at a top-management level. Two to four years of simulated experience can be compressed into as little as a day of intensive play. Or, with correspondingly greater educational effort and benefits, a whole college course is often built around the Executive Game.

The Game is a dynamic business case that develops a life of its own. Its progress is determined by the internal behavior and external interactions of several competing firms in a hypothetical industry. The firms are guided by small teams (or sometimes single players), within a framework created by a course instructor or other Game administrator and by a computerized economic model. The computer model is deterministic (except for certain economic forecasts), but the Game situation is nevertheless loaded with realistic uncertainty. This uncertainty stems partly from imperfect economic predictions and partly from the participants' incomplete knowledge of how the Game works, but most importantly from the unforeseeable, often surprising, and sometimes erratic actions of other firms.

Playing the Executive Game. In the Game, the managers of each firm make the following top-level decisions for the firm:

Selling PRICE of the firm's product
MARKETING budget
R&D (Research and Development) budget
Plant MAINTENANCE budget
Scheduled PRODUCTION VOLUME
PLANT AND EQUIPMENT INVESTMENT budget
ROBOTICS INVESTMENT budget
Raw MATERIALS PURCHASE budget
DIVIDEND to be issued to stockholders

Decisions are made at simulated quarter-year intervals, and apply to one quarter of operations. The simulation normally implements decisions exactly as entered, with rare exceptions if a proposed decision is grossly impractical or impossible to implement. For instance, actual PRODUCTION VOLUME is limited at any time by plant size and by the quantity of raw materials available for processing. Additional details will be spelled out later.

The players' decisions are fed into the computerized model. This model simulates the internal operations of the firms, their interactions with one another, and the ways they are affected by the economy as a whole. The computer prepares several reports for players: profit and loss statements; balance sheets; reports covering cash flow, sales volume, inventories, economic forecasts, limited information about competitors, and various other items that are likely to be useful. A set of reports is normally given to each firm's management each quarter, as a basis for management decisions concerning the next quarter's operations. Annual summary reports are also normally provided, giving more information about competitors than is included in the quarterly reports. (Variations in your Game from these or other "normal" practices, if any, will be explained by your Game administrator.)

The Industry. Once player decisions have been entered, the computer program simulates the workings of a hypothetical consumer goods industry. The results of decisions are determined by applying a set of reasonable economic hypotheses and accounting assumptions. But, as a matter of intentional design, these hypotheses and assumptions do not reflect the details of any specific real-life industry. Like a real manager, the Game manager has to learn how the industry works by observation and analysis of the results of experience.

A good deal of information in available in advance, though. Such information is in fact the main subject of this manual. To get started with this subject matter, the industry portrayed in the Game manufactures and sells a complex technical consumer product which is in demand at all times but is especially salable in the Christmas season. Some players find it helpful to think of the product more specifically as a space-age "solid-state" item that has come into being along with microcomputers, video games and juke boxes, multifunction digital watches, cellular telephones, and the like. But you should be careful not to assume that particular facts about any particular industry can be applied in the Game — or learned from the Game.

To illustrate the general nature of the Game simulation, consider how consumer demand is determined. Subject to influence by general economic conditions, inflation, and seasonal demand cycles, the main determinants of total demand for the Game industry's products (market potential) are industry-wide PRICE patterns, MARKETING expenditures, and R&D (research & development) efforts aimed mainly at product improvement and secondarily at cost reduction. The *share* (percentage) of industry-wide demand attracted by an individual firm depends mainly on the relationship of its own PRICE, MARKETING, and R&D to the industry-wide picture. As is typical in consumer industries, customer reactions to PRICE changes are quick, MARKETING expenditures pay off at once, but have some residual impact over several quarters, and R&D has delayed but longer lasting effects. Moreover, these factors interact significantly, as in real life. Consequently, it may make sense to combine increases in MARKETING and R&D with a decrease in PRICE — thus using all means, simultaneously and in concert, to stimulate increased market potential. Alternatively, it may be appropriate to make tradeoffs among these factors, for instance increasing MARKETING while decreasing R&D, to achieve a more efficient balance between these budgets. A lot of specific information, with a variety of quantitative details, is given in Chapters 2, 3, and 4.

In another direction, although many major costs are directly controlled or implicitly determined by budget decisions, others are only indirectly influenced. For instance, the labor cost of production is directly affected by the degree to which scheduled PRODUCTION VOLUME requires the use of overtime (or the use of multiple shift operations in versions of the Game that permit more that one shift; see Chapter 2). But cost per unit is also influenced by plant MAINTENANCE expenditures, whose main effect is to keep the factory running smoothly. As another example, although the central focus of R&D is on product improvement, the development engineers will also come up with cost-cutting ideas, and, may decide that robotics investment is an excellent idea. And as still more examples, the need for warehousing, insurance, etc., create unbudgeted expenditures connected with inventories; a poor cash position implies possibly large and conceivably overwhelming finance expenses; and so forth. The details of these matters, and many others, are left to later chapters.

It is very important to realize that the character of the Executive Game industry, especially as seen from within any one firm, is largely determined by how the other firms behave. Different runs of the Game vary widely, just as tennis matches and football games differ — even though the rules, and sometimes even the players, remain the same. One Game may, for instance, be characterized by intense price competition, resulting from industry-wide attempts to make large profits through large-volume operations. Another Game may be dominated by large price policies. And in yet another Game, some firms may follow strategies aimed at massive sales volume while other firms use fat markups in order to make large profits per unit sold. Although such variations are important, later chapters will have little to say about alternative styles of competition — mainly because the pertinent theory is not really adequate as a practical tool. The Game in fact created perplexities of competition similar to those encountered in the real business world, and which are similarly resistant to theoretical formulation and analysis.

This illustrates the Game's ability to demonstrate problems that are hard to deal with by theoretical means. And this feature of the Game makes it more than a little bit unpredictable even to experienced players and Game administrators (including the authors!). Because of this, guaranteed "right answers" are simply not available, just as in real life. The uniqueness of each Game run forces its players to *learn from experience* about how their particular industry really works. Thus, the Game requires its players to pay attention to what is actually happening and to make inferences about what these events signify. You can't get away with examining the Game in terms of any preconceived conceptual apparatus or problem solving technique.

Management's Job. In taking a first look at the Executive Game it is satisfactory to focus on profit as the goal, although a closely related but more suitable objective, ownership's "return on investment" (ROI) will be introduced later. This doesn't mean that financial gain is or should be the *sole* target in the modern business world — although it is plain that some profit *is* necessary for any firm's long-run survival. In real life, though, it may often be appropriate to convert opportunities for profit, beyond what is needed for secure survival and reasonable returns to investors, into nonprofit values such as "consumer welfare" or "corporate good citizenship." But even then, it is still reasonable for the firm to think of maximizing *potential* profitability or ROI, with the idea that some of this potential may be diverted to ends other than purely economic gain. But, since the Executive Game situation does not model any such non-profit possibilities, purely economic gain is an appropriate goal in the Game.

Management pursues profits through the use of its firm's resources and opportunities. It is obvious in theory that the ideal would be to make optimal decisions — those that would yield the very largest gains possible. But the situation is so complicated that there is no practical way to jointly optimize the total configuration of interacting decisions that management must make — even for a single quarter, much less over the entire duration of the Game. And the question of optimality becomes almost meaningless when the Game's high levels of uncertainty are brought into the picture.

In any case, whether in the Executive Game or in real life, management's *first* concern is with *consistency* among decisions, and with avoiding outright mistakes. When these concerns are satisfied, it is soon enough to focus on fine tuning the system in order to approximate the best possible results.

"Consistency" is a matter of attaining suitable relationships among related decisions and appropriate coordination in their timing. For instance, in the short run it is usually important to adjust PRICE and MARKETING, so as to make market demand agree at least roughly with the firm's ability to supply goods for sale. A first step in adjusting the relationships among different activities is to seek reasonably efficient allocations among different budgets that have interactions with one another — keeping in mind the need to coordinate the timing of changes in such budgets, which is made tricky by the differences in their built-in time-delay characteristics (for instance, the quick effects of marketing expenditures versus relatively slow effects of research and development).

When the various relatively short-range adjustments have been satisfactorily dealt with, then it is necessary to focus on the longer-range problem of seeking the best overall level of operations. But this effort, especially when it involves substantial expansion, must be timed so that the cost of expansion will not outrun the availability of cash, and to avoid the excessive side costs resulting from overly rapid increases in plant size.

These remarks correctly suggest that *planning* is a central function of management. At first glance, planning in a highly uncertain environment may seem fruitless. You may well wonder what planning is worth when it's often necessary to revise plans every quarter. The fact is that even if plans reaching beyond a quarter or two rarely get implemented in detail, they do provide the best practical assurances of short-run consistency and the most effective safeguards against outright blunders. That would be justification enough for planning. But equally important, a firm's "pointing" at a given plan is similar to a duck hunter's tracking a bird in flight: it's probably the best way to maintain a good direction, even though a continually changing one. Thus, while Chapter 2 stresses the immediate details of the Executive Game, Chapter 3 is devoted to planning in the Game. Chapter 4 provides a systematic procedure for deciding on how immediate decisions and longer-range plans are to be implemented.

Although overall optimization is impractical, there is often a lot to gain from optimal solutions to certain subproblems of management's total problem, both in the Game and in the business world. An important example is the problem of striking a balance between the advantages of small inventories (low costs of storage, insurance, obsolescence, etc.), and the desirability of stocks large enough to minimize the risk of losing sales for lack of goods to sell. This and other opportunities to apply modeling and quantitative analysis are treated in Chapter 5.

The Executive Game Compared with Other Learning Tools

Here are some of the most widely used means for acquiring knowledge and skills aimed at increased managerial capability:

Reading, lectures, drill exercises
Relatively open-ended textbook "word problems"
Analysis of management "cases"
The Executive Game (and similar exercises)
Field research projects
Internships, supervised consulting, and the like
Real-life career experience

This list is arranged so that, as you go from top to bottom, the situations require increasingly independent learner participation, permit less and less reliance on officially "correct" methods or answers, and demand more and more readiness to live with the enduring consequences of past actions. The transition also proceeds from preprogrammed or closely controlled situations, toward situations which more and more have lives of their own — which develop of themselves rather than following prespecified patterns.

We thus place the Executive Game near the midpoint of a continuum extending from the tidily packaged subject matter of a classical textbook, at one extreme, to the turbulent confusion of real life, at the other. This placement correctly suggests that the Executive Game can improve on the textbook as a way of giving lively meaning to complex ideas or as a way to exhibit messy phenomena that are difficult or impossible to intellectualize and analyze satisfactorily. Also, it is a good framework for sharpening skills through realistic practice. Looking in the other direction, compared to real life experience the Game offers a comparatively low-risk environment for the learner, in which high-level responsibilities can be assigned to relatively inexperienced players, where mistakes are not penalized so severely as to prohibit experimentation, and where you can afford to concentrate on learning as such even, at the possible expense of "results."

This does not imply that the Game is a "universal management educator." Quite the contrary: it builds on more traditional academic learning experiences, and its main purpose is to lead toward more "realistic" educational approaches, and ultimately to the actual practice of management. We believe that the Executive Game's wide acceptance, by teachers and students of management alike, demonstrates that it fills important needs in helping students of management to progress from the lecture hall to the executive suite.

The Real Goals in the Executive Game

Although profit (or, more precisely, rate of return on investment) is the "rules of the game" goal within the Executive Game, the player's real objective is of course *learning*. And the real winners are those who learn the most. Because the Game has so much dynamic life, beyond what is built into the computer program, we can't even attempt to describe all the possible learning that it might facilitate. In fact, the total spectrum of learning opportunities is created by Game administrators and by the players themselves, not just by what is built into the computer program. We shall, however, sketch some specific kinds of learning for which the Game has been useful in our experience.

Many of these learning fall into two roughly parallel categories. On the one hand, the Game can help you to become more aware of important aspects of the business world, more familiar with the phenomena of business operations, and better able to understand business situations and how they work. We have more in mind than mere intellectual awareness, familiarity, and understanding — which can generally be conveyed through lectures and reading. The Game in designed to communicate knowledge in such a way that it will work its way down to the learner's "gut level" — where it can become a part of the learner's internalized worldview, and thus be far more pervasive and consequential than the mere ability to recite factual data and theoretical doctrine.

On the other hand, the Executive Game is a valuable "practice ground" on which to develop and exercise useful skills for dealing with important aspects of business systems. Again, the idea is not merely to acquire formal knowledge of specified procedures, but to get practical experience in deciding what approaches should be used and when, and then actually putting them into use.

Table 1

Types of Learning which Can Be Sought through Playing the Executive Game

Awareness, Familiarity, Understanding	*Knowledge and Practice of Skills*
Typical characteristics and uses of the business accounting system, both as a "scorekeeper" indicating how well a firm is doing, and as a basis for management's striving toward improved performance.	Reading and interpreting accounting reports correctly and perceptively, and using the information they provide as a basis for effective management decision making.
Typical basic business functions and their characteristics and interactions.	Estimating the key interactions within the firm of decisions about functional components.
The integrated wholeness of the firm, and the corresponding need for mutual consistency among decisions concerning the various business functions.	Arriving at and pretesting mutually consistent configurations of decisions concerning the functional components of the firm.
Typical characteristics of the competitive environment, and their importance for the effective management of the firm.	Anticipating, evaluating, and coping with competitive factors in the business environment.
Critical economic variables, such as business cycles and inflation.	Anticipating, evaluating, and coping with economic change.
The need for planning as a basis for consistency and for avoiding outright mistakes.	Using planning effectively as the foundation of the entire management decision-making process.
The value of analytic techniques for refining management decisions.	Selection and use of appropriate analytic techniques.
The fundamental need to learn from experience in the business environment.	Learning how to discover and make good use of the lessons offered by experience.

Table 1 gives two parallel lists which briefly sketch types of learning in the two categories described above. You will notice that the lists proceed from the concrete and specific (for instance, accounting practice) to relatively abstract and general ideas (such as the use, in general, of analytic techniques). The last line in each column points to what may be the most important thing that the Executive Game can help you learn to do more effectively — to continue to learn from experience. We'll return to that after a digression on the varied purposes of different Game runs.

Varied Purposes. The sorts of learning that are stressed vary, of course, from one run of the Executive Game to another. The Game is perhaps most widely used as an introduction to business, for students with relatively little pertinent academic knowledge or practical experience. It may then be best, at least in the beginning, to minimize emphasis on last pairs of items in Table 1, so as to concentrate on developing a "map" of what business is about and how it works. Developing such a map may be the main goal of some students who are primarily interested in understanding the business world as a major component of the world in which they are going to live, even those that don't intend to follow business careers. Students who enter the Game with cultural rather than professional goals may, of course, find themselves intrigued, and redirect their career interests. Those who do continue their business studies, whether or not they have originally intended to do so, will find that the map provided by the Game makes it far easier to comprehend such subject matters as accounting, marketing, production, and finance, not only in and of themselves, but also as intertwined components of the overall study of the business firm and the profession of management.

Many Game players, typified by business majors nearing graduation, have a good deal of academic knowledge of business but relatively little practical experience in the business world. Because of the fragmented nature of many business curricula, such students can often benefit greatly from the way the Game puts together the bits and pieces that they have previously studied in separate courses. But an even greater potential value of the Game for such students may be as an arena where ideas and techniques learned elsewhere can be brought to life and put to work. The Game thus serves as a bridge from academia toward the practical world.

Finally, among the almost infinite variety of player populations that could be mentioned, we point to groups of high-level managers — many of whom have played and enjoyed the Executive Game, and have valued its contributions to their own development. For such players, the Game is often most useful as a means for breaking away from the special problems that trouble them on any particular day, thus revitalizing their sense of the wholeness of the business enterprise. To cover this special situation, we might add another pair of items to Table 1:

Awareness, familiarity, understanding: the need to step back frequently from current crises in order to attend to larger issues.	Knowledge, practice of skills: the art of recognizing and responding to needs to step back from current crises and attend to larger issues.

Other player populations will of course suggest still further learning possibilities.

Learning to Learn from Experience. We close this chapter with comments on learning from experience, and on the Executive Game as a means for sharpening skills at learning from experience. This is an important objective. As professors, the authors of the Game of course place great store in book learning. But we clearly recognize that management is a lively art as well as an applied science. Even the most developed science still requires practical experience as a basis for effective practical application. But to the extent that management remains an art, competent management practice is even more importantly based on "learning by doing," that is, upon learning from the lessons of experience. Thus, it is no exaggeration to say that the most useful learning a student can hope to attain (from whatever source, not just the Game) is most likely to be skill at discovering and benefitting from the lessons offered by experience.

Notice that a person doesn't learn much (if anything) by simply "having experience." Otherwise the old would all be wise! To learn from experience you must make yourself aware of opportunities to learn, and you must pay attention to these opportunities, reflecting on what has happened and teasing out whatever lessons you can find. This may be more a matter of habits than of skills. But the need for an effective player in the Executive Game to learn from experience during play makes the Game a natural vehicle for developing the habit of paying attention to potentially meaningful experiences and looking for their useful implications.

We are sure that *learning to learn from experience* is a highly personal process for which no universal formula can be given. But, as a starting point, and as a means for actively attempting to build good habits, we suggest the following procedure, to be gone through whenever something striking occurs — an unpleasant surprise, or a pleasant one, or maybe just an "interesting event":

1. Describe the situation. What happened?

2. Focus on your own part in the situation. What did you do? With what effect?

3. Focus on your own thoughts, not just factual and logical, but also intuitive or emotional:
   a. What did you *think* about the situation? What do you think now?
   b. How did you *feel* about it? How do you feel now?
4. Focus on your options in the situation. What might you have done differently (better or worse)? With what possible effect?
5. Generalize. Find at least one theoretical construct, or another experience (not necessarily your own), to which you can relate the situation at hand. Compare the current experience with its counterparts in theory or previous experience, focusing on similarities and differences.
6. Try to identify, as specifically as possible, what is to be learned from all this. And try to think out, as broadly as possible, how this "lesson" might be useful to you in the future.

This sequence of steps (which we have adapted from the ides of W. E. Torbert) can be viewed as a way of directing your thoughts systematically toward learning as such, in order to improve upon the often hopelessly unstructured process of "thinking over" things that have happened. The sequence also provides an often-useful framework for discussion by a management team of what has happened in the Executive Game, how it happened, and what the team can learn from its experience.

The inclusion in Step 3, above, of the intuitive and emotional, along with the factual and logical, helps toward picking out lessons which have to do with personal values and needs, or which go beyond your ability to think things out completely fully — and these are the very lessons that are probably to be learned *only* from experience.

Among the most valuable such lessons within the Game situation are those concerning effective teamwork among the members of your management group. As an example, you are likely to be annoyed sometimes because your Game teammates don't seem to listen carefully enough, and therefore don't really understand *why* you hold some particular belief. The above procedure would then be likely to turn your thoughts toward related situations where *others* were irritated by *your* not really giving *their* ideas a hearing. Looking at your current annoyance in light of its "mirror image" might then give you valuable personal insights into how you interact with others — and help you to understand, more clearly than any number of lectures on communication or human relations, how to be a better listener as well as a better team player, mentor, and salesperson.

The important thing, of course, is not merely to learn from experience in the Game, but to go forth from the Game with habits and skills that will make effective learning from experience a regular part of your future life — in the business world and elsewhere.

Supplementary Reading

Barnard, Chester I. *The Functions of the Executive.* Boston: Harvard University Press, 1940.

Beebe, Steven A. and John T. Masterson. *Communicating in Small Groups: Principles and Practice.* Glenview, Illinois: Scott-Foresman, 1982.

Bone, Jan. *Opportunities in Robotics Careers.* Lincolnwood, Ill.: Career Horizons, 1987.

Carlson, John G. and Michael J. Misshank, *Introduction to Gaming: Management Decision Simulations.* New York: Wiley, 1972.

Gouran, Dennis S. *Making Decisions in Groups.* Glenview, Illinois: Scott, Foresman and Company, 1982.

Hall, Jay, "Decisions Decisions Decisions," *Psychology Today,* November, 1971.

Henshaw, Richard C. "What's Wrong with the Introduction to Business Course?", *Computing News-letter for Schools of Business,* March, 1970, pp. 1-3.

Jackson, James R. "Learning to Learn from Experience in the Executive Game," *California Management Review, 1,* Winter, 1959, pp. 92-107.

Kolb, David A. "Management and the Learning Process," *California Management Review, 18,* Spring, 1976.

Shubik, Martin. *Games for Society, Business and War: Towards a Theory of Gaming.* New York: Elsevier, 1975.

Simon, Herbert A. *Administrative Behavior, 3rd edition,* New York: Free Press, 1976.

Torbert, W. R., *Learning from Experience: Toward Consciousness.* New York and London: Columbia University Press, 1972.

2

Playing the Executive Game: Basics

This chapter spells out many of the details omitted from the preliminary description of the Executive Game in Chapter 1. For the sake of clarity there will be some repetition here, and again in Chapter 3, on planning, and in Chapter 4 where further specifics are given about how to calculate costs and other numerical quantities and about special rules governing particular circumstances in the Game.

Management's job in the Executive Game is to use its company's resources (cash, plant, workforce, inventories, etc.), to maximize ownership's rate of return on investment (ROI). This idea will be covered thoroughly in the section of this chapter on Performance Criteria. In the meantime, you won't get off the track if you continue to think of profit maximization as the goal.

Each management operates its company by making the following quarterly decisions:

Selling PRICE of the firm's product
MARKETING budget
R&D (research and development budget)
Plant MAINTENANCE budget
Scheduled PRODUCTION VOLUME
PLANT AND EQUIPMENT INVESTMENT budget
ROBOTICS INVESTMENT budget
Raw MATERIALS PURCHASE budget
DIVIDEND for distribution to stockholders

Appendix F includes the form on which decisions are filled in, and Table 2 (page 38) shows how a decision sheet looks after eight quarters of play.

Your Game administrator (for instance, the instructor of the course) will explain various procedures, including the schedule of play, exactly how you are to get your decisions into the computer model, and what sort of "post mortem" will be held to review managerial and company performance in the Game.

As in the real business world, an essential ingredient of successful management of an Executive Game firm is balance and coordination among the various decisions. Efforts to increase sales must properly relate to the quantity of goods available for sale and to production capacity, for instance. Investment programs and dividend policies have to be geared to both profits and cash flow. And so forth. All of the numerous factors must be juggled on a stage marked by continual changes in competitive forces and economic conditions.

This chapter focuses on short-run considerations. But the need for planning, as well as quarter-by-quarter balance and coordination, is emphasized by the fact that evenly paced and smoothly programmed change generally pays off better than erratic fluctuations. For example, consider two firms that behave similarly, except the first holds PRICE constant (in "real dollars," adjusted for inflation), while the second firm's PRICE jumps up and down, above and below the first firm's price, while maintaining the same average level. Although the average PRICE asked by the two firms is the same, the first firm will be able to sell considerably more units, because customers' negative reactions to an increase in price are stronger than their positive reactions to a decrease. To make matters worse for the second firm, a disproportionate fraction of its sales will occur at its lower prices, so that this firm's average sales revenue (and hence its profits) will suffer even more than its average market potential. This example shows why the "basics" covered in this chapter need to be connected together by means of the unifying concept of "planning," presented in Chapter 3, before you can have a really satisfactory picture of how the Executive Game should be played.

Outline of the Present Chapter. We first direct your attention to sample reports that will help you to get a clearer idea of just what goes on in the Executive Game before reading about it more extensively. We then turn to brief comments on different versions of the Executive Game (Models 1 and 2). Next, inflation and deflation are discussed. The ensuing sections explain the Executive Game marketplace, and internal operations and cost generation in Executive Game firms. Then there is a section about the ROI performance criterion, followed by a brief section on management under conditions of risk and uncertainty. Next comes detailed information on the reports that will be provided for your use:

General Economic Information (indices and forecasts)
Information on Competitors (prices, dividends, sales, profits)
Operating Statements (your firm's market potential, sales, production volume, carryover inventory, and production capacity)
Income Statement (cash receipts, expenses, profits before and after income tax, and addition to owners' equity)
Cash Flow Statement (cash receipts, disbursements, and net cash flow)
Financial Statement (assets and owners' equity)
End-of-Fiscal-Year Report (annual information on the assets and operations of all firms)

The chapter closes with some remarks about working together in the Game with your management team, and, finally, a few words to remind you (again) that what seems at first like overwhelming complexity in the Executive Game will be quickly clarified as you get started actually playing.

Game Reports

Before going further, you should examine samples of the reports listed above, and start to become familiar with their organization and content. All of them except the End of Year Fiscal Report are ordinarily provided quarterly, and they are compactly put together on a single page (your Game administrator may make exceptions to these general rules, and if so will explain them to you). Table 2 (page 38) illustrates the form on which decisions will be filled in. Table 4 (page 40) shows the first of many sample quarterly reports. Table 29 (page 65) illustrates the End of Fiscal Year Report.

Table 3 is a particularly important quarterly report. It shows where Executive Games start from, including yours. Ignore the number of firms shown by this table. A report just like it, but with the actual number of firms in your Game, is the Period 0 report for your Game. Table 3 ordinarily serves as the Period 0 report for all firms are in the same situation at the beginning.

Table 4 is special, because rather than illustrating the "real" play of the Game it gives the results of a "trial decision" made to familiarize players with the Game before actual play begins. Such a trial run makes it possible to get a feel for what has to be done in the Game and how to go about doing it. You can be "comfortable" during a trial run, not having to worry about mistakes, since you will throw the practice results away and start over in a "real" (rather than "trial") Period 1. Your Game administrator may choose to eliminate the trial period, or to let you practice for two or even more periods before starting to manage your firm for real.

Tables 5 through 28 follow all six teams through the first year of a particular "Industry 5." Table 29 is the End of Fiscal Year report for this same industry after one year of play. Tables 30 through 32 follow firm 5-4 (Industry 5, Firm 4) through the first three quarters of the second year; and Tables 33 through 38 pick up all six firms for the last quarter of the second year. Table 39 is the second (and final) End of Fiscal Year report for this industry. Finally, Table 40 is a worksheet showing how Firm 5-4 analyzed its problems and made its decisions. (A blank worksheet is supplied for your use, in Appendix F.)

These extensive exhibits are provided to enrich your opportunity for general familiarization with the Game, and also to give you a chance to learn more about the Game by examining past results. You may possibly even want to carry out formal statistical analyses, such as a multiple regression study to estimate the elasticity of the Executive Game market with respect to PRICE, MARKETING, R&D, and ROBOTICS — not yet, of course, but later, when you are more familiar with the Game and its problems.

Models 1 and 2

The Executive Game administrator will choose between two versions of the Game, called Model 1 and Model 2. When Model 1 is used, the manufacturing plant is limited to one-shift operations. Model 2 differs from Model 1 mainly in allowing firms to use up to three shifts. This complicates play in several ways, increasing the need for analysis and the chances of making mistakes. But it also increases the opportunities to earn handsome profits.

The first entry on the quarterly report will tell you whether Model 1 or Model 2 is in use. You can also expect the Game administrator to give you this information, and to notify you ahead of time if the Model is going to be changed. (Many runs start with Model 1 and then switch to Model 2 after about a year of play. By that time players are familiar enough with the elements of the Game to handle Model 2's added complications without difficulty.)

The Game administrator may also introduce special changes in the Game, tailored to fit particular teaching needs or individual preferences. For instance, the carrying costs on raw materials or finished goods inventories may be changed. You can expect, of course, to be told about such modifications, and to be given whatever detailed information is appropriate in view of the teaching objectives concerned.

The discussion that follows applies to the standard version of the Game. Everything said is equally valid for both Model 1 and Model 2, except as amended by a few comments concerned only with Model 2. Such comments are clearly labelled and separated from the mainstream of the text so that players concerned only with Model 1 can easily skip past them.

Inflation and Deflation

Inflation consists of a rise in the general level of prices, and deflation is a decrease. The causes of price-level changes are complex, but rises are usually related to increases in the size of the supply of money, relative to the supply of goods and services available for purchase. Government deficits (expenses larger than tax receipts) are one of the major causes of an increased supply of money, especially in periods when lots of money is distributed through channels that do not create commensurate quantities of consumer goods and services. Government can also, in effect, put more money into circulation by influencing interest rates. Financial institutions such as banks and other major sources of credit also have important roles. When the money supply increases the situation is somewhat like that when the supply of a commodity is enlarged: the "price of money," as measured in goods and services, tends to go down; which is another way of saying that the price of goods and services goes up, as measured in money. In a word, there is inflation.

As this chapter is being written, there have been several years of modest inflation in the United States, and even more severe inflation through most of the world. How long lower inflation rates will continue is widely argued; in fact both political leaders and economic experts are divided as to why 1980 inflation became so extreme, as to what public and private policies should be followed under present circumstances, and as to what levels of inflation are to be expected in the next few years (let alone the relatively long-run future). In any case, most well-informed people believe that continuing pressures to increase the money supply make it almost certain that inflation will remain as the general rule within the foreseeable future — that the question is not "whether" but "how much."

This is why we have built a significant inflationary trend into the Executive Game. This trend does not reflect any specific historic interval. It should by no means be interpreted as the authors' prediction of the real-world future. Nor are the detailed effects of inflation in the Game based on any specific industry. But, as with other economic aspects of the Game, the particulars are realistic, both quantitatively and qualitatively. Thus, the Game will give you an opportunity to face challenges like those stemming from inflation in the business world, and to manage the resolution of the resulting problems. As usual, you must *not* try to transfer highly specific lessons from the Executive Game environment to the business situations in which you find yourself later.

It may help you in the Game to learn something about the history of inflation and deflation, and their interactions with prosperity and recession, changing levels of employment, international pricing, the balance of trade, etc. Not all of this knowledge will be directly applicable in the Game, but a general awareness of the varied phenomena connected with the fluctuating value of money will help you to think of inflation and deflation as a lively process in the economic world rather than as an abstract intrusion into the Game situation. In particular, some knowledge of past economic events involving inflation and deflation may help you to anticipate and plan for changes in the tax structure. The tax structure is controlled by the Game administrator, who will in this context play a sort of Governmental role, determining whether your firm can take investment tax credits or use accelerated depreciation, and whether your taxes will be increased or decreased by a positive or negative surtax. The material on Income Tax in the section of this chapter on Reports in the Executive Game explains these options in detail. The Game administrator will of course give you realistic information when tax changes are made — the sort of information that actual taxpayers get from their actual government. Incidentally, you cannot ignore the realistic possibility that you may not always be given advance knowledge of tax changes, constitutional provisions forbidding *ex post facto* laws to the contrary notwithstanding.

Also, you will learn more from the Game if, rather than seeing inflation and deflation as annoying complications, you view the changeable value of money as just another important fact about the simulated economic world in which you are leading a simulated life as an Executive Game manager — a fact that parallels the realities of the business world. Your firm may even be able to take advantage of inflation, rather than just suffering from it. For instance, you may be able to gain, in both absolute terms and competitive comparisons, if you can see how inflation is affecting or will affect the other firms in your industry, so that you can take advantage of their difficulties. Of course the other firms will be trying to do the same thing to you!

Specific effects of inflation, as they relate to costs and revenues in the Executive Game, are discussed at appropriate points below.

The Market

Total industry market potential is affected by the overall level of economic activity (measured by the economic index), seasonal fluctuations (seasonal index), and the general price level (price index), as well as by the industry-wide constellation of decisions concerning PRICE, MARKETING, and R&D. Each firm's potential share of the total market is determined mainly by the relationship of its PRICE, MARKETING, R&D and ROBOTICS policies to those of its competitors. A firm's share of actual sales is further limited by its ability to supply goods to fill customer orders. In this section we'll look at some of these matters in more detail.

Economic Factors. A percentage change in the economic index is accompanied by a somewhat larger percentage change in the market potential for the products of the Executive Game industry, other things remaining unchanged. Specifically, each one percent increase in the economic index results in about a 1.4 percent increase in industry market potential. That's the good news. The bad news is that much the same thing works in the opposite direction: if the economic index drops one percent, then the industry's market shrinks by somewhat more — about 1.4 percent.

The seasonal index is calculated especially for the industry in which you are involved, and the industry's market potential is directly proportional to this index. For instance, when the seasonal index falls from 100 to 95, then (if other things remain unchanged) sales will drop by about five percent. The standard values of this index are printed at the bottom of the Decision Sheet (Table 2). You will note that the year-round average is 100, and that there is a sharp peak in October-November-December, followed by a deep valley in January-February-March. It is important in the Game to supply this fluctuating market in a cost-efficient way.

Pricing, Marketing, Research and Development, and Robotics. The material in Chapter 3 on Short-range Forecasts of Market Potential includes quantitative information on the sensitivity of an individual firm's potential sales to changes in its decisions and those of its competitors, but this information is accurate only for the initial situation in the Game. Price sensitivity tends to increase with inflation, but to decrease when the industry as a whole increases its research and development, robotics and marketing activity. There are other complicated (and poorly understood) relationships stemming from the possibility of market differentiation through vigorous R&D, ROBOTICS, and to a lesser extent through MARKETING. For instance, as a product becomes more differentiated, its manufacturer sometimes seems to acquire a measure of "administrative power" — which is to say that prices can to some extent be "administered" in accordance with profit objectives, paying less attention to price competition (but not too much less attention: price always remains an important determinant of a firm's share of the industry's total potential sales).

There is a rule in the Game (think of it as a law intended to assure "fair competition") that a firm's PRICE cannot go below its adjusted standard cost ($12 per unit, adjusted for inflation). Also, the maximum permitted price is $36 per unit, adjusted for inflation. The computer program will in fact correct any decisions that violate these limitations. Both of these rules actually protect Executive Game managers from making what would always be poor decisions.

MARKETING budgets are spent mainly for direct selling expenses (advertising, sales commissions, and the like). The effects of these expenditures are intense during the quarter when they are budgeted, and they also have lingering but rapidly decreasing effects in following quarters. Other things being unchanged, to maintain a given level of marketing effectiveness it is necessary to increase MARKETING budgets in proportion to the general price index.

Research and Development (R&D) in the Executive Game is not really concerned with path-breaking fundamental research, but is the function that many firms call "product development" or "product engineering." It is aimed mainly at improving and differentiating the firm's product, and it can also have a significant effect on manufacturing costs. It should not surprise you that R&D expenditures have no *immediate* payoff; however, their effects accumulate and persist over a substantial period of time. In fact, although R&D is considered an expense for accounting purposes (because this is permitted by the tax laws and advantageous for tax purposes), from a managerial point of view the R&D budget might well be considered as a short-run investment, amortized over about two years. *Note well that this point of view will be emphasized when firms are evaluated at the end of the Game. A firm may be penalized, possibly severely, if its longer-run R&D needs have been slighted during the last quarters of play, in order to stress expenditures with more immediate profit payoffs.*

As with MARKETING, the cost of a given level of R&D effectiveness increases in proportion to the price index.

Robotics investment is an important possibility in the Executive Game. The traditional definition of a robot was that it is automation; a mechanical manufactured person that performs all hard work; hence, one who works mechanically and heartlessly. From a creation by Karel Capek, Bohemian playwright, in his *Rossom's Universal Robots* (R.U.R.) in 1921. (Czech. **robots,** work)[1]

Robotics represents an important revolution in the concept of robots in the sense that robotics employ computer-controlled robots to perform tasks. The word 'robotics' was coined by Issac Asimov.

Robots have become increasingly important with the developments of electronics and robotics are as electronic as they are mechanical. Robotics can greatly increase productivity but there have been many disappointments as well as some spectacular successes. In the Executive Game, investments in robotics can increase plant capacity, reduce manufacturing costs, and improve quality. On the other hand, irresponsible investments can cause cash deficits and financing charges and penalties. So extraordinary caution must be exercised with R&D budgets and investments in robotics. For further information see Chapter 5: Research and Development, Investments in Plant and Equipment, and in Robotics, p. 133.

---

[1] From Britannica World Language Edition of Funk & Wagnalls *New Practical Standards Dictionary*, 1955.

Stockouts and Customer Reorders. Sometimes the Game industry as a whole generates more market demand than it can supply. More often, one or two firms will underestimate the effectiveness of their sales efforts and sell out their stocks of goods before all their potential customers have been supplied.

If a firm undersupplies its market, then competing firms may capture some of the sales it thus loses. Some of the customers not supplied by a firm in one quarter return the next quarter to the same firm. But, on the whole, at most, 40 percent of the sales initially lost will be made up in following quarters — and only if enough goods are available then. Also, customers who turn to other suppliers may permanently shift their "brand loyalty," which adds the possible loss of future sales to the immediate loss of sales, and hence profits, suffered by a firm that undersupplies the market. These possibilities are illustrated qualitatively by Chart 1.

Chart 1
Graphic representation of how market potentials are determined in the Executive Game.

A. The size of the "pie" representing industry market potential in any quarter is determined by the industry-wide pattern of prices, marketing effectiveness and research and development effectiveness along with the economic index and the seasonal index. The pie is divided up among individual firms in proportion to their market strengths, which are determined by how individual policies relate to those of the industry as a whole.

B. Suppose Firms 1 and 3 can satisfy all their potential customers, but Firm 2 falls short. Then Firm 2's piece of pie is reduced, as indicated by the shaded area.

C. Parts of the potential sales lost by Firm 2 are acquired by Firms 1 and 3, in proportions determined by their relative market strengths. Part of the lost sales return to Firm 2 in the following quarter. And the rest are simply lost to the industry (the potential customers spend their money on products of other industries).

The third diagram also shows an increment to Firm 3's sales resulting from this firm's hypothesized stockout during the preceding quarter.

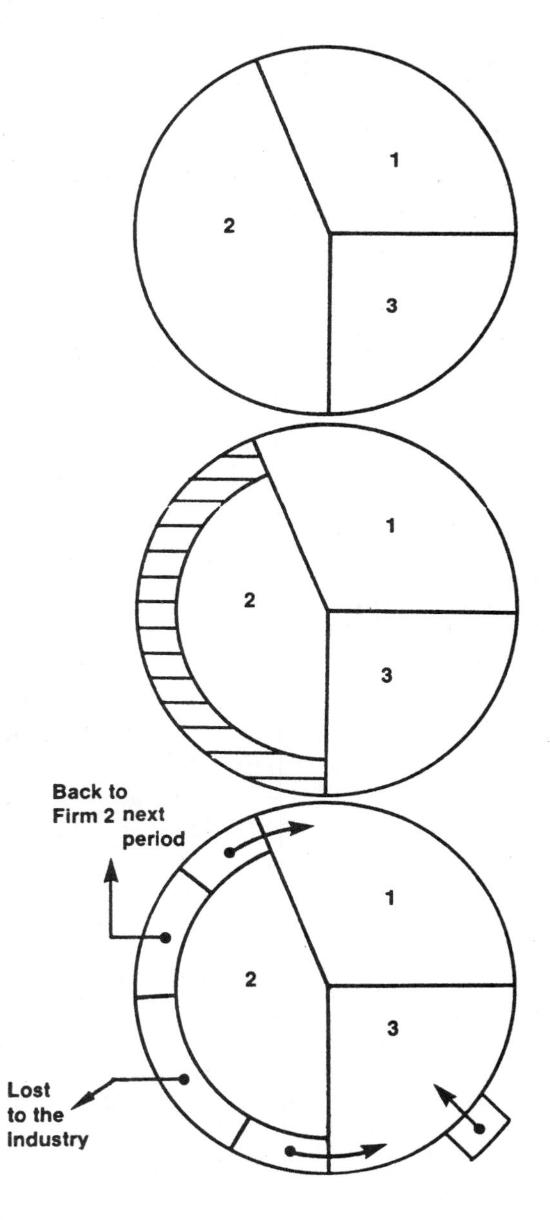

Internal Operations and Costs

This section is about your firm's production system and how costs are generated and accounted for. Questions concerning plant expansion and financing costs are treated separately at the end of the section, because they are linked together in practice. Some of the information given here is enlarged upon later, especially in Chapter 4.

Plant Operations. Production at or below "Plant Capacity, Next Quarter," as given in your Operating Statements, is carried out as directed by your PRODUCTION VOLUME decision provided raw materials are available in sufficient quantity. Such production is accomplished at nearly fixed direct cost per unit, except that:

1. Moderate but possibly significant labor and raw materials cost reductions may result from a vigorous R&D and ROBOTICS programs.
2. Both labor and raw materials cost per unit are affected to a small but often significant degree by MAINTENANCE expenditures, largely because poorly maintained production equipment tends to result in the need for repairs, rework, and even scrapping goods in process, while a really strong plant maintenance effort will have the opposite effects.
3. Manufacturing costs, which consist mainly of wage and raw materials costs, increase with inflation, lagging slightly behind the general price index.

With the next profit per unit sold ordinarily being rather small, even small reductions in cost per unit can have important effects on a firm's profitability.

At the beginning of the game, a normal MAINTENANCE budget is about 75 cents per unit produced. But the wages of the specialized personnel who do maintenance work tend to rise with inflation, the increase generally leading that in the general price index. Money spent (or not spent) on plant maintenance has significant continuing effects. As in real life, if you permit the factory to deteriorate it may be difficult to get its operations back into good shape.

As to the labor component of the cost of production, the Game industry is locked into the practice of adjusting wage scales quarterly, in accordance with the general price index. These adjustments are actually made for you by the computer model. Under this wage policy the industry has avoided strikes in the past, and you will normally be in the happy situation that you can assume your firm will not have labor problems important enough to require top-management attention.

Possible Levels of Production. If you are playing Executive Game Model 1, then PRODUCTION VOLUME decisions up to 40 percent in excess of Plant Capacity will be implemented, raw materials availability permitting. But the direct labor cost of overtime production is 50 percent higher than that of regular-time production. Also, the use of overtime generates added administrative costs (about $50,000 per quarter, adjusted for inflation), but somewhat reduced by research and development expenditures and investments in plant and equipment. Equipment includes computers which are capable of greatly increasing administrative productivity as can innovations brought by research and development. (See step #30, Chapter 4, p. 105.) Since costs also would be larger for a larger plant, you have to reach a balance in answering the question of how you will combine plant expansion and the use of overtime if you want to increase PRODUCTION VOLUME. The tradeoff is complicated by the fact that enlarging the plant uses up money that otherwise might be paid out as DIVIDENDS, or might simply be held as a cushion to protect your firm in case of financial setbacks.

In Model 1, production simply cannot be increased beyond 140 percent of capacity. If you ask for more you just won't get it. However, scheduling production beyond 140 percent of capacity calls for more maintenance which simply will be wasted.

In Model 2, PRODUCTION VOLUME can be increased to as much as 300 percent of Plant Capacity. Production from 100 percent to 140 percent is done on overtime (direct labor cost increased by half, and administrative costs also up), and so is production between 200 and 250 percent of capacity. If you operate two full shifts (140 to 200 percent of capacity) or three full shifts (250-300 percent), then the normal (non-overtime) labor rate applies *but* the extra shifts result in substantially increased administrative costs.

> Also the cost of changing the number of shifts is high: $100,000 per unit change, adjusted for inflation. This expense is incurred each time the number of shifts is changed.
>
> You can see that in Model 2 it is necessary to reach a three-way balance among plant enlargement, the use of overtime, and the use of multiple shifts. Similarly to the situation with Model 1, if you ask for production over 300 percent of capacity, all you can get is 300 percent (and also, of course, no more than you have raw materials to support).

Some specific problems concerned with production scheduling are treated in Chapter 5, under Finished Goods Inventory and Production Scheduling. Even if you don't plan to use the analytic methods stressed there, you'll find it worthwhile at least to skim through Chapter 5, as a source of general information about some of the kinds of problems with which you must somehow cope. Do this later, though, after you are more familiar with the fundamentals of the Game.

Raw Materials. The output actually attained by your plant will be limited by its supply of raw materials, as has been mentioned. The raw materials available for processing in a given quarter are those on hand at the beginning of the quarter — that is, those left over at the end of the preceding quarter plus those ordered by the previous quarter's MATERIAL PURCHASE decision. The current raw MATERIALS PURCHASE order will not be available for processing until "next quarter."

Note that it is generally very important not to overestimate your ability to supply the market. If you do so, you are likely to schedule more production than you can get, and consequently you'll probably overspend on plant maintenance. More important, overestimating your ability to supply the market can lead you to make serious mistakes in PRICE, MARKETING, and MAINTENANCE decisions: it is usually very costly — in terms of profit margin as well as budgeted expenditures — to increase your market potential. If you are unable to fill the market demand that you generate, then you will have paid these costs without getting anything back for them.

Raw materials are paid for at a market price per unit, which goes up with the price index, but lags slightly behind. Every order placed also incurs substantial ordering costs (about $50,000, adjusted for inflation, for paperwork, acceptance sampling, scheduling of labor force problems, setups of processes and equipment, transportation costs, etc.) These added costs do not vary with the size of the order. They do increase with inflation, but with a slight lag behind the general price index.

The most crucial thing to remember about raw materials is that they *must* be ordered a full quarter (or more) before they are needed for processing. If you overlook this, you will find yourself with an expensive factory sitting idle.

Inventories. As we just implied, you *must* carry inventories of raw materials in order to stay in business at all. It is also normal to plan for at least small carryover inventories of finished goods, so you'll have a little extra in case you firm's market potential exceeds your expectations. This can happen, incidentally, if other firms undersupply their markets, even when you have accurately estimated your own market appeal. These inventories of course cost money to maintain — for storage, insurance, etc. And they tie up funds that might better be used elsewhere. So, as Chapter 5 explains in detail, it can be quite important to balance these inventory carrying costs against such other factors as the cost of placing raw materials orders, and the danger of shortages of either raw materials or finished goods.

Budgeted Costs. Executive Game managements are in the pleasant situation, as compared to most managers in real life, that budgets for MARKETING, R&D, and MAINTENANCE are never overspent (or underspent). The figures concerned appear in the quarterly Profit and Loss Statement.

Depreciation, Plant, and Robotics Expansion. In the Executive Game, Plant and Equipment and Robotics normally depreciate at the rate of 2.5 and 5.0 percent per quarter or 10 and 20 percent per year, respectively. Plant and Equipment and Robotics actually deteriorate at two and 3.125 percent per quarter, respectively. To maintain a given capacity, it is necessary to reinvest accordingly. If you should want to reduce capacity, what you do is to invest less than is needed to keep plant capacity unchanged; then plant capacity will gradually shrink. There normally is no way to sell part of your factory and equipment and robotics in the Game. (This is pretty realistic; many businesses cannot in practice sell buildings, plant and equipment, and robotics except perhaps if they sell the whole business.)

The direct cost of production facilities is $70.00 per unit of quarterly production capacity plus adjustments for inflation. These inflation effects tend to follow the general price index. To maintain a fixed production capacity, your PLANT AND EQUIPMENT INVESTMENT each quarter must be about

> 2.0 percent of current Production Capacity,
> multiplied by $70 per unit
> multiplied by adjustment for inflation, and,
> robotics investment must be the same as in the previous quarter.

If you wish to change production capacity next quarter, you may use the formula in step 21 of Chapter 4 in order to determine how much you should invest in plant and equipment and in robotics.

As in the real world, PLANT AND EQUIPMENT and ROBOTICS INVESTMENTS always result in added expenses — not "cost overruns," but side costs connected with making contracts, keeping track of and expediting progress, etc. These are virtually negligible for moderate rates of investment, but they become significant when as much as $1,000,000 is put into plant and equipment and robotics in a single quarter, and they rapidly become prohibitive for one-quarter investments much larger than $1,000,000. The reason costs go up is that "crash programs" are inherently very expensive in the business world. Typically included are unusually high legal fees, costs of architectural and engineering work, costs stemming from the disruption of normal business, and so forth. These appear as expenses rather than as additions to the amount invested because this is permitted by the Government and it is advantageous for tax purposes. The accelerating costs of overly rapid expansion provide a strong reason for planning whatever expansion you want to undertake as a smooth progression of moderate steps.

Don't forget that plant and equipment and robotics budgeted during one quarter is not available for use until the following quarter.

Financing Costs. When a firms's net cash assets fall below zero, then expenses are incurred for loan negotiation, interest, factoring receivables, failure to take advantage of vendor discounts, missed bargains, etc. There "opportunity losses" can greatly exceed normal interest rates. In the Game, such financing costs and penalties are not very important for cash shortages of $100,000 or $200,000; but they grow to hundreds of thousands of dollars per quarter if a shortage reaches the order of magnitude of a million dollars. If the shortage gets much greater than a million dollars, these financing costs can easily wipe out even the healthiest operating profits, and they are likely to lead straight to bankruptcy.

Thus, it is extremely important to keep close control of your cash situation, even if this means being cautious about expansion and especially about declaring dividends. In the Game as in the business world, bankruptcies most often stem from cash flow problems, and bankruptcy is quite possible even when operating profits seem to be up to par.

If your firm sinks into such deep cash difficulties that its recovery is deemed to be impossible, then you can expect the firm to be declared bankrupt by the Game administrator. The administrator *may* be willing to consider special arrangements whereby the failing management can obtain a special loan and continue playing (just as insolvent business firms sometimes continue to operate under a "receivership" formed by their creditors, although usually with a change of management). However, a firm once bankrupted can very rarely recover to the point of being seen as "successfully" managed, although a strong comeback may sometimes deserve a lot of credit.

Performance Criteria

So far we have really treated profit maximization as the criterion of management performance in the Executive Game, although we have often mentioned ownership's rate of return on investment (ROI) as a more satisfactory measure. This section explains ROI.

In real life, and therefore also in the Executive Game, the ideal basis for evaluating a firm's success, from the viewpoint of ownership, is usually its long-run stream of payoffs to the owners; that is, the stream of dividends. In order to evaluate and compare several streams of dividends, it is useful to have an appropriate single number which can be thought of as the "score" deserved by any given stream. Ownership's rate of return on investment (ROI) is such a number.

The idea of ROI is based on drawing a parallel to an ordinary savings account. Ownership's original equity is the one deposit to the account. Dividends distributed to ownership are the withdrawals. In general, ROI is the interest rate that would be necessary for the specified deposit to permit the specified sequence of withdrawals. Comparisons between investments on the basis of ROI have the same logic as comparisons between different savings accounts on the basis of interest rate.

For the purposes of the Executive Game, as well as many real-life applications of ROI, some mechanism must be used to account for what is "left over" at the time when ROI is evaluated; that is, in the Game, to take into account the continuing value of the firm at the end of play. This is done by thinking of ownership as "closing its account" by hypothetically selling the firm for a sum of money equal to its replacement value at the end of the Game. In the analogy with the savings account, the proceeds of this sale count as it they were a final cash withdrawal made by ownership. Within the ROI model, this replacement value — ownership's "economic equity" — can be thought of as a fictitious "final dividend," used to close the outgoing management's books, a dividend which also serves as a plausible indicator of the probable value of the future dividend stream that would be forthcoming if the Game could continue indefinitely. Inflation and the use of accelerated depreciation generally make economic equity substantially larger than ordinary bookkeeping equity.

We have now conceptualized the Executive Game firm's financial dealings with ownership as the equivalent of an initial deposit by ownership followed by a sequence of withdrawals. *ROI is simply the interest rate (figured in the Game as an annual percentage rate, compounded quarterly) for which the same sequence of withdrawals would be possible if the original deposit really had been made to a savings account rather than invested in an Executive Game firm.*

As a simplified example, suppose that the original ownership equity in a firm is $10,000,000. Suppose further that the firm unfailingly pays a $250,000 dividend each quarter, and that the closing value of equity is again $10,000,000. From ownership's point of view the situation is exactly as if $10,000,000 had been on deposit, with interest as a 10.4 percent annual rate paid quarterly (or compounded quarterly), and with the account closed out and the original deposit returned to ownership at the end of the Game. Hence the ROI is 10.4 percent.

The example just given has been simplified to the point where it may be misleading. In practice almost every firm's dividends fluctuate from time to time, and the closing economic equity will probably never be exactly equal to the opening economic equity. Still, a mathematical formulation based on the analogy between an ownership investment and a fictitious bank account leads to a definite and meaningful value for ROI, got by solving an algebraic equation. This equation is derived below. But you don't have to work through the derivation to understand the basic idea of ROI, as explained by analogy in the preceding paragraphs.

In the Executive Game, ROI is computed annually for each firm, and also at the end of play. The results are included in the End of Fiscal Year reports, which also rank the firms from first to last on the basis of ROI to date. This ranking is widely used as the primary measure of comparative success among Executive Game firms.

In addition to permitting comparison with other Game firms, knowing your firm's ROI also gives you the chance to compare its performance as an investment with bank accounts and security holdings in the real world. Savings account interest rates, for instance, are usually advertised in terms that amount to the same thing as ROI, and bond prices are often described in terms of the ROI that will be received if a bond is held until maturity. (ROI is often calculated on the basis of daily or annual compounding, rather than quarterly compounding. Comparisons are still valid, but only as fairly close approximations.)

Management Implications of ROI. Within the Game it is important for you to understand the ROI criterion because it explains why you should bother to declare DIVIDEND payments. If the criterion used to measure management performance were simply total profits over the whole Game, then it would be logical to keep all earnings, so that you would have plenty of money to expand it if that seemed profitable, and otherwise to provide a comfortable cushion to protect your firm from possible cash flow problems. Some businesses do in fact reinvest virtually everything earned. Their stock still finds buyers who can afford to go without current returns in the hope of large long-run capital gains. But this is feasible only in very special situations, usually where there are extraordinary opportunities for growth, as illustrated nowadays by a few leading-edge firms in "high tech" fields. The situation represented by the Game is not one of these. Your owners want a large and consistent stream of income. They want at least a reasonable part of earned profits *now,* to pay their bills and maybe live it up a little if things go well, or perhaps just to put into interest-earning savings deposits or other income-producing investments.

Now profits, whether distributed or not, contribute to ROI by increasing the final value of owner's economic equity. But any money distributed to ownership sooner than the end of the Game has a larger effect on ROI than it would if it were simply held by the firm concerned — and the earlier the distribution the greater the effect. Management, of course, has to decide what balance to strike between reinvesting profits in order to grow, on the one hand, and making liberal DIVIDEND payments in order to satisfy ownership's preference for cash reserves to safeguard against the possibility of unpleasant surprises as events unfold in the Game. As a very rough rule, it seems to be a good idea to play the cash game pretty safe, by issuing dividends up to the point where you feel there is some *small* chance that cash availability or cash deficit problems may follow, but being careful to keep that small chance quite small.

To see why it's worth taking at least some chance here, consider a numerical example illustrating the fact that DIVIDEND payments are good for ROI. Suppose each of Firms 1 and 2 starts out with an owners' equity of $10,000,000, and each of these firms earns a net profit of $2,000,000 in two years of play. The firms differ in that Firm 1 declares a $150,000 dividend each quarter, while Firm 2 keeps all its earnings. For simplicity we suppose that the price level holds constant. It turns out that Firm 1 will have an ROI of 10.03 percent, but Firm 2 will have an ROI of only 9.54 percent. This would be a quite significant difference in many runs of the Game.

The difference in ROI between the two firms in the example just given would not be changed if Firm 2 had declared a huge dividend of $1,200,000 at the end of the Game — equal to all the dividends issued by Firm 1 over the two-year period. This illustrates the fact that early dividends matter more that later ones. One explanation for this difference is that if the investor gets a given dividend "sooner" rather than "later," then it can be earning returns in some other use (say as a savings deposit) during the interval between "sooner" and "later."

Notice that the payoffs represented by ROI generally measure the delivery of ownership of inflated dollars. Ownership isn't earning anything, in purchasing power or "real dollars," until ROI exceeds the average rate of inflation. But real-life investors in non-speculative business often have to be satisfied with quite small profits, measured in "real dollars," when inflation is severe. The same thing often happens to the fictitious owners in the Executive Game.

Exact Algebra of ROI. We now develop the equation from which exact values of ROI can be calculated. Then easier ways to calculate approximations will be given.

Let r denote the (unknown) quarterly ROI, expressed as a proportion. Suppose P is a payment (dividend or final closeout payment) made to ownership t quarters after the beginning of the game (for instance, a $50,000 dividend in the Period 6). Now we ask, how large a deposit, made at the beginning of the Game, and an interest rate r per quarter, compounded quarterly, would grow large enough to make possible this payment of P dollars, t quarters later. The answer is X dollars, where

$$(1+r)^t X = P.$$

This equation simply formalizes the definition of the specified interest arrangement, under which (by definition) the accumulated amount is multiplied each quarter by (1 + r). Solving for X, we get

$$X = P/(1+r)^t.$$

The quantity X is called the *present value,* at the beginning of the game, of the payment of P dollars made t quarters later.

For example, if $r = .025$, $P = \$50{,}000$, and $t = 6$ quarters, then

$$X = 50{,}000/(1.025)^6 = \$43{,}114.84.$$

This means that $43,114.84, on deposit for six quarters, at interest rate 2.5 percent per quarter (or 10.4 percent per annum), compounded quarterly, would yield $50,000.

If r is the quarterly ROI, then its use as an interest rate must make the "initial deposit" (beginning owners' equity) equal to the sum of the amounts needed, at interest rate r, to generate the actual sequence of "withdrawals" (dividends, along with the fictitious final closing payment). Suppose the game has gone on for n quarters. Let E(0) be the initial value of owners' economic equity. For t=1, 2, ..., n let D(t) be the dividend issued in the t quarter. Let E(n) be the value of owners' economic equity after the n quarters. Then the first sentence of this paragraph translates into the following algebraic equation:

$$E(0) = \frac{D(1)}{(1 + r)^1} + \frac{D(2)}{(1 + r)^2} + \ldots + \frac{D(n) + E(n)}{(1 + r)^n}$$

Remember that r is the unknown: all the other symbols represent quantities that are part of the history of the Game at the time when the calculation is to be made. It is not difficult to prove mathematically that there will be exactly one economically meaningful solution to this question (that is one solution with r-1), but the details will not be spelled out here.

When you put in specific numbers, the equation above comes out looking, for example, like this:

$$9{,}700{,}000 = \frac{100{,}000}{(1 + r)^1} + \frac{50{,}000}{(1 + r)^2} + \frac{50{,}000}{(1 + r)^3} + \frac{10{,}100{,}000}{(1 + r)^4}$$

This equation represents a firm that has operated for one year, with initial economic equity \$9,700,000, dividends of \$100,000, \$50,000, \$50,000, and \$100,000 in the four successive quarters, and final economic equity \$10,000,000. It's a formidable looking equation, but can be easily solved with a computer to get the numerical value of the unknown r. The *annualized* rate, R, can then be calculated (also by the computer), using the following equation:

$$R = (1 + r)^4 - 1.$$

Finally, R is multiplied by 100 to convert it from a proportion to a percentage. (The solution to the above equation turns out to be r = .015289, which leads to the final annualized percentage ROI of 6.257 percent.)

So far as the Game is concerned , there's no need for you to solve equations like the above. But you may be interested to know that some "finance" type pocket calculators include hardwired procedures for solving such equations by just punching a few keys. And most "math" auxiliary chips offered with the fancier programmable calculators include "Newton's method," which can be used to solve such equations. Using this method (or almost any other "successive approximation" method for solving equations), the solution process can be coded for any computer in a few lines of BASIC programming language. Those with mathematical interests can find such methods in almost any intermediate calculus text.

One-quarter ROI; Approximations. It is easy to figure *exact* ROI for any one quarter. Using Period 1 in the Game to make the notation as simple as possible, the above general equation becomes

$$E(0) = \frac{D(1) + E(1)}{1 + r}$$

This can easily be solved for r:

$$r = \frac{D(1) + E(1)}{E(0)} - 1.$$

Generalizing the last formula, but expressing it in words, the quarterly ROI for *any* single quarter is gotten as follows: (i) add the dividend issued in the quarter (possible zero) to the value of ownership's economic equity at the end of the quarter; (ii) divide this sum by ownership's economic equity at the end of the preceding quarter; (iii) subtract one from this quotient. The result is the ROI for the quarter concerned, expressed as a proportion.

It is not hard to see that if there is no inflation or deflation, and if book depreciation of plant and equipment equals real depreciation (2.5 percent per quarter), then this non-quarter value of r is simply profit for the quarter expressed as a fraction of initial ownership equity. More generally, it turns out the profit maximization *for a single quarter only* is always the same as ROI maximization for that one quarter. This gives an exact meaning to our earlier statements that profit maximization is a good first approximation to ROI maximization. *But*, in view of ownership's preference for "dividends now," profit maximization is *not* a good enough approximation to ROI maximization over longer intervals of time.

If you want to approximate ROI for a sequence of successive quarters, then: (i) using the procedure spelled out in the paragraph before last, calculate the value of r for each of these quarters; (ii) calculate the average of these values of r; (iii) calculate four times this average; (iv) multiply by 100 if you prefer a percentage. This will give you a pretty good approximation of up to a few quarters, *if* the final answer comes out within the range commonly attained in the Game (up to 16 percent or so), and *if* the individual quarterly values of r don't fluctuate too much. Some improvement, especially if the answer comes out larger than 16 percent, will result from using the following formula in step (iii):

$$R = (1 + \text{average } r)^4 - 1.$$

The final result, as a percentage, is then 100R. This result is exact for a single quarter (in which case the "average" of just one value of r, needed in an early part of the calculation, is just r itself).

Management Under Conditions of Uncertainty and Risk

"Management's job in the Executive Game is to ... maximize ownership's rate of return on investment (ROI)." That's what we said at the beginning of this chapter. Now that ROI has been explained in detail, this sentence tells you exactly what to aim for. But the Game's large measure of uncertainty makes it necessary to give careful thought to just what it means to aim toward maximizing a specific criterion.

The choices you make in the Executive Game will strongly affect how the Game works out, but factors beyond your control will be comparatively important. To some extent you can predict these external factors, but your predictions will at best be reasoned guesses much of the time. And even if you made precise predictions of future economic activity, inflation, and competitive behavior, you would still have only imperfect knowledge of how these factors fit together with one another and with your own firm's decisions, to determine results. So it's clear that you have to manage your firm under conditions of uncertainty. Every decision you make will be a risky decision. In this respect, the Executive Game is like real life. The manager, in the Game or in the business world, is (among other things) a gambler. Good managers are clever gamblers, at least within their own fields of business expertise — good at discovering promising opportunities to gamble, good at estimating the odds of winning or losing and the size of possible gains and losses, good at selecting the best opportunities for gain, and good at avoiding risks with downside possibilities beyond acceptable limits.

The most important thing we want to emphasize here is that, just as in the real business world, you *have to* gamble in the Executive Game. There are no safe paths to follow. For instance, experience with the Game shows that the "conservative" approach of leaving old decisions unchanged is an almost sure road to disaster. To give yourself any worthwhile chance of doing well, you simply must adapt your firm to changes in its environment. And no matter how carefully you read this manual, no matter how carefully you think out your decisions, and no matter how shrewd you are at predicting what other firms are going to do, you still cannot eliminate a significant element of risk — any more than a real-life manager can ever be *sure* of being *exactly* right. The question is not *whether* to gamble, but *how* to gamble profitably.

Operations researchers, statisticians, and management theorists, as well as practicing managers, have given a lot of thought to the question of how risk can best be dealt with. Everyone seems to agree that every business must face a large number of relatively small risks, which can be thought of like a lot of small wagers, and which are best dealt with by counting on the law of averages. Experience bears this out. It means that for each of these small risks, the most sensible policy is to choose the alternative that you believe will give you the best probabilistic expected value (the largest probabilistically expected gain, or the smallest probabilistically expected loss) — where the "expected value" is the average of the possible gains and losses, weighted according to their probabilities. The law of averages (or, more formally, a theorem of mathematical probability called the strong law of large numbers) then makes you almost certain to come very close to the best overall results that you can realistically hope for. Chapter 5 explains in detail how to do this for certain problems of inventory control in the Executive Game.

Every business also involves relatively big risks, which create problems that are less easily dealt with — even in theory. Roughly speaking, in the Executive Game you can comfortably trust the law of averages when you are faced with questions involving possible gains and losses up to a few thousand dollars. That is because the law of averages makes it so very unlikely that you'll suffer a "streak of bad luck" long enough to build losses of a few thousand dollars each up to the level of a financial disaster. That can't be said about potential losses in the range of one hundred thousand dollars or more. A "losing streak" of length only two or three could put your firm in such bad shape that — unless a "lucky streak" happened to come along just when needed — the firm might never be able to get back on its corporate feet. You can't count on the law of averages when the individual bets are so large that just a few losses will knock you out of the Game.

Decision analysts have invented something called "utility theory" to take care of such situations. The idea is to measure potential gains and losses using a "utility scale" explicitly designed to make it right for you to follow the suggestions of the law of averages even when large losses are possible. The basic idea, which is explained fully in texts and treatises on "decision theory," is to evaluate losses and gains in terms of their risk-related importance to the firm (or the manager), rather than simply using dollar figures. The measurement must in fact be subjective, so the measurement scale is "a matter of opinion." That is one of several reasons why the utility concept is difficult to implement (except in some of the simplest cases where it really offers nothing new because the utility measure turns out to be identical, for practical purposes, with plain old money). We think that very few players of the Executive Game, if any, will find it useful or even possible to base their major decisions in the game on formal decision theory. Nevertheless, it will help you to think clearly about risks in the Game if you merely recognize that (for instance) a gain of $100,000 may not be as important a change as a loss of $100,000. This way of thinking about risks can profitably be transferred to the business world and to your personal life.

To illustrate what we mean in personal terms, ask yourself if you'd be willing to accept a fair bet under which you stand to win or lose $1,000 on the toss of an honest coin. Most people would not, because the sudden loss of $1,000 would disrupt their whole lives to a degree that outweighs an equally good chance of whatever comforts and pleasures might result from suddenly winning $1,000. The same thing is true of your firm in the Game, except that the stakes are a bit higher. And the same thing is true, if the stakes are large enough, at McDonald's or Exxon.

The catch, of course, is that the decisive moves that give someone a real shot at winning big are almost always risky moves that create at least the possibility of losing big. We can't offer a prescription for coping sensibly with this troublesome fact of life, but we do very strongly suggest that you think very carefully about your individual attitude toward taking chances, and also that every Executive Game management team talk this subject through in order to reach as clear a consensus as possible. Furthermore, we are sure that every team will also find it worthwhile to return to this subject frequently, regularly reexamining whatever consensus still stands. This will help you to learn valuable *experience-based* lessons, both as a team playing the Executive Game and as individuals looking forward to lives in the business world. (For some further suggestions about how to learn from risk taking or any other experience in the Game, see the last paragraphs of Chapter 1.)

Many Executive Game players feel that a better understanding of business risk is one of the most important learnings attainable from the Game, and that an increased understanding of their own personal feelings about risk may be equally important — or even more important. The opportunities offered in the Game may be especially valuable in this regard precisely because the "real" risks aren't overwhelmingly serious. It's easier to think coolly about what you're doing and to learn from it effectively if you're not paralyzed by fear.

Reports in the Executive Game

This section consists of line-by-line explanations of the quarterly reports prepared by the computer for managers in the Executive Game. You should go through the section carefully, referring constantly to the sample quarterly report for Period 0 (Table 3, page 39). Recall that this report tells you where your firm will start out in a normal run of the Game.

The beginning of the first line of the report reminds you of (i) which Model (No. 1 or No. 2) is currently in use, (ii) the period number, and (iii) which quarter of the year the report covers (JFM — January-February-March, etc.). Then the actual report begins.

General Economic Information. The first line continues with the GENERAL PRICE INDEX for the period just ended and the FORECAST ANNUAL CHANGE (percentage) for the same index in the near future. Remember that while the Price Index is an indicator of price changes of all kinds, some price changes tend to lead or lag the indicator, as indicated in previous sections and again below.

The second line of the report gives the value of the SEASONAL INDEX for the quarter just completed and its value for the quarter just about to start. Following these indices, the general ECONOMIC INDEX is given for the past quarter, and a FORECAST, NEXT QUARTER of the same index follows. If other factors remained unchanged, you could expect Market Potential to change proportionately to the seasonal index, and on top of this to change somewhat more than proportionately to the general economic index.

Information on Competitors. The next report lists the past quarter's PRICE, DIVIDEND, SALES VOLUME, and NET PROFIT for each firm in the industry. Table 3 exhibits this information for a six-firm industry, for Period 0.

This information will obviously help you to keep up to date, to some extent, on what your competitors are doing and how well they are coming out. You will be given more information when the End of Fiscal Year report is distributed — normally at the end of each full year of play. This report is exemplified by Tables 29 and 39.

Operating Statements. Your Operating Statements provide non-financial information about your firm and its potentialities. MARKET POTENTIAL tells you how many units of your product were ordered by customers in the past quarter, and SALES VOLUME is the number of units actually sold. If your potential sales exceeded actual sales, this means your firm ran out of finished goods, and consequently lost sales that would have been made if there had been more goods on hand. If this happens, you'll have to accept the fact that you could have priced higher or spent less money on marketing, and thus increased your profits. Or perhaps you might have produced more and hence sold more and hence profited more.

PERCENT SHARE OF INDUSTRY SALES is self-explanatory. But this line on the report does suggest reviewing the market mechanism. The *total industry market potential* is determined by the interaction among industrywide prices, marketing efforts, and research and development budgets, along with economic conditions measured by the indices discussed above. Your share of market potential (the fraction of the total that you can capture if you've got enough goods available) is determined by how your own firm's pricing, marketing,and research and development policies relate to those of the industry as a whole. Your *final market potential* may in fact be increased a bit by brand-switching customers if other firms run out of stock, and possibly by the return of some customers who were unable to buy your product during the preceding quarter. Your *actual sales* are limited by your final market potential, and also by the quantity of finished goods you have for sale — left-over stock from last quarter, if any, plus current production.

Recall that Price changes and Marketing budget decisions have quick effects, but the effects of Research and Development accumulate slowly over time. The fact that the consequences of R&D are delayed has the important implication that if you put too little into R&D and fall seriously behind your competitors in this area, you may have a very hard time catching up. And if, pursuing what may look like a road to "quick profits" at the end of the Game, you neglect R&D, you will in effect leave your firm in a shambles so far as future potential is concerned — and, as mentioned before, you can expect the final evaluation of your management's performance to penalize you severely for this, even if your ROI looks good. The promising road turns out to be a blind alley.

PRODUCTION, THIS QUARTER will agree with your Production Volume decision for the quarter just completed, unless you asked for more output than your factory could produce or for more than your supply of raw materials would support. Remember that the raw Materials Purchase order must be placed a full quarter in advance: for instance, materials ordered in Period 1 cannot be processed until Period 2. This implies that in Period 1 you *must* formulate at least a preliminary idea of how many units you want to produce in Period 2.

INVENTORY, FINISHED GOODS gives the quantity of finished goods available for sale but not sold during the quarter just completed. This "carryover inventory" drops to zero in case you sell out. As has been mentioned before, that is generally *bad,* because it indicates that you spent money or cut price to generate sales that could never happen. The carryover inventory, if any, will be available for sale during the next quarter, along with goods produced during the next quarter.

PLANT CAPACITY, NEXT QUARTER is basically a measure of plant size. It is equal to the output attainable with a single shift and no overtime, provided enough raw materials are on hand. But you can actually produce more than this if you have more raw materials. The details — which differ between Models 1 and 2 — are spelled out in the section on Internal Operations and Costs (earlier in this chapter), under the subheading Possible Levels of Production. In the same section, under Depreciation and Plant Expansion, you will find information about reducing or increasing plant capacity through your management of the Plant Investment decision.

Income Statement. The dollar figures in this report summarize the revenues and expenses of your firm during the quarter covered. It is important that "expenses" do not always directly represent cash outlays during the quarter, as illustrated in the Executive Game by MATERIALS CONSUMED; REDUCTION, FINISHED GOODS INVENTORY; DEPRECIATION OF PLANT AND EQUIPMENT AND ROBOTICS. Also, cash outlays are not always expenses, as illustrated by PLANT AND EQUIPMENT INVESTMENT (which is not even listed on the Income Statement).

RECEIPTS, SALES REVENUE is equal to the arithmetic product of Sales Volume and Price per Unit. This is the one revenue item in the Executive Game, a separate total for receipts is not needed.

The itemized EXPENSES are in some cases self-explanatory. In particular, MARKETING, RESEARCH AND DEVELOPMENT, AND MAINTENANCE are expenses as budgeted. But remember that these budgets must be increased in proportion to inflation just to maintain unchanged effectiveness. The maintenance budget should ideally increase *ahead* of the inflationary trend, and should also be changed in proportion to Production Volume. All three budgets, but especially R&D, should really be considered as if they were to some extent short-term investments, since their effects continue beyond the quarter in which expenditures are actually made. But tax law permits them to be treated as straight expenses, and they are always so treated in the Game because this reduces or at least postpones taxes. (The same is true in the real business world except that there are *very* special cases where young companies, not yet profitable, may be able to get tax advantages by capitalizing some R&D expenditures as investment. This might in fact sometimes seem desirable in the Executive Game, but the law doesn't permit you to switch from expensing to capitalizing R&D).

ADMINISTRATION consists primarily of overhead costs, largely connected with plant size and production and sales volume. These costs go up in proportion to inflation, but the changes lag one quarter behind the general price index. They vary slightly with plant size, but this source of change is small so long as a ratio between Plant Capacity and Production Volume remains approximately constant and does not cross certain thresholds. However, certain changes in this ratio (such as the introduction of overtime production in Model 1 of the Game) result in large administrative costs. Some information about this is given in the present chapter's section on Internal Operations and Costs; and complete details are explained in a way designed to facilitate worksheet calculations in Chapter 4 (see, in particular, Step #27 of the detailed procedure laid out in that chapter).

LABOR costs for regular-time production vary with inflation, with changes lagging slightly behind the general Price Index. The regular-time labor cost per unit of output is given by the report, as well as the total labor expense. The overtime rate is 50 percent higher thanthe regular time rate. Details for using this information are spelled out in Chapter 4 (Steps #6 and #24).

MATERIALS CONSUMED measures the cost of raw materials processed during the quarter covered by the report. At the beginning of the Game, this cost is about $6.31 per unit of product, but is increases with inflation and will also be affected by research and development, robotics, and maintenance policies. Note that the cost is not a cash outlay: it measures the change in value of the physical inventory of raw materials. This change can of course be either positive or negative. The current cost-per-unit (market price) for raw materials is also given by the report.

REDUCTION, FINISHED GOODS INVENTORY is similar to the preceding item, but relates to finished goods rather than raw materials. This cost again can be either positive or negative. The finished goods inventory is valued according to the current "standard cost" of labor and materials — which is $12.00 per unit, increased in proportion to the price index. Note that this standard cost need not agree with the sum of actual labor and materials costs-per-unit. The difference, in fact, largely reflects the degree to which your research and development, robotics and maintenance policies have been effective in keeping costs down.

DEPRECIATION OF PLANT AND EQUIPMENT is a non-cash expense, normally charged at 2.5 percent of the current (start of quarter) book value of plant and equipment. This 2.5 percent rate slightly exceeds the deterioration of production capacity. The current bookkeeping depreciation rate is given on the report; the actual plant and equipment deterioration rate remains fixed at 2.0 percent per quarter.

DEPRECIATION OF ROBOTICS also is a non-cash expense, normally charged at five percent of the current (start of quarter) book value of robotics equipment. This five percent rate exceeds the deterioration of robotics equipment of 3.125 percent per quarter.

FINISHED GOODS CARRYING COST comes to about $2.00 per unit at the beginning of the Game, and increases proportionate to inflation but with a one-quarter lag. This is a cash expense, to cover the cost of storage, insurance, etc. One of the problems posed by the Executive Game concerns how best to balance the size of planned inventory, with its corresponding carrying cost, against the possibility of selling out and thus losing sales, this being complicated by the desirability of a reasonably stable production rate even though market potential is fluctuating seasonally.

RAW MATERIALS CARRYING COST is similar in nature to the item just discussed. It comes to five percent of the value of raw materials on hand.

ORDERING COSTS for raw materials come to about $50,000 each time an order is placed, subject to increases proportional to the general Price Index lagged one period.

The next item, SHIFTS CHANGE COST, *applies only to Model 2.* This cost comes to about $100,000 for a change from one to two shifts, or from two to three shifts, or vice versa; and about $200,000 for a change from one to three shifts or vice versa — increasing in proportion to the general Price Index lagged one period.

PLANT AND EQUIPMENT and ROBOTICS INVESTMENT EXPENSES are cash outlays incidental to investment in robotics and plant and equipment. From some points of view it might be logical to consider these expenses as part of the investment, but this is not done because it is legally permissible and advantageous from a tax point of view to treat them like any other expense. They can be predicted by the following formula:

$$\text{P\&RIE} = \frac{(\text{PLANT AND EQUIPMENT and ROBOTICS INVESTMENT})^2}{10{,}000{,}000}$$

For instance, an investment of $100,000 produces such costs coming to 100,000 X 100,000/10,000,000 = $1,000 — which is not a very important amount in the Game. But investing $1,000,000 in plant and equipment and robotics in a single quarter produces a side cost of $100,000 — which must be taken very seriously. The rapidly increasing side costs of "crash" expansion strongly motivate you to plan expansion as a series of moderate increments rather than a few large jumps in plant and robotics capacity. (For this expense, inflation need not be considered separately, beyond the fact that it tends to increase the size of the Plant and Equipment and Robotics Investment needed to accomplish any given result.)

FINANCING CHARGES AND PENALTIES only occur when cash assets fall below zero. They are calculated according to the following formula whenever a cash balance goes negative:

$$\text{FCP} = \frac{0.9 \text{ X } (\text{CASH DEFICIT})^2}{10{,}000{,}000} \text{ X } \{1 + \text{pAIR}\}.$$

where pAIR is the Annual Inflation Rate *expressed as a proportion* (that is, .01 times the percentage Annual Inflation Rate). This cost appears on the quarterly report one quarter *after* the cash shortage occurs. A deficit of $100,000 will cost you only about $1,000 per quarter; but a $1,000,000 deficit will produce the very significant expense of about $100,000. If your firm could remain solvent long enough to reach a $2,500,000 deficit, the resulting expenses would generally be almost $1,250,000 — probably enough to be fatal.

SUNDRIES is a category of nearly fixed operating expenses that don't fit into any of the above categories. These expenses go up with production capacity, and also with inflation, and are attenuated somewhat by R&D and plant and equipment expenditures.

TOTAL EXPENSE appears to the right of the SUNDRIES entry, on the same line. It is simply the sum of the expenses listed previously.

PROFIT BEFORE INCOME TAX is equal to RECEIPTS, SALES REVENUE, minus TOTAL EXPENSE. This figure may of course be negative, representing a loss.

INCOME TAX is normally levied on quarterly gross profits at a rate of 34 percent in the Executive Game. If a surtax is in effect, it may be either positive or negative, increasing or decreasing tax liability by a percentage (normally 10 percent). The report itself tells you what surtax (if any) is in effect, but you will normally also be told in advance by the Game administrator. *If profits are negative, the tax is computed as if they were positive but interpreted as a tax refund.*

A second tax option is the investment tax credit. If an investment tax credit is in effect, then your firm's INCOME TAX will be reduced by a percentage of its current Plant and Equipment Investment (normally five percent) since the plant and equipment budget is assumed to be split 50/50 between plant and equipment. However, the investment tax credit for Robotics normally would be a full 10 percent since Robotics are counted as equipment. The effect is always to push the tax liability downward: what would otherwise be a small tax may be pushed downward to the point where you get a refund, and if your tax is already negative (a refund resulting from negative profits), any applicable investment credit will be added to the amount refunded. See Step #40 in Chapter 4 for an explanation of this item.

In the Game, taxes and refunds are actually paid as the liabilities arise, quarter by quarter. That is, any tax on current income is paid out of CASH immediately, and any refund is returned at once into CASH on hand.

(This tax structure, especially the quarter-by-quarter payment and refund system, is a good deal simpler than the Federal tax system now in force. State income and excise taxes may be assumed to be buried in Sundries and Administration expenses.Thus, the Game is not even intended to capture the intricacies of specialized taxation management. But the main tax questions that are central to operating management are still represented fairly realistically.)

NET PROFIT AFTER INCOME TAX is equal to PROFIT BEFORE INCOME TAX minus INCOME TAX. This number — which may be negative, representing a loss — is the celebrated *bottom line.*

DIVIDENDS are paid out as budgeted, except that no dividend will be permitted to reduce OWNERS' EQUITY below $9,000,000; and no dividend at all will be paid if equity is already less than $9,000,000. Think of this as a limitation imposed on management by ownership to guard against the inappropriate distribution of capital.

ADDITION TO OWNERS' EQUITY is the remainder of NET PROFITS AFTER INCOME TAX, when DIVIDENDS have also been paid. This quantity may of course be negative.

Cash Flow Statement. Practical management has to be concerned almost as much with cash flow as with profits (in fact, not just "almost" in many situations), so the Cash Flow Statement should get your close attention.

RECEIPTS, SALES REVENUE is identical to the same item on the Income Statement.

DISBURSEMENTS consist of all cash outlays. This first item on the list includes all CASH EXPENSE — the sum of the cash outlays previously listed as expenses:

MARKETING expense
RESEARCH AND DEVELOPMENT expense
ADMINISTRATION expense
MAINTENANCE expense
LABOR expense
FINISHED GOODS CARRYING COST expense
RAW MATERIALS CARRYING COST expense
ORDERING COSTS expense
SHIFTS CHANGE COST expense (*Model 2 only*)
INVESTMENT expenses
FINANCING CHARGES AND PENALTIES expense
SUNDRIES expense

It is explained above why certain expenses do not appear on this list.

INCOME TAX and DIVIDENDS PAID are identical to the like-named items discussed above.

PLANT and EQUIPMENT and ROBOTICS INVESTMENTS are cash outlays, as budgeted, and so is MATERIALS PURCHASED. None of these items is an "expense" because each is concerned with exchanging one asset (cash) for another (plant and equipment, robotics, or raw materials). The corresponding expenses occur when DEPRECIATION eats into the book values of PLANT and EQUIPMENT and ROBOTICS and when RAW MATERIALS are actually used up in production. It is worth reminding you that investments in plant and equipment and robotics and purchases of materials all must be made a full quarter before the resources involved can be used.

ADDITION TO CASH ASSETS is simply the difference between total receipts and total disbursements. This of course can be negative, in which case it represents a reduction in CASH on hand.

A cash flow statement usually includes both opening and closing values of net cash on hand. In the Game, these are immediately available as the preceding and present quarter's CASH entries, which appear on the Financial Statement (see below).

Financial Statement. In the simplified accounting system of the Executive Game, the Financial Statement (or "balance sheet") simply lists your firm's assets and their total, which is the bookkeeping value of ownership interests in the firm. This simple statement reflects the Game's emphasis on operating management rather than financial management.

CASH is the actual amount of cash on hand, equal to the preceding quarter's value of CASH, plus the current ADDITION TO CASH ASSETS (a reduction, of course in case the "addition" is negative). CASH can of course come out negative. Remember that this can be costly (although the cost won't show up on the reports until the quarter after the shortage occurs), and also that an excessive deficit may be grounds for the Game administrator to declare a company bankrupt.

Comparing the somewhat simplified accounting scheme of the Executive Game with business practice, this CASH item may be thought of as combining the various items that would usually appear under net current assets, including allowances for such accounts as accounts payable and paid-in reserves.

INVENTORY VALUE, FINISHED GOODS is the value of finished goods on hand; and INVENTORY VALUE, RAW MATERIALS is the value of raw materials on hand. Each of these numbers can be got by starting from the preceding report's value for the same item and: (i) adding the cost of increases (labor and materials for finished goods, raw materials purchase for raw materials); (ii) subtracting the value of items removed from inventory (by sales of finished goods, or by processing of raw materials). The same numbers would be obtained if you directly calculated the accounting values of physical stocks on hand. Approximations adequate for most purposes will result if finished goods are figured at $12.00 per unit, corrected for inflation, and raw materials are figured at current cost per unit.

ROBOTICS BOOK VALUE and PLANT AND EQUIPMENT BOOK VALUE are simply the old book values reduced by the applicable depreciation rates, and then increased by the pertinent ROBOTICS and PLANT AND EQUIPMENT INVESTMENTS, respectively. Remember that inflation and depreciation both make the book values of plant and equipment and robotics an imprecise indicator of PLANT CAPACITY — which is however listed elsewhere on the quarterly report.

OWNERS' EQUITY (or "ownership interest") is the sum of the values of the assets, figuring plant and equipment and robotics at book values. This figure is equal to the previous quarterly value plus the current quarter's ADDITION TO OWNER'S EQUITY.

PLANT AND EQUIPMENT REPLACEMENT VALUE is what you would have to pay for the existing capacity at current prices ($70.00 per quarterly unit of production capacity, adjusted for inflation). It would also be reasonable to call this "plant and equipment economic value" (in current dollars).

ROBOTICS REPLACEMENT VALUE is what you would have to pay for the existing system of robotics at current prices. It would also be reasonable to call this "robotics economic value" (in current dollars).

OWNER'S ECONOMIC EQUITY is calculated in the same way as OWNER'S EQUITY except PLANT AND EQUIPMENT REPLACEMENT VALUE and ROBOTICS REPLACEMENT VALUE are used in place of PLANT BOOK VALUE and ROBOTICS BOOK VALUE, respectively. This figure is a more realistic valuation of actual ownership interests when bookkeeping figures have been distorted by inflation and perhaps also by tax accounting practices that may not even be intended to measure "real values" (for example, depreciation). It often turns out, in fact, that "bookkeeping" equity and economic equity differ considerably by the end of two years of play. You can see how this works comparing these figures in the progression of tables at the end of this chapter. Remember that an honest interpretation of OWNERS' ECONOMIC EQUITY cannot ignore the fact that it expresses the value of the firm in terms of "current" dollars — generally inflated dollars relative to those in use at the start of the Game.

Summary. This completes our discussion of the quarterly reports. The first two lines of each report sheet keep you informed about the general situation. The report, Information on Competitors, gives you some idea what other firms are doing and how your performance compares with theirs. The Operating Statements tell you about your market performance and physical assets. The Income Statement tells how you came out, leading to the famous *bottom line* (NET PROFIT AFTER TAXES) — which is actually the third line from the end of the Income Statement. The Cash Flow statement helps you keep track of money as such. Finally, the Financial Statement tells you where you stand financially; its "bottom line," from the viewpoint of ownership, is the economic equity figure.

End of Fiscal Year Report. A special report is normally prepared at the end of each year of play of the Executive Game, and also when the Game ends. Tables 29 and 39 show examples of this End of Fiscal Year report. You will note that each item of this report, except the last two, is extracted directly from either the quarterly reports prepared at the same time (CASH, the values of two inventories, PLANT AND EQUIPMENT REPLACEMENT VALUE, ROBOTICS REPLACEMENT VALUE, and OWNERS' ECONOMIC EQUITY, for each firm), or a four-quarter average of figures from the pertinent four quarterly reports (MARKETING, R&D, SALES VOLUME, NET PROFIT, for each firm).

The last two figures are RATE OF RETURN (ROI) and RANK. ROI was fully explained earlier in this chapter. RANK is simply each firm's current position in the race for maximum ROI.

These last two figures tell you where each firm stands, both in absolute terms (ROI itself) and relative to its competitors (RANK). The other information in this report, together with the Information on Competitors given by the quarterly reports, will help you to see what sorts of policies have been more effective or less effective in your particular Game.

It is easy to infer more from this information than is really justified. For instance, it's natural to suppose that a poor ROI must have resulted from a poor marketing strategy, although the actual cause may have been poor coordination of the marketing strategy with the PRODUCTION VOLUME decision. Still, looking at the leading firms, especially insofar as you can see how these firms differ from the trailing firms, should give you an improved understanding of how the Game works. This understanding, rather than mere imitation of strategies that have been successful in the past, will help you to make good decisions for your own firm's future.

The Management Team

The large Work Sheet provided in Appendix F is designed to facilitate a quarterly "spreadsheet analysis" in the Executive Game. Chapter 4 will guide you through this analysis, step by step. This procedure is a specially tailored version of a technique so widely used by modern management that many of the top-selling computer software items are nothing more than computer programs designed to automate certain parts of the analysis. A powerful hand calculator will give you enough computing power for spreadsheet analysis in the Game, but you'll save a lot of work and learn how to use a very powerful tool if you can get access to one of the pertinent computerized spreadsheets — such as VISICALC, SUPERCALC, PERFECT CALC, MASTER PLANNER, LOTUS 1-2-3, or MULTIPLAN. If such programs are not available at your school, you may be able to find a local businessman who will be willing to help out.

The most successful Executive Game management teams usually rely heavily on the Work Sheet. When reports become available, they meet to review what they've done and how they've come out in the quarter or year just ended. The old Work Sheet provides a focus for this analysis, often making it easy to discover the reasons behind surprising successes or failures, and to sharpen understanding even when events have gone pretty much as expected. The Work Sheet is helpful not only as a basis for analysis, but also because it provides an external focus of attention that makes it much easier for teams to concentrate on resolving problems rather than dwelling on the question of who is to blame. Many of the most capable teams, incidentally, try to separate this review meeting from the later decision-making meeting, sometimes even going so far as to establish the ground rule that people are *not* to talk about "what we should do next quarter" at the review meeting.

For practical reasons, the decision-making meeting is sometimes just the second part of the review meeting. But better results seem to be attained if there is actually an interval between meetings, so that team members can each come to the decision meeting with their own Work Sheets already roughed out, and often annotated to keep track of their reasons for particular entries at the choice points. The team discussion then centers around these choice points, with much more time spent on reasons than on conclusions. It is often important to stop and talk about reasons even at those points where there seems to be initial agreement about conclusions, because (for instance) three different reasons for putting $200,000 into a certain budget may very well add up to a good argument for raising this figure to $300,000.

Experience also suggests that it is worthwhile for each team to take time regularly for general discussion about how the Game is going, what has gone right or wrong and why, and about the goals that the team hopes to gain — such as a target value of ROI, or a target ranking within the industry. This will help team members to learn from each other, both about the Game itself and about what is to be learned from the Game.

Finally, it is worthwhile to take time frequently to talk about how your management team is functioning. Is it really making the best use of the knowledge and talents of all its members in the decision-making process? Are you, as a team, listening to and distilling the best out of different team members' perspectives toward the Game, or is one (probably self-appointed) leader running things with an iron hand and a narrow mind? Are you helping one another to learn, both directly and by the way discussions and decision processes are handled? The more each teammate is concerned with everyone else's learning interests, the better the learning experience for all concerned. To guarantee a really great learning experience, each member of the team should look at the learning process like the three musketeers looked at a fight — all for one and one for all.

Words of Encouragement

The Executive Game *is* complicated. This chapter, on "basics," contains an enormous amount of information — and that on top of a warning to the effect that you'll have to go beyond the chapter before you can really understand what's going on. We hope you are beginning to sense that all this information about the Game does fall into reasonably comprehensible patterns, even though you may not yet have a clear picture of these patterns. But at this moment you may still feel like an unhappy and perhaps unwilling victim of information overload, more overload, and still more overload.

If you do feel that way, take heart! Go on to Chapter 3 where we concentrate on pattern rather than detail, and Chapter 4, where detail again dominates, but in the context of easily followed step-by-step procedures. Then, when you actually start making decisions in the Game, you can be sure that everything will fall together fairly quickly and fairly clearly. Many thousands of people with widely varying aptitudes and knowledge have learned to play the Executive Game, and have in fact found it enjoyable as well as educational. We have no doubt that you will soon join the happy throng.

Supplementary Reading

Business Week magazine.

Fortune magazine.

Wall Street Journal newspaper.

Spreadsheet Computer Programs

There are numerous instructional books, reference manuals, computerized tutorials, etc., for the various spreadsheet programs. The best one for any user depends both upon the program to be applied and the computer with which it is used. Further, the programs, and consequently the instructional materials for them, are updated every year or two (sometimes even more often. Consequently, we shall not reference this material explicitly. Usually what you need will be available wherever a spreadsheet program is available for your use. Supplementary materials can be found in computer stores and the computer sections of large bookstores (especially college bookstores), and some libraries.

Firm No. 5-4

TABLE 2
MASTER COPY–to be detached and handed in at end of Game
EXECUTIVE GAME–DECISION SHEET*

Periods 0 - 4 Model No. 1
Periods 5 - 8 Model No. 2

Period of Year	Period No.	Price $	Marketing Budget $	R & D Budget $	Maintenance Budget $	Prod. Vol. Sch. Maximums: Model 1 1.4xCY1 Model 2 3.0xCY1 units	Investment in Robotics $	Investment in Plant & Equipment $	Purchase of Materials $	Dividend Declared (Max: owners' equity minus $9,000,000 $
AMJ	0	25.60	200,000	100,000	75,000	100,000	,0	500,000	1,000,000	53,000
JAS	Trial 1	25.35	341,750	100,000	88,565	115,206	,0	200,000	285,000	40,000
OND	Trial 2	.	,	,	,	,	,	,	,	,
AMJ	0	25.60	200,000	100,000	75,000	100,000	0	500,000	1,000,000	53,000
JAS	1	23.10	322,500	125,000	107,940	140,410	75,000	375,000	730,000	100,000
OND	2	23.70	265,000	210,000	116,379	151,387	78,750	891,513	975,077	103,333
JFM	3	25.15	394,850	200,000	115,313	150,000	82,500	270,000	865,919	183,333
AMJ	4	26.06	450,000	225,000	115,710	145,000	86,250	270,000	786,130	183,333
JAS	5	26.32	285,000	75,000	127,032	158,000	105,000	216,633	1,023,400	300,000
OND	6	27.05	335,000	101,667	141,095	172,673	109,500	270,000	1,034,287	700,000
JFM	7	27.05	900,000	101,666	141,203	171,000	125,000	270,000	1,600,000	200,000
AMJ	8	30.00	200,000	101,667	149,597	177,853	130,000	270,000	500,000	1,000,000
JAS	9	.	,	,	,	,	,	,	, ,	,
OND	10	.	,	,	,	,	,	,	, ,	,
JFM	11	.	,	,	,	,	,	,	, ,	,
AMJ	12	.	,	,	,	,	,	,	, ,	,

FORECASTS: ECONOMIC AND SEASONAL INDICES

Period of Year	AMJ	JAS	OND	AMJ	JAS	OND	JFM	AMJ	JAS	OND	JFM	AMJ	JAS	OND	JFM	AMJ
Period No.	0	T1	T2	0	1	2	3	4	5	6	7	8	9	10	11	12
Forecast, Econ. Index	100	100	95	100	100	95	93	90	95	97	100	100	103	105	107	107
Changes (if any)																
Seasonal Index	100	95	115	100	95	115	90	100	95	115	90	100	95	115	90	100
Changes (if any)																

* The individual team member should enter his/her team's consolidated decisions for each quarter on this sheet.

Table 3
Executive Game Quarterly Statement, Period 0

0 25.60 200000. 100000. 75000. 100000. 0. 500000. 1000000. 53000.

EXECUTIVE GAME

MODEL 1 PERIOD 0 AMJ PRICE INDEX 100.0 FORECAST,ANNUAL CHANGE 5.0 0/0
SEAS.INDEX 100. NEXT QTR. 95. ECON.INDEX 100. FORECAST,NEXT QTR. 100.

INFORMATION ON COMPETITORS

	PRICE	DIVIDEND	SALES VOLUME	NET PROFIT
FIRM 1	$ 25.60	$ 53000.	109720.	$ 282104.
FIRM 2	$ 25.60	$ 53000.	109720.	$ 282104.
FIRM 3	$ 25.60	$ 53000.	109720.	$ 282104.
FIRM 4	$ 25.60	$ 53000.	109720.	$ 282104.
FIRM 5	$ 25.60	$ 53000.	109720.	$ 282104.
FIRM 6	$ 25.60	$ 53000.	109720.	$ 282104.

FIRM 5 -

OPERATING STATEMENTS

MARKET POTENTIAL	109720.	
SALES VOLUME	109720.	
PERCENT SHARE OF INDUSTRY SALES	16.7	
PRODUCTION,THIS QUARTER	100000.	
INVENTORY,FINISHED GOODS	12750.	
PLANT CAPACITY,NEXT QUARTER	104643.	

INCOME STATEMENT

RECEIPTS,SALES REVENUE		$ 2808832.
EXPENSES,MARKETING	$ 200000.	
RESEARCH AND DEVELOPMENT	100000.	
ADMINISTRATION	278000.	
MAINTENANCE	75000.	
LABOR(COST/UNIT EX.OVERTIME $ 5.74)	573939.	
MATERIALS CONSUMED(COST/UNIT 6.31)	630667.	
REDUCTION,FINISHED GOODS INV.	116638.	
PLANT&EQ.DEPRECIATION(2.500 0/0)	183125.	
ROBOTICS DEPRECIATION(5.000 0/0)	0.	
FINISHED GOODS CARRYING COSTS	25500.	
RAW MATERIALS CARRYING COSTS	41533.	
ORDERING COSTS	50000.	
SHIFTS CHANGE COSTS	0.	
INVESTMENTS EXPENSES	25000.	
FINANCING CHARGES AND PENALTIES	0.	
SUNDRIES	82000.	2381402.
PROFIT BEFORE INCOME TAX		427430.
INCOME TAX(IN.TX.CR. 0. 0/0,SURTAX 0. 0/0)		145326.
NET PROFIT AFTER INCOME TAX		282104.
DIVIDENDS PAID		53000.
ADDITION TO OWNERS EQUITY		229104.

CASH FLOW

RECEIPTS,SALES REVENUE		$ 2808832.
DISBURSEMENTS,CASH EXPENSE	$ 1450972.	
INCOME TAX	145320.	
DIVIDENDS PAID	53000.	
ROBOTICS INVESTMENT	0.	
PLANT&EQ.INVESTMENT	500000.	
MATERIALS PURCHASED	1000000.	3149298.
ADDITION TO CASH ASSETS		-340466.

FINANCIAL STATEMENT

NET ASSETS,CASH		$ 1022000.
INV. VALUE,FINISHED GOODS		153000.
INVENTORY VALUE,MATERIALS		1200000.
ROBOTICS BOOK VALUE(REPLACE.VAL.$	0.)	0.
PLANT&EQ.BOOK VALUE(REPLACE.VAL.	7325000.)	7325000.
OWNERS EQUITY(ECONOMIC EQUITY	9700000.)	9700000.

Table 4
Executive Game Quarterly Statement, Trial Period 1, Firm 5-4, Model 1

```
54 1 25.35  341750.  100000.  88565. 115206.      0. 200000.  285000.   40000.

          TRIAL               EXECUTIVE GAME
MODEL 1 PERIOD  1 JAS PRICE INDEX 101.0 FORECAST,ANNUAL CHANGE  5.3 0/0
SEAS.INDEX  95. NEXT QTR. 115.  ECON.INDEX 101. FORECAST,NEXT QTR.  95.

                  INFORMATION            ON           COMPETITORS
             PRICE              DIVIDEND      SALES VOLUME          NET PROFIT
  FIRM 1    $ 21.00          $    53000.          112750.         $    -36908.
  FIRM 2    $ 25.40          $    50000.           85622.         $     21427.
  FIRM 3    $ 25.49          $    70000.           87684.         $    -58776.
  FIRM 4    $ 25.35          $    40000.          102156.         $     25157.
  FIRM 5    $ 23.10          $    53000.          142750.         $    262901.
  FIRM 6    $ 25.49          $    53000.           88498.         $     76961.

                                    FIRM  5 4
                            OPERATING STATEMENTS
     MARKET POTENTIAL                               102156.
     SALES VOLUME                                   102156.
     PERCENT SHARE OF INDUSTRY SALES                   16.5
     PRODUCTION,THIS QUARTER                        115206.
     INVENTORY,FINISHED GOODS                        25800.
     PLANT CAPACITY,NEXT QUARTER                    105379.
                                 INCOME STATEMENT
     RECEIPTS,SALES REVENUE                                          $  2589658.
     EXPENSES,MARKETING                           $  341750.
       RESEARCH AND DEVELOPMENT                      100000.
       ADMINISTRATION                                330179.
       MAINTENANCE                                    88565.
       LABOR(COST/UNIT EX.OVERTIME $ 5.71)           688538.
       MATERIALS CONSUMED(COST/UNIT  6.30)           725928.
       REDUCTION,FINISHED GOODS INV.                -156599.
       PLANT&EQ.DEPRECIATION(2.500 0/0)              183125.
       ROBOTICS DEPRECIATION(5.000 0/0)                   0.
       FINISHED GOODS CARRYING COSTS                  51600.
       RAW MATERIALS CARRYING COSTS                   60000.
       ORDERING COSTS                                 50000.
       SHIFTS CHANGE COSTS                                0.
       INVESTMENTS EXPENSES                            4000.
       FINANCING CHARGES AND PENALTIES                    0.
       SUNDRIES                                       84459.        2551541.
     PROFIT BEFORE INCOME TAX                                          38117.
     INCOME TAX(IN.TX.CR.  0. 0/0,SURTAX  0. 0/0)                      12960.
     NET PROFIT AFTER INCOME TAX                                       25157.
     DIVIDENDS PAID                                                    40000.
     ADDITION TO OWNERS EQUITY                                        -14843.
                                    CASH FLOW
     RECEIPTS,SALES REVENUE                                          $  2589658.
     DISBURSEMENTS,CASH EXPENSE               $  1799085.
       INCOME TAX                                  12960.
       DIVIDENDS PAID                              40000.
       ROBOTICS INVESTMENT                             0.
       PLANT&EQ.INVESTMENT                        200000.
       MATERIALS PURCHASED                        285000.           2337044.
     ADDITION TO CASH ASSETS                                          252614.
                               FINANCIAL STATEMENT
     NET ASSETS,CASH                                                 $  1274614.
       INV. VALUE,FINISHED GOODS                                        309599.
       INVENTORY VALUE,MATERIALS                                        759072.
       ROBOTICS BOOK VALUE(REPLACE.VAL.$          0.)                       0.
       PLANT&EQ.BOOK VALUE(REPLACE.VAL.   7449239.)                   7341875.
     OWNERS EQUITY(ECONOMIC EQUITY        9792522.)                   9685158.
```

Table 5
Executive Game Quarterly Statement, Period 1, Firm 5-1, Model 1

```
51 1 25.60   205000.  110000.  80445. 104642.  50000. 300000.  700000.   30000.

                              EXECUTIVE GAME
MODEL 1 PERIOD  1 JAS PRICE INDEX 101.0 FORECAST,ANNUAL CHANGE  5.3 0/0
SEAS.INDEX  95. NEXT QTR. 115.  ECON.INDEX 101. FORECAST,NEXT QTR.  95.

                  INFORMATION           ON          COMPETITORS
            PRICE            DIVIDEND       SALES VOLUME          NET PROFIT
  FIRM 1   $ 25.60         $   30000.          70953.          $   -129901.
  FIRM 2   $ 25.40         $   73000.          77604.          $    -96425.
  FIRM 3   $ 23.60         $   60000.         127750.          $     94383.
  FIRM 4   $ 23.10         $  100000.         153160.          $    208386.
  FIRM 5   $ 23.04         $   30000.         127750.          $    179449.
  FIRM 6   $ 21.00         $   40000.         152750.          $    -53381.

                                    FIRM  5 1
                            OPERATING STATEMENTS
     MARKET POTENTIAL                                  70953.
     SALES VOLUME                                      70953.
     PERCENT SHARE OF INDUSTRY SALES                     10.0
     PRODUCTION,THIS QUARTER                          104642.
     INVENTORY,FINISHED GOODS                          46439.
     PLANT CAPACITY,NEXT QUARTER                      107327.
                                INCOME STATEMENT
     RECEIPTS,SALES REVENUE                                           $  1816406.
     EXPENSES,MARKETING                             $  205000.
       RESEARCH AND DEVELOPMENT                        110000.
       ADMINISTRATION                                  280742.
       MAINTENANCE                                      80445.
       LABOR(COST/UNIT EX.OVERTIME $ 5.72)             599003.
       MATERIALS CONSUMED(COST/UNIT  6.30)             659591.
       REDUCTION,FINISHED GOODS INV.                  -404264.
       PLANT&EQ.DEPRECIATION(2.500 0/0)                183125.
       ROBOTICS DEPRECIATION(5.000 0/0)                     0.
       FINISHED GOODS CARRYING COSTS                    92877.
       RAW MATERIALS CARRYING COSTS                     60000.
       ORDERING COSTS                                   50000.
       SHIFTS CHANGE COSTS                                  0.
       INVESTMENTS EXPENSES                             12250.
       FINANCING CHARGES AND PENALTIES                      0.
       SUNDRIES                                         84459.          2013226.
     PROFIT BEFORE INCOME TAX                                          -196820.
     INCOME TAX(IN.TX.CR.  0. 0/0,SURTAX  0. 0/0)                       -66919.
     NET PROFIT AFTER INCOME TAX                                       -129901.
     DIVIDENDS PAID                                                      30000.
     ADDITION TO OWNERS EQUITY                                         -159901.
                                     CASH FLOW
     RECEIPTS,SALES REVENUE                                           $  1816406.
     DISBURSEMENTS,CASH EXPENSE                 $  1574773.
       INCOME TAX                                   -66919.
       DIVIDENDS PAID                                30000.
       ROBOTICS INVESTMENT                           50000.
       PLANT&EQ.INVESTMENT                          300000.
       MATERIALS PURCHASED                          700000.                2587854.
     ADDITION TO CASH ASSETS                                            -771448.
                                FINANCIAL STATEMENT
     NET ASSETS,CASH                                                  $   250552.
       INV. VALUE,FINISHED GOODS                                         557264.
       INVENTORY VALUE,MATERIALS                                        1240409.
       ROBOTICS BOOK VALUE(REPLACE.VAL.$       50000.)                    50000.
       PLANT&EQ.BOOK VALUE(REPLACE.VAL.      7549239.)                  7441875.
     OWNERS EQUITY(ECONOMIC EQUITY           9647463.)                  9540099.
```

Table 6
Executive Game Quarterly Statement, Period 1, Firm 5-2, Model 1

```
52 1 25.40  225000.  125000.  75000. 100000.  10000. 520000. 1000000.   73000.

                              EXECUTIVE GAME
MODEL 1 PERIOD  1 JAS PRICE INDEX 101.0 FORECAST,ANNUAL CHANGE  5.3 0/0
SEAS.INDEX  95. NEXT QTR. 115.  ECON.INDEX 101. FORECAST,NEXT QTR.  95.
```

INFORMATION ON COMPETITORS

	PRICE	DIVIDEND	SALES VOLUME	NET PROFIT
FIRM 1	$ 25.60	$ 30000.	70953.	$ -129901.
FIRM 2	$ 25.40	$ 73000.	77604.	$ -96425.
FIRM 3	$ 23.60	$ 60000.	127750.	$ 94383.
FIRM 4	$ 23.10	$ 100000.	153160.	$ 208386.
FIRM 5	$ 23.04	$ 30000.	127750.	$ 179449.
FIRM 6	$ 21.00	$ 40000.	152750.	$ -53381.

```
                              FIRM  5 2
                         OPERATING STATEMENTS
MARKET POTENTIAL                                   77604.
SALES VOLUME                                       77604.
PERCENT SHARE OF INDUSTRY SALES                      10.9
PRODUCTION,THIS QUARTER                           100000.
INVENTORY,FINISHED GOODS                           35146.
PLANT CAPACITY,NEXT QUARTER                       110016.
                           INCOME STATEMENT
RECEIPTS,SALES REVENUE                                        $  1971141.
EXPENSES,MARKETING                             $  225000.
  RESEARCH AND DEVELOPMENT                        125000.
  ADMINISTRATION                                  280742.
  MAINTENANCE                                      75000.
  LABOR(COST/UNIT EX.OVERTIME $ 5.74)             573677.
  MATERIALS CONSUMED(COST/UNIT  6.31)             630609.
  REDUCTION,FINISHED GOODS INV.                  -268752.
  PLANT&EQ.DEPRECIATION(2.500 0/0)                183125.
  ROBOTICS DEPRECIATION(5.000 0/0)                     0.
  FINISHED GOODS CARRYING COSTS                    70292.
  RAW MATERIALS CARRYING COSTS                     60000.
  ORDERING COSTS                                   50000.
  SHIFTS CHANGE COSTS                                  0.
  INVESTMENTS EXPENSES                             28090.
  FINANCING CHARGES AND PENALTIES                      0.
  SUNDRIES                                         84459.       2117239.
PROFIT BEFORE INCOME TAX                                        -146098.
INCOME TAX(IN.TX.CR.  0. 0/0,SURTAX  0. 0/0)                     -49673.
NET PROFIT AFTER INCOME TAX                                      -96425.
DIVIDENDS PAID                                                    73000.
ADDITION TO OWNERS EQUITY                                       -169425.
                             CASH FLOW
RECEIPTS,SALES REVENUE                                        $  1971141.
DISBURSEMENTS,CASH EXPENSE                 $  1572257.
  INCOME TAX                                   -49673.
  DIVIDENDS PAID                                73000.
  ROBOTICS INVESTMENT                           10000.
  PLANT&EQ.INVESTMENT                          520000.
  MATERIALS PURCHASED                         1000000.          3125583.
ADDITION TO CASH ASSETS                                        -1154442.
                          FINANCIAL STATEMENT
NET ASSETS,CASH                                               $  -132442.
  INV. VALUE,FINISHED GOODS                                       421752.
  INVENTORY VALUE,MATERIALS                                      1569391.
  ROBOTICS BOOK VALUE(REPLACE.VAL.$     10000.)                    10000.
  PLANT&EQ.BOOK VALUE(REPLACE.VAL.    7769239.)                  7661875.
OWNERS EQUITY(ECONOMIC EQUITY         9637940.)                  9530576.
```

Table 7
Executive Game Quarterly Statement, Period 1, Firm 5-3, Model 1

53 1 23.60 250000. 250000. 90000. 115000. 25000. 300000. 500000. 60000.

EXECUTIVE GAME

MODEL 1 PERIOD 1 JAS PRICE INDEX 101.0 FORECAST,ANNUAL CHANGE 5.3 0/0
SEAS.INDEX 95. NEXT QTR. 115. ECON.INDEX 101. FORECAST,NEXT QTR. 95.

INFORMATION ON COMPETITORS

	PRICE	DIVIDEND	SALES VOLUME	NET PROFIT
FIRM 1	$ 25.60	$ 30000.	70953.	$ -129901.
FIRM 2	$ 25.40	$ 73000.	77604.	$ -96425.
FIRM 3	$ 23.60	$ 60000.	127750.	$ 94383.
FIRM 4	$ 23.10	$ 100000.	153160.	$ 208386.
FIRM 5	$ 23.04	$ 30000.	127750.	$ 179449.
FIRM 6	$ 21.00	$ 40000.	152750.	$ -53381.

FIRM 5 3

OPERATING STATEMENTS

MARKET POTENTIAL	135241.	
SALES VOLUME	127750.	
PERCENT SHARE OF INDUSTRY SALES	18.0	
PRODUCTION,THIS QUARTER	115000.	
INVENTORY,FINISHED GOODS	0.	
PLANT CAPACITY,NEXT QUARTER	107061.	

INCOME STATEMENT

RECEIPTS,SALES REVENUE		$ 3014900.
EXPENSES,MARKETING	$ 250000.	
RESEARCH AND DEVELOPMENT	250000.	
ADMINISTRATION	330179.	
MAINTENANCE	90000.	
LABOR(COST/UNIT EX.OVERTIME $ 5.71)	686092.	
MATERIALS CONSUMED(COST/UNIT 6.30)	724483.	
REDUCTION,FINISHED GOODS INV.	153000.	
PLANT&EQ.DEPRECIATION(2.500 0/0)	183125.	
ROBOTICS DEPRECIATION(5.000 0/0)	0.	
FINISHED GOODS CARRYING COSTS	0.	
RAW MATERIALS CARRYING COSTS	60000.	
ORDERING COSTS	50000.	
SHIFTS CHANGE COSTS	0.	
INVESTMENTS EXPENSES	10563.	
FINANCING CHARGES AND PENALTIES	0.	
SUNDRIES	84459.	2871896.
PROFIT BEFORE INCOME TAX		143004.
INCOME TAX(IN.TX.CR. 0. 0/0,SURTAX 0. 0/0)		48621.
NET PROFIT AFTER INCOME TAX		94383.
DIVIDENDS PAID		60000.
ADDITION TO OWNERS EQUITY		34383.

CASH FLOW

RECEIPTS,SALES REVENUE		$ 3014900.
DISBURSEMENTS,CASH EXPENSE	$ 1811287.	
INCOME TAX	48621.	
DIVIDENDS PAID	60000.	
ROBOTICS INVESTMENT	25000.	
PLANT&EQ.INVESTMENT	300000.	
MATERIALS PURCHASED	500000.	2744908.
ADDITION TO CASH ASSETS		269992.

FINANCIAL STATEMENT

NET ASSETS,CASH		$ 1291992.
INV. VALUE,FINISHED GOODS		0.
INVENTORY VALUE,MATERIALS		975517.
ROBOTICS BOOK VALUE(REPLACE.VAL.$	25000.)	25000.
PLANT&EQ.BOOK VALUE(REPLACE.VAL.	7549239.)	7441875.
OWNERS EQUITY(ECONOMIC EQUITY	9841747.)	9734383.

Table 8
Executive Game Quarterly Statement, Period 1, Firm 5-4, Model 1

54 1 23.10 322500. 125000. 107940. 140410. 75000. 375000. 730000. 100000.

EXECUTIVE GAME

MODEL 1 PERIOD 1 JAS PRICE INDEX 101.0 FORECAST,ANNUAL CHANGE 5.3 0/0
SEAS.INDEX 95. NEXT QTR. 115. ECON.INDEX 101. FORECAST,NEXT QTR. 95.

INFORMATION ON COMPETITORS

	PRICE	DIVIDEND	SALES VOLUME	NET PROFIT
FIRM 1	$ 25.60	$ 30000.	70953.	$ -129901.
FIRM 2	$ 25.40	$ 73000.	77604.	$ -96425.
FIRM 3	$ 23.60	$ 60000.	127750.	$ 94383.
FIRM 4	$ 23.10	$ 100000.	153160.	$ 208386.
FIRM 5	$ 23.04	$ 30000.	127750.	$ 179449.
FIRM 6	$ 21.00	$ 40000.	152750.	$ -53381.

FIRM 5 4

OPERATING STATEMENTS

MARKET POTENTIAL	164930.	
SALES VOLUME	153160.	
PERCENT SHARE OF INDUSTRY SALES	21.6	
PRODUCTION,THIS QUARTER	140410.	
INVENTORY,FINISHED GOODS	0.	
PLANT CAPACITY,NEXT QUARTER	108661.	

INCOME STATEMENT

RECEIPTS,SALES REVENUE		$ 3537996.
EXPENSES,MARKETING	$ 322500.	
RESEARCH AND DEVELOPMENT	125000.	
ADMINISTRATION	330179.	
MAINTENANCE	107940.	
LABOR(COST/UNIT EX.OVERTIME $ 5.70)	901657.	
MATERIALS CONSUMED(COST/UNIT 6.30)	884152.	
REDUCTION,FINISHED GOODS INV.	153000.	
PLANT&EQ.DEPRECIATION(2.500 0/0)	183125.	
ROBOTICS DEPRECIATION(5.000 0/0)	0.	
FINISHED GOODS CARRYING COSTS	0.	
RAW MATERIALS CARRYING COSTS	60000.	
ORDERING COSTS	50000.	
SHIFTS CHANGE COSTS	0.	
INVESTMENTS EXPENSES	20250.	
FINANCING CHARGES AND PENALTIES	0.	
SUNDRIES	84459.	3222259.
PROFIT BEFORE INCOME TAX		315737.
INCOME TAX(IN.TX.CR. 0. 0/0,SURTAX 0. 0/0)		107351.
NET PROFIT AFTER INCOME TAX		208386.
DIVIDENDS PAID		100000.
ADDITION TO OWNERS EQUITY		108386.

CASH FLOW

RECEIPTS,SALES REVENUE		$ 3537996.
DISBURSEMENTS,CASH EXPENSE	$ 2001981.	
INCOME TAX	107351.	
DIVIDENDS PAID	100000.	
ROBOTICS INVESTMENT	75000.	
PLANT&EQ.INVESTMENT	375000.	
MATERIALS PURCHASED	730000.	3389331.
ADDITION TO CASH ASSETS		148665.

FINANCIAL STATEMENT

NET ASSETS,CASH		$ 1170665.
INV. VALUE,FINISHED GOODS		0.
INVENTORY VALUE,MATERIALS		1045848.
ROBOTICS BOOK VALUE(REPLACE.VAL.$	75000.)	75000.
PLANT&EQ.BOOK VALUE(REPLACE.VAL.	7624236.)	7516875.
OWNERS EQUITY(ECONOMIC EQUITY	9915748.)	9808387.

Table 9
Executive Game Quarterly Statement, Period 1, Firm 5-5, Model 1

55 1 23.04 210000. 105000. 79000. 115000. 10000. 28000. 725000. 30000.

EXECUTIVE GAME

MODEL 1 PERIOD 1 JAS PRICE INDEX 101.0 FORECAST,ANNUAL CHANGE 5.3 0/0
SEAS.INDEX 95. NEXT QTR. 115. ECON.INDEX 101. FORECAST,NEXT QTR. 95.

INFORMATION ON COMPETITORS

	PRICE	DIVIDEND	SALES VOLUME	NET PROFIT
FIRM 1	$ 25.60	$ 30000.	70953.	$ -129901.
FIRM 2	$ 25.40	$ 73000.	77604.	$ -96425.
FIRM 3	$ 23.60	$ 60000.	127750.	$ 94383.
FIRM 4	$ 23.10	$ 100000.	153160.	$ 208386.
FIRM 5	$ 23.04	$ 30000.	127750.	$ 179449.
FIRM 6	$ 21.00	$ 40000.	152750.	$ -53381.

FIRM 5 5

OPERATING STATEMENTS

MARKET POTENTIAL	142680.	
SALES VOLUME	127750.	
PERCENT SHARE OF INDUSTRY SALES	18.0	
PRODUCTION,THIS QUARTER	115000.	
INVENTORY,FINISHED GOODS	0.	
PLANT CAPACITY,NEXT QUARTER	103049.	

INCOME STATEMENT

RECEIPTS,SALES REVENUE		$ 2943359.
EXPENSES,MARKETING	$ 210000.	
RESEARCH AND DEVELOPMENT	105000.	
ADMINISTRATION	330179.	
MAINTENANCE	79000.	
LABOR(COST/UNIT EX.OVERTIME $ 5.75)	691026.	
MATERIALS CONSUMED(COST/UNIT 6.31)	725536.	
REDUCTION,FINISHED GOODS INV.	153000.	
PLANT&EQ.DEPRECIATION(2.500 0/0)	183125.	
ROBOTICS DEPRECIATION(5.000 0/0)	0.	
FINISHED GOODS CARRYING COSTS	0.	
RAW MATERIALS CARRYING COSTS	60000.	
ORDERING COSTS	50000.	
SHIFTS CHANGE COSTS	0.	
INVESTMENTS EXPENSES	144.	
FINANCING CHARGES AND PENALTIES	0.	
SUNDRIES	84459.	2671466.
PROFIT BEFORE INCOME TAX		271893.
INCOME TAX(IN.TX.CR. 0. 0/0,SURTAX 0. 0/0)		92444.
NET PROFIT AFTER INCOME TAX		179449.
DIVIDENDS PAID		30000.
ADDITION TO OWNERS EQUITY		149449.

CASH FLOW

RECEIPTS,SALES REVENUE		$ 2943359.
DISBURSEMENTS,CASH EXPENSE	$ 1609804.	
INCOME TAX	92444.	
DIVIDENDS PAID	30000.	
ROBOTICS INVESTMENT	10000.	
PLANT&EQ.INVESTMENT	28000.	
MATERIALS PURCHASED	725000.	2495247.
ADDITION TO CASH ASSETS		448112.

FINANCIAL STATEMENT

NET ASSETS,CASH		$ 1470112.
INV. VALUE,FINISHED GOODS		0.
INVENTORY VALUE,MATERIALS		1199463.
ROBOTICS BOOK VALUE(REPLACE.VAL.$	10000.)	10000.
PLANT&EQ.BOOK VALUE(REPLACE.VAL.	7277238.)	7169875.
OWNERS EQUITY(ECONOMIC EQUITY	9956813.)	9849450.

Table 10
Executive Game Quarterly Statement, Period 1, Firm 5-6, Model 1

56 1 21.00 250000. 300000. 80000. 140000. 0. 100000. 600000. 40000.

EXECUTIVE GAME
MODEL 1 PERIOD 1 JAS PRICE INDEX 101.0 FORECAST,ANNUAL CHANGE 5.3 0/0
SEAS.INDEX 95. NEXT QTR. 115. ECON.INDEX 101. FORECAST,NEXT QTR. 95.

INFORMATION ON COMPETITORS

	PRICE	DIVIDEND	SALES VOLUME	NET PROFIT
FIRM 1	$ 25.60	$ 30000.	70953.	$ -129901.
FIRM 2	$ 25.40	$ 73000.	77604.	$ -96425.
FIRM 3	$ 23.60	$ 60000.	127750.	$ 94383.
FIRM 4	$ 23.10	$ 100000.	153160.	$ 208386.
FIRM 5	$ 23.04	$ 30000.	127750.	$ 179449.
FIRM 6	$ 21.00	$ 40000.	152750.	$ -53381.

FIRM 5 6
OPERATING STATEMENTS

MARKET POTENTIAL	208399.	
SALES VOLUME	152750.	
PERCENT SHARE OF INDUSTRY SALES	21.5	
PRODUCTION,THIS QUARTER	140000.	
INVENTORY,FINISHED GOODS	0.	
PLANT CAPACITY,NEXT QUARTER	103965.	

INCOME STATEMENT

RECEIPTS,SALES REVENUE		$ 3207750.
EXPENSES,MARKETING	$ 250000.	
RESEARCH AND DEVELOPMENT	300000.	
ADMINISTRATION	330179.	
MAINTENANCE	80000.	
LABOR(COST/UNIT EX.OVERTIME $ 5.79)	912489.	
MATERIALS CONSUMED(COST/UNIT 6.32)	884383.	
REDUCTION,FINISHED GOODS INV.	153000.	
PLANT&EQ.DEPRECIATION(2.500 0/0)	183125.	
ROBOTICS DEPRECIATION(5.000 0/0)	0.	
FINISHED GOODS CARRYING COSTS	0.	
RAW MATERIALS CARRYING COSTS	60000.	
ORDERING COSTS	50000.	
SHIFTS CHANGE COSTS	0.	
INVESTMENTS EXPENSES	1000.	
FINANCING CHARGES AND PENALTIES	0.	
SUNDRIES	84459.	3288631.
PROFIT BEFORE INCOME TAX		-80881.
INCOME TAX(IN.TX.CR. 0. 0/0,SURTAX 0. 0/0)		-27500.
NET PROFIT AFTER INCOME TAX		-53381.
DIVIDENDS PAID		40000.
ADDITION TO OWNERS EQUITY		-93381.

CASH FLOW

RECEIPTS,SALES REVENUE		$ 3207750.
DISBURSEMENTS,CASH EXPENSE	$ 2068123.	
INCOME TAX	-27500.	
DIVIDENDS PAID	40000.	
ROBOTICS INVESTMENT	0.	
PLANT&EQ.INVESTMENT	100000.	
MATERIALS PURCHASED	600000.	2780623.
ADDITION TO CASH ASSETS		427127.

FINANCIAL STATEMENT

NET ASSETS,CASH		$ 1449127.
INV. VALUE,FINISHED GOODS		0.
INVENTORY VALUE,MATERIALS		915617.
ROBOTICS BOOK VALUE(REPLACE.VAL.$	0.)	0.
PLANT&EQ.BOOK VALUE(REPLACE.VAL.	7349240.)	7241875.
OWNERS EQUITY(ECONOMIC EQUITY	9713984.)	9606619.

Table 11
Executive Game Quarterly Statement, Period 2, Firm 5-1, Model 1

51 2 24.34 155000. 50000. 80813. 105000. 0. 9000. 145000. 0.

EXECUTIVE GAME

MODEL 1 PERIOD 2 OND PRICE INDEX 102.5 FORECAST,ANNUAL CHANGE 5.0 0/0
SEAS.INDEX 115. NEXT QTR. 90. ECON.INDEX 94. FORECAST,NEXT QTR. 93.

INFORMATION ON COMPETITORS

	PRICE	DIVIDEND	SALES VOLUME	NET PROFIT
FIRM 1	$ 24.34	$ 0.	124967.	$ 350651.
FIRM 2	$ 24.79	$ 85000.	118486.	$ 173430.
FIRM 3	$ 23.99	$ 66000.	149150.	$ 138741.
FIRM 4	$ 23.70	$ 183333.	151387.	$ 174208.
FIRM 5	$ 21.90	$ 30000.	144270.	$ 95467.
FIRM 6	$ 22.80	$ 75000.	144818.	$ 18223.

FIRM 5 1

OPERATING STATEMENTS

MARKET POTENTIAL	124967.	
SALES VOLUME	124967.	
PERCENT SHARE OF INDUSTRY SALES	15.0	
PRODUCTION,THIS QUARTER	105000.	
INVENTORY,FINISHED GOODS	26472.	
PLANT CAPACITY,NEXT QUARTER	105296.	

INCOME STATEMENT

RECEIPTS,SALES REVENUE		$ 3041693.
EXPENSES,MARKETING	$ 155000.	
RESEARCH AND DEVELOPMENT	50000.	
ADMINISTRATION	287522.	
MAINTENANCE	80813.	
LABOR(COST/UNIT EX.OVERTIME $ 5.75)	603925.	
MATERIALS CONSUMED(COST/UNIT 6.24)	655260.	
REDUCTION,FINISHED GOODS INV.	235704.	
PLANT&EQ.DEPRECIATION(2.500 0/0)	186047.	
ROBOTICS DEPRECIATION(5.000 0/0)	2500.	
FINISHED GOODS CARRYING COSTS	53594.	
RAW MATERIALS CARRYING COSTS	62020.	
ORDERING COSTS	50614.	
SHIFTS CHANGE COSTS	0.	
INVESTMENTS EXPENSES	8.	
FINANCING CHARGES AND PENALTIES	0.	
SUNDRIES	87402.	2510404.
PROFIT BEFORE INCOME TAX		531289.
INCOME TAX(IN.TX.CR. 0. 0/0,SURTAX 0. 0/0)		180638.
NET PROFIT AFTER INCOME TAX		350651.
DIVIDENDS PAID		0.
ADDITION TO OWNERS EQUITY		350651.

CASH FLOW

RECEIPTS,SALES REVENUE		$ 3041693.
DISBURSEMENTS,CASH EXPENSE	$ 1430892.	
INCOME TAX	180638.	
DIVIDENDS PAID	0.	
ROBOTICS INVESTMENT	0.	
PLANT&EQ.INVESTMENT	9000.	
MATERIALS PURCHASED	145000.	1765530.
ADDITION TO CASH ASSETS		1276163.

FINANCIAL STATEMENT

NET ASSETS,CASH		$ 1526715.
INV. VALUE,FINISHED GOODS		321564.
INVENTORY VALUE,MATERIALS		730149.
ROBOTICS BOOK VALUE(REPLACE.VAL.$	49032.)	47500.
PLANT&EQ.BOOK VALUE(REPLACE.VAL.	7515974.)	7264828.
OWNERS EQUITY(ECONOMIC EQUITY	10143431.)	9890754.

Table 12
Executive Game Quarterly Statement, Period 2, Firm 5-2, Model 1

```
 52 2 24.79  240000.  140000.  83000. 109942.  16000. 532000.  750000.   85000.

                              EXECUTIVE GAME
MODEL 1 PERIOD  2 OND PRICE INDEX 102.5 FORECAST,ANNUAL CHANGE  5.0 0/0
SEAS.INDEX 115. NEXT QTR.  90.  ECON.INDEX '94. FORECAST,NEXT QTR.  93.

                 INFORMATION          ON            COMPETITORS
           PRICE           DIVIDEND     SALES VOLUME         NET PROFIT
  FIRM 1   $ 24.34      $        0.        124967.         $    350651.
  FIRM 2   $ 24.79      $    85000.        118486.         $    173430.
  FIRM 3   $ 23.99      $    66000.        149150.         $    138741.
  FIRM 4   $ 23.70      $   183333.        151387.         $    174208.
  FIRM 5   $ 21.90      $    30000.        144270.         $     95467.
  FIRM 6   $ 22.80      $    75000.        144818.         $     18223.

                                   FIRM  5 2
                             OPERATING STATEMENTS
     MARKET POTENTIAL                                 118486.
     SALES VOLUME                                     118486.
     PERCENT SHARE OF INDUSTRY SALES                     14.2
     PRODUCTION,THIS QUARTER                          109942.
     INVENTORY,FINISHED GOODS                          26602.
     PLANT CAPACITY,NEXT QUARTER                      115421.
                                 INCOME STATEMENT
     RECEIPTS,SALES REVENUE                                             $   2937264.
     EXPENSES,MARKETING                            $   240000.
       RESEARCH AND DEVELOPMENT                        140000.
       ADMINISTRATION                                  290878.
       MAINTENANCE                                      83000.
       LABOR(COST/UNIT EX.OVERTIME $ 5.79)             637052.
       MATERIALS CONSUMED(COST/UNIT  6.27)             688962.
       REDUCTION,FINISHED GOODS INV.                    98609.
       PLANT&EQ.DEPRECIATION(2.500 0/0)                191547.
       ROBOTICS DEPRECIATION(5.000 0/0)                   500.
       FINISHED GOODS CARRYING COSTS                    53857.
       RAW MATERIALS CARRYING COSTS                     78470.
       ORDERING COSTS                                   50614.
       SHIFTS CHANGE COSTS                                 0.
       INVESTMENTS EXPENSES                             30030.
       FINANCING CHARGES AND PENALTIES                   1662.
       SUNDRIES                                         89316.         2674491.
     PROFIT BEFORE INCOME TAX                                            262773.
     INCOME TAX(IN.TX.CR.  0. 0/0,SURTAX  0. 0/0)                         89343.
     NET PROFIT AFTER INCOME TAX                                         173430.
     DIVIDENDS PAID                                                       85000.
     ADDITION TO OWNERS EQUITY                                            88430.
                                    CASH FLOW
     RECEIPTS,SALES REVENUE                                             $   2937264.
     DISBURSEMENTS,CASH EXPENSE                $  1694872.
       INCOME TAX                                   89343.
       DIVIDENDS PAID                               85000.
       ROBOTICS INVESTMENT                          16000.
       PLANT&EQ.INVESTMENT                         532000.
       MATERIALS PURCHASED                         750000.                3167214.
     ADDITION TO CASH ASSETS                                             -229950.
                                FINANCIAL STATEMENT
     NET ASSETS,CASH                                                    $   -362392.
       INV. VALUE,FINISHED GOODS                                          323143.
       INVENTORY VALUE,MATERIALS                                         1630429.
       ROBOTICS BOOK VALUE(REPLACE.VAL.$     25806.)                       25500.
       PLANT&EQ.BOOK VALUE(REPLACE.VAL.   8257733.)                      8002328.
     OWNERS EQUITY(ECONOMIC EQUITY        9874718.)                      9619007.
```

Table 13
Executive Game Quarterly Statement, Period 2, Firm 5-3, Model 1

```
 53 2 23.99  250000.  375000. 111900. 149150. 100000. 500000.  500000.   66000.

                             EXECUTIVE GAME
MODEL 1 PERIOD  2 OND PRICE INDEX 102.5 FORECAST,ANNUAL CHANGE  5.0 0/0
SEAS.INDEX 115. NEXT QTR.  90.  ECON.INDEX  94. FORECAST,NEXT QTR.  93.

                  INFORMATION          ON          COMPETITORS
           PRICE            DIVIDEND     SALES VOLUME          NET PROFIT
  FIRM 1   $ 24.34      $         0.        124967.        $    350651.
  FIRM 2   $ 24.79      $     85000.        118486.        $    173430.
  FIRM 3   $ 23.99      $     66000.        149150.        $    138741.
  FIRM 4   $ 23.70      $    183333.        151387.        $    174208.
  FIRM 5   $ 21.90      $     30000.        144270.        $     95467.
  FIRM 6   $ 22.80      $     75000.        144818.        $     18223.

                                 FIRM  5 3
                           OPERATING STATEMENTS
     MARKET POTENTIAL                                  150775.
     SALES VOLUME                                      149150.
     PERCENT SHARE OF INDUSTRY SALES                     17.9
     PRODUCTION,THIS QUARTER                           149150.
     INVENTORY,FINISHED GOODS                               0.
     PLANT CAPACITY,NEXT QUARTER                       113010.
                               INCOME STATEMENT
     RECEIPTS,SALES REVENUE                                            $  3578109.
     EXPENSES,MARKETING                             $   250000.
       RESEARCH AND DEVELOPMENT                         375000.
       ADMINISTRATION                                   336909.
       MAINTENANCE                                      111900.
       LABOR(COST/UNIT EX.OVERTIME $ 5.70)              970856.
       MATERIALS CONSUMED(COST/UNIT  6.12)              913407.
       REDUCTION,FINISHED GOODS INV.                         0.
       PLANT&EQ.DEPRECIATION(2.500 0/0)                 186047.
       ROBOTICS DEPRECIATION(5.000 0/0)                   1250.
       FINISHED GOODS CARRYING COSTS                         0.
       RAW MATERIALS CARRYING COSTS                      48776.
       ORDERING COSTS                                    50614.
       SHIFTS CHANGE COSTS                                   0.
       INVESTMENTS EXPENSES                              36000.
       FINANCING CHARGES AND PENALTIES                       0.
       SUNDRIES                                          87139.          3367895.
     PROFIT BEFORE INCOME TAX                                             210214.
     INCOME TAX(IN.TX.CR.  0. 0/0,SURTAX  0. 0/0)                          71473.
     NET PROFIT AFTER INCOME TAX                                          138741.
     DIVIDENDS PAID                                                        66000.
     ADDITION TO OWNERS EQUITY                                             72741.
                                   CASH FLOW
     RECEIPTS,SALES REVENUE                                            $  3578109.
     DISBURSEMENTS,CASH EXPENSE                 $  2267190.
       INCOME TAX                                    71473.
       DIVIDENDS PAID                                66000.
       ROBOTICS INVESTMENT                          100000.
       PLANT&EQ.INVESTMENT                          500000.
       MATERIALS PURCHASED                          500000.              3504662.
     ADDITION TO CASH ASSETS                                               73447.
                               FINANCIAL STATEMENT
     NET ASSETS,CASH                                                   $  1365439.
       INV. VALUE,FINISHED GOODS                                                0.
       INVENTORY VALUE,MATERIALS                                           562110.
       ROBOTICS BOOK VALUE(REPLACE.VAL.$   124516.)                        123750.
       PLANT&EQ.BOOK VALUE(REPLACE.VAL.   8006974.)                       7755828.
     OWNERS EQUITY(ECONOMIC EQUITY       10059037.)                       9807126.
```

Table 14
Executive Game Quarterly Statement, Period 2, Firm 5-4, Model 1

54 2 23.70 265000. 210000. 116379. 151387. 78750. 891513. 975077. 183333.

EXECUTIVE GAME

MODEL 1 PERIOD 2 OND PRICE INDEX 102.5 FORECAST,ANNUAL CHANGE 5.0 0/0

SEAS.INDEX 115. NEXT QTR. 90. ECON.INDEX 94. FORECAST,NEXT QTR. 93.

INFORMATION ON COMPETITORS

	PRICE	DIVIDEND	SALES VOLUME	NET PROFIT
FIRM 1	$ 24.34	$ 0.	124967.	$ 350651.
FIRM 2	$ 24.79	$ 85000.	118486.	$ 173430.
FIRM 3	$ 23.99	$ 66000.	149150.	$ 138741.
FIRM 4	$ 23.70	$ 183333.	151387.	$ 174208.
FIRM 5	$ 21.90	$ 30000.	144270.	$ 95467.
FIRM 6	$ 22.80	$ 75000.	144818.	$ 18223.

FIRM 5 4

OPERATING STATEMENTS

MARKET POTENTIAL	161444.
SALES VOLUME	151387.
PERCENT SHARE OF INDUSTRY SALES	18.2
PRODUCTION,THIS QUARTER	151387.
INVENTORY,FINISHED GOODS	0.
PLANT CAPACITY,NEXT QUARTER	119912.

INCOME STATEMENT

RECEIPTS,SALES REVENUE		$ 3587871.
EXPENSES,MARKETING	$ 265000.	
RESEARCH AND DEVELOPMENT	210000.	
ADMINISTRATION	339188.	
MAINTENANCE	116379.	
LABOR(COST/UNIT EX.OVERTIME $ 5.67)	979433.	
MATERIALS CONSUMED(COST/UNIT 6.19)	936856.	
REDUCTION,FINISHED GOODS INV.	0.	
PLANT&EQ.DEPRECIATION(2.500 0/0)	187922.	
ROBOTICS DEPRECIATION(5.000 0/0)	3750.	
FINISHED GOODS CARRYING COSTS	0.	
RAW MATERIALS CARRYING COSTS	52292.	
ORDERING COSTS	50614.	
SHIFTS CHANGE COSTS	0.	
INVESTMENTS EXPENSES	94141.	
FINANCING CHARGES AND PENALTIES	0.	
SUNDRIES	88348.	3323920.
PROFIT BEFORE INCOME TAX		263951.
INCOME TAX(IN.TX.CR. 0. 0/0,SURTAX 0. 0/0)		89743.
NET PROFIT AFTER INCOME TAX		174208.
DIVIDENDS PAID		183333.
ADDITION TO OWNERS EQUITY		-9125.

CASH FLOW

RECEIPTS,SALES REVENUE		$ 3587871.
DISBURSEMENTS,CASH EXPENSE	$ 2195391.	
INCOME TAX	89743.	
DIVIDENDS PAID	183333.	
ROBOTICS INVESTMENT	78750.	
PLANT&EQ.INVESTMENT	891513.	
MATERIALS PURCHASED	975077.	4413807.
ADDITION TO CASH ASSETS		-825936.

FINANCIAL STATEMENT

NET ASSETS,CASH		$ 344729.
INV. VALUE,FINISHED GOODS		0.
INVENTORY VALUE,MATERIALS		1084068.
ROBOTICS BOOK VALUE(REPLACE.VAL.$	152298.)	150000.
PLANT&EQ.BOOK VALUE(REPLACE.VAL.	8473071.)	8220466.
OWNERS EQUITY(ECONOMIC EQUITY	10054165.)	9799263.

Table 15
Executive Game Quarterly Statement, Period 2, Firm 5-5, Model 1

```
 55 2 21.90  225000.  115500.  95000. 145000.     40. 100000.  725536.   30000.

                                 EXECUTIVE GAME
MODEL 1 PERIOD  2 OND PRICE INDEX 102.5 FORECAST,ANNUAL CHANGE  5.0 0/0
SEAS.INDEX 115. NEXT QTR.  90.  ECON.INDEX  94. FORECAST,NEXT QTR.  93.

                     INFORMATION          ON          COMPETITORS
              PRICE             DIVIDEND      SALES VOLUME          NET PROFIT
  FIRM 1    $ 24.34        $          0.          124967.        $    350651.
  FIRM 2    $ 24.79        $      85000.          118486.        $    173430.
  FIRM 3    $ 23.99        $      66000.          149150.        $    138741.
  FIRM 4    $ 23.70        $     183333.          151387.        $    174208.
  FIRM 5    $ 21.90        $      30000.          144270.        $     95467.
  FIRM 6    $ 22.80        $      75000.          144818.        $     18223.

                                     FIRM  5 5
                               OPERATING STATEMENTS
     MARKET POTENTIAL                                 187624.
     SALES VOLUME                                     144270.
     PERCENT SHARE OF INDUSTRY SALES                     17.3
     PRODUCTION,THIS QUARTER                          144270.
     INVENTORY,FINISHED GOODS                              0.
     PLANT CAPACITY,NEXT QUARTER                      102382.
                                   INCOME STATEMENT
     RECEIPTS,SALES REVENUE                                          $  3159502.
     EXPENSES,MARKETING                             $  225000.
       RESEARCH AND DEVELOPMENT                        115500.
       ADMINISTRATION                                  332189.
       MAINTENANCE                                      95000.
       LABOR(COST/UNIT EX.OVERTIME $ 5.84)             963092.
       MATERIALS CONSUMED(COST/UNIT  6.30)             908398.
       REDUCTION,FINISHED GOODS INV.                        0.
       PLANT&EQ.DEPRECIATION(2.500 0/0)                179247.
       ROBOTICS DEPRECIATION(5.000 0/0)                   500.
       FINISHED GOODS CARRYING COSTS                        0.
       RAW MATERIALS CARRYING COSTS                     59973.
       ORDERING COSTS                                   50614.
       SHIFTS CHANGE COSTS                                  0.
       INVESTMENTS EXPENSES                              1001.
       FINANCING CHARGES AND PENALTIES                      0.
       SUNDRIES                                         84345.          3014855.
     PROFIT BEFORE INCOME TAX                                            144647.
     INCOME TAX(IN.TX.CR.  0. 0/0,SURTAX  0. 0/0)                         49180.
     NET PROFIT AFTER INCOME TAX                                          95467.
     DIVIDENDS PAID                                                       30000.
     ADDITION TO OWNERS EQUITY                                            65467.
                                        CASH FLOW
     RECEIPTS,SALES REVENUE                                          $  3159502.
     DISBURSEMENTS,CASH EXPENSE                 $  1926709.
       INCOME TAX                                    49180.
       DIVIDENDS PAID                                30000.
       ROBOTICS INVESTMENT                              40.
       PLANT&EQ.INVESTMENT                          100000.
       MATERIALS PURCHASED                          725536.             2831464.
     ADDITION TO CASH ASSETS                                             328038.
                                   FINANCIAL STATEMENT
     NET ASSETS,CASH                                                 $  1798150.
       INV. VALUE,FINISHED GOODS                                              0.
       INVENTORY VALUE,MATERIALS                                        1016601.
       ROBOTICS BOOK VALUE(REPLACE.VAL.$        9846.)                     9540.
       PLANT&EQ.BOOK VALUE(REPLACE.VAL.    7336487.)                    7090628.
     OWNERS EQUITY(ECONOMIC EQUITY        10161083.)                    9914918.
```

Table 16
Executive Game Quarterly Statement, Period 2, Firm 5-6, Model 1

56 2 22.80 256625. 350000. 111500. 144818. 200000. 300000. 950000. 75000.

EXECUTIVE GAME

MODEL 1 PERIOD 2 OND PRICE INDEX 102.5 FORECAST,ANNUAL CHANGE 5.0 0/0
SEAS.INDEX 115. NEXT QTR. 90. ECON.INDEX 94. FORECAST,NEXT QTR. 93.

INFORMATION ON COMPETITORS

	PRICE	DIVIDEND	SALES VOLUME	NET PROFIT
FIRM 1	$ 24.34	$ 0.	124967.	$ 350651.
FIRM 2	$ 24.79	$ 85000.	118486.	$ 173430.
FIRM 3	$ 23.99	$ 66000.	149150.	$ 138741.
FIRM 4	$ 23.70	$ 183333.	151387.	$ 174208.
FIRM 5	$ 21.90	$ 30000.	144270.	$ 95467.
FIRM 6	$ 22.80	$ 75000.	144818.	$ 18223.

FIRM 5 6

OPERATING STATEMENTS

MARKET POTENTIAL	173591.	
SALES VOLUME	144818.	
PERCENT SHARE OF INDUSTRY SALES	17.4	
PRODUCTION,THIS QUARTER	144818.	
INVENTORY,FINISHED GOODS	0.	
PLANT CAPACITY,NEXT QUARTER	108168.	

INCOME STATEMENT

RECEIPTS,SALES REVENUE		$ 3301850.
EXPENSES,MARKETING	$ 256625.	
RESEARCH AND DEVELOPMENT	350000.	
ADMINISTRATION	332921.	
MAINTENANCE	111500.	
LABOR(COST/UNIT EX.OVERTIME $ 5.75)	950582.	
MATERIALS CONSUMED(COST/UNIT 6.11)	885273.	
REDUCTION,FINISHED GOODS INV.	0.	
PLANT&EQ.DEPRECIATION(2.500 0/0)	181047.	
ROBOTICS DEPRECIATION(5.000 0/0)	0.	
FINISHED GOODS CARRYING COSTS	0.	
RAW MATERIALS CARRYING COSTS	45781.	
ORDERING COSTS	50614.	
SHIFTS CHANGE COSTS	0.	
INVESTMENTS EXPENSES	25000.	
FINANCING CHARGES AND PENALTIES	0.	
SUNDRIES	84903.	3274240.
PROFIT BEFORE INCOME TAX		27610.
INCOME TAX(IN.TX.CR. 0. 0/0,SURTAX 0. 0/0)		9387.
NET PROFIT AFTER INCOME TAX		18223.
DIVIDENDS PAID		75000.
ADDITION TO OWNERS EQUITY		-56777.

CASH FLOW

RECEIPTS,SALES REVENUE		$ 3301850.
DISBURSEMENTS,CASH EXPENSE	$ 2207920.	
INCOME TAX	9387.	
DIVIDENDS PAID	75000.	
ROBOTICS INVESTMENT	200000.	
PLANT&EQ.INVESTMENT	300000.	
MATERIALS PURCHASED	950000.	3742307.
ADDITION TO CASH ASSETS		-440457.

FINANCIAL STATEMENT

NET ASSETS,CASH		$ 1008670.
INV. VALUE,FINISHED GOODS		0.
INVENTORY VALUE,MATERIALS		980345.
ROBOTICS BOOK VALUE(REPLACE.VAL.$	200000.)	200000.
PLANT&EQ.BOOK VALUE(REPLACE.VAL.	7608114.)	7360828.
OWNERS EQUITY(ECONOMIC EQUITY	9797128.)	9549842.

Table 17
Executive Game Quarterly Statement, Period 3, Firm 5-1, Model 1

```
 51 3 24.00  210000.  100000.  96094. 125000.  50000. 400000.  800000.   10000.

                                 EXECUTIVE GAME
MODEL 1 PERIOD  3 JFM PRICE INDEX 104.0 FORECAST,ANNUAL CHANGE  4.8 0/0
SEAS.INDEX  90. NEXT QTR. 100.  ECON.INDEX  95. FORECAST,NEXT QTR.  90.
```

INFORMATION	ON	COMPETITORS		
	PRICE	DIVIDEND	SALES VOLUME	NET PROFIT
FIRM 1	$ 24.00	$ 10000.	113325.	$ 86754.
FIRM 2	$ 24.54	$ 105000.	113335.	$ 77592.
FIRM 3	$ 24.99	$ 75000.	95093.	$ -201354.
FIRM 4	$ 25.15	$ 183333.	123006.	$ 23037.
FIRM 5	$ 23.25	$ 50000.	138697.	$ 167260.
FIRM 6	$ 23.00	$ 125000.	149963.	$ 47742.

```
                                     FIRM  5 1
                              OPERATING STATEMENTS
    MARKET POTENTIAL                                113325.
    SALES VOLUME                                    113325.
    PERCENT SHARE OF INDUSTRY SALES                    15.5
    PRODUCTION,THIS QUARTER                         115632.
    INVENTORY,FINISHED GOODS                         28779.
    PLANT CAPACITY,NEXT QUARTER                     109241.
                                  INCOME STATEMENT
    RECEIPTS,SALES REVENUE                                          $  2719807.
    EXPENSES,MARKETING                            $  210000.
      RESEARCH AND DEVELOPMENT                       100000.
      ADMINISTRATION                                 339191.
      MAINTENANCE                                     96094.
      LABOR(COST/UNIT EX.OVERTIME $ 5.64)            707248.
      MATERIALS CONSUMED(COST/UNIT  6.28)            730149.
      REDUCTION,FINISHED GOODS INV.                  -32304.
      PLANT&EQ.DEPRECIATION(2.500 0/0)               181621.
      ROBOTICS DEPRECIATION(5.000 0/0)                 2375.
      FINISHED GOODS CARRYING COSTS                   58978.
      RAW MATERIALS CARRYING COSTS                    36507.
      ORDERING COSTS                                  51234.
      SHIFTS CHANGE COSTS                                 0.
      INVESTMENTS EXPENSES                            20250.
      FINANCING CHARGES AND PENALTIES                     0.
      SUNDRIES                                        87024.           2588361.
    PROFIT BEFORE INCOME TAX                                            131446.
    INCOME TAX(IN.TX.CR.  0. 0/0,SURTAX  0. 0/0)                         44692.
    NET PROFIT AFTER INCOME TAX                                          86754.
    DIVIDENDS PAID                                                       10000.
    ADDITION TO OWNERS EQUITY                                            76754.
                                       CASH FLOW
    RECEIPTS,SALES REVENUE                                          $  2719807.
    DISBURSEMENTS,CASH EXPENSE                $  1706519.
      INCOME TAX                                   44692.
      DIVIDENDS PAID                               10000.
      ROBOTICS INVESTMENT                          50000.
      PLANT&EQ.INVESTMENT                         400000.
      MATERIALS PURCHASED                         800000.              3011210.
    ADDITION TO CASH ASSETS                                            -291403.
                                  FINANCIAL STATEMENT
    NET ASSETS,CASH                                                 $  1235312.
      INV. VALUE,FINISHED GOODS                                         353866.
      INVENTORY VALUE,MATERIALS                                         800000.
      ROBOTICS BOOK VALUE(REPLACE.VAL.$       98197.)                    95125.
      PLANT&EQ.BOOK VALUE(REPLACE.VAL.     7873599.)                   7483207.
    OWNERS EQUITY(ECONOMIC EQUITY         10360971.)                   9967508.
```

Table 18
Executive Game Quarterly Statement, Period 3, Firm 5-2, Model 1

```
 52 3 24.54  265000.  165000.  86000. 114359.  26000. 552000.       0.  105000.

                                EXECUTIVE GAME
MODEL 1 PERIOD  3 JFM PRICE INDEX 104.0 FORECAST,ANNUAL CHANGE  4.8 0/0
SEAS.INDEX  90. NEXT QTR. 100.  ECON.INDEX  95. FORECAST,NEXT QTR.  90.

                INFORMATION          ON            COMPETITORS
           PRICE             DIVIDEND     SALES VOLUME         NET PROFIT
  FIRM 1   $ 24.00       $    10000.        113325.         $     86754.
  FIRM 2   $ 24.54       $   105000.        113335.         $     77592.
  FIRM 3   $ 24.99       $    75000.         95093.         $   -201354.
  FIRM 4   $ 25.15       $   183333.        123006.         $     23037.
  FIRM 5   $ 23.25       $    50000.        138697.         $    167260.
  FIRM 6   $ 23.00       $   125000.        149963.         $     47742.

                                     FIRM  5 2
                              OPERATING STATEMENTS
     MARKET POTENTIAL                                 113335.
     SALES VOLUME                                     113335.
     PERCENT SHARE OF INDUSTRY SALES                     15.5
     PRODUCTION,THIS QUARTER                          114359.
     INVENTORY,FINISHED GOODS                          27626.
     PLANT CAPACITY,NEXT QUARTER                      121024.
                                  INCOME STATEMENT
     RECEIPTS,SALES REVENUE                                          $  2781241.
     EXPENSES,MARKETING                            $  265000.
       RESEARCH AND DEVELOPMENT                       165000.
       ADMINISTRATION                                 301233.
       MAINTENANCE                                     86000.
       LABOR(COST/UNIT EX.OVERTIME $ 5.84)            668403.
       MATERIALS CONSUMED(COST/UNIT  6.25)            714952.
       REDUCTION,FINISHED GOODS INV.                  -16549.
       PLANT&EQ.DEPRECIATION(2.500 0/0)               200058.
       ROBOTICS DEPRECIATION(5.000 0/0)                 1275.
       FINISHED GOODS CARRYING COSTS                   56615.
       RAW MATERIALS CARRYING COSTS                    81521.
       ORDERING COSTS                                     0.
       SHIFTS CHANGE COSTS                                0.
       INVESTMENTS EXPENSES                            33408.
       FINANCING CHARGES AND PENALTIES                 12469.
       SUNDRIES                                        94293.           2663677.
     PROFIT BEFORE INCOME TAX                                            117564.
     INCOME TAX(IN.TX.CR.  0. 0/0,SURTAX  0. 0/0)                        39972.
     NET PROFIT AFTER INCOME TAX                                          77592.
     DIVIDENDS PAID                                                      105000.
     ADDITION TO OWNERS EQUITY                                           -27408.
                                     CASH FLOW
     RECEIPTS,SALES REVENUE                                          $  2781241.
     DISBURSEMENTS,CASH EXPENSE               $ 1763938.
       INCOME TAX                                 39972.
       DIVIDENDS PAID                            105000.
       ROBOTICS INVESTMENT                        26000.
       PLANT&EQ.INVESTMENT                       552000.
       MATERIALS PURCHASED                            0.                2486909.
     ADDITION TO CASH ASSETS                                             294332.
                                 FINANCIAL STATEMENT
     NET ASSETS,CASH                                                 $    -68060.
       INV. VALUE,FINISHED GOODS                                         339690.
       INVENTORY VALUE,MATERIALS                                         915477.
       ROBOTICS BOOK VALUE(REPLACE.VAL.$     51366.)                      50225.
       PLANT&EQ.BOOK VALUE(REPLACE.VAL.   8763161.)                     8354269.
     OWNERS EQUITY(ECONOMIC EQUITY       10001633.)                     9591600.
```

Table 19
Executive Game Quarterly Statement, Period 3, Firm 5-3, Model 1

```
 53 3 24.99  350000.  400000. 122819. 156734. 112500. 562500.  430000.   75000.

                               EXECUTIVE GAME
MODEL 1 PERIOD  3 JFM PRICE INDEX 104.0 FORECAST,ANNUAL CHANGE  4.8 0/0
SEAS.INDEX  90. NEXT QTR. 100.  ECON.INDEX  95. FORECAST,NEXT QTR.  90.

                  INFORMATION          ON           COMPETITORS
            PRICE            DIVIDEND       SALES VOLUME        NET PROFIT
  FIRM 1    $ 24.00        $   10000.         113325.        $     86754.
  FIRM 2    $ 24.54        $  105000.         113335.        $     77592.
  FIRM 3    $ 24.99        $   75000.          95093.        $   -201354.
  FIRM 4    $ 25.15        $  183333.         123006.        $     23037.
  FIRM 5    $ 23.25        $   50000.         138697.        $    167260.
  FIRM 6    $ 23.00        $  125000.         149963.        $     47742.

                                   FIRM  5 3
                             OPERATING STATEMENTS
     MARKET POTENTIAL                                  112272.
     SALES VOLUME                                       95093.
     PERCENT SHARE OF INDUSTRY SALES                     13.0
     PRODUCTION,THIS QUARTER                            95093.
     INVENTORY,FINISHED GOODS                               0.
     PLANT CAPACITY,NEXT QUARTER                       119844.
                                 INCOME STATEMENT
     RECEIPTS,SALES REVENUE                                           $  2376385.
     EXPENSES,MARKETING                             $  350000.
       RESEARCH AND DEVELOPMENT                        400000.
       ADMINISTRATION                                  297555.
       MAINTENANCE                                     122819.
       LABOR(COST/UNIT EX.OVERTIME $ 5.59)             531626.
       MATERIALS CONSUMED(COST/UNIT  6.28)             562110.
       REDUCTION,FINISHED GOODS INV.                       0.
       PLANT&EQ.DEPRECIATION(2.500 0/0)                193896.
       ROBOTICS DEPRECIATION(5.000 0/0)                  6188.
       FINISHED GOODS CARRYING COSTS                        0.
       RAW MATERIALS CARRYING COSTS                     28106.
       ORDERING COSTS                                   51234.
       SHIFTS CHANGE COSTS                                  0.
       INVESTMENTS EXPENSES                             45563.
       FINANCING CHARGES AND PENALTIES                      0.
       SUNDRIES                                         92376.           2681466.
     PROFIT BEFORE INCOME TAX                                            -305081.
     INCOME TAX(IN.TX.CR.  0. 0/0,SURTAX  0. 0/0)                        -103728.
     NET PROFIT AFTER INCOME TAX                                         -201354.
     DIVIDENDS PAID                                                        75000.
     ADDITION TO OWNERS EQUITY                                           -276354.
                                    CASH FLOW
     RECEIPTS,SALES REVENUE                                           $  2376385.
     DISBURSEMENTS,CASH EXPENSE                $  1919272.
       INCOME TAX                                 -103728.
       DIVIDENDS PAID                               75000.
       ROBOTICS INVESTMENT                         112500.
       PLANT&EQ.INVESTMENT                         562500.
       MATERIALS PURCHASED                         430000.               2995544.
     ADDITION TO CASH ASSETS                                             -619159.
                               FINANCIAL STATEMENT
     NET ASSETS,CASH                                                  $   746280.
       INV. VALUE,FINISHED GOODS                                               0.
       INVENTORY VALUE,MATERIALS                                          430000.
       ROBOTICS BOOK VALUE(REPLACE.VAL.$   234895.)                       230063.
       PLANT&EQ.BOOK VALUE(REPLACE.VAL.   8524312.)                      8124432.
     OWNERS EQUITY(ECONOMIC EQUITY        9935485.)                      9530774.
```

Table 20
Executive Game Quarterly Statement, Period 3, Firm 5-4, Model 1

54 3 25.15 394850. 200000. 115313. 150000. 82500. 270000. 865819. 183333.

EXECUTIVE GAME

MODEL 1 PERIOD 3 JFM PRICE INDEX 104.0 FORECAST,ANNUAL CHANGE 4.8 0/0
SEAS.INDEX 90. NEXT QTR. 100. ECON.INDEX 95. FORECAST,NEXT QTR. 90.

INFORMATION ON COMPETITORS

	PRICE	DIVIDEND	SALES VOLUME	NET PROFIT
FIRM 1	$ 24.00	$ 10000.	113325.	$ 86754.
FIRM 2	$ 24.54	$ 105000.	113335.	$ 77592.
FIRM 3	$ 24.99	$ 75000.	95093.	$ -201354.
FIRM 4	$ 25.15	$ 183333.	123006.	$ 23037.
FIRM 5	$ 23.25	$ 50000.	138697.	$ 167260.
FIRM 6	$ 23.00	$ 125000.	149963.	$ 47742.

FIRM 5 4

OPERATING STATEMENTS

MARKET POTENTIAL	123006.
SALES VOLUME	123006.
PERCENT SHARE OF INDUSTRY SALES	16.8
PRODUCTION,THIS QUARTER	150000.
INVENTORY,FINISHED GOODS	26994.
PLANT CAPACITY,NEXT QUARTER	122216.

INCOME STATEMENT

RECEIPTS,SALES REVENUE		$ 3093592.
EXPENSES,MARKETING	$ 394850.	
RESEARCH AND DEVELOPMENT	200000.	
ADMINISTRATION	357351.	
MAINTENANCE	115313.	
LABOR(COST/UNIT EX.OVERTIME $ 5.62)	927513.	
MATERIALS CONSUMED(COST/UNIT 6.08)	911897.	
REDUCTION,FINISHED GOODS INV.	-331924.	
PLANT&EQ.DEPRECIATION(2.500 0/0)	205512.	
ROBOTICS DEPRECIATION(5.000 0/0)	7500.	
FINISHED GOODS CARRYING COSTS	55321.	
RAW MATERIALS CARRYING COSTS	54203.	
ORDERING COSTS	51234.	
SHIFTS CHANGE COSTS	0.	
INVESTMENTS EXPENSES	12426.	
FINANCING CHARGES AND PENALTIES	0.	
SUNDRIES	97496.	3058687.
PROFIT BEFORE INCOME TAX		34905.
INCOME TAX(IN.TX.CR. 0. 0/0,SURTAX 0. 0/0)		11868.
NET PROFIT AFTER INCOME TAX		23037.
DIVIDENDS PAID		183333.
ADDITION TO OWNERS EQUITY		-160296.

CASH FLOW

RECEIPTS,SALES REVENUE		$ 3093592.
DISBURSEMENTS,CASH EXPENSE	$ 2265701.	
INCOME TAX	11868.	
DIVIDENDS PAID	183333.	
ROBOTICS INVESTMENT	82500.	
PLANT&EQ.INVESTMENT	270000.	
MATERIALS PURCHASED	865819.	3679220.
ADDITION TO CASH ASSETS		-585628.

FINANCIAL STATEMENT

NET ASSETS,CASH		$ -240899.
INV. VALUE,FINISHED GOODS		331924.
INVENTORY VALUE,MATERIALS		1037990.
ROBOTICS BOOK VALUE(REPLACE.VAL.$	232204.)	225000.
PLANT&EQ.BOOK VALUE(REPLACE.VAL.	8695276.)	8284954.
OWNERS EQUITY(ECONOMIC EQUITY	10056493.)	9638968.

Table 21
Executive Game Quarterly Statement, Period 3, Firm 5-5, Model 1

```
 55 3 23.25  200000.  125000. 125000. 144000. 100000. 100000.  200000.   50000.

                                        EXECUTIVE GAME
MODEL 1 PERIOD  3 JFM PRICE INDEX 104.0 FORECAST,ANNUAL CHANGE  4.8 0/0
SEAS.INDEX  90. NEXT QTR. 100.  ECON.INDEX  95. FORECAST,NEXT QTR.  90.

                      INFORMATION           ON           COMPETITORS
              PRICE               DIVIDEND      SALES VOLUME          NET PROFIT
  FIRM 1    $ 24.00        $   10000.          113325.          $     86754.
  FIRM 2    $ 24.54        $  105000.          113335.          $     77592.
  FIRM 3    $ 24.99        $   75000.           95093.          $   -201354.
  FIRM 4    $ 25.15        $  183333.          123006.          $     23037.
  FIRM 5    $ 23.25        $   50000.          138697.          $    167260.
  FIRM 6    $ 23.00        $  125000.          149963.          $     47742.

                                    FIRM  5 5
                              OPERATING STATEMENTS
     MARKET POTENTIAL                                   138697.
     SALES VOLUME                                       138697.
     PERCENT SHARE OF INDUSTRY SALES                      18.9
     PRODUCTION,THIS QUARTER                            143336.
     INVENTORY,FINISHED GOODS                             4638.
     PLANT CAPACITY,NEXT QUARTER                        102718.
                                  INCOME STATEMENT
     RECEIPTS,SALES REVENUE                                            $  3224711.
     EXPENSES,MARKETING                             $  200000.
       RESEARCH AND DEVELOPMENT                        125000.
       ADMINISTRATION                                  335355.
       MAINTENANCE                                     125000.
       LABOR(COST/UNIT EX.OVERTIME $ 5.85)             958637.
       MATERIALS CONSUMED(COST/UNIT  6.32)             906137.
       REDUCTION,FINISHED GOODS INV.                   -57032.
       PLANT&EQ.DEPRECIATION(2.500 0/0)                177266.
       ROBOTICS DEPRECIATION(5.000 0/0)                   477.
       FINISHED GOODS CARRYING COSTS                     9505.
       RAW MATERIALS CARRYING COSTS                     50830.
       ORDERING COSTS                                   51234.
       SHIFTS CHANGE COSTS                                  0.
       INVESTMENTS EXPENSES                              4000.
       FINANCING CHARGES AND PENALTIES                      0.
       SUNDRIES                                         84883.            2971287.
     PROFIT BEFORE INCOME TAX                                              253424.
     INCOME TAX(IN.TX.CR.  0. 0/0,SURTAX  0. 0/0)                           86164.
     NET PROFIT AFTER INCOME TAX                                           167260.
     DIVIDENDS PAID                                                         50000.
     ADDITION TO OWNERS EQUITY                                             117260.
                                     CASH FLOW
     RECEIPTS,SALES REVENUE                                            $  3224711.
     DISBURSEMENTS,CASH EXPENSE              $  1944438.
       INCOME TAX                                  86164.
       DIVIDENDS PAID                              50000.
       ROBOTICS INVESTMENT                        100000.
       PLANT&EQ.INVESTMENT                        100000.
       MATERIALS PURCHASED                        200000.                 2480602.
     ADDITION TO CASH ASSETS                                               744109.
                               FINANCIAL STATEMENT
     NET ASSETS,CASH                                                   $  2542259.
       INV. VALUE,FINISHED GOODS                                            57032.
       INVENTORY VALUE,MATERIALS                                           310464.
       ROBOTICS BOOK VALUE(REPLACE.VAL.$   109678.)                        109063.
       PLANT&EQ.BOOK VALUE(REPLACE.VAL.   7395079.)                       7013362.
     OWNERS EQUITY(ECONOMIC EQUITY       10414511.)                      10032179.
```

Table 22
Executive Game Quarterly Statement, Period 3, Firm 5-6, Model 1

56 3 23.00 264000. 400000. 115285. 149963. 300000. 400000. 950000. 125000.

EXECUTIVE GAME

MODEL 1 PERIOD 3 JFM PRICE INDEX 104.0 FORECAST,ANNUAL CHANGE 4.8 0/0
SEAS.INDEX 90. NEXT QTR. 100. ECON.INDEX 95. FORECAST,NEXT QTR. 90.

INFORMATION ON COMPETITORS

	PRICE	DIVIDEND	SALES VOLUME	NET PROFIT
FIRM 1	$ 24.00	$ 10000.	113325.	$ 86754.
FIRM 2	$ 24.54	$ 105000.	113335.	$ 77592.
FIRM 3	$ 24.99	$ 75000.	95093.	$ -201354.
FIRM 4	$ 25.15	$ 183333.	123006.	$ 23037.
FIRM 5	$ 23.25	$ 50000.	138697.	$ 167260.
FIRM 6	$ 23.00	$ 125000.	149963.	$ 47742.

FIRM 5 6

OPERATING STATEMENTS

MARKET POTENTIAL	176526.	
SALES VOLUME	149963.	
PERCENT SHARE OF INDUSTRY SALES	20.4	
PRODUCTION,THIS QUARTER	149963.	
INVENTORY,FINISHED GOODS	0.	
PLANT CAPACITY,NEXT QUARTER	114744.	

INCOME STATEMENT

RECEIPTS,SALES REVENUE		$ 3449149.
EXPENSES,MARKETING	$ 264000.	
RESEARCH AND DEVELOPMENT	400000.	
ADMINISTRATION	341894.	
MAINTENANCE	115285.	
LABOR(COST/UNIT EX.OVERTIME $ 5.54)	946877.	
MATERIALS CONSUMED(COST/UNIT 5.85)	876611.	
REDUCTION,FINISHED GOODS INV.	0.	
PLANT&EQ.DEPRECIATION(2.500 0/0)	184021.	
ROBOTICS DEPRECIATION(5.000 0/0)	10000.	
FINISHED GOODS CARRYING COSTS	0.	
RAW MATERIALS CARRYING COSTS	49017.	
ORDERING COSTS	51234.	
SHIFTS CHANGE COSTS	0.	
INVESTMENTS EXPENSES	49000.	
FINANCING CHARGES AND PENALTIES	0.	
SUNDRIES	88876.	3376813.
PROFIT BEFORE INCOME TAX		72336.
INCOME TAX(IN.TX.CR. 0. 0/0,SURTAX 0. 0/0)		24594.
NET PROFIT AFTER INCOME TAX		47742.
DIVIDENDS PAID		125000.
ADDITION TO OWNERS EQUITY		-77258.

CASH FLOW

RECEIPTS,SALES REVENUE		$ 3449149.
DISBURSEMENTS,CASH EXPENSE	$ 2306180.	
INCOME TAX	24594.	
DIVIDENDS PAID	125000.	
ROBOTICS INVESTMENT	300000.	
PLANT&EQ.INVESTMENT	400000.	
MATERIALS PURCHASED	950000.	4105774.
ADDITION TO CASH ASSETS		-656625.

FINANCIAL STATEMENT

NET ASSETS,CASH		$ 352045.
INV. VALUE,FINISHED GOODS		0.
INVENTORY VALUE,MATERIALS		1053733.
ROBOTICS BOOK VALUE(REPLACE.VAL.$	496593.)	490000.
PLANT&EQ.BOOK VALUE(REPLACE.VAL.	7965179.)	7576807.
OWNERS EQUITY(ECONOMIC EQUITY	9867549.)	9472585.

Table 23
Executive Game Quarterly Statement, Period 4, Firm 5-1, Model 1

51 4 24.20 230000. 200000. 96000. 125000. 75000. 250000. 800000. 10000.

EXECUTIVE GAME

MODEL 1 PERIOD 4 AMJ PRICE INDEX 104.7 FORECAST,ANNUAL CHANGE 5.0 0/0
SEAS.INDEX 100. NEXT QTR. 95. ECON.INDEX 89. FORECAST,NEXT QTR. 95.

INFORMATION ON COMPETITORS

	PRICE	DIVIDEND	SALES VOLUME	NET PROFIT
FIRM 1	$ 24.20	$ 10000.	124216.	$ 80384.
FIRM 2	$ 24.54	$ 125000.	131216.	$ 130059.
FIRM 3	$ 27.00	$ 0.	72758.	$ 10530.
FIRM 4	$ 26.06	$ 183333.	132708.	$ 128243.
FIRM 5	$ 24.50	$ 0.	54348.	$ -184414.
FIRM 6	$ 23.10	$ 125000.	158389.	$ 208482.

FIRM 5 1

OPERATING STATEMENTS

MARKET POTENTIAL	124216.	
SALES VOLUME	124216.	
PERCENT SHARE OF INDUSTRY SALES	18.4	
PRODUCTION,THIS QUARTER	125000.	
INVENTORY,FINISHED GOODS	29563.	
PLANT CAPACITY,NEXT QUARTER	111288.	

INCOME STATEMENT

RECEIPTS,SALES REVENUE		$ 3006016.
EXPENSES,MARKETING	$ 230000.	
RESEARCH AND DEVELOPMENT	200000.	
ADMINISTRATION	347552.	
MAINTENANCE	96000.	
LABOR(COST/UNIT EX.OVERTIME $ 5.86)	778966.	
MATERIALS CONSUMED(COST/UNIT 6.39)	798867.	
REDUCTION,FINISHED GOODS INV.	-13235.	
PLANT&EQ.DEPRECIATION(2.500 0/0)	187080.	
ROBOTICS DEPRECIATION(5.000 0/0)	4756.	
FINISHED GOODS CARRYING COSTS	61184.	
RAW MATERIALS CARRYING COSTS	40000.	
ORDERING COSTS	51740.	
SHIFTS CHANGE COSTS	0.	
INVESTMENTS EXPENSES	10563.	
FINANCING CHARGES AND PENALTIES	0.	
SUNDRIES	90755.	2884222.
PROFIT BEFORE INCOME TAX		121794.
INCOME TAX(IN.TX.CR. 0. 0/0,SURTAX 0. 0/0)		41410.
NET PROFIT AFTER INCOME TAX		80384.
DIVIDENDS PAID		10000.
ADDITION TO OWNERS EQUITY		70384.

CASH FLOW

RECEIPTS,SALES REVENUE		$ 3006016.
DISBURSEMENTS,CASH EXPENSE	$ 1906751.	
INCOME TAX	41410.	
DIVIDENDS PAID	10000.	
ROBOTICS INVESTMENT	75000.	
PLANT&EQ.INVESTMENT	250000.	
MATERIALS PURCHASED	800000.	3083160.
ADDITION TO CASH ASSETS		-77144.

FINANCIAL STATEMENT

NET ASSETS,CASH		$ 1158168.
INV. VALUE,FINISHED GOODS		367104.
INVENTORY VALUE,MATERIALS		801133.
ROBOTICS BOOK VALUE(REPLACE.VAL.$	171296.)	165369.
PLANT&EQ.BOOK VALUE(REPLACE.VAL.	8023864.)	7546126.
OWNERS EQUITY(ECONOMIC EQUITY	10521561.)	10037897.

Table 24
Executive Game Quarterly Statement, Period 4, Firm 5-2, Model 1

```
 52 4 24.54  290000.  190000. 100000. 130000.  36000. 372000.  800000.  125000.

                                    EXECUTIVE GAME
MODEL 1 PERIOD  4 AMJ PRICE INDEX 104.7 FORECAST,ANNUAL CHANGE   5.0 0/0
SEAS.INDEX 100. NEXT QTR.  95.  ECON.INDEX  89. FORECAST,NEXT QTR.  95.

                    INFORMATION          ON          COMPETITORS
              PRICE             DIVIDEND      SALES VOLUME         NET PROFIT
  FIRM 1    $ 24.20         $   10000.          124216.        $     80384.
  FIRM 2    $ 24.54         $  125000.          131216.        $    130059.
  FIRM 3    $ 27.00         $       0.           72758.        $     10530.
  FIRM 4    $ 26.06         $  183333.          132708.        $    128243.
  FIRM 5    $ 24.50         $       0.           54348.        $   -184414.
  FIRM 6    $ 23.10         $  125000.          158389.        $    208482.

                                          FIRM  5 2
                                    OPERATING STATEMENTS
     MARKET POTENTIAL                                   131216.
     SALES VOLUME                                       131216.
     PERCENT SHARE OF INDUSTRY SALES                       19.5
     PRODUCTION,THIS QUARTER                            130000.
     INVENTORY,FINISHED GOODS                            26410.
     PLANT CAPACITY,NEXT QUARTER                        124130.
                                        INCOME STATEMENT
     RECEIPTS,SALES REVENUE                                            $  3220032.
     EXPENSES,MARKETING                               $  290000.
       RESEARCH AND DEVELOPMENT                          190000.
       ADMINISTRATION                                    362332.
       MAINTENANCE                                       100000.
       LABOR(COST/UNIT EX.OVERTIME $ 5.84)               785968.
       MATERIALS CONSUMED(COST/UNIT  6.18)               803038.
       REDUCTION,FINISHED GOODS INV.                      11741.
       PLANT&EQ.DEPRECIATION(2.500 0/0)                  208857.
       ROBOTICS DEPRECIATION(5.000 0/0)                    2511.
       FINISHED GOODS CARRYING COSTS                      54658.
       RAW MATERIALS CARRYING COSTS                       45774.
       ORDERING COSTS                                     51740.
       SHIFTS CHANGE COSTS                                    0.
       INVESTMENTS EXPENSES                               16646.
       FINANCING CHARGES AND PENALTIES                      437.
       SUNDRIES                                           99277.         3022973.
     PROFIT BEFORE INCOME TAX                                             197059.
     INCOME TAX(IN.TX.CR.  0. 0/0,SURTAX  0. 0/0)                          67000.
     NET PROFIT AFTER INCOME TAX                                          130059.
     DIVIDENDS PAID                                                       125000.
     ADDITION TO OWNERS EQUITY                                              5059.
                                             CASH FLOW
     RECEIPTS,SALES REVENUE                                            $  3220032.
     DISBURSEMENTS,CASH EXPENSE                   $  1996823.
       INCOME TAX                                      67000.
       DIVIDENDS PAID                                 125000.
       ROBOTICS INVESTMENT                             36000.
       PLANT&EQ.INVESTMENT                            372000.
       MATERIALS PURCHASED                            800000.                3396823.
     ADDITION TO CASH ASSETS                                              -176791.
                                        FINANCIAL STATEMENT
     NET ASSETS,CASH                                                   $  -244851.
       INV. VALUE,FINISHED GOODS                                           327950.
       INVENTORY VALUE,MATERIALS                                           912439.
       ROBOTICS BOOK VALUE(REPLACE.VAL.$     86371.)                        83714.
       PLANT&EQ.BOOK VALUE(REPLACE.VAL.   9024177.)                       8517412.
     OWNERS EQUITY(ECONOMIC EQUITY       10106084.)                       9596662.
```

Table 25
Executive Game Quarterly Statement, Period 4, Firm 5-3, Model 1

53 4 27.00 200000. 170000. 58061. 72758. 100000. 25000. 1500000. 0.

EXECUTIVE GAME

MODEL 1 PERIOD 4 AMJ PRICE INDEX 104.7 FORECAST,ANNUAL CHANGE 5.0 0/0
SEAS.INDEX 100. NEXT QTR. 95. ECON.INDEX 89. FORECAST,NEXT QTR. 95.

INFORMATION ON COMPETITORS

	PRICE	DIVIDEND	SALES VOLUME	NET PROFIT
FIRM 1	$ 24.20	$ 10000.	124216.	$ 80384.
FIRM 2	$ 24.54	$ 125000.	131216.	$ 130059.
FIRM 3	$ 27.00	$ 0.	72758.	$ 10530.
FIRM 4	$ 26.06	$ 183333.	132708.	$ 128243.
FIRM 5	$ 24.50	$ 0.	54348.	$ -184414.
FIRM 6	$ 23.10	$ 125000.	158389.	$ 208482.

FIRM 5 3

OPERATING STATEMENTS

MARKET POTENTIAL	86382.	
SALES VOLUME	72758.	
PERCENT SHARE OF INDUSTRY SALES	10.8	
PRODUCTION,THIS QUARTER	72758.	
INVENTORY,FINISHED GOODS	0.	
PLANT CAPACITY,NEXT QUARTER	118864.	

INCOME STATEMENT

RECEIPTS,SALES REVENUE		$ 1964466.
EXPENSES,MARKETING	$ 200000.	
RESEARCH AND DEVELOPMENT	170000.	
ADMINISTRATION	308879.	
MAINTENANCE	58061.	
LABOR(COST/UNIT EX.OVERTIME $ 5.54)	403141.	
MATERIALS CONSUMED(COST/UNIT 5.78)	420863.	
REDUCTION,FINISHED GOODS INV.	0.	
PLANT&EQ.DEPRECIATION(2.500 0/0)	203111.	
ROBOTICS DEPRECIATION(5.000 0/0)	11503.	
FINISHED GOODS CARRYING COSTS	0.	
RAW MATERIALS CARRYING COSTS	21500.	
ORDERING COSTS	51740.	
SHIFTS CHANGE COSTS	0.	
INVESTMENTS EXPENSES	1563.	
FINANCING CHARGES AND PENALTIES	0.	
SUNDRIES	98155.	1948512.
PROFIT BEFORE INCOME TAX		15954.
INCOME TAX(IN.TX.CR. 0. 0/0,SURTAX 0. 0/0)		5424.
NET PROFIT AFTER INCOME TAX		10530.
DIVIDENDS PAID		0.
ADDITION TO OWNERS EQUITY		10530.

CASH FLOW

RECEIPTS,SALES REVENUE		$ 1964466.
DISBURSEMENTS,CASH EXPENSE	$ 1313033.	
INCOME TAX	5424.	
DIVIDENDS PAID	0.	
ROBOTICS INVESTMENT	100000.	
PLANT&EQ.INVESTMENT	25000.	
MATERIALS PURCHASED	1500000.	2943457.
ADDITION TO CASH ASSETS		-978991.

FINANCIAL STATEMENT

NET ASSETS,CASH		$ -232711.
INV. VALUE,FINISHED GOODS		0.
INVENTORY VALUE,MATERIALS		1509136.
ROBOTICS BOOK VALUE(REPLACE.VAL.$	330347.)	318560.
PLANT&EQ.BOOK VALUE(REPLACE.VAL.	8441345.)	7946321.
OWNERS EQUITY(ECONOMIC EQUITY	10048116.)	9541305.

Table 26
Executive Game Quarterly Statement, Period 4, Firm 5-4, Model 1

54 4 26.06 450000. 225000. 115710. 145000. 86250. 270000. 786130. 183333.

EXECUTIVE GAME

MODEL 1 PERIOD 4 AMJ PRICE INDEX 104.7 FORECAST,ANNUAL CHANGE 5.0 0/0
SEAS.INDEX 100. NEXT QTR. 95. ECON.INDEX 89. FORECAST,NEXT QTR. 95.

INFORMATION ON COMPETITORS

	PRICE	DIVIDEND	SALES VOLUME	NET PROFIT
FIRM 1	$ 24.20	$ 10000.	124216.	$ 80384.
FIRM 2	$ 24.54	$ 125000.	131216.	$ 130059.
FIRM 3	$ 27.00	$ 0.	72758.	$ 10530.
FIRM 4	$ 26.06	$ 183333.	132708.	$ 128243.
FIRM 5	$ 24.50	$ 0.	54348.	$ -184414.
FIRM 6	$ 23.10	$ 125000.	158389.	$ 208482.

FIRM 5 4

OPERATING STATEMENTS

MARKET POTENTIAL	132708.	
SALES VOLUME	132708.	
PERCENT SHARE OF INDUSTRY SALES	19.7	
PRODUCTION,THIS QUARTER	145000.	
INVENTORY,FINISHED GOODS	39286.	
PLANT CAPACITY,NEXT QUARTER	124499.	

INCOME STATEMENT

RECEIPTS,SALES REVENUE		$ 3458378.
EXPENSES,MARKETING	$ 450000.	
RESEARCH AND DEVELOPMENT	225000.	
ADMINISTRATION	363664.	
MAINTENANCE	115710.	
LABOR(COST/UNIT EX.OVERTIME $ 5.57)	871403.	
MATERIALS CONSUMED(COST/UNIT 6.02)	872633.	
REDUCTION,FINISHED GOODS INV.	-155910.	
PLANT&EQ.DEPRECIATION(2.500 0/0)	207124.	
ROBOTICS DEPRECIATION(5.000 0/0)	11250.	
FINISHED GOODS CARRYING COSTS	81305.	
RAW MATERIALS CARRYING COSTS	51900.	
ORDERING COSTS	51740.	
SHIFTS CHANGE COSTS	0.	
INVESTMENTS EXPENSES	12691.	
FINANCING CHARGES AND PENALTIES	5471.	
SUNDRIES	100097.	3264070.
PROFIT BEFORE INCOME TAX		194308.
INCOME TAX(IN.TX.CR. 0. 0/0,SURTAX 0. 0/0)		66065.
NET PROFIT AFTER INCOME TAX		128243.
DIVIDENDS PAID		183333.
ADDITION TO OWNERS EQUITY		-55090.

CASH FLOW

RECEIPTS,SALES REVENUE		$ 3458378.
DISBURSEMENTS,CASH EXPENSE	$ 2328972.	
INCOME TAX	66065.	
DIVIDENDS PAID	183333.	
ROBOTICS INVESTMENT	86250.	
PLANT&EQ.INVESTMENT	270000.	
MATERIALS PURCHASED	786130.	3720749.
ADDITION TO CASH ASSETS		-262371.

FINANCIAL STATEMENT

NET ASSETS,CASH		$ -503270.
INV. VALUE,FINISHED GOODS		487830.
INVENTORY VALUE,MATERIALS		951487.
ROBOTICS BOOK VALUE(REPLACE.VAL.$	313958.)	300000.
PLANT&EQ.BOOK VALUE(REPLACE.VAL.	8855137.)	8347830.
OWNERS EQUITY(ECONOMIC EQUITY	10105142.)	9583877.

Table 27
Executive Game Quarterly Statement, Period 4, Firm 5-5, Model 1

```
 55 4 24.50  160000.   75000. 100000.  82000.  50000. 100000.  663600.          0.

                                    EXECUTIVE GAME
MODEL 1 PERIOD  4 AMJ PRICE INDEX 104.7 FORECAST,ANNUAL CHANGE  5.0 0/0
SEAS.INDEX 100. NEXT QTR.  95.  ECON.INDEX  89. FORECAST,NEXT QTR.  95.

                   INFORMATION            ON             COMPETITORS
             PRICE              DIVIDEND       SALES VOLUME           NET PROFIT
  FIRM 1    $ 24.20        $   10000.            124216.          $     80384.
  FIRM 2    $ 24.54        $  125000.            131216.          $    130059.
  FIRM 3    $ 27.00        $       0.             72758.          $     10530.
  FIRM 4    $ 26.06        $  183333.            132708.          $    128243.
  FIRM 5    $ 24.50        $       0.             54348.          $   -184414.
  FIRM 6    $ 23.10        $  125000.            158389.          $    208482.

                                       FIRM  5 5
                                  OPERATING STATEMENTS
     MARKET POTENTIAL                                      81998.
     SALES VOLUME                                          54348.
     PERCENT SHARE OF INDUSTRY SALES                         8.1
     PRODUCTION,THIS QUARTER                               49710.
     INVENTORY,FINISHED GOODS                                 0.
     PLANT CAPACITY,NEXT QUARTER                          102518.
                                      INCOME STATEMENT
     RECEIPTS,SALES REVENUE                                           $  1331537.
     EXPENSES,MARKETING                                $  160000.
       RESEARCH AND DEVELOPMENT                            75000.
       ADMINISTRATION                                     287899.
       MAINTENANCE                                        100000.
       LABOR(COST/UNIT EX.OVERTIME $ 5.72)                284311.
       MATERIALS CONSUMED(COST/UNIT  6.25)                310464.
       REDUCTION,FINISHED GOODS INV.                       57029.
       PLANT&EQ.DEPRECIATION(2.500 0/0)                   175334.
       ROBOTICS DEPRECIATION(5.000 0/0)                     5453.
       FINISHED GOODS CARRYING COSTS                          0.
       RAW MATERIALS CARRYING COSTS                        15523.
       ORDERING COSTS                                      51740.
       SHIFTS CHANGE COSTS                                     0.
       INVESTMENTS EXPENSES                                 2250.
       FINANCING CHARGES AND PENALTIES                         0.
       SUNDRIES                                            85953.          1610952.
     PROFIT BEFORE INCOME TAX                                             -279415.
     INCOME TAX(IN.TX.CR.  0. 0/0,SURTAX  0. 0/0)                          -95001.
     NET PROFIT AFTER INCOME TAX                                          -184414.
     DIVIDENDS PAID                                                             0.
     ADDITION TO OWNERS EQUITY                                            -184414.
                                          CASH FLOW
     RECEIPTS,SALES REVENUE                                           $  1331537.
     DISBURSEMENTS,CASH EXPENSE                    $  1062670.
       INCOME TAX                                      -95001.
       DIVIDENDS PAID                                       0.
       ROBOTICS INVESTMENT                              50000.
       PLANT&EQ.INVESTMENT                             100000.
       MATERIALS PURCHASED                             663600.             1781268.
     ADDITION TO CASH ASSETS                                               -449731.
                                      FINANCIAL STATEMENT
     NET ASSETS,CASH                                                  $  2092528.
       INV. VALUE,FINISHED GOODS                                                0.
       INVENTORY VALUE,MATERIALS                                           663600.
       ROBOTICS BOOK VALUE(REPLACE.VAL.$    157554.)                       153610.
       PLANT&EQ.BOOK VALUE(REPLACE.VAL.   7401396.)                       6938028.
     OWNERS EQUITY(ECONOMIC EQUITY       10315077.)                       9847765.
```

Table 28
Executive Game Quarterly Statement, Period 4, Firm 5-6, Model 1

```
 56 4 23.10  250000.  350000. 126395. 158389. 200000. 300000.  925000.  125000.

                              EXECUTIVE GAME
MODEL 1 PERIOD  4 AMJ PRICE INDEX 104.7 FORECAST,ANNUAL CHANGE  5.0 0/0
SEAS.INDEX 100. NEXT QTR.  95.  ECON.INDEX  89. FORECAST,NEXT QTR.  95.

                  INFORMATION          ON          COMPETITORS
            PRICE            DIVIDEND       SALES VOLUME         NET PROFIT
  FIRM 1   $ 24.20        $   10000.          124216.        $      80384.
  FIRM 2   $ 24.54        $  125000.          131216.        $     130059.
  FIRM 3   $ 27.00        $       0.           72758.        $      10530.
  FIRM 4   $ 26.06        $  183333.          132708.        $     128243.
  FIRM 5   $ 24.50        $       0.           54348.        $    -184414.
  FIRM 6   $ 23.10        $  125000.          158389.        $     208482.

                               FIRM  5 6
                         OPERATING STATEMENTS
    MARKET POTENTIAL                              204019.
    SALES VOLUME                                  158389.
    PERCENT SHARE OF INDUSTRY SALES                  23.5
    PRODUCTION,THIS QUARTER                       158389.
    INVENTORY,FINISHED GOODS                           0.
    PLANT CAPACITY,NEXT QUARTER                   118737.
                           INCOME STATEMENT
    RECEIPTS,SALES REVENUE                                       $  3658786.
    EXPENSES,MARKETING                          $  250000.
      RESEARCH AND DEVELOPMENT                     350000.
      ADMINISTRATION                               353260.
      MAINTENANCE                                  126395.
      LABOR(COST/UNIT EX.OVERTIME $ 5.25)          946830.
      MATERIALS CONSUMED(COST/UNIT  5.55)          878632.
      REDUCTION,FINISHED GOODS INV.                     0.
      PLANT&EQ.DEPRECIATION(2.500 0/0)             189420.
      ROBOTICS DEPRECIATION(5.000 0/0)              24500.
      FINISHED GOODS CARRYING COSTS                     0.
      RAW MATERIALS CARRYING COSTS                  52687.
      ORDERING COSTS                                51740.
      SHIFTS CHANGE COSTS                               0.
      INVESTMENTS EXPENSES                          25000.
      FINANCING CHARGES AND PENALTIES                   0.
      SUNDRIES                                      94443.          3342904.
    PROFIT BEFORE INCOME TAX                                         315882.
    INCOME TAX(IN.TX.CR.  0. 0/0,SURTAX  0. 0/0)                     107400.
    NET PROFIT AFTER INCOME TAX                                      208482.
    DIVIDENDS PAID                                                   125000.
    ADDITION TO OWNERS EQUITY                                         83482.
                                CASH FLOW
    RECEIPTS,SALES REVENUE                                       $  3658786.
    DISBURSEMENTS,CASH EXPENSE             $  2250350.
      INCOME TAX                                107400.
      DIVIDENDS PAID                            125000.
      ROBOTICS INVESTMENT                       200000.
      PLANT&EQ.INVESTMENT                       300000.
      MATERIALS PURCHASED                       925000.             3907749.
    ADDITION TO CASH ASSETS                                          -248963.
                          FINANCIAL STATEMENT
    NET ASSETS,CASH                                              $   103082.
      INV. VALUE,FINISHED GOODS                                           0.
      INVENTORY VALUE,MATERIALS                                     1100100.
      ROBOTICS BOOK VALUE(REPLACE.VAL.$    686978.)                  665500.
      PLANT&EQ.BOOK VALUE(REPLACE.VAL.   8164331.)                  7687386.
    OWNERS EQUITY(ECONOMIC EQUITY       10054490.)                  9556067.
```

Table 29
Executive Game Year-End Information on Competitors, Industry 5, Fiscal Year 1

EXECUTIVE GAME

END OF FISCAL YEAR 1.

FIRM NO.	NET CASH ASSETS ($)	INVENTORY VALUE FIN.GOODS ($)	INVENTORY VALUE MATERIALS ($)	ROBOTICS REPLACE. VALUE ($)	PLANT&EQ. REPLACE. VALUE ($)	OWNERS ECONOMIC EQUITY ($)
51	1158168.	367104.	801133.	171296.	8023864.	10521565.
52	-244851.	327950.	912439.	86371.	9024177.	10106086.
53	-232711.	0.	1509136.	330347.	8441345.	10048117.
54	-503270.	487830.	951487.	313958.	8855137.	10105142.
55	2092528.	0.	663600.	157554.	7401396.	10315078.
56	103082.	0.	1100100.	686978.	8164331.	10054491.

AVERAGES PER QUARTER FOR FISCAL YEAR 1. ONLY

FIRM NO.	MARKET-ING ($)	R AND D ($)	SALES VOLUME (UNITS)	NET PROFIT ($)	RATE OF RETURN* (0/0)	RANK*
51	200000.	115000.	108365.	96972.	9.01	2
52	255000.	155000.	110160.	71164.	8.29	3
53	262500.	298750.	111188.	10575.	5.72	6
54	358088.	190000.	140065.	133469.	11.12	1
55	198750.	105125.	116266.	64441.	7.51	4
56	255156.	350000.	151480.	55267.	7.49	5

* RANK AND ANNUAL RATE OF RETURN ARE BASED UPON DIVIDEND PAY-OUT FOR ALL 4 PERIODS AND OWNERS ECONOMIC EQUITY AT THE END OF FISCAL YEAR 1.

Table 30
Executive Game Quarterly Statement, Period 5, Firm 5-4, Model 2

54 5 26.32 285000. 75000. 127032. 158000. 105000. 216633. 1023400. 300000.

EXECUTIVE GAME

MODEL 2 PERIOD 5 JAS PRICE INDEX 106.3 FORECAST,ANNUAL CHANGE 5.3 0/0
SEAS.INDEX 95. NEXT QTR. 115. ECON.INDEX 96. FORECAST,NEXT QTR. 97.

INFORMATION ON COMPETITORS

	PRICE	DIVIDEND	SALES VOLUME	NET PROFIT
FIRM 1	$ 24.50	$ 20000.	131398.	$ 139838.
FIRM 2	$ 25.03	$ 130000.	128862.	$ 54670.
FIRM 3	$ 24.75	$ 100000.	192839.	$ 567483.
FIRM 4	$ 26.32	$ 300000.	127303.	$ 240900.
FIRM 5	$ 24.50	$ 0.	100508.	$ 126763.
FIRM 6	$ 23.20	$ 125000.	190000.	$ 467909.

FIRM 5 4

OPERATING STATEMENTS

MARKET POTENTIAL	127303.	
SALES VOLUME	127303.	
PERCENT SHARE OF INDUSTRY SALES	14.6	
PRODUCTION,THIS QUARTER	158000.	
INVENTORY,FINISHED GOODS	69983.	
PLANT CAPACITY,NEXT QUARTER	126167.	

INCOME STATEMENT

RECEIPTS,SALES REVENUE		$ 3350619.
EXPENSES,MARKETING	$ 285000.	
RESEARCH AND DEVELOPMENT	75000.	
ADMINISTRATION	371762.	
MAINTENANCE	127032.	
LABOR(COST/UNIT EX.OVERTIME $ 5.57)	972540.	
MATERIALS CONSUMED(COST/UNIT 5.95)	940067.	
REDUCTION,FINISHED GOODS INV.	393930.	
PLANT&EQ.DEPRECIATION(2.500 0/0)	208696.	
ROBOTICS DEPRECIATION(5.000 0/0)	15000.	
FINISHED GOODS CARRYING COSTS	146961.	
RAW MATERIALS CARRYING COSTS	47574.	
ORDERING COSTS	52499.	
SHIFTS CHANGE COSTS	0.	
INVESTMENTS EXPENSES	10345.	
FINANCING CHARGES AND PENALTIES	23878.	
SUNDRIES	103202.	2985619.
PROFIT BEFORE INCOME TAX		365000.
INCOME TAX(IN.TX.CR. 0. 0/0,SURTAX 0. 0/0)		124100.
NET PROFIT AFTER INCOME TAX		240900.
DIVIDENDS PAID		300000.
ADDITION TO OWNERS EQUITY		-59100.

CASH FLOW

RECEIPTS,SALES REVENUE		$ 3350619.
DISBURSEMENTS,CASH EXPENSE	$ 2215784.	
INCOME TAX	124100.	
DIVIDENDS PAID	300000.	
ROBOTICS INVESTMENT	105000.	
PLANT&EQ.INVESTMENT	216633.	
MATERIALS PURCHASED	1023400.	3984916.
ADDITION TO CASH ASSETS		-634297.

FINANCIAL STATEMENT

NET ASSETS,CASH		$ -1137567.
INV. VALUE,FINISHED GOODS		881764.
INVENTORY VALUE,MATERIALS		1034820.
ROBOTICS BOOK VALUE(REPLACE.VAL.$	412879.)	390000.
PLANT&EQ.BOOK VALUE(REPLACE.VAL.	9022017.)	8355767.
OWNERS EQUITY(ECONOMIC EQUITY	10213912.)	9524783.

Table 31
Executive Game Quarterly Statement, Period 6, Firm 5-4, Model 2

54 6 27.05 335000. 101667. 141095. 172673. 109500. 270000. 1034287. 700000.

EXECUTIVE GAME

MODEL 2 PERIOD 6 OND PRICE INDEX 107.1 FORECAST,ANNUAL CHANGE 6.0 0/0
SEAS.INDEX 115. NEXT QTR. 90. ECON.INDEX 95. FORECAST,NEXT QTR. 100.

INFORMATION ON COMPETITORS

	PRICE	DIVIDEND	SALES VOLUME	NET PROFIT
FIRM 1	$ 25.00	$ 30000.	153165.	$ 315996.
FIRM 2	$ 25.33	$ 150000.	168332.	$ 253661.
FIRM 3	$ 25.00	$ 250000.	216052.	$ 761209.
FIRM 4	$ 27.05	$ 700000.	143870.	$ 264871.
FIRM 5	$ 24.50	$ 20000.	108800.	$ 142161.
FIRM 6	$ 24.00	$ 150000.	231018.	$ 947298.

FIRM 5 4

OPERATING STATEMENTS

MARKET POTENTIAL	143870.	
SALES VOLUME	143870.	
PERCENT SHARE OF INDUSTRY SALES	14.1	
PRODUCTION,THIS QUARTER	171307.	
INVENTORY,FINISHED GOODS	97421.	
PLANT CAPACITY,NEXT QUARTER	128567.	

INCOME STATEMENT

RECEIPTS,SALES REVENUE		$ 3891673.
EXPENSES,MARKETING	$ 335000.	
RESEARCH AND DEVELOPMENT	101667.	
ADMINISTRATION	377819.	
MAINTENANCE	141095.	
LABOR(COST/UNIT EX.OVERTIME $ 5.55)	1076098.	
MATERIALS CONSUMED(COST/UNIT 6.04)	1034820.	
REDUCTION,FINISHED GOODS INV.	-357802.	
PLANT&EQ.DEPRECIATION(2.500 0/0)	208894.	
ROBOTICS DEPRECIATION(5.000 0/0)	19500.	
FINISHED GOODS CARRYING COSTS	206595.	
RAW MATERIALS CARRYING COSTS	51741.	
ORDERING COSTS	53016.	
SHIFTS CHANGE COSTS	0.	
INVESTMENTS EXPENSES	14402.	
FINANCING CHARGES AND PENALTIES	121993.	
SUNDRIES	105517.	3490353.
PROFIT BEFORE INCOME TAX		401320.
INCOME TAX(IN.TX.CR. 0. 0/0,SURTAX 0. 0/0)		136449.
NET PROFIT AFTER INCOME TAX		264871.
DIVIDENDS PAID		700000.
ADDITION TO OWNERS EQUITY		-435129.

CASH FLOW

RECEIPTS,SALES REVENUE		$ 3891673.
DISBURSEMENTS,CASH EXPENSE	$ 2584939.	
INCOME TAX	136449.	
DIVIDENDS PAID	700000.	
ROBOTICS INVESTMENT	109500.	
PLANT&EQ.INVESTMENT	270000.	
MATERIALS PURCHASED	1034287.	4835174.
ADDITION TO CASH ASSETS		-943501.

FINANCIAL STATEMENT

NET ASSETS,CASH		$ -2081068.
INV. VALUE,FINISHED GOODS		1239567.
INVENTORY VALUE,MATERIALS		1034287.
ROBOTICS BOOK VALUE(REPLACE.VAL.$	513417.)	480000.
PLANT&EQ.BOOK VALUE(REPLACE.VAL.	9177339.)	8416872.
OWNERS EQUITY(ECONOMIC EQUITY	9883542.)	9089658.

Table 32
Executive Game Quarterly Statement, Period 7, Firm 5-4, Model 2

54 7 27.05 900000. 101666. 141203. 171000. 125000. 270000. 1600000. 200000.

EXECUTIVE GAME

MODEL 2 PERIOD 7 JFM PRICE INDEX 108.9 FORECAST,ANNUAL CHANGE 6.5 0/0
SEAS.INDEX 90. NEXT QTR. 100. ECON.INDEX 101. FORECAST,NEXT QTR. 100.

INFORMATION ON COMPETITORS

	PRICE	DIVIDEND	SALES VOLUME	NET PROFIT
FIRM 1	$ 26.50	$ 400000.	132000.	$ 236621.
FIRM 2	$ 26.29	$ 150000.	122678.	$ 177532.
FIRM 3	$ 26.75	$ 200000.	168665.	$ 411740.
FIRM 4	$ 27.05	$ 200000.	201222.	$ 274680.
FIRM 5	$ 24.60	$ 25000.	105992.	$ 124271.
FIRM 6	$ 27.00	$ 600000.	153751.	$ 580037.

FIRM 5 4

OPERATING STATEMENTS

MARKET POTENTIAL	201222.	
SALES VOLUME	201222.	
PERCENT SHARE OF INDUSTRY SALES	22.8	
PRODUCTION,THIS QUARTER	170849.	
INVENTORY,FINISHED GOODS	67048.	
PLANT CAPACITY,NEXT QUARTER	131057.	

INCOME STATEMENT

RECEIPTS,SALES REVENUE		$ 5443054.
EXPENSES,MARKETING	$ 900000.	
RESEARCH AND DEVELOPMENT	101666.	
ADMINISTRATION	386616.	
MAINTENANCE	141203.	
LABOR(COST/UNIT EX.OVERTIME $ 5.57)	1069269.	
MATERIALS CONSUMED(COST/UNIT 6.05)	1034287.	
REDUCTION,FINISHED GOODS INV.	373920.	
PLANT&EQ.DEPRECIATION(2.500 0/0)	210422.	
ROBOTICS DEPRECIATION(5.000 0/0)	24000.	
FINISHED GOODS CARRYING COSTS	144275.	
RAW MATERIALS CARRYING COSTS	51714.	
ORDERING COSTS	53795.	
SHIFTS CHANGE COSTS	0.	
INVESTMENTS EXPENSES	15603.	
FINANCING CHARGES AND PENALTIES	411209.	
SUNDRIES	108899.	5026872.
PROFIT BEFORE INCOME TAX		416182.
INCOME TAX(IN.TX.CR. 0. 0/0,SURTAX 0. 0/0)		141502.
NET PROFIT AFTER INCOME TAX		274680.
DIVIDENDS PAID		200000.
ADDITION TO OWNERS EQUITY		74680.

CASH FLOW

RECEIPTS,SALES REVENUE		$ 5443054.
DISBURSEMENTS,CASH EXPENSE	$ 3384243.	
INCOME TAX	141502.	
DIVIDENDS PAID	200000.	
ROBOTICS INVESTMENT	125000.	
PLANT&EQ.INVESTMENT	270000.	
MATERIALS PURCHASED	1600000.	5720744.
ADDITION TO CASH ASSETS		-277690.

FINANCIAL STATEMENT

NET ASSETS,CASH		$ -2358758.
INV. VALUE,FINISHED GOODS		865651.
INVENTORY VALUE,MATERIALS		1600000.
ROBOTICS BOOK VALUE(REPLACE.VAL.$	628476.)	581000.
PLANT&EQ.BOOK VALUE(REPLACE.VAL.	9417830.)	8476450.
OWNERS EQUITY(ECONOMIC EQUITY	10153199.)	9164343.

Table 33
Executive Game Quarterly Statement, Period 8, Firm 5-1, Model 2

51 8 28.50 250000. 350000. 116543. 150500. 250000. 300000. 800000. 50000.

EXECUTIVE GAME

MODEL 2 PERIOD 8 AMJ PRICE INDEX 110.5 FORECAST,ANNUAL CHANGE 7.0 0/0
SEAS.INDEX 100. NEXT QTR. 95. ECON.INDEX 99. FORECAST,NEXT QTR. 103.

INFORMATION ON COMPETITORS

	PRICE	DIVIDEND	SALES VOLUME	NET PROFIT
FIRM 1	$ 28.50	$ 50000.	133900.	$ 438220.
FIRM 2	$ 26.55	$ 150000.	120258.	$ 85650.
FIRM 3	$ 28.00	$ 200000.	197036.	$ 724530.
FIRM 4	$ 30.00	$ 1000000.	101716.	$ -220891.
FIRM 5	$ 24.80	$ 30000.	131736.	$ 290060.
FIRM 6	$ 29.00	$ 500000.	164295.	$ 597594.

FIRM 5 1

OPERATING STATEMENTS

MARKET POTENTIAL	133900.	
SALES VOLUME	133900.	
PERCENT SHARE OF INDUSTRY SALES	15.8	
PRODUCTION,THIS QUARTER	150500.	
INVENTORY,FINISHED GOODS	16600.	
PLANT CAPACITY,NEXT QUARTER	128841.	

INCOME STATEMENT

RECEIPTS,SALES REVENUE		$ 3816148.
EXPENSES,MARKETING	$ 250000.	
RESEARCH AND DEVELOPMENT	350000.	
ADMINISTRATION	385123.	
MAINTENANCE	116543.	
LABOR(COST/UNIT EX.OVERTIME $ 5.49)	897262.	
MATERIALS CONSUMED(COST/UNIT 6.28)	863585.	
REDUCTION,FINISHED GOODS INV.	-216946.	
PLANT&EQ.DEPRECIATION(2.500 0/0)	200423.	
ROBOTICS DEPRECIATION(5.000 0/0)	33602.	
FINISHED GOODS CARRYING COSTS	36158.	
RAW MATERIALS CARRYING COSTS	44765.	
ORDERING COSTS	54454.	
SHIFTS CHANGE COSTS	0.	
INVESTMENTS EXPENSES	30250.	
FINANCING CHARGES AND PENALTIES	0.	
SUNDRIES	106964.	3152179.
PROFIT BEFORE INCOME TAX		663969.
INCOME TAX(IN.TX.CR. 0. 0/0,SURTAX 0. 0/0)		225749.
NET PROFIT AFTER INCOME TAX		438220.
DIVIDENDS PAID		50000.
ADDITION TO OWNERS EQUITY		388220.

CASH FLOW

RECEIPTS,SALES REVENUE		$ 3816148.
DISBURSEMENTS,CASH EXPENSE	$ 2271514.	
INCOME TAX	225749.	
DIVIDENDS PAID	50000.	
ROBOTICS INVESTMENT	250000.	
PLANT&EQ.INVESTMENT	300000.	
MATERIALS PURCHASED	800000.	3897263.
ADDITION TO CASH ASSETS		-81115.

FINANCIAL STATEMENT

NET ASSETS,CASH		$ 614984.
INV. VALUE,FINISHED GOODS		216946.
INVENTORY VALUE,MATERIALS		831717.
ROBOTICS BOOK VALUE(REPLACE.VAL.$	941236.)	888432.
PLANT&EQ.BOOK VALUE(REPLACE.VAL.	9145052.)	8116492.
OWNERS EQUITY(ECONOMIC EQUITY	11749933.)	10668570.

Table 34
Executive Game Quarterly Statement, Period 8, Firm 5-2, Model 2

52 8 26.55 350000. 100000. 112800. 141000. 50000. 600000. 900000. 150000.

EXECUTIVE GAME

MODEL 2 PERIOD 8 AMJ PRICE INDEX 110.5 FORECAST,ANNUAL CHANGE 7.0 0/0
SEAS.INDEX 100. NEXT QTR. 95. ECON.INDEX 99. FORECAST,NEXT QTR. 103.

INFORMATION ON COMPETITORS

	PRICE	DIVIDEND	SALES VOLUME	NET PROFIT
FIRM 1	$ 28.50	$ 50000.	133900.	$ 438220.
FIRM 2	$ 26.55	$ 150000.	120258.	$ 85650.
FIRM 3	$ 28.00	$ 200000.	197036.	$ 724530.
FIRM 4	$ 30.00	$ 1000000.	101716.	$ -220891.
FIRM 5	$ 24.80	$ 30000.	131736.	$ 290060.
FIRM 6	$ 29.00	$ 500000.	164295.	$ 597594.

FIRM 5 2

OPERATING STATEMENTS

MARKET POTENTIAL	132453.	
SALES VOLUME	120258.	
PERCENT SHARE OF INDUSTRY SALES	14.2	
PRODUCTION,THIS QUARTER	79674.	
INVENTORY,FINISHED GOODS	0.	
PLANT CAPACITY,NEXT QUARTER	148185.	

INCOME STATEMENT

RECEIPTS,SALES REVENUE		$ 3192848.
EXPENSES,MARKETING	$ 350000.	
RESEARCH AND DEVELOPMENT	100000.	
ADMINISTRATION	356119.	
MAINTENANCE	112800.	
LABOR(COST/UNIT EX.OVERTIME $ 5.94)	473465.	
MATERIALS CONSUMED(COST/UNIT 6.33)	504617.	
REDUCTION,FINISHED GOODS INV.	523974.	
PLANT&EQ.DEPRECIATION(2.500 0/0)	241220.	
ROBOTICS DEPRECIATION(5.000 0/0)	10824.	
FINISHED GOODS CARRYING COSTS	0.	
RAW MATERIALS CARRYING COSTS	25231.	
ORDERING COSTS	54454.	
SHIFTS CHANGE COSTS	0.	
INVESTMENTS EXPENSES	42250.	
FINANCING CHARGES AND PENALTIES	147347.	
SUNDRIES	120778.	3063075.
PROFIT BEFORE INCOME TAX		129773.
INCOME TAX(IN.TX.CR. 0. 0/0,SURTAX 0. 0/0)		44123.
NET PROFIT AFTER INCOME TAX		85650.
DIVIDENDS PAID		150000.
ADDITION TO OWNERS EQUITY		-64350.

CASH FLOW

RECEIPTS,SALES REVENUE		$ 3192848.
DISBURSEMENTS,CASH EXPENSE	$ 1782439.	
INCOME TAX	44123.	
DIVIDENDS PAID	150000.	
ROBOTICS INVESTMENT	50000.	
PLANT&EQ.INVESTMENT	600000.	
MATERIALS PURCHASED	900000.	3526561.
ADDITION TO CASH ASSETS		-333713.

FINANCIAL STATEMENT

NET ASSETS,CASH		$ -1575042.
INV. VALUE,FINISHED GOODS		0.
INVENTORY VALUE,MATERIALS		900000.
ROBOTICS BOOK VALUE(REPLACE.VAL.$	276379.)	255665.
PLANT&EQ.BOOK VALUE(REPLACE.VAL.	11158599.)	10007570.
OWNERS EQUITY(ECONOMIC EQUITY	10759934.)	9588192.

Table 35
Executive Game Quarterly Statement, Period 8, Firm 5-3, Model 2

```
 53 8 28.00  600000.  150000.  95000. 127660. 100000. 300000.  750000.  200000.

                                 EXECUTIVE GAME
MODEL 2 PERIOD  8 AMJ PRICE INDEX 110.5 FORECAST,ANNUAL CHANGE  7.0 0/0
SEAS.INDEX 100. NEXT QTR.  95.  ECON.INDEX  99. FORECAST,NEXT QTR. 103.

                  INFORMATION          ON          COMPETITORS
            PRICE           DIVIDEND      SALES VOLUME         NET PROFIT
  FIRM 1   $ 28.50       $   50000.          133900.         $    438220.
  FIRM 2   $ 26.55       $  150000.          120258.         $     85650.
  FIRM 3   $ 28.00       $  200000.          197036.         $    724530.
  FIRM 4   $ 30.00       $ 1000000.          101716.         $   -220891.
  FIRM 5   $ 24.80       $   30000.          131736.         $    290060.
  FIRM 6   $ 29.00       $  500000.          164295.         $    597594.

                                     FIRM  5 3
                             OPERATING STATEMENTS
     MARKET POTENTIAL                                197036.
     SALES VOLUME                                    197036.
     PERCENT SHARE OF INDUSTRY SALES                    23.2
     PRODUCTION,THIS QUARTER                         127660.
     INVENTORY,FINISHED GOODS                         74818.
     PLANT CAPACITY,NEXT QUARTER                     130237.
                                 INCOME STATEMENT
     RECEIPTS,SALES REVENUE                                         $  5517002.
     EXPENSES,MARKETING                            $  600000.
       RESEARCH AND DEVELOPMENT                       150000.
       ADMINISTRATION                                 335760.
       MAINTENANCE                                     95000.
       LABOR(COST/UNIT EX.OVERTIME $ 5.50)            701823.
       MATERIALS CONSUMED(COST/UNIT  5.75)            734504.
       REDUCTION,FINISHED GOODS INV.                  883868.
       PLANT&EQ.DEPRECIATION(2.500 0/0)               205339.
       ROBOTICS DEPRECIATION(5.000 0/0)                32081.
       FINISHED GOODS CARRYING COSTS                  162966.
       RAW MATERIALS CARRYING COSTS                    66054.
       ORDERING COSTS                                  54454.
       SHIFTS CHANGE COSTS                            108908.
       INVESTMENTS EXPENSES                            16000.
       FINANCING CHARGES AND PENALTIES                163147.
       SUNDRIES                                       109330.          4419229.
     PROFIT BEFORE INCOME TAX                                          1097773.
     INCOME TAX(IN.TX.CR.  0. 0/0,SURTAX  0. 0/0)                       373243.
     NET PROFIT AFTER INCOME TAX                                        724530.
     DIVIDENDS PAID                                                     200000.
     ADDITION TO OWNERS EQUITY                                          524530.
                                       CASH FLOW
     RECEIPTS,SALES REVENUE                                         $  5517002.
     DISBURSEMENTS,CASH EXPENSE               $  2563435.
       INCOME TAX                                  373243.
       DIVIDENDS PAID                              200000.
       ROBOTICS INVESTMENT                         100000.
       PLANT&EQ.INVESTMENT                         300000.
       MATERIALS PURCHASED                         750000.             4286677.
     ADDITION TO CASH ASSETS                                           1230325.
                                 FINANCIAL STATEMENT
     NET ASSETS,CASH                                                $   -75864.
       INV. VALUE,FINISHED GOODS                                        977798.
       INVENTORY VALUE,MATERIALS                                       1336573.
       ROBOTICS BOOK VALUE(REPLACE.VAL.$   777367.)                     709544.
       PLANT&EQ.BOOK VALUE(REPLACE.VAL.  9373455.)                     8308220.
     OWNERS EQUITY(ECONOMIC EQUITY      12389327.)                    11256270.
```

Table 36
Executive Game Quarterly Statement, Period 8, Firm 5-4, Model 2

54 8 30.00 200000. 101667. 149597. 177853. 130000. 270000. 500000. 1000000.

EXECUTIVE GAME

MODEL 2 PERIOD 8 AMJ PRICE INDEX 110.5 FORECAST,ANNUAL CHANGE 7.0 0/0
SEAS.INDEX 100. NEXT QTR. 95. ECON.INDEX 99. FORECAST,NEXT QTR. 103.

INFORMATION ON COMPETITORS

	PRICE	DIVIDEND	SALES VOLUME	NET PROFIT
FIRM 1	$ 28.50	$ 50000.	133900.	$ 438220.
FIRM 2	$ 26.55	$ 150000.	120258.	$ 85650.
FIRM 3	$ 28.00	$ 200000.	197036.	$ 724530.
FIRM 4	$ 30.00	$ 1000000.	101716.	$ -220891.
FIRM 5	$ 24.80	$ 30000.	131736.	$ 290060.
FIRM 6	$ 29.00	$ 500000.	164295.	$ 597594.

FIRM 5 4

OPERATING STATEMENTS

MARKET POTENTIAL	101716.	
SALES VOLUME	101716.	
PERCENT SHARE OF INDUSTRY SALES	12.0	
PRODUCTION,THIS QUARTER	177853.	
INVENTORY,FINISHED GOODS	143185.	
PLANT CAPACITY,NEXT QUARTER	133526.	

INCOME STATEMENT

RECEIPTS,SALES REVENUE		$ 3051481.
EXPENSES,MARKETING	$ 200000.	
RESEARCH AND DEVELOPMENT	101667.	
ADMINISTRATION	394734.	
MAINTENANCE	149597.	
LABOR(COST/UNIT EX.OVERTIME $ 5.55)	1117845.	
MATERIALS CONSUMED(COST/UNIT 6.08)	1080487.	
REDUCTION,FINISHED GOODS INV.	-1005636.	
PLANT&EQ.DEPRECIATION(2.500 0/0)	211911.	
ROBOTICS DEPRECIATION(5.000 0/0)	29050.	
FINISHED GOODS CARRYING COSTS	311880.	
RAW MATERIALS CARRYING COSTS	80000.	
ORDERING COSTS	54454.	
SHIFTS CHANGE COSTS	0.	
INVESTMENTS EXPENSES	16000.	
FINANCING CHARGES AND PENALTIES	532028.	
SUNDRIES	112149.	3386164.
PROFIT BEFORE INCOME TAX		-334683.
INCOME TAX(IN.TX.CR. 0. 0/0,SURTAX 0. 0/0)		-113792.
NET PROFIT AFTER INCOME TAX		-220891.
DIVIDENDS PAID		1000000.
ADDITION TO OWNERS EQUITY		-1220890.

CASH FLOW

RECEIPTS,SALES REVENUE		$ 3051481.
DISBURSEMENTS,CASH EXPENSE	$ 3070350.	
INCOME TAX	-113792.	
DIVIDENDS PAID	1000000.	
ROBOTICS INVESTMENT	130000.	
PLANT&EQ.INVESTMENT	270000.	
MATERIALS PURCHASED	500000.	4856557.
ADDITION TO CASH ASSETS		-1805076.

FINANCIAL STATEMENT

NET ASSETS,CASH		$ -4163834.
INV. VALUE,FINISHED GOODS		1871282.
INVENTORY VALUE,MATERIALS		1019513.
ROBOTICS BOOK VALUE(REPLACE.VAL.$	747770.)	681950.
PLANT&EQ.BOOK VALUE(REPLACE.VAL.	9634711.)	8534538.
OWNERS EQUITY(ECONOMIC EQUITY	9109441.)	7943448.

Table 37
Executive Game Quarterly Statement, Period 8, Firm 5-5, Model 2

```
 55 8 24.80  205000.    90000.  90000. 132500.  60000. 100000.  650000.   30000.

                                   EXECUTIVE GAME
MODEL 2 PERIOD  8 AMJ PRICE INDEX 110.5 FORECAST,ANNUAL CHANGE  7.0 0/0
SEAS.INDEX 100. NEXT QTR.  95.  ECON.INDEX  99. FORECAST,NEXT QTR. 103.

                  INFORMATION         ON          COMPETITORS
            PRICE             DIVIDEND      SALES VOLUME        NET PROFIT
  FIRM 1    $ 28.50      $    50000.         133900.        $    438220.
  FIRM 2    $ 26.55      $   150000.         120258.        $     85650.
  FIRM 3    $ 28.00      $   200000.         197036.        $    724530.
  FIRM 4    $ 30.00      $ 1000000.          101716.        $   -220891.
  FIRM 5    $ 24.80      $    30000.         131736.        $    290060.
  FIRM 6    $ 29.00      $   500000.         164295.        $    597594.

                                     FIRM  5 5
                               OPERATING STATEMENTS
     MARKET POTENTIAL                                  144515.
     SALES VOLUME                                      131736.
     PERCENT SHARE OF INDUSTRY SALES                      15.5
     PRODUCTION,THIS QUARTER                           131736.
     INVENTORY,FINISHED GOODS                               0.
     PLANT CAPACITY,NEXT QUARTER                       103541.
                                   INCOME STATEMENT
     RECEIPTS,SALES REVENUE                                         $  3267043.
     EXPENSES,MARKETING                              $  205000.
       RESEARCH AND DEVELOPMENT                          90000.
       ADMINISTRATION                                   358225.
       MAINTENANCE                                       90000.
       LABOR(COST/UNIT EX.OVERTIME $ 5.94)              864876.
       MATERIALS CONSUMED(COST/UNIT  6.38)              840039.
       REDUCTION,FINISHED GOODS INV.                         0.
       PLANT&EQ.DEPRECIATION(2.500 0/0)                 169541.
       ROBOTICS DEPRECIATION(5.000 0/0)                  19598.
       FINISHED GOODS CARRYING COSTS                         0.
       RAW MATERIALS CARRYING COSTS                      42002.
       ORDERING COSTS                                    54454.
       SHIFTS CHANGE COSTS                                   0.
       INVESTMENTS EXPENSES                               2560.
       FINANCING CHARGES AND PENALTIES                       0.
       SUNDRIES                                          91267.        2827559.
     PROFIT BEFORE INCOME TAX                                           439484.
     INCOME TAX(IN.TX.CR.  0. 0/0,SURTAX  0. 0/0)                       149425.
     NET PROFIT AFTER INCOME TAX                                        290060.
     DIVIDENDS PAID                                                      30000.
     ADDITION TO OWNERS EQUITY                                          260060.
                                       CASH FLOW
     RECEIPTS,SALES REVENUE                                         $  3267043.
     DISBURSEMENTS,CASH EXPENSE                 $  1798379.
       INCOME TAX                                   149425.
       DIVIDENDS PAID                                30000.
       ROBOTICS INVESTMENT                           60000.
       PLANT&EQ.INVESTMENT                          100000.
       MATERIALS PURCHASED                          650000.             2787803.
     ADDITION TO CASH ASSETS                                            479240.
                                  FINANCIAL STATEMENT
     NET ASSETS,CASH                                                $  2661562.
       INV. VALUE,FINISHED GOODS                                             0.
       INVENTORY VALUE,MATERIALS                                        650001.
       ROBOTICS BOOK VALUE(REPLACE.VAL.$  470115.)                      432354.
       PLANT&EQ.BOOK VALUE(REPLACE.VAL.  7657762.)                     6712108.
     OWNERS EQUITY(ECONOMIC EQUITY      11439437.)                    10456024.
```

Table 38
Executive Game Quarterly Statement, Period 8, Firm 5-6, Model 2

56 8 29.00 600000. 200000. 101426. 124182. 0. 150000. 350000. 500000.

EXECUTIVE GAME

MODEL 2 PERIOD 8 AMJ PRICE INDEX 110.5 FORECAST,ANNUAL CHANGE 7.0 0/0
SEAS.INDEX 100. NEXT QTR. 95. ECON.INDEX 99. FORECAST,NEXT QTR. 103.

INFORMATION ON COMPETITORS

	PRICE	DIVIDEND	SALES VOLUME	NET PROFIT
FIRM 1	$ 28.50	$ 50000.	133900.	$ 438220.
FIRM 2	$ 26.55	$ 150000.	120258.	$ 85650.
FIRM 3	$ 28.00	$ 200000.	197036.	$ 724530.
FIRM 4	$ 30.00	$ 1000000.	101716.	$ -220891.
FIRM 5	$ 24.80	$ 30000.	131736.	$ 290060.
FIRM 6	$ 29.00	$ 500000.	164295.	$ 597594.

FIRM 5 6

OPERATING STATEMENTS

MARKET POTENTIAL	164295.	
SALES VOLUME	164295.	
PERCENT SHARE OF INDUSTRY SALES	19.4	
PRODUCTION,THIS QUARTER	124182.	
INVENTORY,FINISHED GOODS	39820.	
PLANT CAPACITY,NEXT QUARTER	127352.	

INCOME STATEMENT

RECEIPTS,SALES REVENUE		$ 4764567.
EXPENSES,MARKETING	$ 600000.	
RESEARCH AND DEVELOPMENT	200000.	
ADMINISTRATION	336000.	
MAINTENANCE	101426.	
LABOR(COST/UNIT EX.OVERTIME $ 5.46)	678529.	
MATERIALS CONSUMED(COST/UNIT 5.75)	713636.	
REDUCTION,FINISHED GOODS INV.	511601.	
PLANT&EQ.DEPRECIATION(2.500 0/0)	207384.	
ROBOTICS DEPRECIATION(5.000 0/0)	28529.	
FINISHED GOODS CARRYING COSTS	86734.	
RAW MATERIALS CARRYING COSTS	73750.	
ORDERING COSTS	54454.	
SHIFTS CHANGE COSTS	108908.	
INVESTMENTS EXPENSES	2250.	
FINANCING CHARGES AND PENALTIES	46408.	
SUNDRIES	109515.	3859121.
PROFIT BEFORE INCOME TAX		905446.
INCOME TAX(IN.TX.CR. 0. 0/0,SURTAX 0. 0/0)		307852.
NET PROFIT AFTER INCOME TAX		597594.
DIVIDENDS PAID		500000.
ADDITION TO OWNERS EQUITY		97594.

CASH FLOW

RECEIPTS,SALES REVENUE		$ 4764567.
DISBURSEMENTS,CASH EXPENSE	$ 2397967.	
INCOME TAX	307852.	
DIVIDENDS PAID	500000.	
ROBOTICS INVESTMENT	0.	
PLANT&EQ.INVESTMENT	150000.	
MATERIALS PURCHASED	350000.	3705818.
ADDITION TO CASH ASSETS		1058749.

FINANCIAL STATEMENT

NET ASSETS,CASH		$ 362103.
INV. VALUE,FINISHED GOODS		520402.
INVENTORY VALUE,MATERIALS		1111364.
ROBOTICS BOOK VALUE(REPLACE.VAL.$	635286.)	542054.
PLANT&EQ.BOOK VALUE(REPLACE.VAL.	9280084.)	8237990.
OWNERS EQUITY(ECONOMIC EQUITY	11909236.)	10773911.

Table 39
Executive Game Year-End Information on Competitors, Industry 5, Fiscal Year 2

EXECUTIVE GAME

END OF FISCAL YEAR 2.

FIRM NO.	NET CASH ASSETS ($)	INVENTORY VALUE FIN.GOODS ($)	INVENTORY VALUE MATERIALS ($)	ROBOTICS REPLACE. VALUE ($)	PLANT&EQ. REPLACE. VALUE ($)	OWNERS ECONOMIC EQUITY ($)
51	614984.	216946.	831717.	941236.	9145052.	11749935.
52	-1575042.	0.	900000.	276379.	11158599.	10759936.
53	-75864.	977798.	1336573.	777367.	9373455.	12389329.
54	-4163834.	1871282.	1019513.	747770.	9634711.	9109442.
55	2661562.	0.	650001.	470115.	7657762.	11439440.
56	362103.	520402.	1111364.	635286.	9280084.	11909239.

AVERAGES PER QUARTER FOR FISCAL YEAR 2. ONLY

FIRM NO.	MARKET-ING ($)	R AND D ($)	SALES VOLUME (UNITS)	NET PROFIT ($)	RATE OF RETURN* (0/0)	RANK*
51	262500.	312500.	137616.	282669.	12.73	3
52	318750.	161250.	135033.	142878.	10.31	5
53	426250.	206250.	193648.	616241.	17.70	2
54	430000.	95000.	143528.	139890.	11.86	4
55	201250.	97500.	111759.	170814.	9.55	6
56	362500.	237500.	184766.	648210.	19.28	1

* RANK AND ANNUAL RATE OF RETURN ARE BASED UPON DIVIDEND PAY-OUT FOR ALL 8 PERIODS AND OWNERS ECONOMIC EQUITY AT THE END OF FISCAL YEAR 2.

TABLE 40
WORK SHEET FOR ANALYSIS OF OPERATIONS

-to be detached and handed in at the end of the Game-the individual team member should enter his/her team's consolidated decision and forecasts on this sheet each quarter.

Firm 5-4 Periods 0 - 4 Model # 1
Periods 5 - 8 Model # 2

	Trial Period 2 Actual	Trial Period 2 Forecast	Trial Period 1 Actual	Trial Period 1 Forecast	Period 0 Actual
I (a) Price Index (Period 0=100%)/(b) Forecast, Annual Change (%)	/	/	101.0/5.3	101.25/5.0	100.0/5.0
II (a) Calendar Quarter/(b) Seasonal Index (Average Period=100%)	OND/	OND/	JAS/95	JAS/95	AMJ/100
III Economic Index (Period=100%)			101	100	100
IV (a) Inv. Tax Cr. %/(b) Surtax %/(c) Pl & Eq. Depr. %/(d) Robotics Depr. %	/ / /	/ / /	0/0/12.5/5	0/0/12.5/5	0/0/12.5/5
1 (a) Firm's Price/(b) Average Industry Price ($)	/	/	25.35/24.31	25.35/25.00	25.60/25.60
2 Total Industry Sales - in units (not dollars)			619,460	650,000	658,120
3 Market Potential (units)			102,156	120,000	109,720
4 Sales Volume (units)			102,156	120,000	109,720
5 Percent Share of Industry Sales (%)			16.5	18.5	16.7
6 Production, This Quarter (units)			115,206	115,206	100,000
7 (a) Labor Cost per Unit/(b) Material Cost per Unit ($)	/	/	5.71/6.30	5.74/6.31	5.74/6.31
8 Inventory, Finished Goods (units)			25,800	7,956	12, 750
9 Plant Capacity, Next Quarter (units)			105,379	105,372	104,643
10 INCOME (and expense) STATEMENT ($)					
11 Receipts, Sales Revenue			2,589,658	3,042,000	2,808,832
12 Expenses, Marketing Expense			341,750	341,750	200,000
13 Research and Development Expense			100,000	100,000	100,000
14 Administration Expense			330,179	330,514	278,000
15 Maintenance Expense			88,565	88,565	75,000
16 Labor Expense			688,538	691,598	573,939
17 Materials Expense			725,928	726,950	630,667
18 Reduction, Finished Goods Inventory Value			-156,599	57,528	116,638
19 Plant and Equipment Depreciation			183,125	183,125	183,125
20 Robotics Depreciation			0	0	0
21 Finished Goods Carrying Costs			51,600	15,912	25,500
22 Raw Materials Carrying Costs			60,000	60,000	41,533
23 Ordering Costs			50,000	50,000	50,000

24 Shifts Change Costs			0	0	0
25 Investment Expenses			4,000	4,000	25,000
26 Financing Charges and Penalties			0	0	0
27 Sundries Expenses			84,459	86,159	82,000
28 Total Expenses			2,551,541	2,736,101	2,381,402
29 Profit Before Income Taxes			38.117	305.898	427,430
30 Income Tax			12,969	104.605	145,326
31 Net Profit After Income Tax			25.157	201,893	282,104
32 Dividends Paid			40,000	40,000	53,000
33 Addition to Owners' Equity			- 14,843	161,893	229,104
34 CASH FLOW STATEMENT ($)					
35 Receipts, Sales Revenue			2,589,658	3,042,000	2,808,832
36 Disbursements, Cash Expense			1,799,085	1,768,498	1,450,972
37 Income Tax			12,960	104,005	145,326
38 Dividends Paid			40,000	40.000	53,000
39 Robotics Investments			0	0	0
40 Plant and Equipment Investments			200,000	200,000	500,000
41 Materials Purchased			285,000	285,000	1,000,000
42 Total Disbursements			2,337,041	2,397,503	3,149,298
43 Addition to Cash Assets			252,614	644,497	-340,466
44 FINANCIAL STATEMENT ($)					
45 Net Assets, Cash			1,274,614	1,666,497	1.022,000
46 Inventory Value, Finished Goods			309,599	95,472	153,000
47 Inventory Value, Materials			759,072	758.010	1,200,000
48 Robotics Book Value			0	0	0
49 Plant and Equipment Book Value			7,341,875	7,341,875	7,325,000
50 Owners' Equity			9,685,158	9,811,854	9,700,000
51 Plant and Equipment Replacement Value			7,449,239	7,468,241	7,325,000
52 Robotics Replacement Value			0	0	0
53 Owners' Economic Equity			9,192,522	9,938,200	9,700,000

TABLE 40 (continued)
WORK SHEET FOR ANALYSIS OF OPERATIONS

-to be detached and handed in at the end of the Game-the individual team member should enter his/her team's consolidated decision and forecasts on this sheet each quarter.

Periods 0 - 4 Model # 1
Periods 5 - 8 Model # 2

	Period 1		Period 2		Period 3	
	Forecast	Actual	Forecast	Actual	Forecast	Actual
I (a) Price Index (Period 0=100%)/(b) Forecast, Annual Change (%)	101.0 / 5.3	101.0 / 5.3	102.3 / 5.3	102.5 / 5.0	103.8 / 5.0	104.0 / 4.8
II (a) Calendar Quarter/(b) Seasonal Index (Average Period=100%)	JAS/95	JAS/95	OND/115	OND/115	JFM/90	JFM/90
III Economic Index (Period=100%)	101	101	95	94	94	95
IV (a) Inv. Tax Cr. %/(b) Surtax %/(c) Pl & Eq. Depr. %/(d) Robotics Depr. %	0 / 0 / 2.5 / 5	0 / 0 / 2.5 / 5	0 / 0 / 2.5 / 5	0 / 0 / 2.5 / 5	0 / 0 / 2.5 / 5	0 / 0 / 2.5 / 5
1 (a) Firm's Price/(b) Average Industry Price ($)	23.10 / 24.00	23.10 / 23.62	23.70 / 23.60	23.70 / 23.59	25.15 / 23.00	25.15 / 24.22
2 Total Industry Sales - in units (not dollars)	700,000	709,967	800,000	833,078	760,000	733,419
3 Market Potential (units)	153,160	164,930	151,387	161,444	138,000	123,006
4 Sales Volume (units)	153,160	153,160	151,387	151,387	138,000	123,006
5 Percent Share of Industry Sales (%)	21.9	21.6	18.9	18.2	18.2	16.8
6 Production, This Quarter (units)	140,410	140,410	151,387	151,387	150,000	150,000
7 (a) Labor Cost per Unit/(b) Material Cost per Unit ($)	5.71 / 6.30	5.70 / 6.30	5.70 / 6.30	5.67 / 6.19	5.67 / 6.19	5.62 / 6.08
8 Inventory, Finished Goods (units)	0	0	0	0	12,000	26,994
9 Plant Capacity, Next Quarter (units)	108,660	108,661	119,870	119,912	122,226	122,216
10 INCOME (and expense) STATEMENT ($)						
11 Receipts, Sales Revenue	3,537,996	3,537,996	3,587,872	3,587,871	3,470,700	3,093,592
12 Expenses, Marketing Expense	322,500	322,500	265,000	265,000	394,850	394,850
13 Research and Development Expense	125,000	125,000	210,000	210,000	200,000	200,000
14 Administration Expense	330,179	330,179	338,463	339,188	357,382	357,351
15 Maintenance Expense	107,440	107,940	116,379	116,379	115,313	115,313
16 Labor Expense	903,856	901,657	984,675	979,433	935,799	927,513
17 Materials Expense	884,583	884,152	953,738	936,856	928,500	911,987
18 Reduction, Finished Goods Inventory Value	153,000	153,000	0	0	-147,600	-331,924
19 Plant and Equipment Depreciation	183,125	183,125	187,922	187,922	205,512	205,512
20 Robotics Depreciation	0	0	3,750	3,750	7,500	7,500
21 Finished Goods Carrying Costs	0	0	0	0	24,600	55,321
22 Raw Materials Carrying Costs	60,000	60,000	52,292	52,292	54,203	54,203
23 Ordering Costs	50,000	50,000	50,500	50,614	51,250	51,234

24 Shifts Change Costs	0	0	0	0	0	0
25 Investment Expenses	20,250	20,250	94,141	94,141	12,426	12,426
26 Financing Charges and Penalties	0	0	0	0	0	0
27 Sundries Expenses	84,459	84,459	88,217	88,348	97,492	97,496
28 Total Expenses	3,224,892	3,222,259	3,345,077	3,323,920	3,237,227	3,058,657
29 Profit Before Income Taxes	313,014	315,737	242,795	263,951	233,473	34,905
30 Income Tax	106,455	107,351	82,550	89,743	79,381	11,868
31 Net Profit After Income Tax	206,559	208,386	160,245	174,208	154,092	23,037
32 Dividends Paid	100,000	100,000	183,333	183,333	183,333	183,333
33 Addition to Owners' Equity	106,559	108,386	-23,088	-9,125	-29,241	-160,296
34 CASH FLOW STATEMENT ($)						
35 Receipts, Sales Revenue	3,537,996	3,537,996	3,587,872	3,587,871	3,470,700	3,093,592
36 Disbursements, Cash Expense	2,004,184	2,001,981	2,199,667	2,195,391	2,243,315	2,265,701
37 Income Tax	106,457	107,351	82,550	89,743	79,381	11,868
38 Dividends Paid	100,000	100,000	183,333	183,333	183,333	183,333
39 Robotics Investments	75,000	75,000	78,750	78,750	82,500	82,500
40 Plant and Equipment Investments	375,000	375,000	891,513	891,513	270,000	270,000
41 Materials Purchased	730,000	730,000	975,077	975,077	865,819	865,819
42 Total Disbursements	3,390,639	3,389,331	4,410,890	4,413,807	3,724,348	3,679,220
43 Addition to Cash Assets	147,357	148,665	-823,018	-825,936	-253,848	-585,628
44 FINANCIAL STATEMENT ($)						
45 Net Assets, Cash	1,169,357	1,170,665	347,647	344,729	91,081	-240,899
46 Inventory Value, Finished Goods	0	0	0	0	147,600	331,924
47 Inventory Value, Materials	1,045,417	1,045,843	1,067,182	1,084,068	1,021,387	1,037,990
48 Robotics Book Value	75,000	75,000	150,000	150,000	225,000	225,000
49 Plant and Equipment Book Value	7,516,875	7,516,875	8,220,466	8,220,466	8,284,954	8,284,954
50 Owners' Equity	9,806,649	9,808,387	9,785,295	9,799,263	9,770,022	9,638,968
51 Plant and Equipment Replacement Value	7,643,244	7,624,236	8,463,378	8,473,071	8,679,897	8,695,276
52 Robotics Replacement Value	75,000	75,000	152,369	152,298	231,994	232,204
53 Owners' Economic Equity	9,933,015	9,915,748	10,030,576	10,054,165	10,171,959	10,056,493

TABLE 40 (continued)
WORK SHEET FOR ANALYSIS OF OPERATIONS

-to be detached and handed in at the end of the Game-the individual team member should enter his/her team's consolidated decision and forecasts on this sheet each quarter.

Periods 0 - 4 Model # 1
Periods 5 - 8 Model # 2

	Period 4		Period 5		Period 6	
	Forecast	Actual	Forecast	Actual	Forecast	Actual
I (a) Price Index (Period 0=100%)/(b) Forecast, Annual Change (%)	105.2 / 4.8	104.7 / 5.0	106.0 / 5.0	106.3 / 5.3	107.6 / 5.3	107.1 / 6.0
II (a) Calendar Quarter/(b) Seasonal Index (Average Period=100%)	AMJ/100	AMJ/100	JAS/95	JAS/95	OND/115	OND/115
III Economic Index (Period=100%)	90	89	95	96	97	95
IV (a) Inv. Tax Cr. %/(b) Surtax %/(c) Pl & Eq. Depr. %/(d) Robotics Depr. %	0 / 0 / 2.5 / 5	0 / 0 / 2.5 / 5	0 / 0 / 2.5 / 5	0 / 0 / 2.5 / 5	0 / 0 / 2.5 / 5	0 / 0 / 2.5 / 5
1 (a) Firm's Price/(b) Average Industry Price ($)	26.06 / 25.00	26.06 / 24.90	26.32 / 24.75	26.32 / 24.85	27.05 / 25.00	27.05 / 25.15
2 Total Industry Sales - in units (not dollars)	700,000	673,619	800,000	870,907	1,030,000	1,021,237
3 Market Potential (units)	142,000	132,708	140,000	127,303	148,000	143,370
4 Sales Volume (units)	142,000	132,708	140,000	127,303	148,000	143,870
5 Percent Share of Industry Sales (%)	20.3	19.7	17.5	14.6	14.4	14.1
6 Production, This Quarter (units)	145,000	145,000	158,000	158,000	172,673	171,307
7 (a) Labor Cost per Unit/(b) Material Cost per Unit ($)	5.62 / 6.08	5.57 / 6.02	5.57 / 6.02	5.57 / 5.95	5.57 / 5.95	5.55 / 6.04
8 Inventory, Finished Goods (units)	29,994	39,286	57,286	69,983	94,656	97,421
9 Plant Capacity, Next Quarter (units)	124,498	124,499	126,234	126,167	128,604	128,567
10 INCOME (and expense) STATEMENT ($)						
11 Receipts, Sales Revenue	3,700,520	3,458,578	3,684,800	3,350,619	4,003,400	3,891,673
12 Expenses, Marketing Expense	450,000	450,000	285,000	285,000	335,000	335,000
13 Research and Development Expense	225,000	225,000	75,000	75,000	101,667	101,667
14 Administration Expense	365,573	363,664	370,787	371,762	379,853	377,819
15 Maintenance Expense	115,710	115,710	127,032	127,032	141,095	141,095
16 Labor Expense	878,923	871,403	973,360	972,540	1,091,308	1,076,098
17 Materials Expense	881,600	872,633	951,160	940,067	1,027,404	1,034,820
18 Reduction, Finished Goods Inventory Value	-37,400	-155,910	-226,152	-393,930	-314,742	-357,802
19 Plant and Equipment Depreciation	207,124	207,124	208,696	208,696	208,892	208,894
20 Robotics Depreciation	11,250	11,250	15,000	15,000	19,500	19,500
21 Finished Goods Carrying Costs	62,388	81,305	119,957	146,961	201,239	206,595
22 Raw Materials Carrying Costs	51,900	51,900	47,574	47,574	51,741	51,741
23 Ordering Costs	52,000	51,740	52,350	52,499	53,150	53,016

24 Shifts Change Costs	0	0	0	0	0	0
25 Investment Expenses	12,691	12,691	10,345	10.345	14,402	14,402
26 Financing Charges and Penalties	5,474	5,471	23.935	23,878	122.638	121,993
27 Sundries Expenses	100,620	100,097	102,929	103,202	106,061	105,507
28 Total Expenses	3,382,753	3,264,070	3,636,973	2,985,619	3,539,210	3,490,353
29 Profit Before Income Taxes	317,767	194,308	547,827	365,000	464,190	401,320
30 Income Tax	108,041	66,065	186,261	124,100	157,825	136,499
31 Net Profit After Income Tax	209,626	128,243	361,566	240,900	306,365	264,871
32 Dividends Paid	1,833,333	1,833,333	300,000	300,000	700,000	700,000
33 Addition to Owners' Equity	26,293	-55,090	61,566	-59,100	-393,635	-435,129
34 CASH FLOW STATEMENT ($)						
35 Receipts, Sales Revenue	3,700,520	3,458,378	3,684,800	3,350,619	4,003,400	3,891,673
36 Disbursements, Cash Expense	2,320,179	2,328,972	2,635,661	2,215,784	2,598,654	2,584,939
37 Income Tax	108,041	66,065	186,260	124,100	157,825	136,449
38 Dividends Paid	1,833,333	1,833,333	300,000	300,000	700,000	700,000
39 Robotics Investments	86,250	86,250	105,000	105,000	109,500	109,500
40 Plant and Equipment Investments	270,000	270,000	216,633	216,633	270,000	270,000
41 Materials Purchased	786,130	786,130	1,023,400	1,023,400	1,034,287	1,034,287
42 Total Disbursements	3,753,933	3,720,749	4,466,955	3,984,916	4,869,766	4,835,174
43 Addition to Cash Assets	-53,413	-262,371	-782,155	-634,297	-861,366	-943,501
44 FINANCIAL STATEMENT ($)						
45 Net Assets, Cash	-294,312	-503,270	-1,285,425	-1,137,567	-2,003,933	-2,081,068
46 Inventory Value, Finished Goods	62,388	487,830	719,741	881,764	1,207,432	1,239,567
47 Inventory Value, Materials	942,520	951,487	1,023,727	1,034,820	1,041,703	1,034,287
48 Robotics Book Value	300,000	300,000	390,000	390,000	480,000	480,000
49 Plant and Equipment Book Value	8,347,830	8,347,830	8,355,767	8,355,767	8,416,872	8,416,872
50 Owners' Equity	9,365,945	9,583,877	9,203,810	9,524,783	9,142,075	9,089,658
51 Plant and Equipment Replacement Value	8,896,019	8,855,137	8,999,004	9,022,017	9,146,834	9,177,339
52 Robotics Replacement Value	314,009	313,958	412,949	412,879	514,776	513,417
53 Owners' Economic Equity	9,920,624	10,105,142	9,869,996	10,213,912	9,906,812	9,883,542

TABLE 40 (continued)
WORK SHEET FOR ANALYSIS OF OPERATIONS

-to be detached and handed in at the end of the Game–the individual team member should enter his/her team's consolidated decision and forecasts on this sheet each quarter.

Periods 0 - 4 Model # 1
Periods 5 - 8 Model # 2

	Period 7 Forecast	Period 7 Actual	Period 8 Forecast	Period 8 Actual	Period 9 Forecast	Period 9 Actual
I (a) Price Index (Period 0=100%)/(b) Forecast, Annual Change (%)	108.6 / 6.0	108.9 / 6.5	110.5 / 6.5	110.5 / 7.0	/	/
II (a) Calendar Quarter/(b) Seasonal Index (Average Period=100%)	JFM/ 90	JFM/ 90	AMJ/ 100	AMJ/ 100	JAS/	JAS/
III Economic Index (Period=100%)	100	101	100	99		
IV (a) Inv. Tax Cr. %/(b) Surtax %/(c) PI & Eq. Depr. %/(d) Robotics Depr. %	0 / 0 / 2.5 / 5	0 / 0 / 2.5 / 5	0 / 0 / 2.5 / 5	0 / 0 / 2.5 / 5	/ / /	/ / /
1 (a) Firm's Price/(b) Average Industry Price ($)	27.05 / 26.00	27.05 / 26.36	30.00 / 27.00	30.00 / 26.48	/	/
2 Total Industry Sales - in units (not dollars)	900,000	884,308	950,000	848,941		
3 Market Potential (units)	190,000	201,222	150,000	101,716		
4 Sales Volume (units)	190,000	201,222	150,000	101,716		
5 Percent Share of Industry Sales (%)	21.1	22.8	15.8	12.0		
6 Production, This Quarter (units)	171,000	170,849	177,853	177,853		
7 (a) Labor Cost per Unit/(b) Material Cost per Unit ($)	5.55 / 6.04	5.57 / 6.05	5.57 / 6.05	5.55 / 6.08	/	/
8 Inventory, Finished Goods (units)	78,421	67,048	94,901	143,185		
9 Plant Capacity, Next Quarter (units)	131,157	131,057	133,630	133,526		
10 INCOME (and expense) STATEMENT ($)						
11 Receipts, Sales Revenue	5,139,500	5,443,054	4,500,000	3,051,481		
12 Expenses, Marketing Expense	900,000	900,000	200,000	200,000		
13 Research and Development Expense	101,666	101,666	101,667	101,667		
14 Administration Expense	385,451	386,616	395,483	394,734		
15 Maintenance Expense	141,203	141,203	149,597	149,597		
16 Labor Expense	1,066,802	1,069,269	1,120,968	1,117,845		
17 Materials Expense	1,032,840	1,034,287	1,076,011	1,080,487		
18 Reduction, Finished Goods Inventory Value	244,188	373,920	-363,983	-1,005,636		
19 Plant and Equipment Depreciation	210,422	210,422	211,911	211,911		
20 Robotics Depreciation	24,000	24,000	29,050	29,050		
21 Finished Goods Carrying Costs	167,976	144,275	206,694	311,880		
22 Raw Materials Carrying Costs	51,714	51,714	80,000	80,000		
23 Ordering Costs	53,550	53,795	54,450	54,454		

24 Shifts Change Costs	0	0	0	0		
25 Investment Expenses	15,603	15,603	16,000	16,000		
26 Financing Charges and Penalties	413,163	411,209	533,284	532,028		
27 Sundries Expenses	108,557	108,899	112,344	112,149		
28 Total Expenses	4,917,141	5,026,872	3,923,476	3,386,164		
29 Profit Before Income Taxes	222,359	416,182	576,524	-334,683		
30 Income Tax	75,604	141,502	196,018	-113,792		
31 Net Profit After Income Tax	146,757	274,680	380,506	-220,891		
32 Dividends Paid	200,000	200,000	1,000,000	1,000,000		
33 Addition to Owners' Equity	-53,243	74,680	-619,496	-1,220,891		
34 CASH FLOW STATEMENT ($)						
35 Receipts, Sales Revenue	5,139,500	5,443,054	4,500,000	3,051,481		
36 Disbursements, Cash Expense	3,405,690	3,384,243	2,970,487	3,070,350		
37 Income Tax	75,602	141,502	196,018	-113,792		
38 Dividends Paid	200,000	200,000	1,000,000	1,000,000		
39 Robotics Investments	125,000	125,000	130,000	130,000		
40 Plant and Equipment Investments	270,000	270,000	270,000	270,000		
41 Materials Purchased	1,600,000	1,600,000	500,000	500,000		
42 Total Disbursements	5,676,292	5,720,744	5,066,505	4,856,557		
43 Addition to Cash Assets	-536,992	-277,690	-566,505	-1,805,076		
44 FINANCIAL STATEMENT ($)						
45 Net Assets, Cash	-2,617,860	-2,358,758	-2925,213	-4,163,834		
46 Inventory Value, Finished Goods	1,007,867	865,651	1,240,166	1,871,282		
47 Inventory Value, Materials	1,601,987	1,600,000	1,023,989	1,019,513		
48 Robotics Book Value	581,000	581,000	681,950	681,950		
49 Plant and Equipment Book Value	8,476,449	8,476,450	8,534,539	8,534,538		
50 Owners' Equity	9,049,443	9,164,343	8,555,381	7,943,448		
51 Plant and Equipment Replacement Value	9,400,633	9,417,830	9,648,488	9,634,711		
52 Robotics Replacement Value	629,833	628,476	748,730	747,770		
53 Owners' Economic Equity	10,022,458	10,153,199	9,736,210	9,109,441		

3

Planning in the Executive Game

Sometimes the Executive Game is run at breakneck speed, as a demonstration, or as an icebreaker, or as a quick and dramatic way of getting across a few basic ideas about how a business firm works and how competing firms interact with one another. It may then make sense for players just to go ahead and enjoy themselves, giving in to the temptation to fool around rather than working at the Game. They can nudge the various budgets this way or that, in the hope of doing something right by pure accident. Or they can take some big leaps motivated by the spirit of adventure rather than thoughtful analysis. Or they can play follow the leader, trying to do well by imitating their most successful competitor (but what if everyone tried to follow the leader?). However, even when there isn't really time to think things out fully, almost all players seem to find the Game much more interesting as well as a great deal more valuable if they do the best they can, rather than just fooling around. And when there is enough time, and there are substantial educational objectives, the Game really demands careful analysis. It's always possible, though not too likely, that players who fail to take the Game seriously will come up with a great record of profit and ROI by sheer luck; but even if they happened to finish in first place, such players will really be the losers, in terms of the *real* objective of the Game: *learning.*

And the most important part of the decision-making process, if you want to get the most out of the Executive Game, is *planning.*

Planning is nothing new to you, although planning for a business probably is. The basic ideas of business planning are pretty much like those of planning in everyday life. Suppose you have a vacation coming up. If you want to make the most of it, your first thoughts aren't about what route to take, but about where you want to go, or even if you want to go anywhere further away than the nearest swimming pool (or whatever nearby facility suits your tastes). When alternatives come to mind, you think about their feasibility, as well as their enjoyability, asking about whether there is enough time to hike the John Muir trail, for instance, or whether you have enough money to visit Italy. As an experienced vacationer, you undoubtedly carry out "thought experiments" in which you try to imagine just how various things might work out, perhaps ruling out a long stay at home when you remember how bored you got last year, or thinking more seriously about camping in the mountains when you consider how nice it would be to have a couple of weeks of cool weather at the end of August. What you try to do is think through the reasonable possibilities, and from among those that are really practical you try to pick out the alternative that you think you'll enjoy most, taking into account such factors as expense and the effect these factors will have on you later. This thought experimentation has the purpose of clarifying your values as well as working through the probable facts implicit in a given choice.

And, being realistic, you know that most of the details of your plan won't come out just the way you expect. So you maintain flexibility to review and revise your plans if unanticipated difficulties or opportunities turn up, or if you find something less or more enjoyable than you'd anticipated.

Now business planning has much the same character. The first question is about what is desirable and possible, rather than what specific actions to take. Interesting goals are checked out to see if ways can really be found to pursue them effectively. When a tentative plan of action is conceived, then it's very important to think out what might happen if the plan were followed — what might go wrong as well as what you hope will go right, whether the proposal will leave you a chance to roll with the punches if things do go wrong, and whether you'll maintain the flexibility to seize unexpected opportunities. And it's just as important as it is in personal matters to remember that anticipation and experience have much to teach you about goals as well as about the way choices and outcomes are linked.

Planning can be looked at many ways, each with a certain validity. It is a top-down approach, concerned with setting up guidelines for specific actions. It is a process of thought experimentation in which your imagination reaches out to examine alternative possible futures. But it's less a matter of designing the future than one of choosing premises on which to act in the present. The plan is not a fact of the future, but an hypothesis that will help you to decide just what to do now. The plan may be most valuable as a framework for evaluating and improving your firm's behavior as events unfold — and often for replanning.

Planning is largely the business of testing and guiding the continuing implications of current actions. A plan, even a bad one, makes for consistency and coordination. It gives you a sense of direction — something you may be able to get along without on a personal vacation, if you are easygoing enough, but something always needed in running a business. Planning is so important in the organizational world that governance without planning can hardly be called management.

This chapter will suggest some specific guidelines that *may* help you to score well (profit, ROI) in the Executive Game, and that *will* help you to make the Game an invaluable learning experience. The chapter is divided into three main sections, on Short-range Planning, Long-range Planning, and Cash Projection. A brief section will remind you again of something also worth noting here: that, while the three main sections of this chapter treat three different subjects of study, the management process to which they refer really forms one single inseparable whole.

This chapter should not be viewed as a comprehensive coverage of planning in the business world. It concentrates on the what, how, and why of planning in the Executive Game. The Game reflects one sort of business situation, in which the organizations are rather simple and in which they are basically symmetric in their mutual relationships. The internal workings of the firms are givens, so that in the Game, you won't have to think about personnel evaluation, technical decisions, merchandising methods, organization structure, etc., etc., etc. Perhaps most important, you won't have to deal with "people problems," and with developing a personal network of business relationships — except in the limited though important context of getting the most out of your own small top-management team. Still, significant components of business planning are represented by the Game. Most important, the Game stresses kinds of decision making and planning that are centrally important to managers, but that seem far removed from most non-managers' ordinary experiences.

Short-Range Planning

A short-range plan is a scenario for the near future, which extends just far enough in time to be a basis for consistency among current decisions, and coordination among these current decisions and between them and further actions to be taken soon. The short-range plan must also maintain consistency with long-range plans, at least after they are adjusted and updated to keep in step with current realities.

The long-range plan in the Executive Game should ordinarily provide close guidance concerning PLANT AND EQUIPMENT AND ROBOTICS INVESTMENT. It should also pretty much nail down the R&D budget. It should include a clearly stated DIVIDEND policy — although projected distributions to stockholders are one of the first things to think about changing, either upward or downward, if profit or cash on hand turns out to deviate substantially from planned levels. MAINTENANCE budgets are pretty much determined by the current level of output, and RAW MATERIALS PURCHASE budgets by anticipated short-run-future output levels.

Thus, among the decisions required in the Executive Game, we are left with PRICE, MARKETING, and PRODUCTION VOLUME as the decisions on which the short-range planning effort must focus. These are the decisions with which the present section will be mainly concerned. The key lies in adjusting MARKETING, PRICE, and PRODUCTION VOLUME so that there will be a match between market potential and goods available for sale.

This adjustment is complicated by the fact that the most profitable operations generally involve PRODUCTION VOLUME decisions which come close to using full regular-time production capacity, or close to the full use of overtime (or, *in Model 2 only,* close to maximum regular-time output or full use of overtime for whatever number of shifts is to be used). Thus, at least as a first approximation, in the short run you can ordinarily think of there being a small number of relatively attractive output levels — although intermediate levels are sometimes best, especially if you have an unusually large stock of finished goods on hand. The central short-range problems can be thought of as those of deciding simultaneously (i) which of these preferred output levels will be best and (ii) how to influence market potential accordingly by means of MARKETING and PRICE decisions. We turn first to the second of these problems, approaching it via the question of how you can estimate the effects of your decisions, and the other relevant factors, on your market potential.

Short-range Forecasts of Market Potential. Chapters 1 and 2 point the way to qualitative estimates of the effects of market potential: other things being unchanged, if you increase MARKETING or decrease PRICE, your market potential will go up, and vice versa. Also, if your decisions are unchanged, while your competitors increase MARKETING or decrease PRICE, then the total industry market potential will go up, but the increasing market shares captured by your competitors will result in a net decrease in your own market potential.

Luckily, information is available that will enable you to estimate these changes quantitatively. Specifically, test-market studies have recently been made of the short-range effects of small changes in decisions and certain other variables. The industry has not yet got around to using these research findings, but you may be able to profit from them:

> A one percent increase in the economic index will tend to increase your market potential by about 1.4 percent. This is a constant elasticity which means that it remains constant over time and is independent of other factors affecting market potential.
>
> A one percent increase in the seasonal index will tend to increase your market potential by about 1 percent. This also is a constant elasticity.

A one percent increase in your PRICE will tend to decrease your market potential by about 5 percent. This is a point elasticity which means that it changes slowly as other factors affecting market potential change.

A one percent increase in the average PRICE of the other firms will tend to increase your market potential by about 2 percent. This also is a point elasticity.

A one percent increase in your MARKETING budget will tend to increase your market potential by about 0.25 percent. This also is a point elasticity.

A one percent increase in the average MARKETING budget of the other firms will tend to decrease your market potential by about 0.1 percent. This also is a point elasticity.

Changes in the opposite directions have effects of about the same size, but of course also in the opposite directions. The research results assume that MARKETING budgets are measured in "real dollars," in the sense that keeping up with inflation is not viewed as a budget increase but as a zero percent change; and they assume that PRICE figures are automatically raised to keep step with inflation.

The research study of course merely verifies things you already knew about the relationships between your market potential and the economic and seasonal indices. The specified effects of changes in these indices are believed to be correct, at least for practical purposes, for changes of any size and from any starting point. And these effects are believed to represent the full consequences of changes in the indices, with no residual effects in later periods. (Of course, the indices will continue to change and thus to generate new effects.)

But the results concerning pricing and marketing policies are of more limited use. First, they concern only the *immediate* effects of changes. It is estimated that the indicated effects of price changes will shrink slightly in the quarter after the changes are made, while the effects of marketing changes will grow by about half over the next couple of quarters (assuming that the changed marketing budget is not changed further).

Also, the results for MARKETING and PRICE can only be assumed valid under the circumstances that prevail at the beginning situation in the Game. As various factors change substantially, it is to be expected that further changes in MARKETING and PRICE will have effects at least a little different from those specified above, and possibly a lot different.

Further, the accuracy of these results is only assured for fairly small changes in the decisions — up to somewhere around plus or minus ten percent. The researchers think, in fact, that forecasts of the effects of large changes in your own decisions are likely to be on the optimistic side — overestimates of the increase in market potential that will stem from a large increase in MARKETING or a large decrease in PRICE, but underestimates of the market shrinkage that will follow from large changes in the opposite directions. However, there is not enough data to prove whether this theoretical interpretation of the "law of diminishing returns" actually holds in the Game situation.

To turn to some good news, you can approximate the effects of a whole pattern of small changes by adding up their individual effects. Suppose, for instance, that you hypothesize that the economic index will increase by 2 percent; the seasonal index will decrease by 3 percent; that you will cut PRICE by 2 percent, while other firms' average PRICE will go down only one percent; and that you will cut your MARKETING budget by 6 percent (after first incrementing it by 2 percent to keep pace with inflation, for an approximate effect upon your market potential of -1.5

percent), while, on the average, the other firms will make no change in MARKETING except for a 2 percent increment to keep up with inflation. The estimated effect on your market potential will then be as follows:

Cause	*Approximate effect*		
economic index up 2 percent	(+2) x (+ 1.4) =	+	2.8%
seasonal index down 3 percent	(–3) x (+ 1.0) =	–	3.0
your 2 percent price cut	(–2) x (– 5.0) =	+	10.0
others' 1 percent avg. price cut	(–1) x (+ 2.0) =	–	2.0
your 6 percent marketing cut	(–6) x (+ 0.25) =	–	1.5
others, unchanged marketing			0.0
NET EFFECT ON YOUR MARKET POTENTIAL		+	6.3%

We have algebraically determined the sign (plus or minus) of each contribution in the right-hand column. But you can get the same results by using common sense to decide whether a given contribution will result in a "plus" (an index up, your price down, competitive prices up, your marketing up, or competitive marketing down), or a "minus" (changes in the opposite directions).

It is important to remember that the research results are approximate. They are based on statistical studies, and therefore subject to sampling error as well as imprecisions arising from the use of underlying models that may not accurately reflect the full complexity of the market factors and their interactions. Thus, the above calculations can at best lead only to an estimate. As indicated before, you can expect this estimate to become less and less accurate as circumstances change, or if you are concerned with larger and larger changes in MARKETING or PRICE. Further inaccuracies will of course stem from imperfect forecasts of economic variables, and also from the residual effects in any given quarter of past changes in your decisions and those of other firms.

The most important errors in market-potential forecasts will often stem from bad guesses about what your competitors are going to do. It makes a lot of sense, in fact, to keep this uncertainty up front by making "worst case" and "best case" estimates, along with "most likely case" estimates of competitive activity. Players who are familiar with probability theory and comfortable with numerical analysis may find it worthwhile to make probability estimates of the variables that are inputs to the forecasting model, and to use these to make probability forecasts of market potential.

Note that the results just reported do not cover R&D and ROBOTICS INVESTMENT. The market potential consequences of change in R&D budgets and ROBOTICS INVESTMENT were, in fact, estimated to be somewhat smaller that the effects of changes in MARKETING budgets, and *delayed* — only beginning to appear after a full quarter has passed, and then building up over several subsequent quarters. This means, of course, that if you increase R&D and ROBOTICS INVESTMENT the payoff will not be immediate, *and also that if you "get behind" other firms in R&D and ROBOTICS INVESTMENT it will be difficult to "catch up"* — perhaps impossible within the short time frame of most Games. Remember also that R&D and ROBOTICS INVESTMENT have total payoff may some effect on manufacturing costs, so that be significantly greater than that implied by their effect on market potential alone.

Using the Short-range Forecast. In spite of the shortcomings of the market-potential forecasting procedure just sketched, it will enable you to make fairly good predictions of how many units you can sell, depending on how you set your PRICE and how much you budget for MARKETING.

To use this procedure you need to have forecasts of the economic index and the seasonal index. Fortunately, these are readily available. You also need to estimate what your competitors are going to do in pricing and setting their marketing budgets. This is pretty much a matter of guesswork, in practice, but you may find it helpful to keep in mind that these competitors are guided by the same information that is available to you — although they may interpret this information differently, and they may make their choices with different ideas in mind as to what they hope to accomplish. It helps a little that you do not have to predict each competitor's individual choices, but only to estimate their average behavior. It is also helpful that, although your competitors' MARKETING and PRICE averages are important, they are only two of the six inputs to the short-range market-potential forecast — and not the most important inputs, either, since your market potential is considerably more sensitive to your own decisions than to the decisions of your competitors. In this regard, the information in Tables 3 through 40 may be very useful.

In any case, we suppose now that you have somehow made these necessary forecasts (perhaps including best case and worst case estimates, as suggested above). Then, given any hypothesized values of your own PRICE level and MARKETING budget, it is a straightforward matter to work out the corresponding forecast of your market potential. The most obvious way to use the forecasting model is simply to fish around among different possible prices and budgets until you come up with a market potential that is reasonably related to your ability to supply the market. Then you'll at least be able to make a mutually consistent set of decisions on MARKETING, PRICE and PRODUCTION VOLUME. Such decisions may be far from the best possible, but they are unlikely to be really bad. If you want to use these decisions without further analysis (*not* recommended), you can easily determine a reasonable MAINTENANCE budget; and a simple calculation using general information about seasonal fluctuations will enable you to work out a reasonable raw MATERIALS PURCHASE decision. If you are careful to avoid plain mistakes such as arithmetical errors, you need do no more to reach decisions good enough to keep your firm in business.

But of course you should do better than that. First, you can save some work and be *sure* of good results if you are systematic about the process of "fishing around" among different possible prices and budgets. For instance, suppose your indicated PRODUCTION VOLUME decision turned out to be 10,000 units higher that you think makes sense (perhaps 10,000 units above plant capacity, or possibly above some other threshold such as the maximum possible production including overtime output — or *in Model 2 only* the level where a new shift would have to be started). In order to reduce your output level, while avoiding the undesirable situation where your market potential exceeds your ability to supply goods, you might then want to decrease MARKETING and/or increase PRICE enough to reduce your market potential by 10,000 units. You can easily convert this into a percentage change. Suppose it turns out to be a 6 percent reduction in market potential. The research results listed above indicate how you can make such a change. You might, for instance, increase PRICE by 1.2 percent, since (+1.2) x (-5.0) = 6%. Or you might decrease MARKETING by 24 percent, since (-24) x (+0.25) = 6% (although the effect of so large a change may be poorly predicted). Or you might feel better about some weighted mixture of these changes such as the 50-50 mixture, "increase PRICE by 0.6 percent and decrease MARKETING by 12 percent."

Notice how much you can gain by making such changes. Suppose, for instance,that volume is going to be around 150,000 units, with PRICE somewhere near $25.00. A 0.6 percent PRICE increase comes to 0.006 x 2,500 = 15 cents per unit, for a total increase in revenue of .15 x 150,000 = $22,500. And, if your estimates are valid, so that actual sales volume will not suffer as a result of the price increase, then this $22,500 is "pure gravy" — an increase in profit before taxes as compared with what you would have got at the lower price. Similarly, if the 24 percent decrease is applied to a $200,000 MARKETING budget, you would add .24 x 200,000 = $48,000 to profit before taxes. These are *very* important profit improvements for a company the size of your firm, and well within the range of improvements that may actually result from carefully carrying through the indicated analysis.

The illustrative figures just given should make it clear that it can be important to make a correct decision about *how* to adjust market potential to a desired level. In the hypothesized situation, adjusting PRICE would increase revenues by $22,500, while adjusting MARKETING would cut costs by $48,000. In this case the MARKETING change appears to be more than twice as profitable as the PRICE change — although this may be an exaggeration in view of the fact that the 24 percent indicated change in the marketing budget is too large for the forecasting model to be considered reliable.

Still more systematically, and with increasing assurance that you will be approaching the best possible combinations of MARKETING, PRICE, and PRODUCTION VOLUME, you can carry through the sort of analysis suggested above for various proposed levels of output — ordinarily including PRODUCTION VOLUME equal to capacity and equal to the maximum possible with overtime, in Model 1, but also checking out values a bit lower than these thresholds, and continuing to search "downward" if one of these should turn out to be best — which can easily happen if you have an unusually large stock of finished goods. You can improve further upon this approach by actually working out profit estimates for each possibility, using the detailed procedures set forth in Chapter 4, or one of the simpler (but perhaps less reliable) procedures given in the section on Profit models in Chapter 5.

Analytically inclined players further systematize this search process by carefully analyzing the profit as a mathematical function defined over the MARKETING, PRICE, PRODUCTION VOLUME "phase space." Such a search procedure might in fact be computerized in whole or in part, or perhaps set up for interactive use with a person guiding the computer's explorations. It would, however, take us far afield to explore such possibilities in depth.

Regardless of how far you go in systematizing the search, what you come up with is a MARKETING, PRICE, PRODUCTION VOLUME combination that "looks good on paper." Given the imperfection of the forecasting procedure and the fact that different kinds of inaccuracies may lead to different degrees of risk, you may want to temper the analytical conclusions so reached. In any case, once these three decisions are made you can easily go on to make reasonable current decisions about MAINTENANCE and raw MATERIALS PURCHASE.

Planning for a One-year Period. Except for passing comments, attention has so far been focused on the one-quarter period that is immediately at hand. The length of this period is long enough so that every operating decision can be considered to fall within the category of (very) short-range planning. But in the Executive Game it is the one-year period for which the word "planning" really begins to have a meaning beyond that of "decision making."

The main one-year issue that is significantly different from those arising in either quarter-by-quarter decision making or longer-range planning is the matter of managing output in the face of the seasonal cycle. It is nice that this cycle is consistent and predictable (by the seasonal index) so that it does not in itself add serious difficulty to the problem of forecasting for four quarters instead of one. Our best answer to the one-year forecasting problem is simply to project estimates for the coming quarter into the future, taking into account predictable changes (among which the seasonal cycle itself may be the most important), and squarely facing the fact that when you look more than one quarter ahead you have to expect to make large errors.

Even a very crude forecast will enable you to estimate roughly the magnitudes of the fluctuations in market potential to which your firm will be subjected during the year. From this you can prepare at least a general picture of desirable buildups and sell-offs of finished goods inventory during the year, so as to meet customer demand without incurring unjustified overtime cost (and *in Model 2 only,* shift-change costs), or excessive inventory carrying charges. This information will then enter into your judgments each quarter about the suitability of alternative PRODUCTION VOLUME decisions, and about what sort of market potential you'll want to develop each quarter in order to pursue a sensible inventory policy. Generally speaking, it is a good idea to manufacture more than you can sell during the low-demand quarters, and to sell off the excess during the high-demand quarters.

The preceding paragraph contains an important message, in that it doesn't even suggest working out a fully detailed "one year plan." It's necessary only to go far enough to learn what you need to know about the effects on current decisions of taking into account the whole of the coming year. Of course this full-year look-ahead should be repeated every quarter, at least in the sense of updating previous plans in accordance with current facts.

Improving Your Short-range Forecasts. You need not be satisfied with the short-range forecasting model presented above, and you may be able to improve on it — especially as its performance deteriorates with the passage of time and changes in the Game situation. At a common-sense level, you should at least keep your eyes open, looking for situations where the effects of PRICE or MARKETING seem to be separable from other effects, so that the numbers given above can be tested against up-to-date information. (But don't be in a hurry to give a lot of weight to one or two observations.)

At a more sophisticated level, statistical analysis may be applicable, perhaps using data supplied by the tables in Chapter 2, or data from your own run, or preferably both. Players who are mathematically trained and knowledgeable about computer programs may also be able to squeeze useful information out of the Executive Game FORTRAN program (Appendix C), although Game participants who have tried this in the past have most often been led astray. And remember that you will never have such a program to analyze in the business world.

A Final Word About Short-range Planning. The incremental approach emphasized above conceals the process of balancing between PRICE and MARKETING, by making it part of the search process. And, except for a parenthetical comment, R&D and ROBOTICS INVESTMENT have been left out of the balance entirely. These omissions should not be serious if you are content to move slowly in the improvement of your firm. But they may be serious for those who wish to make larger jumps. We hope that this difficulty will not deter adventurous players from carefully conceived risk taking. In the Game, if you do want (for example) to make a try at developing a novel product based on massive R&D and ROBOTICS INVESTMENT intended to justify a high markup, you've got to accept the fact that it will be a big gamble: you may win big, but you may lose big. If you lose, you won't be in such bad company: CBS's cultural cable TV channel was a total failure, and Mazda's rotary engine automobiles were a great mistake. It is a fact that a large percentage of highly successful business entrepreneurs failed once or more before they tasted success. And if you win with a big gamble, the sky's the limit!

Any major change in policy should of course be viewed as a key element, or *the* key element, in a long-range plan. But some short-range "pussyfooting" may give you a better idea about whether you want to take the plunge. For instance, you might tentatively move part way across the large gap you are thinking about jumping — far enough to provide a significant test, but not so far that you can't get back to safety. This illustrates an extreme case in which short-run considerations may provide crucial inputs to long-range planning. More will be said about that below.

Long-Range Planning

A long-range plan is a "plausible future," worked out far enough ahead of time and in enough detail to adequately indicate how future problems and opportunities will be relevant to current decisions. Ideally, a plan should not be a narrowly conceived single-path scenario, but should be expressed in terms of possibilities and contingencies, so as to keep in mind the importance of flexibility as opposed to fixed commitment. It's often more practical, though, just to keep in mind that you must allow for the likelihood that events will turn out quite a bit different from anticipations. You may want to make irrevocable commitments in some situations, where this can be done realistically. In the Executive Game, though, one thing you can be sure of is that the future will offer unimagined surprises. Therefore you should at least understand that your plans are tentative and subject to revision at any time.

Executive Game players are sometimes discouraged by the whole idea of long-range planning, feeling that the uncertainties are so great that even the main outlines of their plans may not be carried through. They contrast this with the business world, where it seems as if plans often do work out. But the fact is that long-range plans in real life rarely come true as they were originally set forth, but only after they are redrawn to reflect what has actually happened. The revision of plans, like revisions of history, is often motivated by someone's desire for self-glorification. In such cases the original details of the plan, or the facts of history, are "stonewalled" — hidden away with the pretense that they never existed. But honest revisions are labelled as such, and even in the case of history may be legitimate reinterpretations rather than reprehensible lies. And it is quite proper, even necessary, to revise plans as a matter of course, in order that the "current version" will be an up-to-date basis for the continuing choice of future directions.

Legitimate revision of plans does not, of course, involve throwing away earlier versions of the plans concerned, at least in any situation where there is genuine interest in improving future performance. More specifically, the revision process is one of the crucial opportunities for learning. The most important part of planning is often what can be got out of the process of comparing unrevised plans with actual performance. Much of the value of planning is realized precisely when such comparison processes are given purpose by the need to make new judgments about what should be planned for the future.

What a Long-range Plan Looks Like. Most long-range plans, in business or elsewhere, start from broad statements about what goals are sought and through what means. In the Executive Game, a long-range plan usually revolves around a verbally expressed general strategic posture, like "increasing profitability through growth made possible by offering a good product at a low price," or "maintaining a solid profit and dividend record based on a strongly marketed quality product for which customers will pay a little extra." The customer focus is important — in real life as well as in the Game, as has been demonstrated by recent studies of the most successful American companies. It helps to keep in mind that, even though the purpose of a business may be to make money, that purpose can only be achieved by doing something that someone is willing to pay for, and that the more the firm does for its customers the more they'll be willing to pay.

Aside from a general sense of direction, the most important results of planning are policies concerning R&D, ROBOTICS and PLANT AND EQUIPMENT INVESTMENTS. The working core of the plan is a sequence of goals, which should extend several years into the future even when you know that your run of the Game will soon end. These goals typically include hoped-for annual sales volumes, profits, and intended dividend distributions. Such targets must of course be guesses as to what will be possible, rather than logically calculated benchmarks that can be reached by following some clearly marked path. The point is to make *educated* guesses. As a start toward educating your guesses you can hardly do better than carefully absorbing the information in this manual.

The working core of the long-run plan usually centers on anticipated sales volumes. A progression of planned sales volumes, together with information about the relationships among production volume, plant size, and costs, will largely determine the needed progression of plant size, and hence the schedule of PLANT AND EQUIPMENT INVESTMENT decisions. General price policy, with sales volumes and cost estimates, will enable you to estimate future profits. Estimated profits, with information about related cash flows (see below), will provide bases for determining what dividend payments will be feasible. To construct a consistent plan, you have to get these various elements to fit together, so that they form a unified picture of a future stream of company operations and money flows — and a picture in which related things match up; for instance, intended DIVIDENDS and expected cash surpluses.

Research and Development and Robotics Investment are an important part of the long-range plan, but in the Game (as is typical of real life) there are no really satisfactory guidelines for planning R&D and robotics efforts. A paragraph at the end of the subsection on Short-range Forecasts (see above) gives you some idea of how R&D and robotics influence market potential. We also can say that the initial R&D budget ($100,000 per quarter) and about $50,000 for robotics in period 1 seem to be in the "reasonable" range. Some additional general suggestions are given at the end of Chapter 5, under the heading, Research and Development, Investments in Plant and Equipment, and in Robotics. But perhaps the most important thing to remember (or maybe we should describe it as the most important things that are easiest to forget) is the difficulty of recovering from inadequate R&D and robotics policies, a difficulty stemming from the slowness with which R&D and robotics take effect.

The delayed consequences of R&D and ROBOTICS and the impracticability of changing capacity rapidly by means of huge PLANT AND EQUIPMENT decisions are the key factors that make long-range planning both necessary and difficult. But you must remember that it makes no sense to plan for these three decisions without developing a general plan for the firm as a whole, any more than it would make sense in your personal life to plan to build a house without considering your finances and lifestyle.

The "broad brush" long-range planning process, as briefly sketched above, is all there is to it. If this seems disappointing, remember that the purpose of the long-range plan is mainly to give the firm consistent — but probably not fixed — general directions. In the Executive Game, as in so many real-life situations, this quarter's long-range plan is more often useful as the starting point for next quarter's replanning than as a blueprint for the future.

Replanning the Long-range Plan. Replanning is virtually a must when the actual progress of your own firm differs substantially from the existing plan. At such a point your first concern should be with figuring out what assumptions led you astray — what factors in the business situation or in the economy were misunderstood, what unexpected competitive actions might have been responsible, etc. The worst thing a management team, or any individual team member, can do is to focus attention on the question of who is to blame when something hasn't worked out well. Whenever a working group gets to arguing about its members' competence, rather than about facts and their interpretation, the team's abitity to do its work at all, much less to do it well, is jeopardized; and potential disaster is just around the corner.

Many of the surprises you'll have in the Game will result from unexpected competitive actions. But as time goes by you should become increasingly capable of anticipating what other firms are going to do. As a simple rule, successful firms will of course most often do "more of the same," continuing their profitable policies, with variations but usually without major turnabouts. On the other hand, the less successful firms are likely to change their courses radically, and often in directions similar to those taken by their more successful competitors. As the Game goes on, most firms will probably exhibit reasonably good guesses about what they are going to do next. But your guesses will sometimes be wrong, and possibly very much wrong. Competitive surprises are ultimately part of the irreducible risk that you have to accept in the Game.

Many of the surprises that are not matters of competitors' behavior can be resolved by reviewing this manual. Such surprises will be minimized if you regularly step through the procedure given in Chapter 4, but you may still miss something important.

One class of surprises, those resulting from faulty arithmetic or misreading formulas, will teach you little except to be more careful. You can minimize the occurrence of such errors by following the procedure closely, especially if you are able to computerize it (using, say, one of the spreadsheet software packages mentioned near the end of Chapter 2).

Finally, you will undoubtedly be troubled sometimes by the lack of complete information on just how the Executive Game works. You will of course be stuck with similar difficulties in real life. There is no remedy that can be routinized, but you can do your best by making the most of the information that flows from the Game as time goes by. For example, it was pointed out above that you may be able to improve upon the short-range forecasting model presented above.

Replanning should be considered whenever any major surprise occurs: not just when something goes wrong, but also when something goes unexpectedly well; and also when you are surprised by the relationship between some other firm's actions and the results. In any such case it's worth trying to figure out where your faulty assumptions lay. And then you should see whether your corrected assumptions call for changed plans. More generally (and not just in the Game), you will profit by alertness to whatever is going on around you, examining events in light of your beliefs about how things work, trying to learn from whatever discrepancies you can find, and trying to convert what you learn into better payoffs.

Cash Projection

Both short-range and long-range plans should be supplemented by (or include) cash projections, which are simply predictions of your firm's cash position over the term of the plan. These projections are made by estimating revenues and disbursements for each quarter, and then using the following equation:

cash, end of quarter (t)
= cash, end of quarter (t-1)
+ revenue during quarter (t)
– cash disbursements during quarter (t)

Don't forget that not all expenses are cash disbursements, nor are all cash disbursements expenses (see Chapter 2 for details). And be sure to carry out the computation quarter-by-quarter, rather than trying to lump several quarters of revenue and disbursements together; because you need to consider each quarter's cash position separately, at least to take into account the fact that if you run short at any time, then the corresponding financing charges and penalties must be added into disbursements for the next quarter.

Cash planning is important in the Game, as in real life, because the large costs of financing can become crucial and also because a lack of funds takes away a firm's chance to take advantage of unexpected opportunities. Note that bankruptcy is not a matter of being "in the red" on the profit and loss statement, but one of being unable to pay your bills. Paper profits are not negotiable, and it is quite possible for an overexpanded firm in the Executive Game to collapse financially even though its *operating* profits (before financing costs are considered) are positive.

Deficits larger than a few thousand dollars point to the urgent need for replanning. Even small shortages suggest caution, lest unexpected setbacks lead to serious shortages, made ever more serious by the snowball effects of financing costs.

In general, the sort of replanning called for when unacceptable cash deficits are projected will emphasize reduced DIVIDENDS, and often less money put into PLANT AND EQUIPMENT and ROBOTICS INVESTMENTS. This usually implies reducing projected values of PRODUCTION VOLUME, whence appropriate cuts can be made in planned MAINTENANCE budgets. Also, when you reduce your market potential goals, small cuts in R&D and ROBOTICS will be reasonable, along with the generally small cuts in MARKETING and small increases in PRICE made appropriate by the planned reductions in volume. But if you raise PRICE or lower MARKETING beyond the levels justified by less ambitious plans for sales volume, this can only intensify your difficulties. If you should find you are tempted to lower budgets below the levels needed to support your operations properly, then it's time to re-plan, cutting sales objectives still further.

Incidentally, there may be occasions where cutting back is desirable, even though current and projected operations are profitable, especially if your industry gets involved in a major price war or excessively energetic marketing battles, much as the best way to avoid injury in a barroom brawl is usually to walk out the door.

The opposite of a cash shortage is a cash excess. If you have any substantial amount of cash on hand, beyond what is needed as reasonable protection against setbacks, then you're treating your stockholders poorly. Such funds should either be invested in operations, if this can be done profitably enough, or distributed. We leave to you the decisions as to what cash position can be considered reasonably safe, and where the line should be drawn between investing excess funds and distributing them as dividends.

A Closing Comment

It should be obvious that short-range planning, long-range planning, and cash projection are part of a single indivisible management process, and this combined planning process cannot even be separated from quarter-by-quarter decision making. We emphasize this fact because experience shows that it is often forgotten. Even in otherwise well-managed companies, long-range planning is sometimes hidden away as if it were shameful. And neglect of proper cash planning is said to account for more bankruptcies than inability to produce profits. Executive Game managements seem to be no better than real life in these regards. Plans are often simply forgotten in the heat of battle, especially when something goes wrong. Frantic attempts to make a "quick fix," with planning neglected, cause most of the gross errors that get Executive Game firms into serious trouble.

There's no way you can guarantee that your firm will come out on top in the Game, but careful planning and regular updating of plans will make it almost certain that you'll do better than last place, and will virtually eliminate the possibility of bankruptcy. Most important, careful planning will provide a focus that will make the Executive Game into an interesting and valuable learning experience.

Supplementary Reading

Steiner, G.A. *Comprehensive Management Planning.* Oxford, Ohio: Planning Executive Institute, 1972.

Webber, Ross A. *Management.* Homewood, Illinois: Richard D. Irwin, 1976. (See especially Chapter 12, "Strategic Planning," and the bibliography.)

4

Step-By-Step Procedure for Decisions in the Executive Game

This chapter lays out a procedure for using the large columnar Work Sheet provided in Appendix F to systematize the steps in making decision in the Executive Game. Most of these calculations can be made with a simple hand calculator although we recommend the use of a scientific calculator with the exponential function, or, ideally, a spreadsheet program on a personal computer.

In what follows, the subscript "t-1" refers to the most recent past period of play in the Game, and to the "actual" Work Sheet column for that period. Subscript "t" refers to the period for which decisions are currently being made, and to the corresponding "forecast" column. These subscripts are appended to numbers which indicate Work Sheet rows, such as Ia, Ib, 1a, 13, etc. The entire subscripted notation is used like an algebraic symbol to refer to the number in the square indicated. For instance, the notation

$$16_{t-1} \div 6_{t-1}$$

means to divide the number in square 16_{t-1} by the number in square 6_{t-1}; that is to calculate the following quotient:

$$\frac{\text{actual labor expense, for most recent period}}{\text{actual production this period, for most recent period}}$$

Similarly, $7_t \times 6_t$ means to multiply the contents of row 7, "forecast" column t, by the contents of row 6, "forecast" column t. And so forth. This notation - which is unusual as "algebraic" notation - is one of the standard styles used in the preparation of spreadsheet programs.

In many cases, the formulae given produce exact results. In every instance they are accurate enough for the purposes of cost forecasting, cash projection, profit prediction, etc. Precise results can be obtained by using the formulae implicit in the flow chart in Appendix A or the FORTRAN computer program in Appendix C.

Some of the steps below are not actually computational, but require judgments or decisions.

Examples include #3 (a qualitative judgment), #10 (a decision), and #15 (market forecasts). In many such instances specific guidance is to be found in Chapters 2, 3, or 5. However, it is the very nature of the Game that *you* are responsible for the content of the Work Sheet squares concerned, rather than merely for following programmed instructions.

The word "widgets" is used below as shorthand for "units of production." Note that inflation indices, wherever they appear, are generally divided by 100, to convert them from percentage figures (e.g., 107) to absolute proportions (e.g., 107/100 = 1.07).

Steps

1 Examine *results of last period* operations on sheet from computer.

2 Copy these results in proper "actual" column of your big work sheets in Appendix F or onto your spreadsheet. Most of the spaces under period 0 "actual" are filled in. Your Game administrator will tell you what to put in spaces Ib_0, 2_0, and 5_0, based on Tables 3 and 40.

3 Compare "actual" with your "forecast" and make further tentative plans.

4 Fill in following blanks in your "actual" column: I_{t-1}, II_{t-1}, III_{t-1}, IV_{t-1}, 1_{t-1}, 2_{t-1}. Compute 1_{t-1}, 2_{t-1}.

5 Fill in corresponding spaces in "forecast" column. In spaces I_t, 1_t, and 2_t enter your best predictions after considering the inflation forecast, seasonal and economic indices, and your estimate of total industry marketing, robotics and R&D expenditures. For further information on the effects of seasonal and economic indices and total industry marketing expenditures, see page 87, Chapter 3. A forecast of the general price index can be made by the following formula: $Ia_t = Ia_{t-1} \times (1 + Ib_{t-1} \div 400)$, where Ib_{t-1} is the forecast at time t-1 of the annual inflation rate for the next four quarters.

6 Compute: $7a_{t-1}$, Labor cost per unit.
$7b_{t-1}$, Materials cost per unit.

Calculated by the computer, but you should know how. Ordinarily, to obtain the labor cost of production per unit, divide labor expense by production ($16_{t-1} \div 6_{t-1}$). To obtain materials cost, divide materials expense by production ($17_{t-1} \div 6_{t-1}$). However, if you have been producing beyond normal plant capacity at overtime wage rates in a game using Model 1, this calculation gives you an erroneous answer for regular time labor cost-per-unit. It is too high because the labor expenses include overtime for the extra production. Hence, to obtain regular time labor cost-per-unit divide labor expense by production at plant capacity plus 1-1/2 times production in excess of plant capacity.

$$\text{Formula: } 16_{t-1} \div [9_{t-2} + 1.5 \times (6_{t-1} - 9_{t-2})].$$

In Model 2 operations at rates: (1) greater than capacity up to and including 40% above capacity or, (2) at more than twice capacity up to and including two and one half times capacity, are considered to take place on an overtime basis. The formula presented just above for Model 1 also applies for this case of (1) while the formula for computing straight time labor cost for this case (2) is:

$$16_{t-1} \div [2 \times 9_{t-2} + 1.5 \times (6_{t-1} - 2 \times 9_{t-2})]$$

There are no overtime charges for labor in Model 2 with operations at rates: (3) from 0 percent up to and including 100 percent or, (4) at greater than 40 percent above capacity up to and including two times capacity, or (5) at greater than two and one half times capacity up to and including three times capacity. Therefore, the formula for cases (3), (4), and (5) is:

$$16_{t-1} \div 6_{t-1}.$$

$7a_{t-1}$ and $7b_{t-1}$ are fairly good approximations to $7a_t$ and $7b_t$. However, during periods of severe inflation, or if large changes in R&D, robotics investment and maintenance are budgeted, appropriate adjustments should be made. Changes in labor scales and costs of raw materials lag the general price index in the Game by one quarter, but *costs per*

Steps

unit of finished products produced also depend upon levels of R&D, robotics investment and maintenance support.

7 Reexamine your general plan - "style," specific policies, etc. Remember you are top management making major plans and decisions. Think!

8 Your next jobs are (1) to make eight new major decisions and two major estimates and (2) to make forecast calculations resulting from these decisions and estimates.

Enter your decisions, estimates, and calculations in the proper spaces in the "forecast" column.

9 Your next decisions should be the price you are going to charge; how much you are going to spend on marketing, R&D, robotics investment, maintenance; how many "widgets" you hope to sell; and how many you will want to produce, in addition to the inventory of finished goods now on hand. (Steps 10 through 17, inclusive. Don't forget the forecasts of inflation, seasonal demand, and economic activity while carrying out these steps.)

10 *Decide price*, consulting $1a_{t-1}$ and $1b_{t-1}$. Note your sales volume and profits at your last price, marketing, robotics investment, and R&D expenditures. Demand is quite elastic. At high prices sales fall off sharply. But low price may not cover total cost per unit. Remember that price elasticity in the Game varies directly with the level of inflation, i.e., customers resist paying a price for the firm's product which is proportional to increases over the past six months in the general price index. Compute your marketing. What do you think the average industry price will be? Will your price be competitive considering your R&D, robotics investment and marketing program? Enter in spaces $1a_t$ and $1b_t$. Don't forget that marketing, robotics investment and R&D can differentiate your product and make possible profit-based pricing with reduced attention to price competition ("administered prices"). For further information on price effects, see page 88, Chapter 3.

11 *Decide marketing expenditure*. This is an expense, so don't waste your money. But remember it is a major weapon in fighting competition for your share of the market and to bring your product to the attention of the public. But don't go to extremes. Law of diminishing returns applies. Large expenditures may bring less than proportionate increase in sales. Beware of a profit squeeze. Costs of marketing change in direct proportion in the Game to changes in the general price index. For further information on marketing effects, see page 88, Chapter 3. Enter your decision in space 12_t.

12 *Decide R&D*. Also an expense. But you must keep your product modern and well designed and your production and sales techniques efficient. So, do research and development to keep costs down and quality up. Costs of R&D in the Game also change in direct proportion to changes in the general price index. For further information on R&D effects, see page 134, Chapter 5. Enter your decision in space 13_t.

13 *Decide maintenance expense*. You must keep your plant operating efficiently. Otherwise, labor and materials cost-per-unit will rise. Correlate maintenance expenditures with changes in production. The costs of maintenance change at a slightly faster rate than the general price index. Use one half of the forecast of the *annual* inflation rate as a rough approximation. Enter your decision in space 15_t.

Steps

14 *Decide robotics investment.* This is an investment — not an expense. In the long run it will keep costs down and quality up. It also will increase production capacity; and, decrease the price elasticity as does R&D and marketing. Sensitivity is another word for elasticity. For further information on the effects of robotics investment see page 135, Chapter 5. Enter your decision in space 39_t.

15 *Estimate (a) total industry sales, (b) your expected market potential, and (c) your sales volume.* It is expensive to create a greater market potential than the volume you can sell. Sales cannot be greater than finished goods on hand plus production. Enter your estimates in spaces 2_t, 3_t, and 4_t.

16 *Compute* your hoped-for Percent Share of Industry Sales ($4_t \div 2_t$). Enter in space 5_t.

17 *Decide proposed production.* Enter in space 6_t. In Model 1 games production cannot be larger than the smaller of: (1) $47_{t-1} \div 7b_t$ or (2) $1.4 \times 9_{t-1}$. That is, you can't produce more than will use up the raw materials you now have on hand at the beginning of this quarter. Purchases made during the coming quarter can't be used until the following quarter. Also, you cannot work your plant further into overtime than 1.4 times normal plant capacity.

For a method of determining a good production schedule see pages 124-133, Chapter 5.

In Model 2, production cannot be larger than the smaller of (1) $47_{t-1} \div 7b_t$ or (2) $3 \times 9_{t-1}$; i.e., you can't produce more than to use up raw materials you now have on hand at the beginning of the quarter. Also, you cannot work your plant further into overtime than three times normal plant capacity. Note: It is expensive to add or terminate extra shifts, and overtime and additional shifts affect administrative overhead. See step 30.

Note: You have now made all the major *decisions* and *estimates* necessary for this quarter's operations. Two of the three remaining decisions, *viz.*, new investment in plant and purchase of materials, prepare for next quarter's operations. The last, viz., dividend, you may wish to decide after you see how large your expected profits after taxes are and how much cash you have on hand. From now on your work is mostly making simple *computations.*

18 *Decide plant and equipment investment* and enter in 40_t. See also page 134, Chapter 5.

19 *Decide raw materials purchase* and enter in 41_t. See also page 116, Chapter 5.

20 *Compute Inventory of Finished Goods* at end of forecast period as follows: Beginning inventory plus planned production minus expected sales ($8_{t-1} + 6_t - 4_t$). Enter in 8_t.

21 Compute 9_t *Plant capacity, next quarter* (in "widgets"). This is a big one because in this one operation you will also get forecast figures for depreciation, new investment in plant and equipment, net book value, and replacement value of the plant and equipment, and robotics replacement value.

First compute net plant and equipment book value, next quarter (49_t), which is equal to what it was at the beginning of the quarter (49_{t-1}), less the amount of depreciation during the quarter (19_t), plus your new investment in plant and equipment (40_t). In short, beginning plant and equipment minus depreciation plus new investment; adjust this figure for the effects of robotics replacement value in the past (history) period.

Steps

Only approximations of plant capacity next quarter and replacement value of the plant and equipment can be calculated because they are affected by the intensity of inflationary pressures. *The Calculations: Compute* 19_t, Depreciation 2.5% of 49_{t-1}. Enter in space 19_t.

Note: In deciding how much to invest in new plant, remember that it must make up for the quarter's deterioration of 2.2 percent, plus whatever expansion in plant capacity you wish to make which is affected by price changes due to inflation or deflation. Better also take a look to see if you have the cash. It might be expensive to borrow it. Now compute net Plant and Equipment Book Value, next quarter. Enter in space 49_t.

Formula: $49_t = 49_{t-1} - 19_t + 40_t$
or = beginning plant minus depreciation plus new investment.

Now you are ready to compute Plant Capacity, next quarter (approximation only):

Formula: $9_t = .98 \times 9_{t-1} + 40_t \div [\$70 \times .01 \times Ia_{t-1} \times (1 + Ib_{t-1} \div 400)] \times [2 - 2.718^{-39_t/10,000,000}]$

Enter in space 9_t.

Finally you are ready to compute Plant and Equipment Replacement Value, next quarter (approximation only):

Formula: $51_t = .98 \times [9_t \times \$70 \times .01 \times Ia_{t-1} \times [1 + Ib_{t-1} \div 400] \div (2 - 2.718^{-52_{t-1}/10,000,000})] + 40_t$

Enter in space 51_t.

Note 1: $(2.718)^0 = 1$. Since the exponential e = 2.718, on some scientific calculators or spreadsheet programs you may find it easier to use e instead of its approximation 2.718.

Note 2: In the Game, Plant and Equipment Replacement Value and Plant and Equipment Book Value in Period 0 are set equal as a matter of convenience.

22 Compute Robotics Replacement Value, next quarter.

Formula: $52_t = 52_{t-1} \times 0.96875 \times (1 + Ib_{t-1}/400) + 39_t$

Enter in 52_t.

23 Compute Depreciation of Robotics.

Formula: $20_t = 0.05 \times 48_{t-1}$

Enter in 20_t.

24 You have now completed the preliminary calculations dealing with operations in general. Next compute the entire *"Income and Expense"* statement which includes the *profit* you expect to make. Do this as outlined in Steps 25 and 42, inclusive.

25 Compute your expected receipts, sales revenue first. You have only one source of income, which is receipts from sales of widgets. Price times expected sales volume: $1a_t \times 4_t$. You decided on price in Step 10 and estimated expected sales volume in Step 15. Enter in spaces 11_t and 35_t.

Steps

26 Now compute the remainder of your expected expenses: Steps 27 to 37, inclusive.

27 *Labor expense:*

A. If no overtime is used, multiply labor cost per unit ($7a_t$) times production during the quarter (6_t); i.e., the formula is $7a_t \times 6_t$.

B. If you go into overtime, at wage rates of time and a half, the formula is ($7a_t \times 9_{t-1}$) + ($1.5 \times 7a_t$) x ($6_t - 9_{t-1}$). Read it in words as follows: Labor cost per unit ($7a_t$) times plant capacity at the beginning of the quarter (9_{t-1}) plus 1.5 times labor cost per unit, i.e., ($1.5 \times 7a_t$), multiplied by the amount you produce in excess of plant capacity ($6_t - 9_{t-1}$). Enter in space 16_t.

In Model 2 use the formula in A above if production is: (1) from 0 percent up to and including 100 percent of capacity or (2) at greater than 40 percent above capacity up to and including two times capacity or (3) at greater than two and one half times capacity up to and including three times capacity. However, if operations are at rates: (4) greater than capacity up to and including 40 percent above capacity or (5) at more than twice capacity up to and including two and one half times capacity, they are considered to take place at overtime rates. The formula for computing labor expense in the case of (4) is $7a_t \times 1 \times 9_{t-1} + 1.5 \times 7a_t \times (6_t - 9_{t-1})$. *For case (5) the formula is:* $7a_t \times 2 \times 9_{t-1} + 1.5 \times 7a_t \times (6_t - 2 \times 9_{t-1})$.

28 *Materials Consumed expense:* $7b_t \times 6_t$. Enter in space 17_t.

Note: However, the figures in Steps 24 and 25 give us the estimated labor and materials expenses of the widgets *to be produced during the three-month period,* this is not what we want. We should have the labor and materials expenses of widgets sold *during this period.* If production and sales are equal *during this period,* there is no problem. But two other possibilities exist and are very probable:

A. Sales may exceed production with the extra widgets taken out of inventory.

B. Production may exceed sales with the extra widgets put into inventory.

Hence, the next expense item "Reduction, Finished Goods Inventory Value" is included to correct this situation.

29 *Reduction, Finished Goods Inventory Value expense* (positive or negative):

A. If sales are greater than production, our labor and materials figure which include only goods produced *understates the labor and materials expenses of those sold.* It does not include the labor and materials costs of the "widgets" taken out of inventory and sold. These costs must be added. To correct, multiply "standard" cost per unit of raw materials and labor times ($4_t - 6_t$). Use \$12 x .01 x Ia_{t-1} as an approximatiion to "standard" cost per unit. Thus, "Reduction, Finished Goods Inventory Value" is a positive number. Enter in space 18_t.

B. If production is greater than sales, our labor and materials expenses figure *overstates the labor and materials costs* of widgets sold since it includes the labor and materials costs of the widgets added to inventory. These costs must be subtracted. To correct, multiply standard cost per unit of raw materials and labor per unit times ($4_t - 6_t$) as before. However, this time use \$12 x .01 x Ia_{t-1} as an approximation to "standard" cost per unit. "Reduction, Finished Goods Inventory Value" will be a negative number. Enter in space 18_t.

Steps

Note I: These extra unsold "widgets" are put into "finished goods inventory" and carried as an asset at the average "standard" cost per unit at which they were put into inventory until they are sold, which is normally the next period (because sales are filled first out of any carryover inventory). See Step 49.

Note: Make sure when you get to Step 49 that your asset, viz., "Inventory Value of Finished Goods" was reduced (if sales exceed production) or increased (if production exceeds sales) by this same amount in dollars; that is, reduced or increased from what it was at the end of the previous period. Also check that in Step 20, your inventory of finished goods was changed by the corresponding number of "widgets."

30 *Administration expense:* In Model 1, for regular time basis, use ($150,000+$1.28x9_{t-1}) x Ia_{t-1}/[(2-2.718$^{(-13_{t-1}\text{-}51_{t-1}/20)/45,000,000}$].

For overtime use $200,000 instead of $150,000 in the above formula.

In Model 2 use the above formula for regular time and overtime. For more than 40 percent above capacity up to and including two full shifts use $250,000 instead of $200,000 in the formula above. For more than two and a half times capacity up to and including three times capacity use $350,000 in the above formula. These are approximations only. The calculations can be made on a scientific hand calculator.

Enter in space 14_t.

31 *Finished Goods Carrying Costs expense:* Charged on finished goods carryover inventory at the end of the forecast period. $2 x .01 x Ia_{t-1} x 8_t will give a good approximation, i.e., $2.00 per unit times effects due to inflation. Enter in space 21_t.

32 *Raw Materials Carrying Costs expense:* .05 x 47_{t-1}; i.e., 5 percent of the value of the raw materials in stock at the beginning of the period (end of last period). Enter in space 22_t.

33 *Ordering Costs expense* (on raw materials): $50,000 x Ia_{t-1} x .01, i.e., $50,000 times effects due to inflation if raw materials are to be ordered during the forecast period. Enter in space 23_t.

34 *Model 2 only - Shifts Change Costs expense:* $100,000 x Ia_{t-1} x .01; i.e., $100,000 times effects of inflation for each unit change in number of shifts employed. Enter in space 24_t.

35 *Investment Expenses* (and penalties): $(39_t + 40_t)^2$/10,000,000; i.e., square the amount budgeted for plant and equipment and robotics investments and divide by 10,000,000. Enter in space 25_t.

36 *Financing Charges and Penalties Expense:* Effective only when 45_{t-1} was negative. Therefore, if $45_{t-1} < 0$, calculate $(45_{t-1})^2$ x (1 + .01 x Ib_{t-1}) x .9/10,000,000. Enter in space 26_t.

37 *Sundries Expenses:* ($10,000 + .72 x 9_{t-1}) x .01 x Ia_{t-1}/(2 - 2.718$^{(-13_{t-1}\text{-}51_{t-1}/20)/49,000,000}$). This is an approximation only. Enter in space 27_t.

38 Add all your expenses (12_t to 27_t) and enter in space 28_t.

39 Subtract total expenses 28_t from total receipts 11_t and enter in space 24_t. This is your *profit before income tax.*

Steps

40 Compute your *tax*. Taxes are levied on quarterly gross profit (if there is a loss the profit will be negative and the firm receives a tax credit equal to the amount of the taxes it would have been required to pay if the profit had been positive) at 34 percent. This is only an approximatiion to the real tax code. In addition, if the tax credit on investments in new equipment is ever again in effect the firm will be granted a tax credit on any investments in plant and equipment (which are assumed to be divided equally between building and equipment each quarter) and on an investment in robotics. From the early 1960s through 1986 a 10 percent investment tax credit on equipment and robotics was in effect.

Furthermore, if the surtax is in effect ever again it will have the effect of increasing or reducing income taxes depending upon whether the surtax is positive or negative. In the late 1960s and the first half of the year 1970, a 10 percent positive surtax was in effect. Obviously a negative surtax of 10 percent would reduce taxes. Thus, the surtax in the Game simply amounts to an across-the-board change in taxes either up or down depending on whether it is positive or negative. Enter in spaces 30_t and 37_t.

Subtract tax to get net profit after taxes. Remember when you subtract a negative number you change its negative sign to positive and add it algebraically to the other numbers in the problem. Enter in space 31_t.

Decide on the dividends you are going to pay to your stockholders and enter in space 32_t and 38_t. Watch your cash. Dividends are limited to excess of owners' equity over $9,000,000. See page 24, Chapter 2, for a discussion of issues to consider when declaring dividends.

41 Compute "addition to owners' equity" by subtracting dividends from profits after taxes. (Enter in space 33_t. It may be negative.)

42 You have now completed your "income and expense" statement (see Step 24). Next your *cash flow statement*, most of which is already done. Steps 43 to 46.

43 Compute cash expenses: Sum of 12_t through 16_t and 21_t through 27_t. Enter in space 36_t. Cash expenses include all expenses except materials consumed and reduction, finished goods inventory value, which are inventory adjustment items, and depreciation, none of which are cash expenses.

44 Decide on "purchase of materials." This is your last major operating decision. Enter in 41_t. You are now ordering for period $t + 1$. See 17_{t-1} material expense for the amount you have been using up per quarter.

45 Add up all cash disbursements (36_t through 41_t) and enter in space 42_t.

46 *Compute "addition to cash assets"* by subtracting total disbursements from cash receipts, 35_t-42_t, and enter this figure in space 43_t (may be negative). This completes your *cash flow statement*.

47 Make out your *financial statement*, first the assets. Steps 48 to 54.

48 Net cash assets equal the cash you had on hand (from previous "Actual") plus (or minus) addition to cash assets, 45_{t-1} - 43_t. Enter in space 45_t.

Steps

49 *Inventory value, finished goods:* number of units of finished goods on hand x "standard" cost of raw materials and labor per unit. Use \$12 x .01 x Ia_{t-1} as an approximation to "standard" cost per unit. Enter in space 46_t.

50 *Inventory value, materials.* Computation: Value of materials on hand at beginning of forecast period less materials consumed plus purchased, $47_{t-1} - 17_t + 41_t$. Enter in space 47_t.

51 *Robotics book value* (net). Computation: Its value at the beginning of the period less depreciation (5%) plus new investments in robotics. Formula: $48_t = 48_{t-1} - 20_t + 39_t$. Enter in space 48_t.

52 *Plant and Equipment book value* (net). Computation: Its value at beginning of the period less depreciation (2.5) plus new investment in plant and equipment. This was done in Step 21.

53 Next add all your assets and, since you have no listed liabilities (debts), this is your *Owners' Equity*. Formula: $45_t + 41_t + 47_t + 48_t + 49_t$.

Also: $50_{t-1} + 33_t$ should give the same result. Check it. Enter in space 50_t.

54 *Plant and Equipment Replacement Value.* Computation: 9_t x \$70 x adjustment for effects of inflation. This was done in Step 21.

55 *Robotics Replacement Value.* Computation: 52_{t-1} x effects of deterioration x adjustment for effects of inflation + investments in robotics. This was done in Step 22.

56 *Owners' Economic Equity.* Same as Owners' Equity, except substitute robotics replacement value and plant and equipment replacement value for robotics book value and plant and equipment book value. More accurately measures the true economic or replacement value of the company's assets. Used to make a more valid estimate of rate of return earned on the company's assets at the end of each year (i.e., 4 quarters) of play.

Your job should now be done. Study it. If your expected profit is not as large as you think it should be, possibly you may wish to make some changes in your decisions and calculate their effects.

Supplementary Reading

Spreadsheet Computer Programs. See comments under "Supplementary Readings" at the end of Chapter 2.

5

Quantitative Modeling and Analysis

Many significant problems of business management can profitably be subjected to quantitative modeling and analysis. The same is true in the Executive Game. This chapter gives some examples, both to help your firm improve its "score" in the Game and to help you toward making similar applications in the business world. It should be understood that the chapter illustrates the possibilities for modeling and analysis in the Game, and that numerous other opportunities are waiting for you to find them. And, of course, the opportunities available in the Game are merely illustrative of those to be found in the practical work of management.

The first example is a simplified (and in fact simple) model for estimating Profit Before Income Tax, once certain basic decisions and forecasts have been made. This model involves no abstract "theory." It is a straightforward computing procedure, similar to but much less complicated than that given in Chapter 4, above. It will not in itself "solve" your decision problems, but it will greatly reduce the work of evaluating and comparing proposed solutions. A "comparison model" is also provided, which is still more efficient (in fact far more) for the special problem to which it applies.

These profit models illustrate how you can construct other similar models for different purposes, such as Cash Flow Projection.

Following the Profit Models, a brief section introduces the subject of Inventory Analysis. Then two sections are devoted to Executive Game problems centering around inventories of raw materials and of finished goods. This is followed by a section on research and development and investment in plant and equipment. The chapter closes with a short final section pointing toward some other potentially fruitful uses of quantitative modeling and analysis in the Executive Game.

Profit Models

The section on "Short-range Planning" in Chapter 3 indicates why it would be useful to be able to compare the profitability of alternative decision proposals, with corresponding forecasts of market potential, in order to choose the best among them. The computational procedure of Chapter 4 can, of course, be used to make such comparisons, but this complicated sequence of calculations is so tedious as to discourage repeated use in a single decision cycle. The idea of what follows is merely to extract the essence of Chapter 4 calculation of Profit Before Income Tax, accepting some degree of approximation in order to save work.

We shall then go one step further, to extract a very simple model for the comparative evaluation of alternative proposals for PRICE, MARKETING, and PRODUCTION VOLUME. Recall from Chapter 3 that such comparisons can be viewed as the main step in systematic short-range planning and decision making, once procedure for short-range forecasting of market potential is available.

The Profit Model: Construction. We suppose now that you are starting from a proposed set of Executive Game decisions (except that DIVIDEND will not be needed), plus a prediction of market potential. We suppose further that the proposed PRODUCTION VOLUME decision is large enough so that you are confident that actual sales volume will be identical with market potential. To simplify the analysis we shall use the following notations:

Y = predicted market potential
= expected sales

$$I = \frac{\text{The current quarter's predicted inflation index}}{100}$$

The letter Y, suggesting a "variable," is used intentionally, because the model will permit you to answer some questions which do not start from the assumption that the predicted value of Y is exact. Dividing the inflation index by 100 simply converts it from a percentage (for instance, 107%) to an absolute proportion (107/100 = 1.07).

Table 41, (page 111) gives the procedure for estimating Profit Before Income Tax, for Model 1 of the Executive Game. We won't explain the sources of the specific formulae, but you will be able to find them in Chapter 4 if you want to make the effort. (If your run of the Game is currently using Model 2, you should also be able to revise the procedure accordingly, by changing steps B5 and B13.

The Profit Model: Forecasting. Given last quarter's reports, this quarter's proposed decisions, and estimates of Y and I, the model can be used straightforwardly to calculate an estimate of Profit Before Income Tax. We have done this for the actual Period 1 decisions made by Firm 5-4 in the run from which Tables 3 and 8 (pp. 39 and 44) were obtained. In order to test the validity of Table 41, we hypothesized an accurate sales forecast (153,160 vs. actual results of 153,160) and forecast of general price index. The calculation is summarized in Table 42 (page 112). Comparison with the actual outcome of Period 1 shows that the estimate of Receipts is extremely accurate (as was assured by the accurate sales "forecast"), that Total Expense is over estimated by only 1.0 percent. The calculation took about 30 minutes, using a hand calculator and paper and pencil; this required time could easily be cut to at most 15 minutes by arranging the needed data efficiently. Of course, for those players who have access to a micro-computer, a spreadsheet program will be more beneficial than a hand calculator.

Given the needed resources, there would, of course, be no difficulty in computerizing Table 41 or even programming it for computation into one of the more sophisticated hand calculators. Then typing the required data into the computer (or keying data into an interactive node) should not take more than two minutes (9 long numbers at 10-15 seconds each).

Real period 1 was particularly easy to estimate because market potential was very likely to exceed production plus inventory of finished goods in stock. Thus, it is unlikely that players will be able to estimate quite as accurately as this, but they should be able to estimate accurately enough for this procedure to be helpful. One of the reasons why real period 1 was easy to estimate for Firm 5-4 was that the players constituting Firm 5-4 were fairly inept at managing their firm. They didn't use the large worksheet (Table 40). The authors constructed Table 40 for this edition as an example for players. However, Firm 5-4 did forecast their market potential each quarter which is a minimum requirement of Game administrators.

Table 41

Procedure for Estimating Profit Before Income Tax, Executive Game Model 1.

The letter Y denotes market potential, assumed to be equal to expected sales. The letter I denotes the inflation index for the past quarter, divided by 100.

A. *Receipts*

1. Sales Revenue = PRICE x Y.

B. *Expenses*

1. Marketing = MARKETING budget.
2. Research and Development = R&D budget.
3. Administration Expense = ($150,000 + 1.28 x PLANT CAPACITY) x I / [2 - 2.718 $^{(\text{-R\&D-Plant \& Equipment Replacement Value/20)/45,000,000}}$] If overtime is scheduled add: $50,000 x I / [2 - 2.718$^{(\text{-R\&D-Plant \& Equipment Replacement Value/20)/45,000,000}}$] (See step 30, p. 105, Chapter 4 and blocks 277, 282, and 298, p. 151, Appendix A).
4. Maintenance = MAINTENANCE budget.
5. Labor = (labor cost/unit, last quarter) x (PRODUCTION VOLUME); but if there is overtime in the present quarter, add
   0.5 x (labor cost/unit, last quarter) x (PRODUCTION VOLUME - PLANT CAPACITY).
6. Materials Consumed = (materials cost/unit, last quarter) x (PRODUCTION VOLUME).
7. Reduction, Finished Goods Inventory = 12 x I x [Y - (PRODUCTION VOLUME)]. (See Step 29, p. 104, Chapter 4.)
8. Plant and Equipment Depreciation = 0.025 x (Plant and Equipment Book Value, last quarter)
9. Robotics Depreciation = 0.05 x (Robotics Book Value, last quarter)
10. Finished Goods Carrying Cost = 2 x I x [(Inventory, Finished Goods, last quarter) + (PRODUCTION VOLUME) - Y]. (See Step 31, p. 105, Chapter 4.)
11. Raw Materials Carrying Costs = 0.05 x Inventory Value, Materials, last quarter.
12. Ordering Costs = $50,000 x I, if a MATERIALS PURCHASE ORDER is being placed; otherwise zero. (See Step 33, p. 105, Chapter 4).
13. Shifts Change Cost = $0.
14. Plant Investment Expenses = $\frac{(\text{PLANT AND EQUIPMENT + ROBOTICS INVESTMENT})^2}{10{,}000{,}000}$
15. Financing Charges and Penalties = $0 if Cash, last quarter, is positive or zero; otherwise 0.0000001X.9X (Cash Deficit, last quarter)^2 x (1 + Forecast of the Annual Percentage Change in the General Price Index/100).
16. Sundries = ($10,000 + 0.72 x PLANT CAPACITY) x I / (2 - 2.718$^{(\text{-R\&D - Plant and Equipment Replacement Value/20)/49,000,000}}$)
17. Total Expense = sum of items B1 through B16.

C. *Profit Before Income Tax* = (Item A1) - (Item B17).

Table 42

Profit Before Income Tax, Estimated by the Procedure of Table 41 for Firm 5-4, Period 1.

All numbers needed in the calculation and all "actual" results are shown in Tables 3 and 8 (pp. 39 and 44); except that "forecast" of actual potential = 153,160 was hypothesized. "Actual" results are shown after predicted results, in parenthesis.

A. *Receipts*

1. Sales Revenue = $23.1 x 153,160 = $3,537,996 (3,537,996)

B. *Expenses*

1. Marketing = $322,500 (322,500)
2. Research and Development = $125,000 (125,000)
3. Administration = $330,179 (330,179)
4. Maintenance = $107,440 (107,440)
5. Labor = $5.71 x 140,410 + 0.5 x $5.71 x (140,410 - 104,643) = $903,854 (901,657)
6. Materials consumed = $6.30 x 140,410 = $884,583 (884,152)
7. Reduction, Finished Goods Inventory = $12 x 1.00 x (153,160 - 140,410) = $153,000 (153,000)
8. Plant and Equipment Depreciation = 0.025 x $7,325,000 = $183,125 (183,125)
9. Robotics Depreciation = 0.05 x $0 = $0 (0)
10. Finished Goods Carrying Cost = $2 x 1.00 x (12,750 + 140,410 - 153,160) = $0 (0)
11. Raw Materials Carrying Cost = .05 x $1,200,000 = $60,000 (60,000)
12. Ordering Costs = $1.00 x $50,000 = $50,000 (50,000)
13. Shifts Change Costs = $0 (0)
14. Investment Expenses = ($375,000 + $75,000)^2 / 10,000,000 = $20,250 (20,250)
15. Financing Charges and Penalties = $0 (0)
16. Sundries = $84,459 (84,459)
17. Total Expense = $3,224,892 (3,222,259)

C. *Profit Before Income Tax* = $3,537,996 - $3,224,892 = $313,044 (315,737)

Market Potential as a Variable. In Table 41 you can think of Y as a variable, and carry through all the calculations to get Profit Before Income Tax as a mathematical function of Y; that is, expressed in terms of a formula in which Y appears as a variable. If you work out the details for the example of Table 42 (by replacing "153,160" with "Y," throughout), the result is the following formula:[1]

$$\text{Profit Before Income Tax} = 13.10Y - 1{,}585{,}352.$$

Such expressions enable management to inquire about the consequences of various hypotheses as to what market potential will actually be (up to Y equal to the total quantity of finished goods to be offered for sale, carryover inventory plus PRODUCTION VOLUME). For instance, profit will be zero if

$$13.10Y - 1{,}585{,}352 = 0;$$

that is, if Y = 121,019. For smaller values of Y, the firm will obviously suffer a loss, and for larger values it will earn a positive profit.

The same idea, carried somewhat further, leads to the idea of "break-even analysis," which is usually based, however, on assumptions that manufacturing output and all the variances which naturally go along with it will be geared to actual sales (including, for instance, purchases of raw materials). Break-even analysis is most useful for exploring the potential profitability of a proposed new product. This technique may be useful in the Game when a product is to be radically changed (for instance, by sharply increasing both PRICE and R&D). We suspect, though, that the details of suitable models should be tailored to specific situations, and we shall not go further with this subject here.

A Quick Comparison Model. Suppose you wish to compare several alternatives for PRICE, MARKETING, and PRODUCTION VOLUME, where we assume that the PRODUCTION VOLUME proposals are well tuned to actual market potentials, and also that buffer-stock decisions will not depend importantly on which alternative is chosen. To make the comparison, we need only consider those items in Table 41 which will vary according to which alternative is selected, and we need only consider those components of these items which will actually change between alternatives. Items A1 and B1 are, of course, to be counted. In Item B3 we need only consider the overtime cost, since the "actual, last quarter" part of the formula will not change from one alternative to another. We should consider item B4 as a variable, since MAINTENANCE should be geared to PRODUCTION VOLUME. Items B5 and B6 are obviously important. But the rest of the expense items are simply not directly affected by the choice among PRICE, MARKETING, PRODUCTION VOLUME combinations.

Here is a list of the pertinent items sorted out in the preceding paragraph (again using the notations Y and I as before, but with the understanding now that Y is also equal to PRODUCTION VOLUME, and again treating the case of Model 1):

A. Receipts

   1. Sales revenue = PRICE x Y.

B. 1. Marketing = MARKETING budget.

   3. Administration, variable part only = $50{,}000 \times I / [2 - 2.718^{(-R\&D\ -\ Plt\ Eq\ Repl\ Val/20)}]$ if overtime is scheduled.

---

[1] This formula assumes overtime production, in conformity with the plans of Firm 5-4. The expression on the right would be different for values of Y that do not imply overtime.

4. Maintenance (desirable level) = 0.75 x I x Y.
5. Labor = (labor cost/unit, last quarter) x Y; but if overtime is scheduled add 0.5 x (labor cost/unit, last quarter) x [Y - (Plant Capacity)].
6. Materials consumed = (materials cost/unit, last quarter) x Y.
16. Total expense, variable part only = sum of B1, B3, B4, B5, B6, above.

C. *Profit Before Income Tax*, variable part only = (Item A1) - (Item B16).

Now we can combine the elements listed above to get simple formulae for the variable part of Profit Before Income Tax - the exact formula depending on whether overtime is scheduled or not. We will not trouble you with the algebraic details of developing these formulae, but present the results in Table 43. Table 44 illustrates the application of Table 43 for the firm in a normal period 0 situation (Table 3, page 39) - which is the same situation to which Table 42 applies except with PRICE, MARKETING, and PRODUCTION VOLUME all viewed as variables whose values are to be proposed.

About five minutes with a pocket calculator were needed to produce the formulae in Table 44. Each calculation of "Variable Part of Profit Before Income Tax" takes about one minute, once proposed PRICE, MARKETING, and PRODUCTION VOLUME decisions are on hand. So fifteen such combinations can be compared in a quarter of an hour. But remember that the comparison is meaningful only if the proposed PRODUCTION VOLUME, Y, really is reasonably close to what market potential will turn out to be. The section on "Short-range Planning" in Chapter 3 provides bases for estimating market potential.

As a numerical example based on Table 44, consider the following two proposals:

	#1	#2
PRICE	$25.40	$25.50
MARKETING	$200,000	$250,000
PRODUCTION VOLUME	104,000	110,000

Proposal #1 does not require overtime, so the first formula of Table 44 applies:

Variable part of
Profit Before Income Tax = (25.40 - 12.76) x 104,000 - 200,000
= $1,114,560

Since Proposal #2 does require overtime, the second formula is the correct one:

Variable part of
Profit Before Income Tax = (25.50 - 15.62) x 110,000 - 250,000 + 248,756
= $1,085,556

Thus, insofar as the predictions are valid, and within the accuracy of Table 43, Proposal #1 can be expected to be over $29,000 more profitable than Proposal #2. But note well that the calculation must not be understood to suggest that Proposal #1 will yield a profit of $1,114,560; the computed figures have no meaning except as bases for comparison of the relative profitabilities of alternative proposals. And it is quite possible that such comparisons will be substantially in error, mainly because even the best estimates of market potential are not very trustworthy.

Table 43
Formulae for Estimating the Variable Part of Profit Before Income Tax, for the Purpose of Comparing Alternative Combinations of Price, Marketing, and Production Volume, Executive Game Model 1.

The letter Y denotes PRODUCTION VOLUME, assumed to be equal to market potential. The letter I denotes the inflation index for the past quarter. Also, parameters A, B, C, and D are defined as follows:

A = PRICE - (0.75 X I)

– I x (labor cost/unit, last quarter)

– I x (materials cost/unit, last quarter)

B = MARKETING BUDGET

C = A - 0.5 x I x (labor cost/unit, last quarter)

D = B + (50,000 x I)

– 0.5 x I x (labor cost/unit, last quarter) x (Production Capacity, this quarter)

If no overtime is scheduled; that is, if PRODUCTION VOLUME, Y does not exceed Plant Capacity, then
Variable part of
Profit Before Income Tax = AY – B.

Otherwise; that is, if PRODUCTION VOLUME, Y exceeds Plant Capacity (by at most 40%), then
Variable part of
Profit Before Income Tax = CY – D.

Table 44
Variable Part of Profit Before Income Tax; Dependent upon Price, Marketing, and Production Volume, for the Normal Period 0 Situation in Executive Game Model 1. Formulae Derived from Table 43.

The letter Y denotes PRODUCTION VOLUME. assumed to be equal to market potential.

A = PRICE - 0.75 x 1.00 - 1.00 x 5.71 - 1.00 x 6.30

= PRICE - 12.76

B = MARKETING

C = A - 0.5 x 1.00 x 5.71

= PRICE - 15.62

D = B + 50,000 x 1.00 - 0.5 x 1.00 x 5.71 x 104,643

= MARKETING - 248,756

If PRODUCTION VOLUME, Y, does not exceed 104,643, then
Variable part of
Profit Before Income Tax = (PRICE – 12.76) x Y – MARKETING.

If PRODUCTION VOLUME, Y, does exceed 104,643 (but is not more than the maximum possible, 146,500), then
Variable part of
Profit Before Income Tax = (PRICE – 15.62) x Y – MARKETING + 248,756.

Inventory Analysis

Numerous practical problems concerned with inventories and related purchasing and manufacturing activities can be solved through modeling and analysis. In fact, the large body of published work in this field has acquired its own name, "inventory theory." And the use of inventory analysis has become so important in recent years that the phrase "inventory revolution" has been coined, and has appeared frequently in such magazines as *Business Week* and *Fortune*.

The most sophisticated applications of inventory analysis generally require the joint efforts of line managers and technically trained staff specialists or specialized consultants. But managers without specialized technical training can often apply common-sense analytic approaches to their own practical problems, to obtain better solutions than could be expected from nonanalytic judgment. In fact, the greatest gains are often attained in this way - although inventory experts may be essential, especially when complicated computerized inventory systems are called for.

In the following sections, we shall explore ways in which you can analyze the inventory problems of your firm in the Executive Game. In some cases the solution will be laid out for you. In others we shall give clues as to how you can deal with the question at hand for yourself. And in some instances we shall frankly admit that one issue or another simply does not seem to be suitable for analytic treatment, at least short of advanced methods beyond the scope of this chapter. We shall first consider questions concerned with raw materials inventories and purchase ordering policies, and then turn to questions concerned with finished goods inventories and manufacturing schedules.

Ordering Raw Materials

Management in the Executive Game must decide how often to order raw materials, and how large each order should be. Their problem is special, as compared with the possibilities in the business world, in two ways:

1) The only intervals between orders which can be considered are multiples of one quarter; it simply isn't possible to space orders 75 days or 8 months apart.

2) The quantity ordered is always actually supplied, and on time; there are no shortages or delays in the supply process.

These features make the raw-materials-ordering problem in the Game somewhat simpler than most similar problems in the business world. But this very simplification makes the Game problem a good starting point from which to begin learning how to make practical use of inventory analysis.

Frequency of Orders. What criteria determine how frequent raw MATERIALS PURCHASE orders should be placed? In the long run we want to make ROI as large as possible. In the short run, this amounts to much the same thing as maximizing the expected value of profits. Since the frequency of purchases does not directly affect revenues (which in the Game arise solely from sales), this reduces to minimizing costs. But what costs are affected by the frequency with which orders are placed? A careful search through Chapter 4 reveals one obvious cost: the Ordering Cost itself, of $50,000 for each order placed, over and above the purchase price itself (and subject to adjustment for inflation). Neglecting inflation for the moment, if an order were placed every quarter, this cost would create an expense of $50,000 per quarter. Ordering every second quarter would result in average expense of 50,000/2 = $25,000 per quarter; ordering every third quarter would make the quarterly average $50,000/3 = $16,666.67; etc. If this were the only relevant cost, you'd want to order as infrequently as possible, It would be best to place one huge order at the beginning, to cover all future needs. This hardly seems a reasonable policy, but it emphasizes the fact that the Ordering Cost expense, considered alone, motivates you to place MATERIALS PURCHASE orders infrequently rather than frequently.

What is wrong with the "one huge order" idea? First and most obvious is its effect on the *Raw Materials Carrying Cost* (see Chapter 4 again), which is 5 percent of the value of raw materials in stock at the end of any given period. "One huge order" would make the average raw materials stock very large over the entire game, and would, therefore, lead to a very large *average* Raw Materials Carrying Cost expense. It should be obvious in fact that if you wanted solely to minimize this average expense, then the best thing to do would be to keep the raw materials stock as small as possible, by ordering for just one quarter at a time, and ordering just enough to satisfy predicted needs for processing during the "next quarter" (when the present quarter's order will become available for use).[2]

But this policy would actually *maximize* the average Ordering Cost expense. Thus, one consideration pushes you one way and the other shoves in the opposite direction. What you must do is to select the frequency of ordering which will provide the best possible *balance* between these opposing forces, in the sense of minimizing the total of average Ordering Cost expense and average Raw Material Carrying Cost expense.

We can solve this problem on the basis of two simplifying "steady state" assumptions: (i) that prices will be stable (no inflation); and (ii) that future raw materials needs will be stable (PRODUCTION VOLUME per quarter will be constant). We shall later see that these assumptions can be unrealistic and detract from the utility of the solution obtained - thus following a sequence which is common in the practical application of analytic approaches. We shall also indicate how to "generalize" the solution in order to bring into the picture two factors which we have so far neglected; to wit, the question of uncertainty about future needs for raw materials, and the question of how your cash situation affects the desirability of investing in more raw materials than you actually need to stay in business.

Steady State Solution: Part 1. We first answer the question of whether it is better to place an order every quarter, or to order every other quarter, to indicate the method of analysis. Then we shall turn to the question of what frequency of ordering is actually best.

We want to select the frequency of ordering so as to minimize the sum of two expenses:

average Ordering Cost

\+

average Raw Materials Carrying Cost

As a basis for doing this, we start by expressing this sum in specific terms.

First, suppose an order will be placed every quarter. Then average Ordering Cost = $50,000. The order must be large enough to leave raw materials in stock at the end of each quarter for the next quarter's production, and this carryover will be the same at the end of every quarter. Thus, average Raw Materials Carrying Cost will be as follows:

0.05 x (value of raw materials required for one quarter's production) = 0.05V.

---

[2] The blindly unthinking cost minimizer would simply place no orders at all (and hence incur no expenses); but we implicitly assume that what you want to do is minimize expenses subject to doing what is necessary to maximize ROI.

The symbol,

$$V = \text{value of raw materials required for one quarter's production,}$$

is introduced not for the sake of being "mathematical," but in accordance with the rule that algebraic abbreviations are worthwhile to stop formulae from becoming bulky and clumsy to write.

The total of the average costs specified in the preceding paragraph is as follows:

$$\text{Sum (order every quarter)} = 50{,}000 + 0.05V.$$

To decide whether it is better to order every quarter or every second quarter, we need a similar formula for the every-second-quarter case, so that we can compare costs. Which policy is better may, of course, depend on V.

If an order is placed every second quarter, then the average Ordering Cost expense per quarter = 50,000/2 = $25,000. It will be necessary to order enough to leave raw materials for two quarters' production in stock at the end of the quarter, and at the end of the next quarter there will be enough in stock for one quarter's production. Then another order will be placed, and the cycle will start over again. Thus, the average amount of raw materials in stock at the end of a quarter will be enough for (2 + 1)/2 = 1.5 quarters; so the average value of this turnover inventory will be 1.5V, and the average Raw Materials Carrying Cost expense will be

$$0.05 \times 1.5V = 0.075V.$$

The total of these average costs thus turns out to be as follows:

$$\text{Sum (order every 2nd quarter)} = 25{,}000 + 0.075V.$$

(Remember that V is not a "mysterious" algebraic symbol, but simply an *abbreviation* for the "value of raw materials required for one quarter's production.")

Suppose now that you estimate that V = $800,000. Then average costs can be calculated as follows:

$$\begin{aligned}\text{Sum (order every quarter)} &= 50{,}000 + 0.05 \times 800{,}000\\ &= 90{,}000\\ \text{Sum (order every 2nd quarter)} &= 25{,}000 + 0.075 \times 800{,}000\\ &= 85{,}000\end{aligned}$$

Thus, under the present assumptions, if V = $800,000, it will be better to order every second quarter than to order every quarter ($5,000 per quarter better).

Similarly, if V = $1,300,000, then it turns out, by calculations parallel to those above, that

$$\begin{aligned}\text{Sum (order every quarter)} &= 115{,}000\\ \text{Sum (order every 2nd quarter)} &= 122{,}500\end{aligned}$$

Thus, in this instance, it will be $7,500 better to order every quarter.

Next, it turns out that if V = $1,000,000, then both of the above sums come out $100,000; in this instance it doesn't matter whether you order every quarter or every other quarter. Finally, it is in fact not difficult to show that

Sum (order every 2nd quarter)

will be smaller than

Sum (order every quarter)

if and only if V, the value of raw materials required for one quarter's production, is less than \$1,000,000. We conclude that, under the present assumptions, the policy "order every second quarter" is superior to "order every quarter" if and only if $V < \$1,000,000$.

Steady State Solution: Part II. Now what about the possibility of ordering every third quarter, every fourth quarter, etc.? To generalize, let

$$N = \text{the number of quarters between orders.}$$

If orders are placed every N quarters, then the average Ordering Cost expense per quarter will be \$50,000/N. It will be necessary to order enough raw materials each time for N quarters of production, so that the carryover inventory during the N quarters of one ordering cycle will shift stepwise from NV down to V (for instance, with N = 3: 3V,2V,V; and with N = 4: 4V,3V,2V,V). It can be proved mathematically (and you can easily verify for small values of N) that the average carryover inventory will then be (NV + V)/2 (for instance, with N = 3, (3V + V)/2 = 2V; and with N = 4, (4V + V)/2 = 2.5V. Thus, the average Raw Materials Carrying Cost expense will be

$$0.05 \times \frac{NV + V}{2} = 0.025(NV + V).$$

Putting together the two expressions obtained in this paragraph, we conclude as follows:

$$\text{Sum (order every N-th quarter)} = \frac{50{,}000}{N} + 0.025(NV + V).$$

This looks complicated, but you can easily check that the two "Sum" formulae given previously are simply the cases N = 1 and N = 2. Substituting N = 3 and N = 4, we get the following new formulae:

$$\text{Sum (order every 3rd quarter)} = 16{,}666.67 + 0.10V$$
$$\text{Sum (order every 4th quarter)} = 12{,}500 + 0.125V$$

And so forth.

Now you can verify that V = \$333,333.33 is the point where "order every third quarter" is a policy equally as good as "order every second quarter," and that the former alternative is the better of the two if and only if V is smaller than \$333,333.33. Similarly, "order every fourth quarter" becomes better than "order every third quarter" if and only if V drops below \$166,666.67. These results are summarized and interpreted, with commentary, in Table 45 (where we also round the money figures to whole dollars).

Dropping the "Steady State" Assumption. Inflation enters into the raw MATERIALS PURCHASE issue in two ways. First, the "Sum" formulae above should all be corrected at any given time by applying the current inflation index to the \$50,000 ordering cost.

The presence of inflation suggests the desirability of "stocking up" at current low prices. In effect, price inflation during any given quarter can be viewed as deductible from the 5 percent Raw Materials Carrying Cost rate. For instance, if inflation is 2 percent per quarter, then the carrying cost rate, in real dollar terms, is 5% - 2% = 3%. The analytically-oriented player can easily apply this correction (using the best available estimate of near-future inflation rates).

The ordering cost also must be adjusted for inflation. For example, in trial period 1, Firm 5-4 in Table 4, the price index equals 101 (%) or 1.01 as a ratio to one. If we wish to calculate for a hypothetical period 2, we would multiply the average ordering cost per quarter, \$50,000 divided by N (the number of periods), by 1.01 to adjust for the effects of inflation; the formula would be (101/100)(\$50,000/N). Of course, we also have to adjust the carrying costs of raw materials for the effects of inflation and the opportunity cost of capital. This formula will be presented following a discussion of the opportunity cost of capital.

An exact analysis of the effects of anticipated future changes in PRODUCTION VOLUME would be extremely complicated. A rough approximation, adequate for the purposes of the Game, is to base the estimate of V upon anticipated average needs over the next two quarters. Slightly greater refinement can be attained by using more complicated quarter-by-quarter models for costing policies other than "order every quarter." Again, we suggest the exploration of such models as an exercise of possible interest to the mathematically-oriented player, rather than as a basis for significant improvements in profitability.

(Note that while we have easily brushed aside the steady state assumptions for the raw materials problem of the Game, this is not always possible for similar problems in the business world.)

Uncertainty. If circumstances change unexpectedly between the time when you order raw materials and the quarter in which they are processed, then you may want to change your anticipated PRODUCTION VOLUME decision - and thus wind up with a shortage or an overage of raw materials. Since the profit lost by missing a potential sale is generally very much greater than the cost of carrying an added unit of raw materials, it makes sense to "stay on the safe side" by keeping a buffer stock of raw materials, over and above what you expect to process. Very roughly speaking, you should plan for large enough raw material stocks to fulfill your most "optimistic" guesses about how you may wish to increase PRODUCTION VOLUME. The mathematically-minded game player can develop an analytic model, based on the same ideas as those in the discussion (below) of the effect of uncertainty on decisions about finished goods inventory and production scheduling.

Table 45

Optimal Raw Materials Ordering Policies under Steady State Conditions, Dependent upon Production Volume per Quarter.

The inflation index is assumed to be 1.00, and the effects of uncertainly about future needs for raw materials are ignored, as are questions concerning the desirability of investing in more raw materials than are actually neded to stay in business.

Dollar value of raw materials required per quarter for the needed PRODUCTION VOLUME.	Frequency of raw MATERIALS PURCHASE decisions (other than "zero" = no purchase)
$1,000,000 or more	every quarter
$333,333 - $999,999	every second quarter
$166,667 - $333,332	every third quarter
$100,000 - $166,666	every fourth quarter
less than $100,000	less often than every fourth quarter*

*Any firm in the Executive Game which actually anticipates needing less than $100,000 per quarter in raw materials will be in such disastrous shape that such niceties as optimal purchasing policy will be of little concern. In fact, the first two lines of this table will probably be sufficient for any viable firm.

In principle, such a model could also cover the tendency of uncertainty to favor delaying decisions until they are really needed, but we frankly do not see how to take advantage of this possibility. In any case, we do not judge it to be an important matter, in terms of profitability. A rough qualitative analysis indicates that this tendency militates for frequent rather than infrequent raw MATERIALS PURCHASE orders.

Cash Flow Considerations. The biggest gap in the above analysis, both within the Game and in terms of practical applications in the business world, is the neglect of cash flow considerations. "Stocking up" on two or more quarters' needs of raw materials would tie up money which might be better used - for other operating budgets, for dividends, or to minimize the costs of current cash shortages or the possible dangers of future shortages. The 5 percent Raw Materials Carrying Cost covers only the out-of-pocket expenses of raw materials inventories (warehousing, insurance, and the like). Your firm's "opportunity cost" of capital should really be added to this 5 percent, to determine the true level of the Raw Materials Carrying Cost. This is another factor which will tend to militate for frequent rather than infrequent ordering.

This opportunity cost of capital represents the percentage return (or equivalent in terms of stockholder satisfaction or risk reduction) that you could get from the best alternative use of the money concerned. It may be as low as zero (for instance, when you are holding unused cash in anticipation of future expansion). But if you are short of cash and must consequently slash budgets, it is not unlikely that judicious assignments to MARKETING or R&D will in effect return the amount spent, plus 10 percent or 20 percent per annum, and possibly more. At the higher rate (5 percent per quarter), the Raw Materials Carrying Cost should be increased from 5 percent to 10 percent. You can easily check that this change will make it optimal to place raw MATERIALS PURCHASE orders every quarter if quarterly consumption exceeds $500,000 - which means "almost always" for a successful firm in the Executive Game.

It is almost impossible to accurately forecast the ROI for a marketing, R&D, etc. incremental expenditure. Therefore, let's consider some practical methods of estimating the opportunity cost of capital. It may be as high as the financing charges and penalties that must be paid for a cash deficit if there were to be a cash deficit. However, assuming that the best alternative investment of the money to be invested in raw materials would yield a higher ROI than the cost rate for financing charges and penalties, how can such a ROI be estimated? It is suggested that the firm's ROI per quarter before taxes be used as a rough approximation to the opportunity cost of capital. Assuming that the firm's management attempts to invest in an optimal fashion and has already made all of the decisions except for the purchase of raw materials, the average ROI before taxes should be a rough approximation to the opportunity cost of capital from the standpoint of the firm's management.

In spite of the difficulties and erratic nature of forecasting, firms may choose to estimate the opportunity cost of capital from the latest forecasts available. For example, if a firm's forecasted owner's economic equity at the end of trial period 1 was $10,017,622, the dividends paid in trial period 1 were $53,000, and the forecasted income taxes for trial period 1 were $128,549; thus, the equation for calculating the estimated ROI before taxes was $9,700,000 = (10,017,622 + 53,000 + 128,549)/(1 + (.01)ROI), so 9,700,000(1 + (.01)(ROI) = 10,017,622 + 53,000 + 128,549. Therefore, the forecasted ROI per quarter before taxes = 5.1%. Since the firm did not have a projected cash deficit at the end of trial period 1, the financing charges and penalties would be zero ($0). Therefore, the firm should use 5.1 percent per quarter for its opportunity cost of capital for a decision involving the purchase of raw materials in trial period 1.

In order to demonstrate how to calculate the financing charges and penalties rate, let's pretend that the firm had a forecasted cash deficit of $379,147 at the end of trial period 1. The financing charges and penalties for a subsequent hypothetical period 2 would be .9 x (-379,147) x [1 + .05] / 10,000,000 = $13,585; therefore, the rate per quarter = 13,585 / 379,149 = 3.6%. Again, 3.6 percent is less than 5.1 percent so the firm should use 5.1 percent per quarter as a rough estimate of the opportunity cost of capital.

Obviously, the opportunity cost of capital must at least equal the rate of financing charges and penalties since this would be the cost to carry a cash deficit in order to purchase raw materials. In fact we really would like to know the marginal opportunity cost of capital but this may be impractical to figure in the Game. The ROI before taxes is an average rate and if it is higher than the financing charges and penalties rate we might use it as the estimated opportunity cost of capital (even if there is no cash deficit). Because this size of a cash deficit is unlikely to exceed the amount invested in raw materials, and, based upon the assumptions stated in the next paragraph, we believe that these average ROIs and financing charges and penalties rates will be a good approximation to the opportunity cost of capital.

A positive cash position may be considered to be a buffer stock of money which certainly has a tangible value as a hedge against a cash deficit. We are assuming that the firm's management operates the company as near optimally as possible; thus, they are budgeting as much as they think is optimal for marketing, R&D, maintenance, production, investments in plant and equipment and robotics, purchase of raw materials, and dividends. Likewise, they also have set their price at what they consider to be an optimal level.

Now, if they still have a huge cash surplus, then they have not been doing a good job. In such an instance, their opportunity cost of capital may be considered to be zero even if there is a sharp inflation. The smallest possible value for the opportunity cost of capital is zero.[3]

However, in most instances firms will not have a large cash surplus. Thus, the projected quarterly ROI before taxes will frequently be the best available estimate of the opportunity cost of capital. Alternatively, one might calculate the financing charges and penalties for the subsequent quarter if the firm has a projected cash deficit for that quarter, and use the larger of financing charges and penalties and ROI as the estimated opportunity cost of capital.

Remember, the opportunity cost of capital can only be approximated subjectively. In general it is not possible to forecast it precisely, but even a crude approximation can be very valuable.

The complete formula for the average carrying cost of raw materials per quarter follows:

$$(.05 - \text{quarterly inflation rate} + \text{quarterly opportunity cost of capital})(NV + V)/2.$$

The complete formula for the average ordering cost per quarter follows:

$$\$50{,}000(.01PI1)/N.$$

Upon substituting the estimated value of the value of raw materials needed per quarter, V, and the price index for the period just completed, PI1, then you simply calculate the carrying costs and ordering costs for values of N = 1,2,3,etc. and select the number of periods N for which you will order raw materials such that the sum of ordering costs and carrying costs per quarter are minimized. This is demonstrated in Table 46 for a case where the inflation rate equals 2 percent per quarter and the opportunity cost of capital equals 6 percent per quarter.

---

[3] In the real world, the quarterly opportunity cost of capital would never fall below, say, the ROI on a 91 day treasury bill.

A Final Word About Raw Materials. Most of the considerations not explicitly reflected in Table 46 are either of small importance or tend to favor frequent purchases of raw materials. With this in mind, we judge that successful firms (usually operating at fairly high production levels) should almost always place purchase orders every quarter. On the other hand, a firm operating at a low production level is likely to be in trouble, and suffering from a lack of cash - so that the opportunity cost of money (needed perhaps to cut losses rather than to enhance profits) is likely to be large, and quarterly purchases are again likely to be best. In summary, we recommend that "order every quarter" be considered the norm, with consideration given to less frequent purchases only under exceptional conditions (no serious cash shortage in spite of low-volume operations, or lots of cash on hand combined with moderate volume).

You may well wonder if the lengthy discussion just concluded was worthwhile, since the final conclusion is that you should almost always follow the most obvious and natural policy with respect to ordering raw materials. The answer is that this conclusion has only become clear after the analysis. By changing some of the numbers in the Game we could change this conclusion - and of course your Game administrator might choose to make such changes - although we assume that this will not be done without giving proper warnings to the players, and appropriate suggestions concerning the sort of responses they should make.

Table 46

Optimal Raw Material Ordering Policies under an Inflation Rate of 2 Percent per Quarter and an Opportunity Cost of Capital Of 5.1 Percent per Quarter, Dependent upon Value of Raw Materials Consumed per Quarter.

The effects of uncertainty about future needs for raw materials are ignored, as are questions concerning the desirability of investing in more raw materials than are actually needed to stay in business. For a hypothetical period 1.

FORMULAE:

CARRYING COSTS	ORDERING COSTS
=(.05-.02+.051) (NV+V)/2	=.01P11(50,000)/N
=.0405 (NV+V)	=1.00(50,000)/N

Dollar value of raw materials required per quarter for the needed PRODUCTION VOLUME	Frequency of raw Materials PURCHASE decisions (other than "zero"=no purchase)
$617,284 or more	every quarter
$205,761 - $617,283	every second quarter
$102,881 - $205,760	every third quarter
$61,728 - $102,880	every fourth quarter*
Less than $61,728	less often than every fourth quarter*

*Any firm in the Executive Game which actually anticipates needing less than $100,000 per quarter in raw materials will be in such disastrous shape that such niceties as optimal purchasing policy will be of little concern.

Finished Goods Inventory and Production Schedules

A long-range plan normally centers around sales volume objectives, and corresponding management of plant size through PLANT AND EQUIPMENT INVESTMENT decisions. As the time approaches for actually supplying the goods, sales objectives give way to forecasts of market potential, taking into account policies and specific decisions about such quantities as PRICE, MARKETING, and R&D - and often giving cause for reconsideration of these decisions when market potential is judged to be out of step with plant size. In this maze of interacting plans, decisions, and anticipations, it is often natural for the actual PRODUCTION VOLUME decisions to be the last ones made (except possibly for the size of raw MATERIALS PURCHASE orders), because they most insistently demand close adjustment to the latest available information.

For instance, as perhaps the most obvious example, suppose that market potential has been overestimated in the past, so that a large stock of finished goods remains unsold in the inventory carried over from "last quarter." Then, ordinarily, at least, PRODUCTION VOLUME should be cut sharply, in order to reduce the excessive inventory in spite of realistically lowered estimates of market potential. In rare cases it may even make sense to stop production completely. But, of course, it is far better not to get into such situations in the first place.

PRODUCTION VOLUME is not the only decision which should respond to the most recent information. For instance, a poor sales record suggests cutting PRICE, or intensifying MARKETING efforts, with the complication that poor sales often imply a shortage of cash, which viewed separately, suggests budget cuts. But it is still natural and desirable to make a final review of the PRODUCTION VOLUME decision after the other decisions are in, and after short-run forecasts of market potential have been updated in accordance with these decisions as well as recent sales information - remembering, though, that the hoped-for "final" PRODUCTION VOLUME decisions may point to the need to reconsider other decisions, and then again to look for genuinely "final" PRODUCTION VOLUME choices. This section is primarily concerned with the questions which need to be considered in making these "final" choices.

We have noted that PRODUCTION VOLUME should be affected by the carryover inventory of finished goods as well as by the anticipated market potential. More precisely, the quantity which should be more or less directly related to market potential is the total quantity of finished goods available for sale during the quarter; that is, the following sum:

PRODUCTION VOLUME
+
Carryover inventory of finished
goods, from "last quarter"

In the simplest possible manufacturing/marketing situation, this sum should be equated to anticipated market potential, thus supplying all the demand created without incurring any Finished Goods Carrying Cost expense (see Chapter 4). But the PRODUCTION VOLUME decision in the Game is much more complicated. You must of course stay within the availability of raw materials and within your plant's capability to produce goods. The large costs associated with overtime (and, in Model 2, with changing the number of shifts) are often important considerations. Especially in view of these costs, predicted seasonal effects should be anticipated, rather than taken into account at the last moment. Finally, the uncertain accuracy of forecasts of market potential must be taken into account. Except in regard to uncertainty, this section will focus on clarifying the problems to be dealt with, so that you can handle them for yourself, rather than presenting neatly packaged answers. In the case of uncertainty we shall suggest answers, but because of the inherent difficulties of the problems concerned, the answers will by no means be "neatly packaged."

Limits on Production. If anticipated market potential exceeds your firm's ability to supply finished goods, then you are not yet ready to attempt a PRODUCTION VOLUME decision. Usually it is appropriate in these circumstances to reconsider PRICE and MARKETING decisions (see Chapter 3). If you can only supply so many units of your product, then there is no point in pricing so low that more would be bought if available, or in paying good money to stimulate demand which your firm cannot satisfy.

Overtime and Shift Changes. Even though you might be able to afford overtime labor rates, the substantial administrative costs of scheduling overtime production may not be worthwhile (see Chapter 4, and the "Profit Models" earlier in this chapter). Thus, if anticipated market potential indicates a need for overtime production, it is sensible to consider an alternative, usually with increased PRICE or a decreased MARKETING budget, in which overtime will not be necessary. In effect, you hypothesize an alternative in which PRODUCTION VOLUME is limited to "regular-time" (nonovertime) production capacity.

In Model 2, the cogent "normal capacity" is the "regular-time" capacity of the number of shifts currently employed. You may also have to consider increasing (or possibly decreasing) the number of shifts. If such a change is temporary, it is quite likely that a new plan, not requiring the change, will be better, because of the large costs of changing the number of shifts (see Chapter 4 again). On the other hand, the cost of a relatively permanent change in the number of shifts can be spread over many quarters, and therefore may be a relatively minor consideration.

Seasonal Cycles. If your plant size is closely tuned to market potential, taking a quarter-by-quarter aim at current market potential may lead to the need for overtime production at the crest of the seasonal cycle, with corresponding "undertime" at the trough. You can easily verify that, in such a situation, it will be economical to overproduce during the slack season and thus build up a stock of goods to satisfy peak demand. This policy will generate Finished Goods Carrying Cost expense, but (with possible rare exceptions) this will be justified by the resulting savings in overtime costs.

As an alternative, you may wish to consider enlarging plant capacity so that even peak demand can be satisfied by current production, without the use of overtime. The key question is whether the resulting savings (mainly in Finished Goods Carrying Cost expenses) are sufficient to justify the needed capital investment. This is a question concerning the "opportunity cost" of capital, and is thus related to the issues raised under the heading "Cash flow considerations," near the end of the above section on "Ordering Raw Materials."

Uncertainty: The Basic Issue. The problems discussed up to this point in the present section, although not necessarily easy to solve at all or possible to solve precisely, can reasonably be attacked without special technical tools. Now we turn to the somewhat more difficult question of coping with the uncertain accuracy of forecasts of market potential. Unfortunately, our treatment of this matter, although unavoidably complex, cannot possibly be complete, even within the artificial limits of the difficulties posed by the Executive Game.

The most obvious response to uncertainty is to ignore it, by acting as if your guesses about the future were actually accurate predictions. Such a procedure can even be made to seem "scientific," at least on the surface - by calling your guess an "estimate" of the mode, or mean, or median of the "probability distribution of demand." But no matter how soundly based such an estimate may be, to treat it as an exact prediction is hardly more logical than deciding not to carry automobile insurance on the ground that "zero" is the most likely number of accidents you'll have during the coming year. Just as you should consider the (ordinarily small) possibility that you will have accidents, so should you consider the (surely large) likelihood that your firm's actual market potential in the Game will be significantly different from whatever advance estimate you can make.

A rough-and-ready approach which does face uncertainty head-on, but with no attempt at precision of formulation or solution, starts from the observation that the profit lost by missing a potential sale is ordinarily quite a bit greater than the cost of carrying an added unit of finished product in carryover inventory. This suggests (and a more precise analysis to be developed below validates the suggestion) that a firm should generally guard against finished goods shortages, by supplying enough goods for sale to make "selling out" unlikely. This is expressed by the following:

Rule of thumb. Set PRODUCTION VOLUME so that you judge it to be unlikely (but not impossible) that your firm will "sell out" its stock of finished goods.

This rule is quite frankly ambiguous. Making it a matter of what "you judge" is certainly not solving the problem; and the phrase "unlikely (but not impossible)" has at best a fuzzy meaning. Still, the idea of the rule is clear. As it stands it is surely better than no rule at all.

Uncertainty: The Critical Ratio Rule. It turns out that we can give a precise probability meaning to the phrase "unlikely (but not impossible)," a meaning which, in fact, can be numericized with enough accuracy for practical use. We shall now derive the resulting "critical ratio rule." At first reading the analysis may seem somewhat tricky, but it will be worth your while to stick with it until you fully understand the procedure, since the same approach applies to a wide variety of business problems.

The basic idea, in its application to the problem at hand, is that *if* you can find a general rule for deciding whether a hypothetical PRODUCTION VOLUME decision would be improved if it were increased by one (1 unit of product), *then* this rule can be used to identify the best possible PRODUCTION VOLUME - below which additions are desirable and above which they are undesirable. To search for the general rule, suppose we start with an unrealistically small PRODUCTION VOLUME decision. Under what conditions will an increase of one (1 unit of product) lead to a resulting increase in the probabilistic expected value of profits?

To help toward answering this question, we define the following algebraic notations:

1) Let $P(D<i)$ be the probability that the added unit i will not be sold if it is manufactured. Then $P(D \geq i)$ is also the probability that the unit i will be sold.

2) Let X be the loss of underage which results from failure to manufacture one unit which could have been sold. This is called the "opportunity loss" from failing to manufacture a salable unit. (As a first approximation, X is the gross profit per unit; selling price minus cost of manufacture. But see below.)

3) Let Y be the loss of overage which results from manufacturing one unit which cannot be sold. This is called the "opportunity loss" from manufacturing an unsalable unit. (As a first approximation, Y is the cost of carrying a leftover in inventory.)

Now we can use these notations to calculate the probabilistic expected value of the change in opportunity losses which will result from adding the extra unit to the original PRODUCTION VOLUME:

— With probability $P(D \geq i)$ an extra unit would have been sold, resulting in an opportunity loss of X which resulted from the failure to manufacture the unit.

—With probability $P(D<i)$ the extra unit will not be sold, resulting in an opportunity loss of Y which resulted from the failure to sell the unit.

Clearly we wish to manufacture those units and only those units for which the loss of stocking is less than the loss of not stocking; so it follows that

$$YP(D < i) < XP(D \geq i).$$

It is easier to find the highest value i* which satisfies the above inequation by dealing with only one cumulative probability so we replace $P(D \geq i)$ by $[1-P(D< i)]$.

By a little elementary algebraic manipulation this can be put into the following convenient form

$$P(D < i) < X / (X + Y).$$

The optimal stock level is the highest value of i, i*, which satisfies the above inequation. Or expressed in another way, we should choose the total stock to be made available (PRODUCTION VOLUME plus carryover inventory of finished goods from "last quarter") so that the probability of "not stocking out" will be as close as possible below and to $X/(X+Y)$.

The last ratio is called the critical ratio. In mixed algebraic notation and words, it is defined by the following:

$$\text{Critical ratio} = \frac{\text{Opportunity loss from failing to manufacture a salable unit}}{\text{Opportunity loss from failing to manufacture a salable unit} + \text{Opportunity loss from manufacturing an unsalable unit}}$$

Putting aside the need to "round off" to whole units of product (which is insignificant in the Game, but not in all applications), we now interpret the last statement in the preceding paragraph, as follows:

> Critical ratio rule. Set PRODUCTION VOLUME so that you judge the probability of "not selling out" to be equal to the critical ratio.
>
> In applications, the specific value of the critical ratio is estimated numerically. If, for instance, this estimate turns out to be 0.75, then the rule takes the following more definite form: Set PRODUCTION VOLUME so that you judge the probability of 'not selling out' to be 0.75; or, conversely, so that you judge the probability of 'selling out' to be 0.25; (i.e., 1-0.75=0.25).

Uncertainty: Estimating the Critical Ratio. In the Executive Game, the opportunity loss from manufacturing an unsalable unit is, at least to a satisfactorily close approximation, equal to the cost of carrying the unit in inventory. The main component of this cost is the out-of-pocket Finished Goods Carrying Cost of $2.00 per unit, adjusted for inflation (see Chapter 4). But this figure should really be augmented by an allowance for the opportunity value of money invested in the unit - a percentage of the following sum:

Direct cost per unit = Cost per unit of labor
\+ Cost per unit of raw materials
\+ Cost per unit of maintenance.

Guidelines for estimating the correct percentage (normally less than 10 percent, in our judgment) were sketched under the heading "Cash Flow considerations," near the end of the earlier section on "Ordering Raw Materials."

The opportunity loss from failing to manufacture a salable unit is somewhat more complicated. A natural starting point is the immediate short-run loss from not making the sale:

Gross profit per unit = Selling PRICE per unit − Direct cost per unit.

(Direct cost per unit is defined above.) This is only a "starting point," first because about 40 percent of the buyers left unsatisfied by a stockout return to the same firm to make their purchase in the following quarter, so a second approximation is 60 percent of the gross profit. In fact, though, this figure should be adjusted upward to account for the loss of "goodwill" when customers are turned away, to about 70 percent of the gross profit (see the material in Chapter 2 under the heading "Stockouts and Customer Reorders" p. 19).

This (70 percent of the gross profit per unit) is our final estimate of the opportunity loss from failing to manufacture a salable unit. It is still not, however, a really "hard" figure, mainly because of complicated factors concerned with quarter-to-quarter interactions - relating especially to the fact that units stockpiled to fulfill future demand can to some extent "double" as safeguards against current stockouts. It appears that this last phenomenon may sometimes be significant, but we simply have not been able to find a workable way to bring it within the scope of analysis.

As a numerical example, consider the situation sketched for forecast period 5, page 80, in a past run of the Executive Game. The out-of-pocket Finished Goods Carrying Cost is 2.00 x 1.047 = $2.09 per unit. Assuming for the moment that Firm 5-4 will be manufacturing entirely in "regular time," we calculate:

$$\text{Direct cost per unit} = 5.57 + 6.02 + 0.75 \times 1.072 = \$12.39.$$

Noting that Firm 5-4 would have projected a cash deficit of $1,285,425 in period 5, we estimate the current opportunity cost of cash to be $156,144/$1,285,425 = 0.121 or 12.1 percent per quarter, based upon the projected financing charges and penalties in period 6, divided by the estimated cash deficit in period 5 before taxes is only ($9,869,996 + $300,000 + $186,261)/$10,105,142 = 1.025. Since 2.5% < 12.1% we use 12.1% as the estimated cost of capital. The carrying cost augmentation for the opportunity cost of money is, hence, 12.39 x .121 = $1.50. We conclude that the opportunity loss from manufacturing an unsalable unit is about 2.09 + 1.50 = $3.59. Now we calculate:

$$\text{Gross profit per unit} = 26.32 - 12.39 = \$13.93$$

Our estimate of the opportunity loss from failing to manufacture a salable unit is thus 0.70 x 13.93 = $9.75. Hence, we estimate the critical ratio as follows:

$$\text{Critical ratio} = \frac{9.75}{9.75 + 3.59} = 0.73$$

Our advice for the management of Firm 5-4 would thus be as follows: "Assuming you will be producing only on 'regular time,' set PRODUCTION VOLUME so that you judge the probability of 'not selling out' to be 0.73."

Now let's estimate the critical ratio for the overtime situation. If "regular time" labor cost ($5.57 per unit) is replaced by the overtime cost (1.5($5.57) = $8.36 per unit) the new estimate of direct cost per unit becomes:

Direct cost per unit = 1.5($5.57) + $6.02 + 0.75(1.072) = $15.18.

The carrying cost augmentation for the opportunity cost of capital is, hence, $15.18(.121) = $1.84. We conclude that the opportunity loss from manufacturing an unsalable unit at overtime is about $2.09 + $1.84 = $3.93. Now we calculate:

Gross profit per unit (overtime) = $26.32 - $15.18 = $11.14.

Our estimate of the opportunity loss from failing to manufacture a salable unit is thus 0.70($15.18) = $7.80. Hence, we estimate the critical ratio as follows:

$$\text{Critical ratio (overtime)} = \frac{7.80}{7.80 + 3.93} = 0.66$$

An Approach to Error Estimation.

Let's pretend that you have used the very subjective approach outlined above for the trial period 1 and the first four periods of the Game. Thus you will have forecasted market potential five times. Possibly you have been a bit discouraged with your forecasting results. But, assuming that you have done a conscientious job, you should be in a good position to exploit the error distribution of your forecasts.

In fact, most suggestions for computing the "fudge" factors have been based upon a historical record of the firm's forecasting errors and we subscribe to that method also as soon as a historical record becomes available to the firm. By the end of the first four quarters of play, including trial period 1, you should have a record of five of your own forecasting errors, and these together should put you in a better position to "fudge" sensibly. Also, at the end of the fiscal year you will receive information about other firms' carryover inventories, which at least will give you some hints about the errors they have been making, and hence about the sort of errors you should also expect to make.

As the Game proceeds, your records of the errors of earlier estimates become more and more significant. In fact, when the number of sample errors M has become large enough you can apply a formal procedure for estimating the correct "fudge factor." This is based on the hypothesis that the past record of the magnitude of your errors is the best available indicator of current performance - which may be a pessimistic assumption, in case you are learning to forecast better, or an optimistic one in case your forecasting procedure is deteriorating as the action of the Game moves away from the initial situation to which the material in Chapter 3 is most directly applicable.

From Table 40, pp. 76-83, we can calculate the forecasting errors made by Firm 5-4 in trial period 1, real periods 1,2,3,&4, respectively. For this purpose we define the forecasting errors as the actual market potentials minus the corresponding forecasted market potentials, which gives

102,156 - 120,000 = -17,844; 164,930 - 153,160 = +11,770;
161,444 - 151,387 = +10,057; 123,006 - 138,000 = -14,994;
and, 132,708 - 142,000 = -9,292.

These "errors" are arranged in order of ascending size and applied to Firm 5-4's forecasted market potential for period 5 of 140,000 units from Table 40, p. 80. This procedure produces the fractiles in column (3) of Table 47, below. Fractiles are like percentiles except they are ratios to one instead of percentages which are ratios to 100. These fractiles represent projected levels of the market potentials for Firm 5-4's finished goods in period 5. In column (4) of Table 47 we present cumulative relative frequencies which we shall use as a basis for estimating probabilities that the actual market potential for Firm 5-4 in period 5 will be less than or equal to the corresponding fractiles in column (3).

The cumulative frequencies in this kind of a problem in column (4) of Table 47 are computed as $k/(M+1), k=1,2,...,M$; $M=5$, rather than k/M. Intuitively it is easy to understand that a random sample of only 5 market potentials contains neither the lowest nor the highest possible market potentials; therefore, 122,156 and 151,770 are not sensible estimates of the lowest and highest market potentials for Firm 5-4 in period 5; thus, computing the cumulative relative frequencies as k/M would not be logical. It is easy to see that k/M must be wrong but seeing that $k/(M+1)$ is correct is not so easy. A good discussion of this matter (as well as most of the other concepts that we are utilizing in this section of Chapter 5) may be found in Robert Schlaifer's book *Introduction to Statistics for Business Decisions,* McGraw-Hill, 1961, pp. 111-12.

The next question for which the solution must be found is whether to use the "absolute" forecasting errors or the "relative" forecasting errors as a basis for calculating the fractiles. The absolute forecasting errors were defined (in Table 47) to be the actual market potentials minus the forecasted market potentials, while the relative forecasting errors are defined to be the actual market potentials minus the forecasted market potentials all divided by the forecasted market potentials.

Conceptually the relative forecasting errors are more appealing while the absolute forecasting errors are somewhat easier to work with. Experience with this kind of problem has shown that both methods work about equally well in the XGAME because of the rather constrained nature of the fractiles therein. Therefore, we shall use the absolute forecasting errors to analyze this problem.

Table 47

Computing Procedure for using the Records of your Past Forecasting Errors to Answer the "key Question" in the use of the Critical Ratio Method

(1) Forecast, Market Potential, Per. 5		(2) Forecast Errors		(3) Fractiles	(4) Cumulative Relative Frequencies
140,000	–	17,844	=	122,156	1/(5+1) = 0.167
"	–	14,994	=	125,006	2/(5+1) = 0.333
"	–	9,292	=	130,708	3(5+1) = 0.500
"	+	10,057	=	150,057	4/(5+1) = 0.667
"	+	11,770	=	151,770	5/(5+1) = 0.833
		Average	=	135,939	

Source of Data: Table 40, pp. 76-83.

First we would like to suggest a simple rule of thumb for deciding whether to produce at regular time or overtime in models 1 and 2, or, in model 2 only, at two shifts, two shifts with overtime, or at three shifts. As a simple rule of thumb, we shall decide to operate in whichever one of the above ranges that our best estimate of average market potential minus inventory of finished goods in stock, falls within (see Table 48).

Table 48
Application of the Rule of Thumb for a Firm 5-4 in Period 5. Compare Average Market Potential Minus Stock with Ranges Shown.

(1)	(2)	(3)	(4)	(5)
Regular Time Basis Prod. Vol.	Overtime Basis Prod. Vol.	2-Shift Basis Prod. Vol.	2-Shift with Overtime Basis Prod. Vol.	3-Shift Basis Prod. Vol.
0 - 124,499	124,500 - 174,299	174,300 - 248,998	248,999 - 311,247	311,248 - 373,497

Source: Based upon data from Tables 20 and 40, pp. 56 and 76-83.

In order to estimate the average market potential, take the simple unweighted average of the fractiles. For example, from column (3) of Table 47, the average is 135,939. If this average minus inventory of finished goods in stock at the end of period 4 is less than normal plant capacity next quarter (124,499 units for period 5, Table 40, p. 80) use the critical ratio (regular time) of 0.73 and place a limit on production of finished goods up to normal plant capacity.

Actually the projected average market potential for period 5 (135,939 from column (3) of Table 47) minus the stock of finished goods at the end of period 4 (39,286 from Table 40, p. 80) equals 135,939 - 39,286 = 96,653 < 124,499. Therefore, using the rule of thumb, the maximum production during period 5 should be 124,499.

The fractiles and cumulative probabilities from Table 47, columns (3) and (4), respectively, are plotted on Chart 2. Stairsteps are drawn through these points and a smooth curve, bisecting the stairsteps, has been plotted thereon. Reading 0.73 on the vertical axis and drawing a line parallel to the horizontal axis over to the curve and dropping a perpendicular to the horizontal axis locates the 0.73 fractile. As can be seen, the 0.73 fractile is about 152,000 units. Subtracting 39,286 units of inventory gives 112,214 units of production. Since our rule of thumb tells us that 124,499 is the maximum production level, you should end up producing all 112,214 units. Note that Firm 5-4 didn't use the critical ratio method for period 5 and they ended up producing 158,000 units. Obviously if they had produced only 112,214 units, they would have achieved much better results (see p. 80, Table 40).

Table 48 shows the relevant range for application of the rule of thumb.

In the above example, average market potential of 135,939 minus stock of 39,286 = 96,653 which is less than 124,499, so production volume is constrained by the rule of thumb to be less than or equal to 124,499 units in period 5 (see column (2) of Table 48).

Chart 2
Absolute Error Distribution for a Firm 5-4 for Period 5, Estimation of the 0.73 Fractile

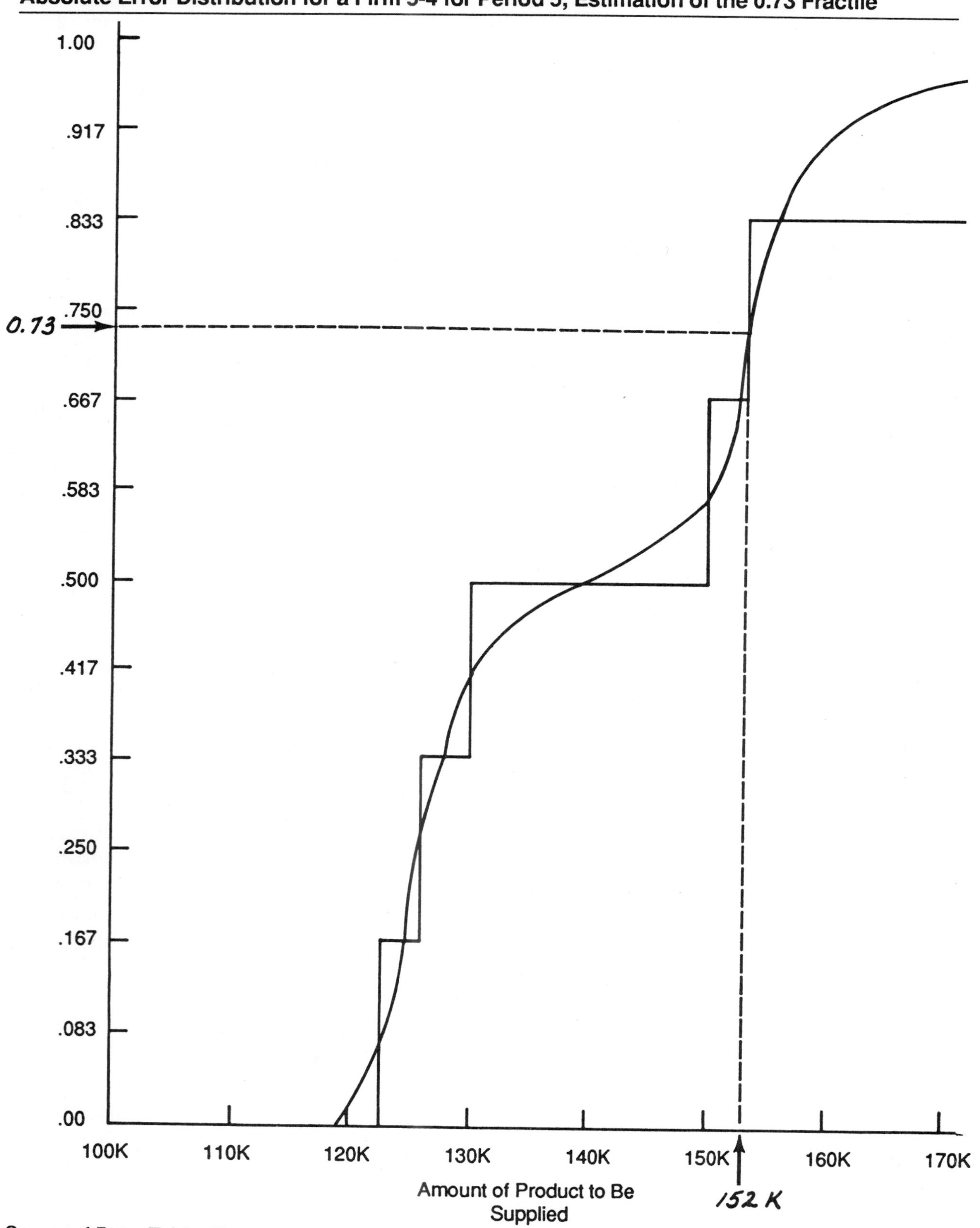

Source of Data: Table 47, p. 130.

Amount of Instability in the Critical Ratio.

An important question is whether the critical ratio should be forecasted for each quarter. It depends on how much work you are willing to do. We recommend that you forecast the critical ratio for each quarter. In order to give you some guidance, we calculated the critical ratio for each quarter of a Game for a specific firm and present them in Table 49.

Table 49
Fluctuations in the Critical Ratios for a Specific Firm in a Game.

Period		Regular time basis		Overtime basis			Forecast
	X	Y	X/(X+Y)	X'	Y'	X'/(X'+Y')	Infl. Rate
T1	$8.97	$2.32	0.79	$6.97	$2.39	0.74	5.0%
1	8.70	2.46	0.78	6.63	2.57	0.72	5.0
2	8.84	3.03	0.74	6.83	3.25	0.68	5.3
3	9.14	2.29	0.80	7.11	2.35	0.75	5.0
4	8.24	2.32	0.78	6.10	2.36	0.72	4.3
5	8.58	2.63	0.77	6.43	2.73	0.70	4.0
6	8.61	2.61	0.77	6.32	2.70	0.70	4.0
7	9.29	2.81	0.77	7.01	2.93	0.71	4.3
8	9.29	2.93	0.76	6.94	3.07	0.69	4.8

As can be seen from Table 49, the critical ratio for the firm ranged from 0.77 to 0.82 on a regular time basis and from 0.72 to 0.78 on an overtime basis. The annual inflation rate forecast ranged from 4.0 percent to 5.3 percent. With greater inflation, the variability can be expected to be greater.

You can start using the critical ratio as soon as real period 1 results are available; i.e, for real period 2. This may be before many Game administrators are ready for you to use it. We frequently don't suggest that players start using it before period 5. It just depends on how much emphasis the Game gets in a particular class.

A very important rule for every class, however, is that players should make a forecast of their market potential every quarter beginning with trial period 1. Of course, if you fill out the large worksheet in Appendix F, which we strongly recommend, you will automatically make a forecast of your market potential each quarter.

RESEARCH AND DEVELOPMENT, INVESTMENTS IN PLANT AND EQUIPMENT, AND IN ROBOTICS

We have combined these two transactions for discussion purposes because both are definitely oriented toward a long-range horizon.

A multi-faceted variable like R&D seems difficult to analyze. It increases the firm's market share and reduces the firm's labor and materials cost per unit of production. Also, in the long run it reduces the price elasticity of the industry's product more than the marketing budget does.

However, it can be difficult to determine these effects because there are no effects whatsoever in the period in which the expenditure is made. The effects begin in the next period and are cumulative for a sustained program.

In a hypothetical situation in which a firm increased its R&D budget by $25,000 in period 1 and then reduced it by $25,000 to its original level for the next three periods, the net payoff after taxes turned out to be over 12 percent per quarter through period 4. This hypothetical situation assumed no inflation, no seasonal variation, a constant economic index, and, except for the additional $25,000 expenditure on R&D in period 1, the same decisions on price, marketing, R&D, maintenance, production, investment in plant (and equipment), purchase of raw materials, and dividends declared by the competitors. Furthermore, there were no significant stockouts or instances of overstocking.

A net payoff of 12 percent per quarter after taxes seems very profitable but remember that this was a hypothetical situation where there was a balance between availability of product and market potential, the correct amount of raw materials were ordered, an optimum maintenance program was followed, etc. There is no way that a real firm in the Game can match these decisions.

In order to have a profitable R&D budget program you have to implement a policy of stable to increasing production, a good balance between the availability of goods and market potential, and a moderate to aggressive plant and equipment investment program. The risks are large; an aggressive program combined with erratic results can lead to large losses. It is well worth considering a modest R&D program combined with a strong effort to be competitive in price and marketing programs.

Now let's consider the opportunities associated with investment in plant and equipment. This is the most multifaceted problem in the Game. If the Game administrator has put the investment tax credit into effect it will make investments in plant and equipment more attractive. In the Game we assume that investments in plant are divided 50/50 between plant and equipment. Equipment gets a 10 percent credit so it's easy to see that this amounts to 5 percent of the total investment which is abbreviated in the Game as investment in plant.

It is much better in the Game to program your investments in plant and equipment smoothly. Erratic programs consisting of big variations in investments from huge amounts in some quarters to little or no investments in other quarters will be penalized by the plant investment expenses function. Remember that this function reflects legal, architectural, and consulting engineering firms' fees for planning purposes, and, costs of disruptions due to new plant additions and new equipment installations and start-up costs. It is equal to $(\$\text{Plant Investment})^2/(10{,}000{,}000)$.

Another thing to consider when evaluating plant investment is the system. Average depreciation is 2.5 percent per quarter of plant net book value whereas the plant (and equipment) in the Game actually deteriorates at 2.0 percent per quarter. This makes current expenses appear spuriously large, but, actually has the effect of reducing taxes which, of course, makes real income larger; of course, it makes investments in plant and equipment more profitable.

Further, inflation is a strong incentive for plant and equipment investment particularly since the plant replacement value grows with the general price index.

Now in a hypothetical situation, a firm invested the following amounts in plant and equipment and the annual inflation rate per quarter also are shown. As you can see the inflation rates are modest by the standards of the late 70s and 1980-81 but in line with 1988-89.

Periods	*Hypothetical Firm's Plant Investment*	*Annual Inflation Rate*
1	$500,000	4%
2	400,000	5
3	400,000	6
4	350,000	5
5	350,000	5
6	250,000	4
7	250,000	3
8	250,000	4

The other firms invested nothing in plant and equipment. Each firm sold the same amount of goods each quarter and varied price in order to prevent a stockout. There were no seasonal variations and no economic index fluctuations.

The hypothetical firm made approximately 1.22 percent ROI per year after taxes on its investments in plant and equipment. With different inflation and depreciation rates the ROI would change significantly.

In another hypothetical situation, a firm invested $50,000 per quarter in robotics while the other firms invested nothing in robotics. The inflation, seasonal and economic fluctuations were as in the case of the plant and equipment example above. The firm made approximately 4.84 percent per year on its investment in robotics after taxes.

Now what can we learn from all this? Large investments in R&D and in plant and equipment, and in robotics, are risky. In order for them to pay off you have to do a good job of managing your firm. Erratic programs can be costly.

On the other hand if you manage your firm well and are able to operate at overtime rates, or at two or three shifts, the rewards can be very handsome.

Further Examples

Various users of the Executive Game have explored a number of problem areas in which analytic techniques can be useful. What seems to us the most interesting cases, with the most valuable results, have centered around fairly comprehensive models of individual firms or of the industry market. Such models generally abstract from many of the details of the Game, and conclusions reached using them are expected to be approximate rather than exact.

The individual firm models most often start from the idea of reducing the effort needed to predict profits, cash flows, and the like. The "Profit Models" presented early in the present chapter are simple examples.

The models of the industry market generally focus on ways in which market potentials are determined. These models permit experimentation to explore how the policies of different firms will interact - as bases, for instance, for judging the riskiness as well as the promise of various proposed policies. The forecasting procedure of Chapter 3 is a very simple illustration.

The most ambitious models combine models of individual firms and of the Game market, to represent the Executive Game industry as a whole. Such models (along with many of the less ambitious ones) are usually programmed for high-speed computation. In some cases, where plenty of computer time is readily available, Game players have actually been encouraged to experiment using the Executive Game program itself - a simulation of the Game situation which is essentially error-free except for the impossibility of anticipating what competition will do. Of course, no such opportunity is ever available in the business world; but it may be very instructive to learn from experience about what even such an unrealistically "perfect" simulation will and won't do for you.

The advanced analytic tools which seem most often to be valuable in the development of models like those discussed above (excluding, of course, the use of the Executive Game computer code itself) are techniques of statistical inference, including multivariate analysis in particular. The large volume of data supplied in Chapter 2 provides opportunities for properly prepared persons to undertake statistical studies. These same statistical tools are also useful for analyzing experimental results obtained with complicated models. Such applications are generally quite sophisticated, and far beyond the scope of the present chapter.

Elementary Analytical Procedures. In the Executive Game, as in the business world, the most important analytic procedures need not be the complex and sophisticated ones, but may be those which can be worked out on a piece of scratch paper or the back of an envelope. Straightforward cash projections are perhaps most important of all. Simple averaging is probably the most important statistical method, and basic arithmetic is the most useful part of mathematics. A Game firm whose management makes the most of such elementary techniques may do far better than one which emphasizes correct solutions to subtle problems but overlooks some of the elementary problems which really matter most. The use of spreadsheet programs on micro-computers will greatly increase the players' efficiency in calculating and can lead naturally to more sophisticated aplications.

Supplementary Reading

Anderson, David R., Dennis J. Sweeney and Thomas A. Williams. *Quantitative Methods for Business, 2nd edition.* St. Paul, Minnesota: West Publishing Co., 1986.

Budnick, Frank S., Richard Mojena, and Thomas E. Vollman. *Principles of Operations Research for Management.* Homewood, Illinois: Richard D. Irwin, Inc., 1977.

Buffa, Elwood S. and James S. Dyer. *Management Science / Operations Research,* 2nd edition. New York: Wiley, 1981.

Tummala, V. M. Rao and Richard C. Henshaw (eds.). *Concepts and Applications of Modern Decision Models.* East Lansing: Michigan State University, 1976.

Van Matre, Joseph G. and Glenn H. Gilbreath, *Statistics for Business and Economics*; 2nd ed, Dallas: Business Publications, Inc., 1983.

Wagner, Harvey M. *Principles of Operations Research, 2nd edition.* Englewood Cliffs, N.J.: Prentice-Hall, Inc., 1975.

APPENDICES: Mathematical Models and FORTRAN Programs

APPENDIX A

Mathematical Models and Computer Programs

This appendix describes the mathematical models underlying the Executive Game *et al.,* and, by means of flow charts, outlines the FORTRAN computer programs, through which the models are realized. A brief introduction to FORTRAN programming is also included.

The programs and test data are listed in Appendices B and D; the present appendix will satisfy the needs of those who are interested in the models.

Note that in addition to the FORTRAN programs discussed here, BASIC programs are available to run the XGAME on the IBM line of desk-top computers and numerous "IBM-compatible" computers such as those in the COMPAQ line. These programs are logically equivalent to the FORTRAN programs, but they take advantage of the interactive capacities of modern desk-top computers, to simplify things for the user. Their clearly explained menus and onscreen instructions make the Game directly usable by any teacher or assistant who knows how to turn the computer on and insert a diskette. Further details are given in the XGAME Instructor's Manual, and step-by-step instructions are included with the program diskettes.

However, the discussion in this chapter is primarily devoted to the initial FORTRAN program. Since computer operating systems vary so widely, each Game administrator — or perhaps a computer specialist working with him or her — must give players whatever instructions are needed about how to input data, collect output reports, etc.

Section I, below, describes the input FORTRAN formats for the Executive Game XGAME program. Sections 2-8, inclusive, outline the FORTRAN computer program (by means of flow charts) and the mathematical models (by means of formulae). For examples of quarterly outputs see Chapter 2, Tables 3-28 and 30-38.

Section 9 describes the input FORTRAN formats for the Executive Game Year-End XRATE program. Sections 10-12, inclusive, outline the FORTRAN computer program (by means of flow charts) and the mathematical model (by means of formulae). For examples of annual outputs see Chapter 2, Tables 29 and 39. This introduction is devoted to a few general comments on the ensuing sections concerned with the programs and the mathematical models. In the flow charts for both the Executive Game XGAME program and the Year-End XRATE program, the number to the upper left of each block is the serial number in the program listing of the first instruction represented.

FORTRAN: A Brief Description

FORTRAN is a formula translation computer language which can be easily learned by persons who understand high school algebra and can be efficiently translated into computing machine language by an electronic computer via a FORTRAN compiler.

The most difficult FORTRAN statements to understand in the accompanying programs are the DO loops and the IF instructions. The meanings of the DO loops and IF instructions, as well as the GO TO, CONTINUE, and STOP statements, can be readily understood by the reader if he will trace their effects via graphical representations in the corresponding flow charts. Following the IF statements, the program branches to one of the three statement numbers contained therein, depending upon whether the argument in the IF statement is negative, zero, or positive, respectively.

The FORTRAN order of operations philosophy is easy to learn. Quantities within parentheses are computed first and the resultant values are considered in the simplified expression. All operations are performed from left to right in the following order:

(1) Exponentation (**) (i.e., exponentation is the raising of a number to a power)

(2) Multiplication (*) and Division (/)

(3) Addition plus (+) and Subtraction (-).

While a FORTRAN arithmetic statement closely resembles a conventional mathematical formula, an important conceptual exception is the equal (=) sign. In FORTRAN, "=" means "is to be replaced by" rather than "is equal to." Thus, in FORTRAN, the statement:

FFM = FFM + FM2(J)/FN

means that the new value of FFM (on left), after this statement is executed, will become the current value of FFM plus the current value of FM2(J) divided by the value of FN.

Variables whose names begin with one of the six letters I, J, K, L, M, or N represent fixed point numbers (integers). Variables whose names begin with any of the remaining 20 letters represent floating point (i.e., decimal) numbers.

Some versions of FORTRAN allow arithmetic in which fixed and floating point numbers are combined, but some do not. In order to make these programs as universal as possible, no "mixed mode" arithmetic has been used; that is, fixed point numbers that are to be used in calculations with floating point numbers are first converted to floating point numbers by appending the letter F to the beginning of their names. Thus, for example, N, the number of firms in the industry (section) becomes FN in calculations with floating point numbers but remains N in calculations with other fixed point numbers.

Each line in the program listings (Appendices C and E) corresponds to a separate line in the program. The lines are numbered sequentially at the far right.

In the program listings the first line contains the program name. The next set of lines consist of the dimension statements. These statements are too long for one line, so they are continued on successive lines. Continuation statements in Fortran language are achieved by punching any single digit number in column 6 of the continuation line. The dimension statements reserve sufficient space in the computer's memory for storing the values of the variables whose names appear therein. The number of spaces reserved for each variable is equal to the product of the numbers punched in parentheses following the variable's name. Thus ACA(9) reserves space for nine valued of ACA(J) — one for each Firm J, while DV(16,9) reserves 144 spaces, that is, for 9 values of DV(1,J) and 9 values of DV(2,J), and so on, through DV(16,J).

The dimension statements are designed to accommodate an industry with nine firms maximum and a game length of 16 periods (4 years) maximum. (Alphabetical lists of definitions of variables may be found in Appendices B and D.) The format statements, which follow the dimension statements in the programs, are used in reading the data into the computer and they are used also along with the format statements near the end of the programs in printing the results or filing the histories for subsequent use.

The READ statements specify which variables are being read — the F or I specifications in the corresponding FORMAT statements designate whether floating point or fixed point numbers are being read — I2 means that a 2-digit fixed point number is being read, while F7.2 means that a 7-digit floating point number containing 2 decimal places is being read (if decimals are punched in the numbers in the data *per se,* the number of decimals indicated in the F specification is ignored and the number of decimals actually punched in the data are read into the computer).

The FORMAT statements near the end of the programs are executed by the corresponding PRINT and WRITE statements. PRINT 905, JZ, J, II, CA2(J), FIV(J), etc., means print the values of the fixed and floating point variables specified according to FORMAT statements #905. However, WRITE (94,915) JZ, J, II, CA2(J), etc., means store the values of the specified variables according to FORMAT statement #915 in a file on tape #94.

Many of the other FORMAT statements such as #815 are more complicated since they store the alphabetical material specified therein along with the values in sequence of the variables listed in the corresponding WRITE statement in spaces indicated by the I and F specifications in the statements. The 1HO (or a /) and 1H1 in the FORMAT statments call for a new line and a new page, respectively. Specifications in FORMAT statements such as 3X direct the computer to skip three spaces before printing subsequent alphabetical or numerical material. Finally, specifications in FORMAT statements such as 14H direct the computer to print whatever alphabetical or numerical material immediately follows in the next 14 spaces in this FORMAT statement.

Readers who wish to pursue the study of FORTRAN will find books such as the following very helpful:

Standard FORTRAN Programming: AStructured Style; 4th ed., by Donald H. Ford and Joseph Rue; Richard D. Irwin, Inc.,: Homewood, Ill., 1982. Written by professors of Business and Public Administration.

A Structured Approach to FORTRAN, by J. Winston Crowley and Charles E. Miller; Reston Publishing Company: Englewood Cliffs, N.J., 1983.

Note: The discussion above is limited to FORTRAN because it is one of the most machine-independent languages.

The Executive Game XGAME Program Flow Charts

The general format of the flow charts given on the subsequent pages is self-explanatory.

The program is organized so that it can be easily segmented in one or two places if necessary for running on small computers. The number of firms, N, can be varied between one and nine (maximum), inclusive. The tax and depreciation rates are automatically input by the computer programs and easily may be changed by the Game administrator. Appropriate values of a general price index are used throughout the models to simulate the effects of inflation upon the operations of the firms.

The Executive Game Models

The mathematical models are summarized by the formulae placed in the blocks in which they are calculated. Definitions or descriptions of some of the literal symbols are also inserted. (A complete alphabetical list of definitions of variables may be found in Appendix B.) Because the models are very straightforward, no general verbal descriptions will be given. However, a few comments which can be referred to as the programs and the models are examined, are in order.

As a practical matter, firms will not attempt to raise their price above $36 times an adjustment for inflation, since prices approaching that level drastically suppress the firms' potential sales. However, as a program safeguard against errors, jokers, etc., prices in excess of $36 times an adjustment for inflation are automatically set back to that level by the computer.

The calculation of the firm's product price index P(J) represents an overreaction of the market to price changes. If a deflated price is reduced, say, from $27.00 to $26.00, market potential reacts for a single quarter *as if* the reduction were to $25.80.

The FM2(J), R2(J), and T2(J) calculations represent carryover from quarter to quarter of part of the effects of past marketing, research and development, and maintenance, respectively.

The maintenance adjustment factor TCA has the apparent effect of requiring a less than proportionate increase in maintenance when production volume scheduled PV(J) rises above normal plant capacity CY1(J). Technically, the adjustment factor probably should be based upon production volume produced, which might be less than that scheduled, but we haven't done so because we want to make it as important as possible that production volume scheduled be carefully calculated.

The harmonic mean calculation of FP (average industry price index), which is used in the calculation of industry market potential, tends to emphasize the relative importance of a low-pricing firm in determining industry market potential.

The weighting factors, $\frac{W(J)}{FW}$, used in calculating individual firms' marketing potentials (i.e., PS1(J) and PS22(J), should be studied by the Game Administrator. He/she should also study the relation of the factors in the PS1(J) and PS22(J) formulae in order to understand the sort of market mechanism which the models create.

In regard to the above, it should be especially noted that some of the firm's lost sales may be captured by its competitors, but a maximum of 40 percent of customers' demands that are not filled in a given period will carry over into the subsequent period if the firm does not change its price. The actual amount of carryover of unsatisfied demand for a firm is inversely proportional to its current deflated price cubed, divided by its previous deflated price cubed.

The report calculations are largely self-explanatory, but should be examined carefully. In particular, the two-step calculation and the multistep calculation of direct labor expense EL(J) in Models 1 and 2, respectively, call for attention. Please note also the stairstep escalation in administrative expenses AL(J) which is associated with production at rates in excess of normal plant capacity CY1(J) in Model 2. In addition, it would be wise to be especially familiar with three terms in total expenses EX(J), that is, cash shortage costs and penalties FC(J), costs and penalties associated with plant construction and purchase of equipment VPE(J), and robotics equipment VR(J), and ordering costs incurred when raw materials are purchased FOC(J).

Computation of income taxes was described in Chapter 4, Step #40, and reduction, finished goods inventory was described in Step #29. The Game administrator should be thoroughly familiar with these items as the Game participants may need assistance in order to understand them.

1. Inputs in The Executive Game Program (XGAME)

Input data, symbols used in flow charts and FORTRAN programs, and formats for the input data are as follows. All numbers appear as far to the right in their respective fields as possible. The Game administrator may change these inputs as she/he sees fit. A complete list of variables may be found in Appendix B.

Calendar Quarter of the Year String (line 11)

Col. 7-114 Calendar quarter of the year abbreviated, QTR(K) — a sequence of 16 three-letter abbreviations starting in Col. 7; e.g., DATA QTR/'JAS', 'OND', 'JFM'., 'AMJ', etc.

Seasonal Indices Data (line 12)

Col. 7-90 S(K) — a sequence of 17 numbers, each appearing in the line; e.g., DATA S/95., 115., 90., 100., etc.

Annual Inflation Factors Data (line 13)

Col. 7-73 F(K) — a sequence of 20 numbers, each appearing in the line, e.g., DATA F/4., 5., 6., 5., etc.

Economic Indices Forecast Data (line 14)

Col. 7-37 FE(K) — a sequence of 17 numbers, each appearing in the line, DATA FE/100., 95., 93., 90., etc.

Erratic Error Numbers Data (line 15)

Col. 7-6 EN(K) — a sequence of 16 numbers, each appearing in the line, e.g., DATA EN/1., -1,. 2., -1., etc.

Industry No., Model No., No. of Firms, Period No., Depreciation Rates, and Tax Options Data (lines 29-88)

Execution of the XGAME program by the Game administrator or her/his keyboard operator will prompt her/him to enter the Industry No., the Model No., No. of Firms, Period No., and the Depreciation Rates, and the Tax Rates.

History Data (two lines per firm each quarter after period 0 — filed by the computer after period 0. The computer stores the data as far to the right in each field as possible.

Period 0
line 89 e.g., II-1=0

line 90 e.g., PR1(J) = 25.6

line 91 e.g., FM1(J) = 240000.

" " " "

line 106 e.g., NS1 (J) = 1

Subsequent Periods

line 151 e.g., READ (92, 745) JZ, JJ, III, PR1(J), FM1(J) etc.

wherein III = II-1

line 153 e.g., READ (92, 755) JZ, JJ, III, ST1(J), PS21(J) etc.

2. The Executive Game Program: Reading input data

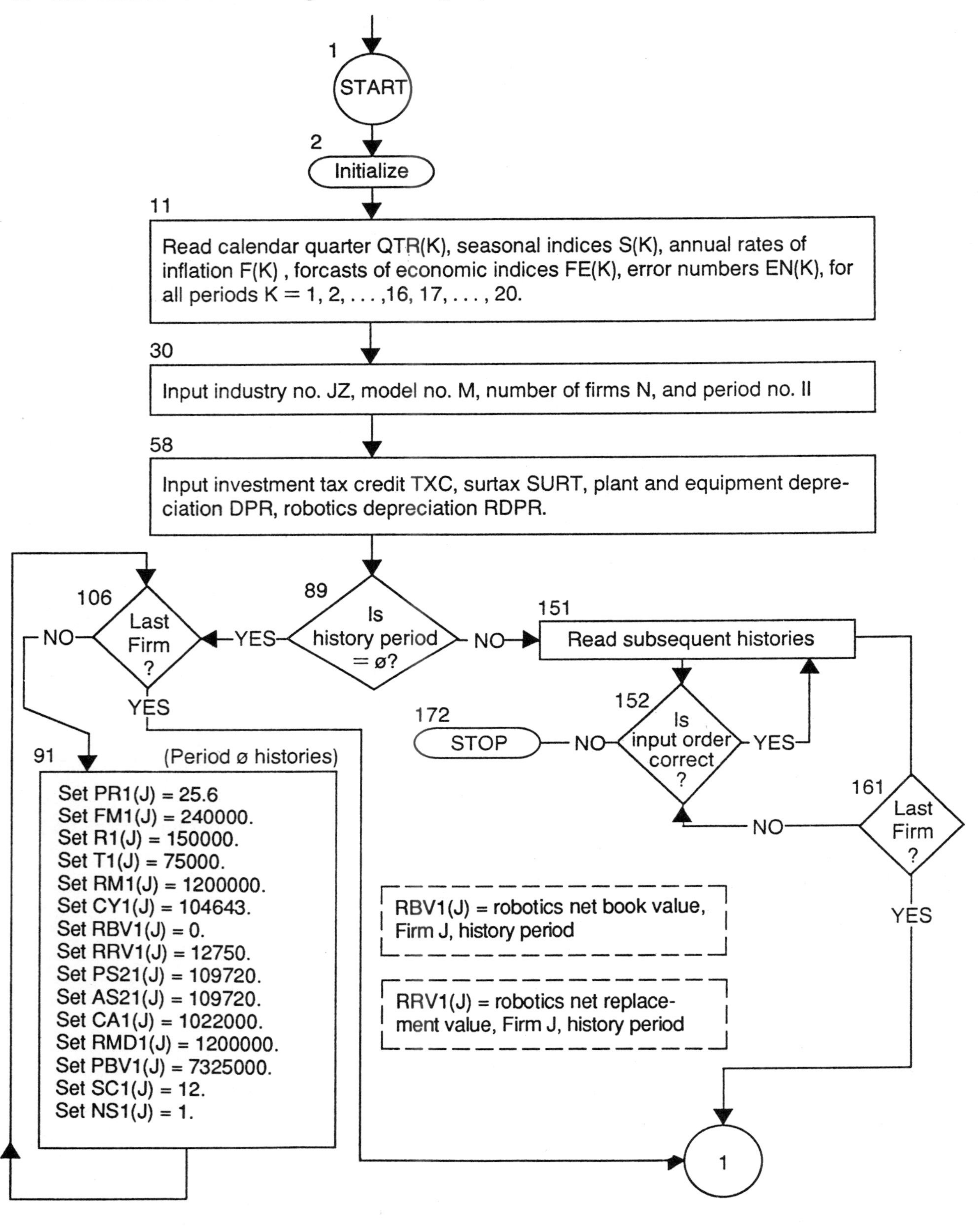

3. Reading decisions and calculation of general price, deflator, and economic "indices" and forecast of annual rate of inflation

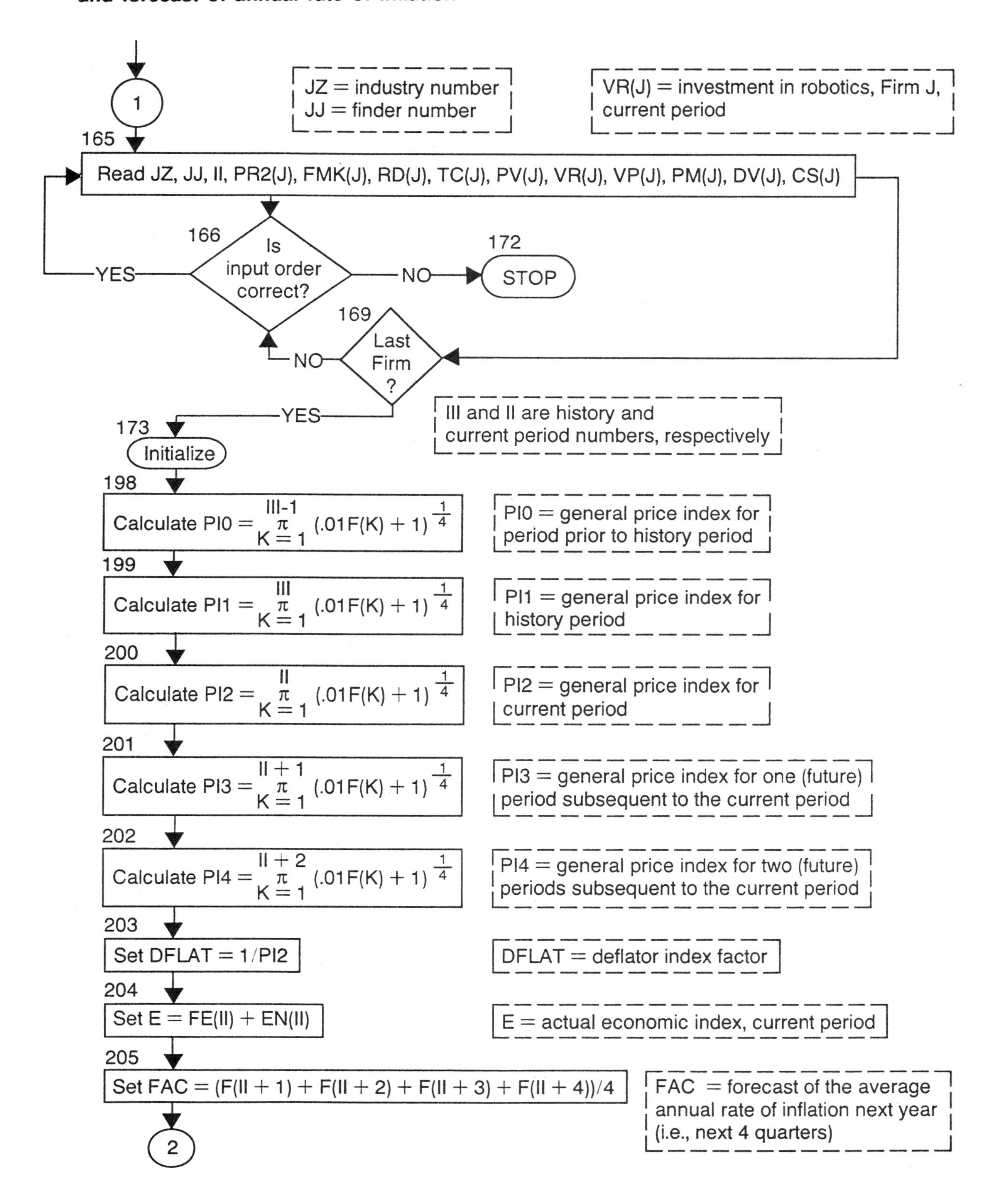

4. Calculation of firm and industry "indices" and firm market share weighting factors

(2) →

207 Is PR2(J)≤SC1(J)? — YES → 208 Set PR2(J) = SC1(J); NO → 210

210 Is PR2(J)>$36P10? — YES → 211 Set PR2(J) = $36P10; NO → 212

P(J), FM2(J), R2(J), and T2(J) are firm "indices"
FFM and FR are industry "indices"

SC1(J) = "standard" cost of direct labor and raw materials per unit of finished goods, Firm J, history period

PR2(J) = price per unit of finished goods, Firm J, current period

PR1(J) = deflated price per unit of finished goods, Firm J, history period

212 Set P(J) = 1.2 PR2(J)/P10 -.2PR1(J)

213 Set FP = FP +1/P(J)

at the completion of this DO loop

$$FP = \sum_J \frac{1}{P(J)}$$

214 Set FM2(J) = .7(FMK(J) + 40,000)DFLAT +.3 FM1(J)

215 Set FFM = FFM + FM2(J)/N

at the completion of this DO loop

$$FFM = \frac{\sum_J FM2(J)}{N}$$

216 Set RRV2 = RRV2 + RRV1(J)/N

at the completion of this DO loop

$$RRV2 = \frac{\sum_J RRV1(J)}{N}$$

217 Set R2(J) = .3(RD(J) + 50,000)DFLAT + .7 R1(J)

218 Set FR = FR + R1(J)/N

at the completion of this DO loop

$$FR = \frac{\sum_J R1(J)}{N}$$

219 Set $CY2(J) = CY1(J) \cdot (2-e^{-RRV1(J)/10{,}000{,}000}) + 1$

CY2(J) = plant capacity, current period, Firm J
Note: e ≃ 2.718

220 Set PRVI(J) = 70 CY2(J) PI1

221 Set TCA = TC(J) PI3(CY2(J) + 50,000)/(PV(J) + 50,000)

TCA = maintenance adjustment factor, Firm J

222 Set T2(J) = .5TCA + .5T1(J)

222 Last Firm? — NO → return to 207; YES → 223

FP = industry price "index" . . . the harmonic mean of individual firms' price "indices"

223 Set $FP = \frac{N}{\sum_J \frac{1}{P(J)}}$

224 Set $PRICEL = 6e^{-(FFM+FR+RRV2)/1{,}000{,}000}$ → (3)

PRICEL = price elasticity variable
Note: e ≃ 2.718

5. Calculation of firm market share factors, market potentials, sales, production, unit materials costs, and stocks

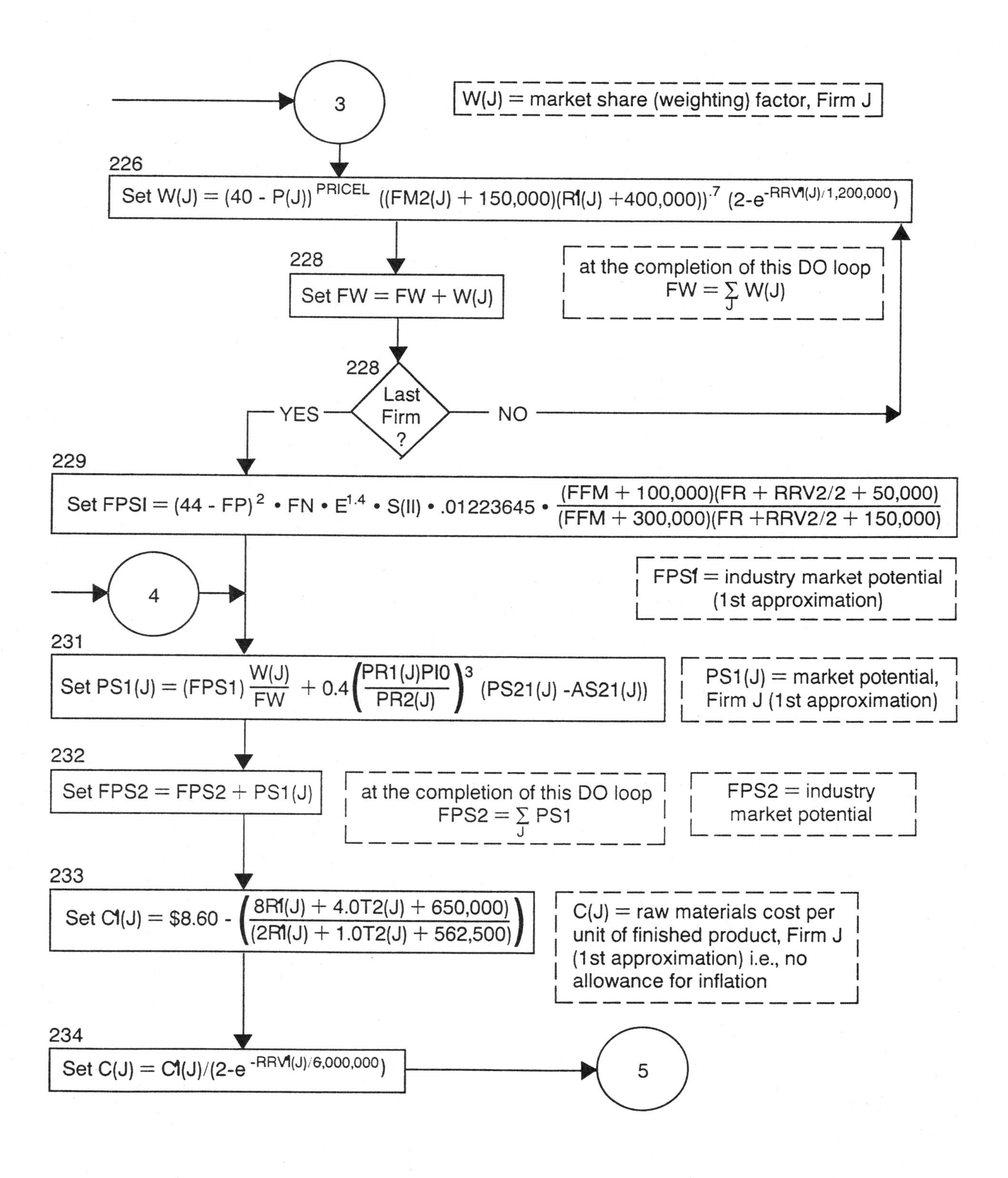

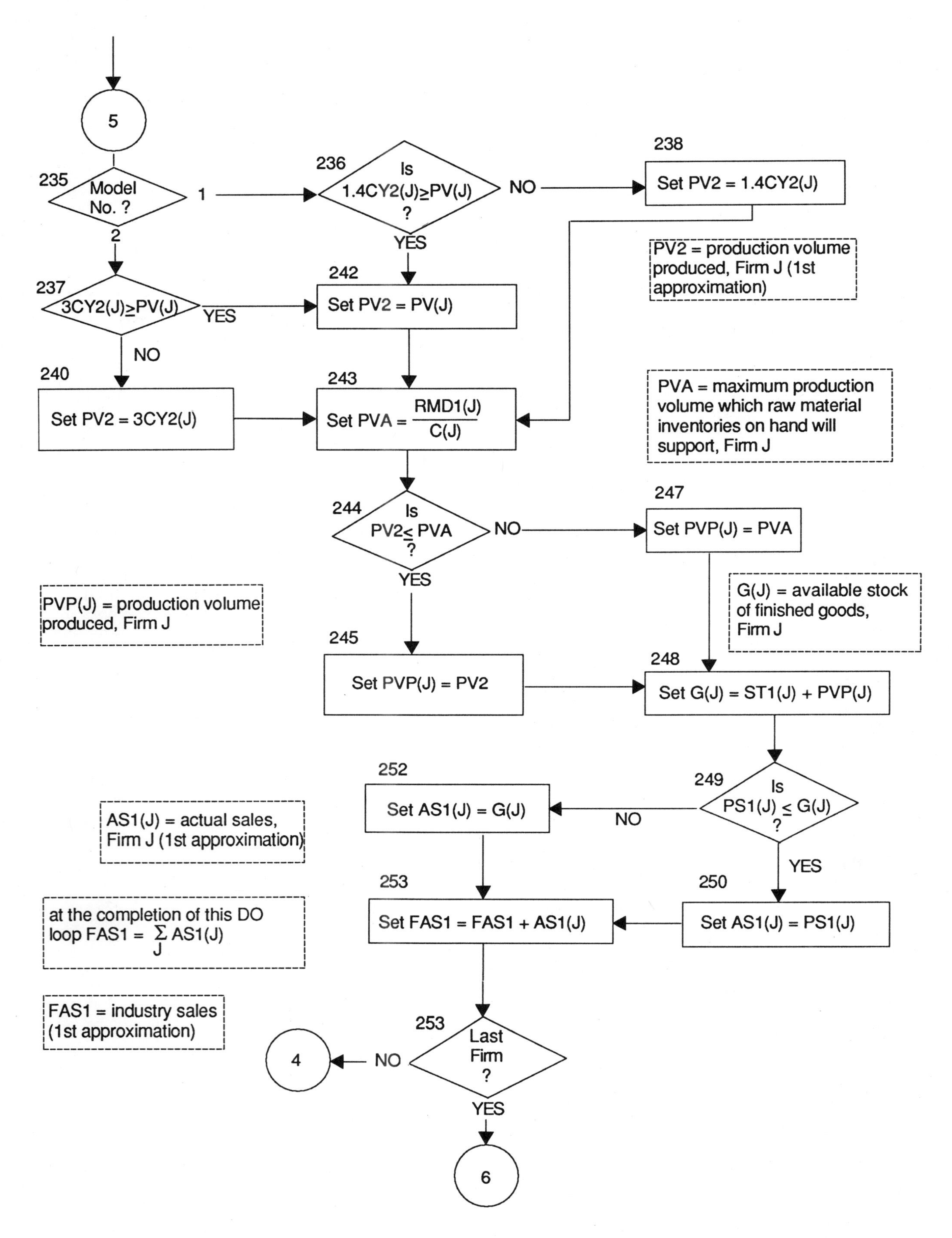
5
235
Model No. ?
1
2
236
Is 1.4CY2(J)≥PV(J) ?
NO
YES
238
Set PV2 = 1.4CY2(J)
PV2 = production volume produced, Firm J (1st approximation)
237
3CY2(J)≥PV(J)
YES
NO
242
Set PV2 = PV(J)
240
Set PV2 = 3CY2(J)
243
Set PVA = RMD1(J) / C(J)
PVA = maximum production volume which raw material inventories on hand will support, Firm J
244
Is PV2≤ PVA ?
NO
YES
247
Set PVP(J) = PVA
PVP(J) = production volume produced, Firm J
G(J) = available stock of finished goods, Firm J
245
Set PVP(J) = PV2
248
Set G(J) = ST1(J) + PVP(J)
252
Set AS1(J) = G(J)
249
Is PS1(J) ≤ G(J) ?
NO
YES
AS1(J) = actual sales, Firm J (1st approximation)
253
Set FAS1 = FAS1 + AS1(J)
250
Set AS1(J) = PS1(J)
at the completion of this DO loop FAS1 = Σ AS1(J) J
FAS1 = industry sales (1st approximation)
253
Last Firm ?
4
NO
YES
6

6. **Calculation of stockouts, market potentials, actual sales, and remaining stocks of finished goods**

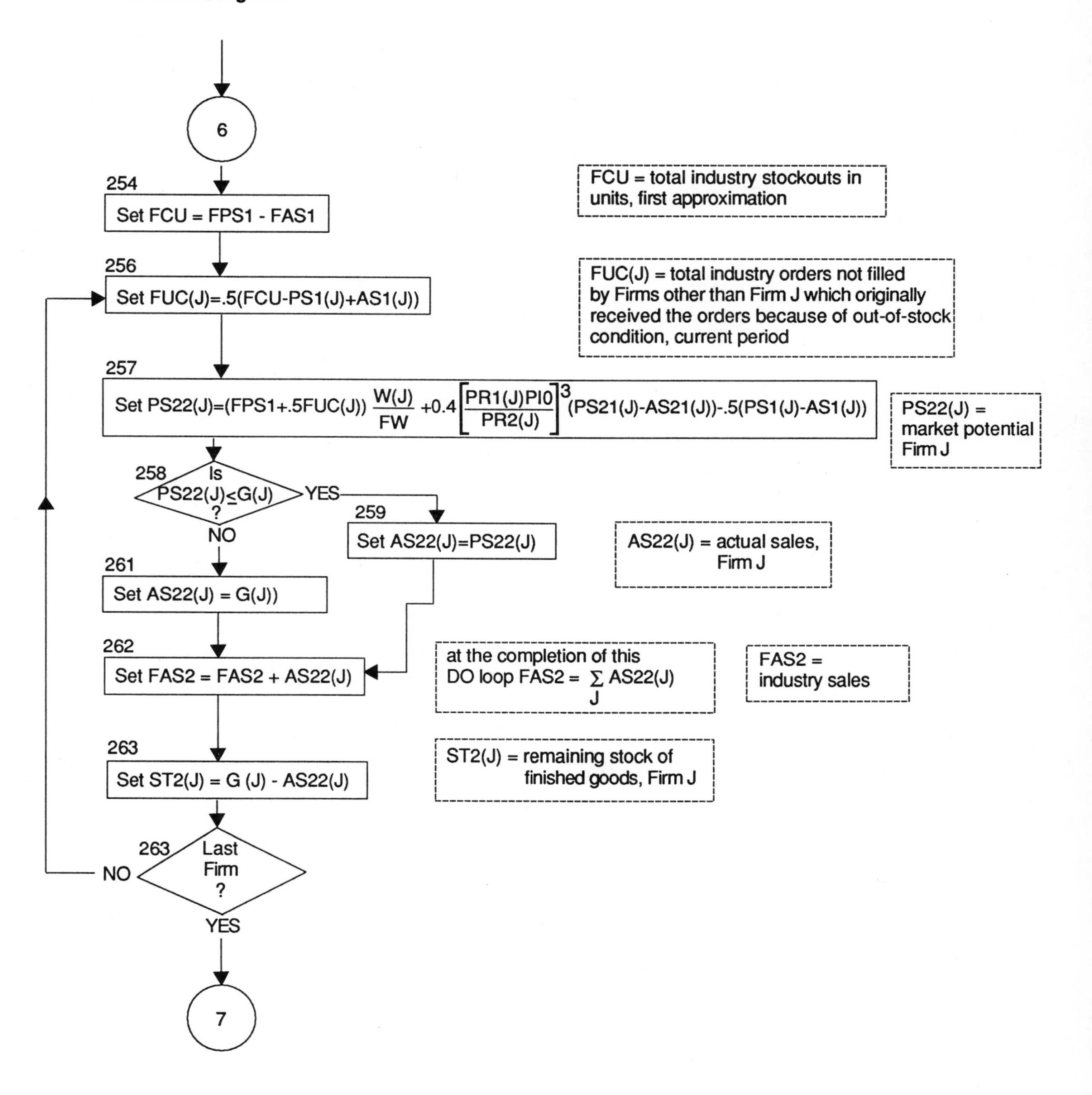

7. Calculation of remaining output data

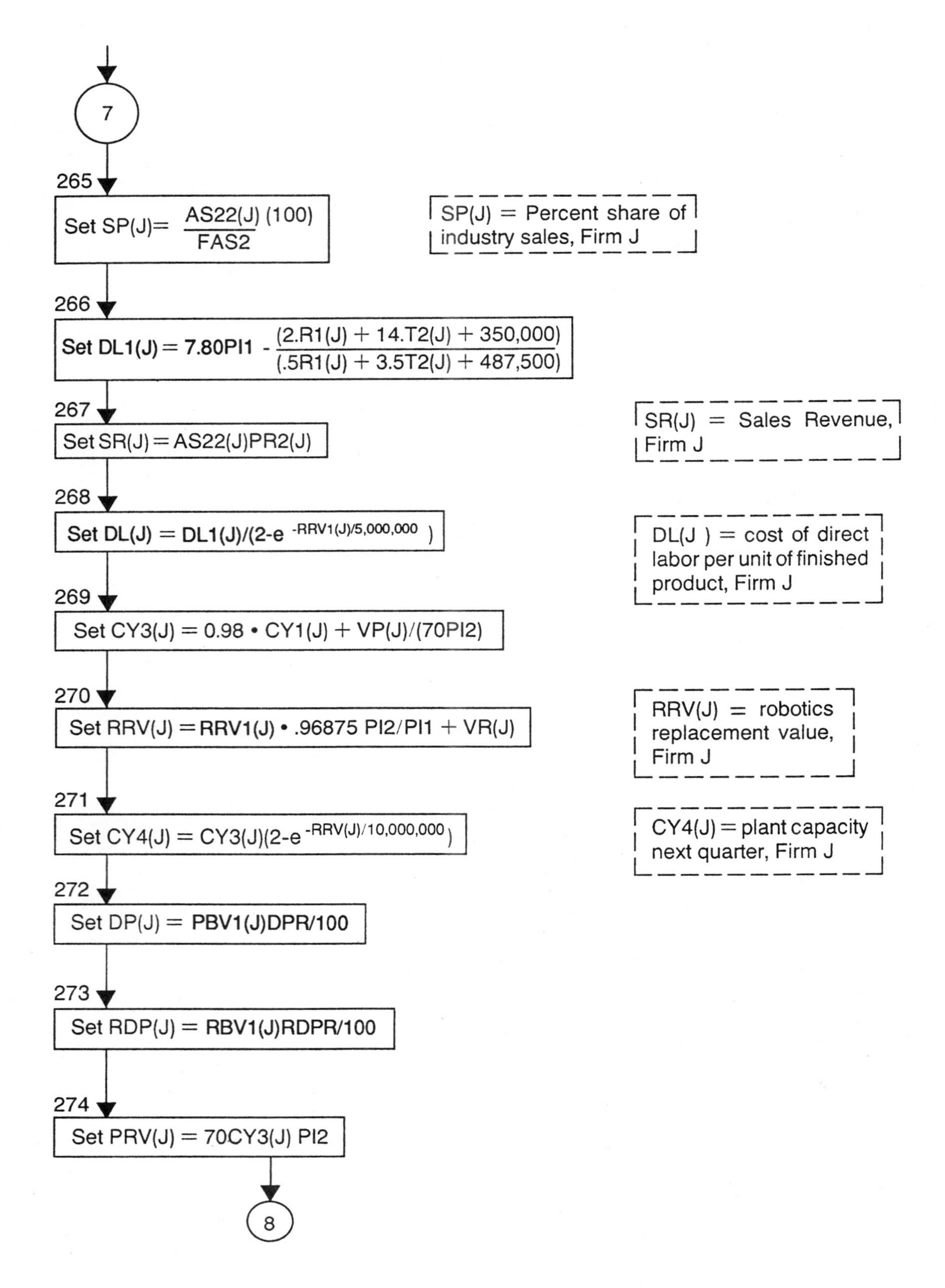

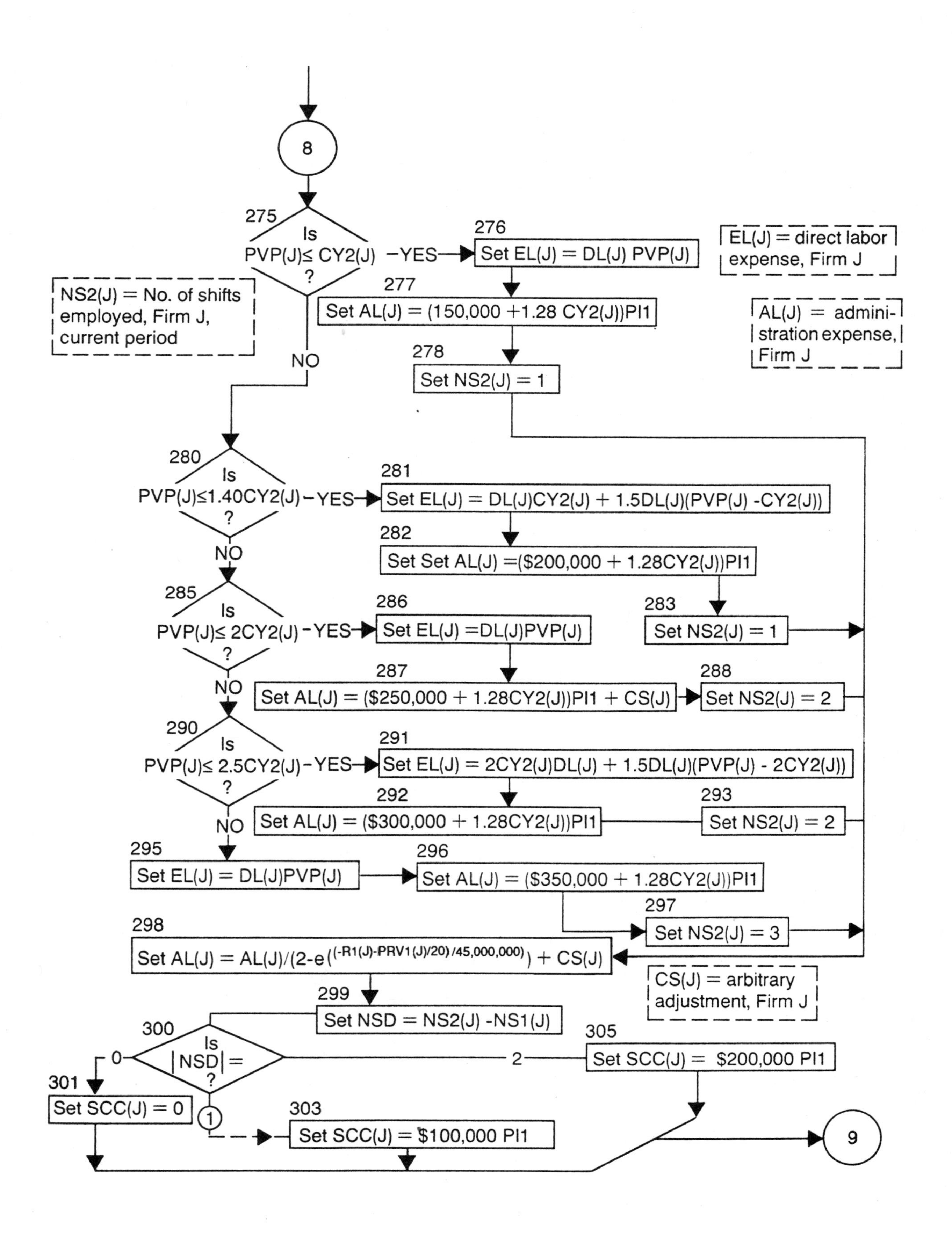

8
275
Is PVP(J)≤ CY2(J) ?
YES
NO
276
Set EL(J) = DL(J) PVP(J)
EL(J) = direct labor expense, Firm J
277
Set AL(J) = (150,000 +1.28 CY2(J))PI1
AL(J) = administration expense, Firm J
NS2(J) = No. of shifts employed, Firm J, current period
278
Set NS2(J) = 1
280
Is PVP(J)≤1.40CY2(J) ?
281
Set EL(J) = DL(J)CY2(J) + 1.5DL(J)(PVP(J) -CY2(J))
282
Set Set AL(J) =($200,000 + 1.28CY2(J))PI1
283
Set NS2(J) = 1
285
Is PVP(J)≤ 2CY2(J) ?
286
Set EL(J) =DL(J)PVP(J)
287
Set AL(J) = ($250,000 + 1.28CY2(J))PI1 + CS(J)
288
Set NS2(J) = 2
290
Is PVP(J)≤ 2.5CY2(J) ?
291
Set EL(J) = 2CY2(J)DL(J) + 1.5DL(J)(PVP(J) - 2CY2(J))
292
Set AL(J) = ($300,000 + 1.28CY2(J))PI1
293
Set NS2(J) = 2
295
Set EL(J) = DL(J)PVP(J)
296
Set AL(J) = ($350,000 + 1.28CY2(J))PI1
297
Set NS2(J) = 3
298
Set AL(J) = AL(J)/(2-e((-R1(J)-PRV1(J)/20)/45,000,000)) + CS(J)
CS(J) = arbitrary adjustment, Firm J
299
Set NSD = NS2(J) -NS1(J)
300
Is |NSD| = ?
0
1
2
301
Set SCC(J) = 0
303
Set SCC(J) = $100,000 PI1
305
Set SCC(J) = $200,000 PI1
9

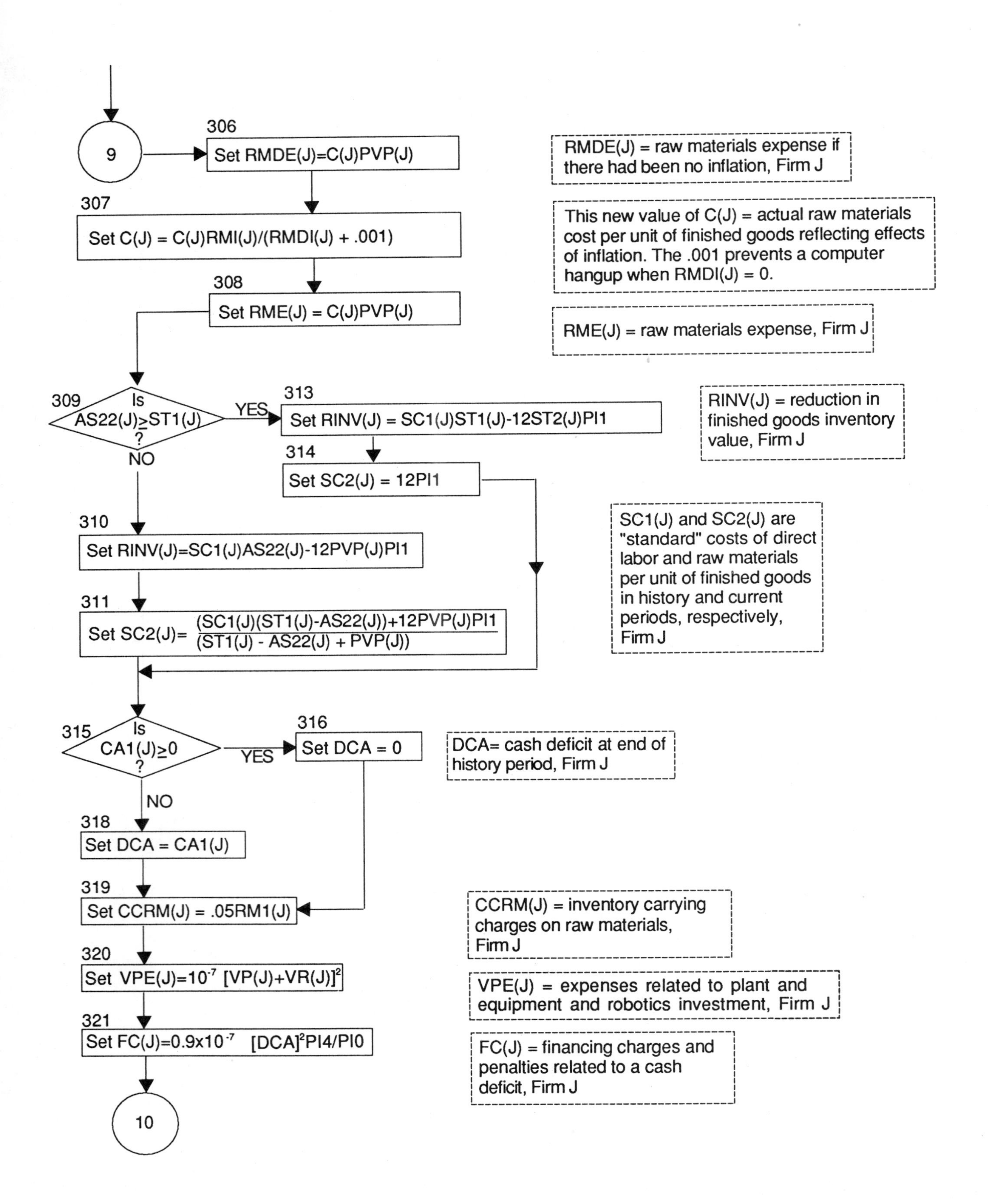
9
306
Set RMDE(J)=C(J)PVP(J)
RMDE(J) = raw materials expense if there had been no inflation, Firm J
307
Set C(J) = C(J)RMI(J)/(RMDI(J) + .001)
This new value of C(J) = actual raw materials cost per unit of finished goods reflecting effects of inflation. The .001 prevents a computer hangup when RMDI(J) = 0.
308
Set RME(J) = C(J)PVP(J)
RME(J) = raw materials expense, Firm J
309
Is AS22(J)≥ST1(J) ?
YES
NO
313
Set RINV(J) = SC1(J)ST1(J)-12ST2(J)PI1
RINV(J) = reduction in finished goods inventory value, Firm J
314
Set SC2(J) = 12PI1
310
Set RINV(J)=SC1(J)AS22(J)-12PVP(J)PI1
SC1(J) and SC2(J) are "standard" costs of direct labor and raw materials per unit of finished goods in history and current periods, respectively, Firm J
311
Set SC2(J)= (SC1(J)(ST1(J)-AS22(J))+12PVP(J)PI1 / (ST1(J) - AS22(J) + PVP(J))
315
Is CA1(J)≥0 ?
YES
NO
316
Set DCA = 0
DCA= cash deficit at end of history period, Firm J
318
Set DCA = CA1(J)
319
Set CCRM(J) = .05RM1(J)
CCRM(J) = inventory carrying charges on raw materials, Firm J
320
Set VPE(J)=10^-7 [VP(J)+VR(J)]^2
VPE(J) = expenses related to plant and equipment and robotics investment, Firm J
321
Set FC(J)=0.9x10^-7 [DCA]^2PI4/PI0
FC(J) = financing charges and penalties related to a cash deficit, Firm J
10

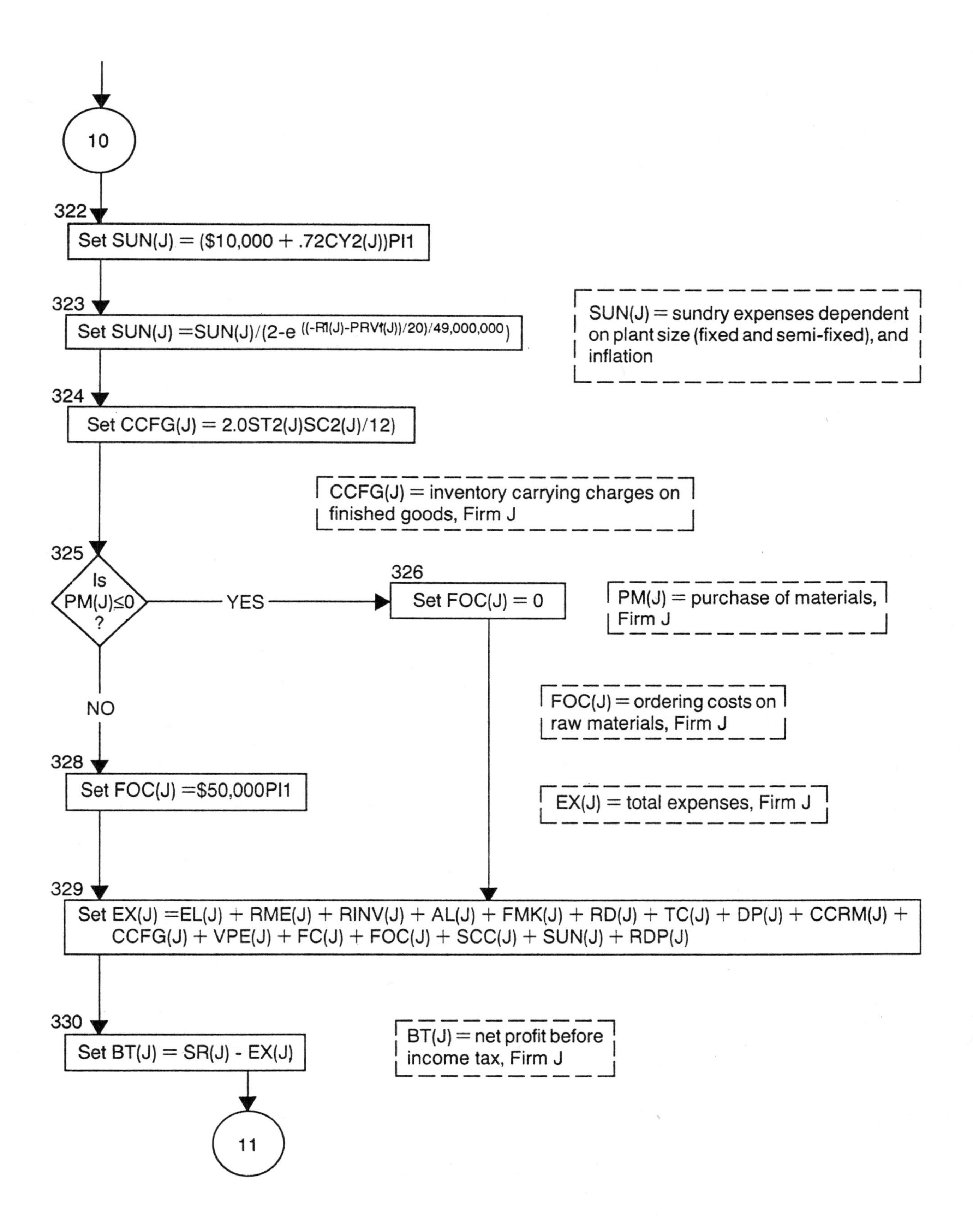
10
322
Set SUN(J) = ($10,000 + .72CY2(J))PI1
323
Set SUN(J) =SUN(J)/(2-e ((-RI(J)-PRVI(J))/20)/49,000,000)
SUN(J) = sundry expenses dependent on plant size (fixed and semi-fixed), and inflation
324
Set CCFG(J) = 2.0ST2(J)SC2(J)/12)
CCFG(J) = inventory carrying charges on finished goods, Firm J
325
Is PM(J)≤0 ?
YES
326
Set FOC(J) = 0
PM(J) = purchase of materials, Firm J
NO
FOC(J) = ordering costs on raw materials, Firm J
328
Set FOC(J) =$50,000PI1
EX(J) = total expenses, Firm J
329
Set EX(J) =EL(J) + RME(J) + RINV(J) + AL(J) + FMK(J) + RD(J) + TC(J) + DP(J) + CCRM(J) + CCFG(J) + VPE(J) + FC(J) + FOC(J) + SCC(J) + SUN(J) + RDP(J)
330
Set BT(J) = SR(J) - EX(J)
BT(J) = net profit before income tax, Firm J
11

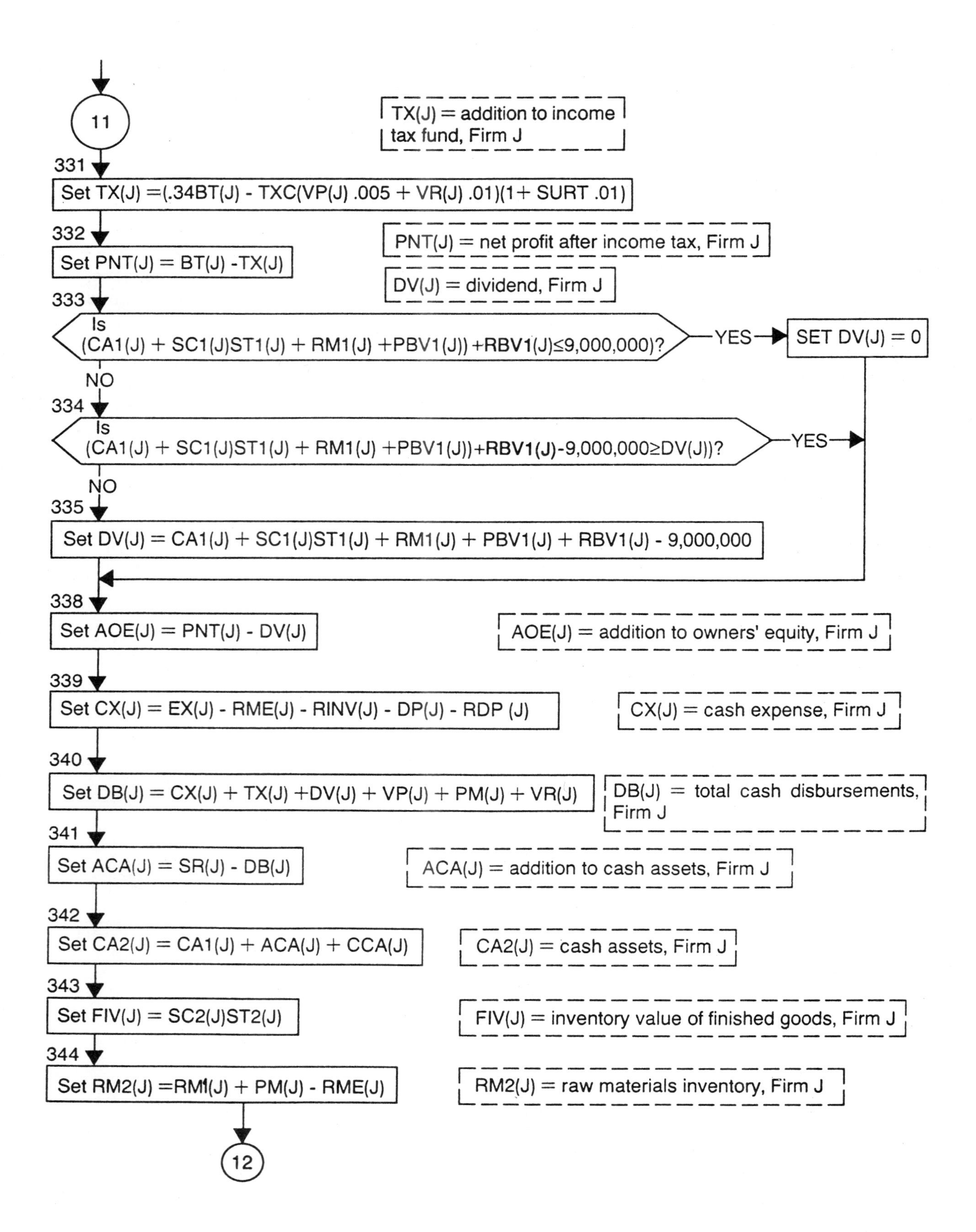
11
TX(J) = addition to income tax fund, Firm J
331
Set TX(J) =(.34BT(J) - TXC(VP(J) .005 + VR(J) .01)(1+ SURT .01)
332
Set PNT(J) = BT(J) -TX(J)
PNT(J) = net profit after income tax, Firm J
DV(J) = dividend, Firm J
333
Is (CA1(J) + SC1(J)ST1(J) + RM1(J) +PBV1(J)) +RBV1(J)≤9,000,000)?
YES
SET DV(J) = 0
NO
334
Is (CA1(J) + SC1(J)ST1(J) + RM1(J) +PBV1(J))+RBV1(J)-9,000,000≥DV(J))?
YES
NO
335
Set DV(J) = CA1(J) + SC1(J)ST1(J) + RM1(J) + PBV1(J) + RBV1(J) - 9,000,000
338
Set AOE(J) = PNT(J) - DV(J)
AOE(J) = addition to owners' equity, Firm J
339
Set CX(J) = EX(J) - RME(J) - RINV(J) - DP(J) - RDP (J)
CX(J) = cash expense, Firm J
340
Set DB(J) = CX(J) + TX(J) +DV(J) + VP(J) + PM(J) + VR(J)
DB(J) = total cash disbursements, Firm J
341
Set ACA(J) = SR(J) - DB(J)
ACA(J) = addition to cash assets, Firm J
342
Set CA2(J) = CA1(J) + ACA(J) + CCA(J)
CA2(J) = cash assets, Firm J
343
Set FIV(J) = SC2(J)ST2(J)
FIV(J) = inventory value of finished goods, Firm J
344
Set RM2(J) =RM1(J) + PM(J) - RME(J)
RM2(J) = raw materials inventory, Firm J
12

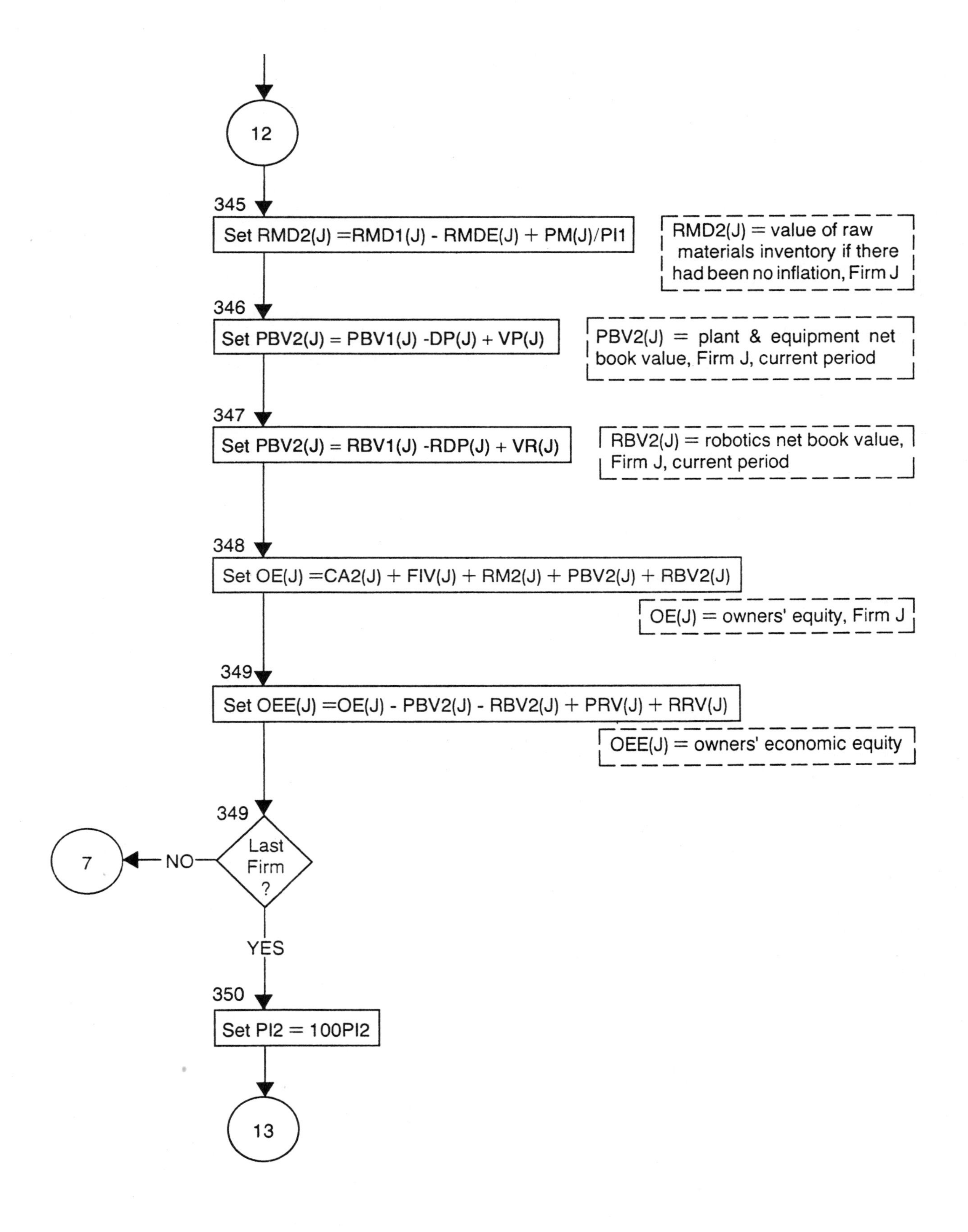
12
345
Set RMD2(J) =RMD1(J) - RMDE(J) + PM(J)/PI1
RMD2(J) = value of raw materials inventory if there had been no inflation, Firm J
346
Set PBV2(J) = PBV1(J) -DP(J) + VP(J)
PBV2(J) = plant & equipment net book value, Firm J, current period
347
Set PBV2(J) = RBV1(J) -RDP(J) + VR(J)
RBV2(J) = robotics net book value, Firm J, current period
348
Set OE(J) =CA2(J) + FIV(J) + RM2(J) + PBV2(J) + RBV2(J)
OE(J) = owners' equity, Firm J
349
Set OEE(J) =OE(J) - PBV2(J) - RBV2(J) + PRV(J) + RRV(J)
OEE(J) = owners' economic equity
349
Last Firm ?
NO
7
YES
350
Set PI2 = 100PI2
13

8. Storing of Results and History Data

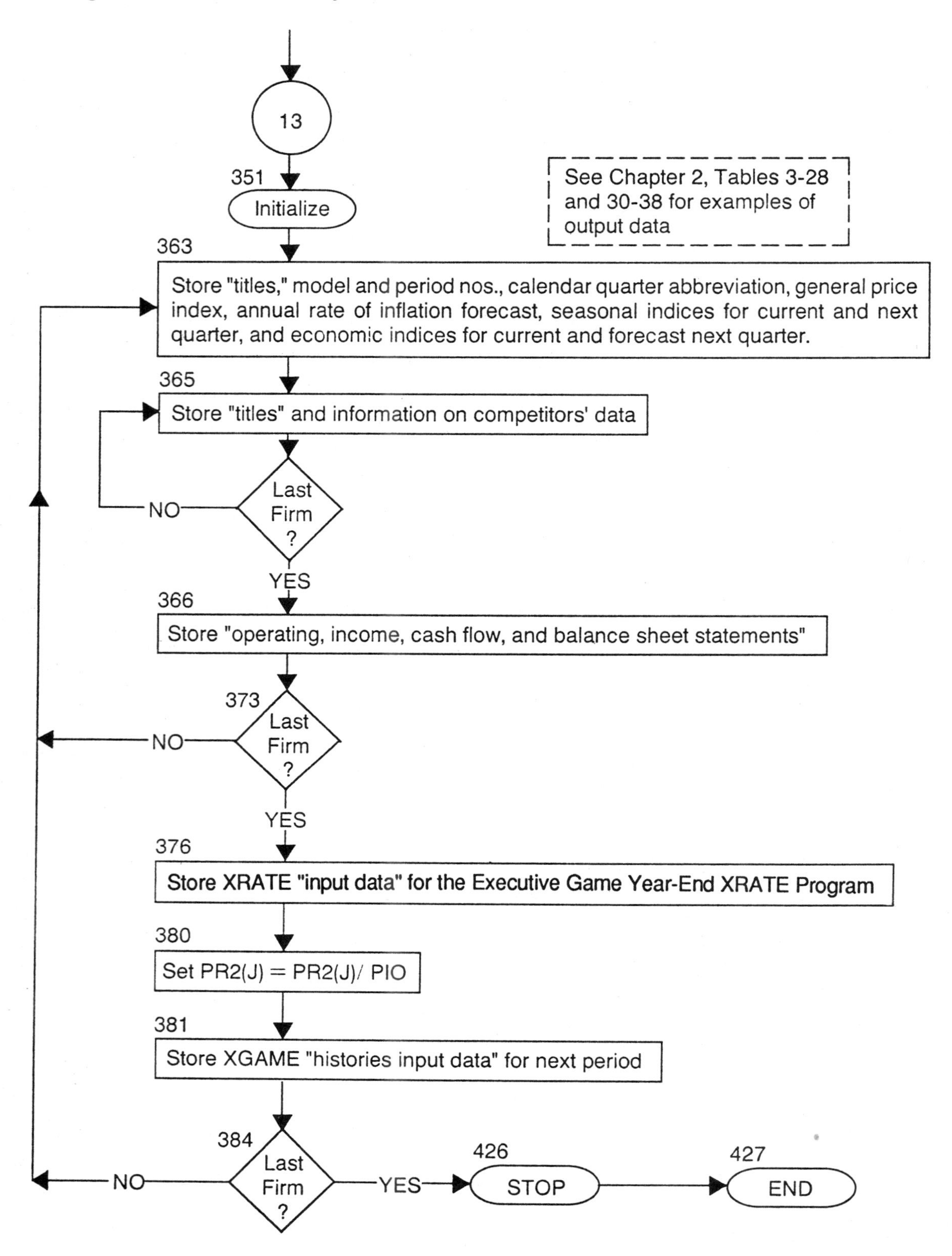

The Executive Game Year-End XRATE Program Flow Charts

As in the case of the Executive Game program, the general format of the Year-End XRATE program flow charts given on the subsequent pages is self-explanatory.

The Year-End XRATE Model

The mathematical model is summarized by the formulae placed in the blocks in which they are calculated. Definitions or descriptions of some of the literal symbols are also inserted. (A complete alphabetical list of definitions of variables may be found in Appendix D.) Because the calculations are fairly straightforward no general verbal description will be given.

9. Inputs to the Executive Game Year-End XRATE Program

Input data, symbols used in flow charts and FORTRAN program, and formats for the input data are as follows: All numbers appear as far to the right in their respective fields as possible. The following line is typed by the Game administrator or keyboard operator.

Industry No., Number of firms, and Fiscal year No. (lines 18-50)

Execution of the XRATE program by the Game administrator or her/his keyboard operator will prompt her/him to enter the industry No., the number of periods, and the Fiscal year No. (note: enter the number of the fiscal year being played or just completed).

Beginning Owners' Economic Equity (line 51) e.g., BOE = 9700000. = Beginning Owners' Equity = Beginning Owners' Economic Equity.

History Data (one line per firm for each quarter completed to date in the Game — output by the computer each quarter preceding the Executive Game history data). The computer outputs the data as far to the right in each field as possible.

line 70 e.g., READ (TAPE(I), 747) JZ, JJ, II, CA(J), FIV(J), etc.

10. The Executive Game Year-end XRATE Program: Reading input data and calculation of fiscal year averages

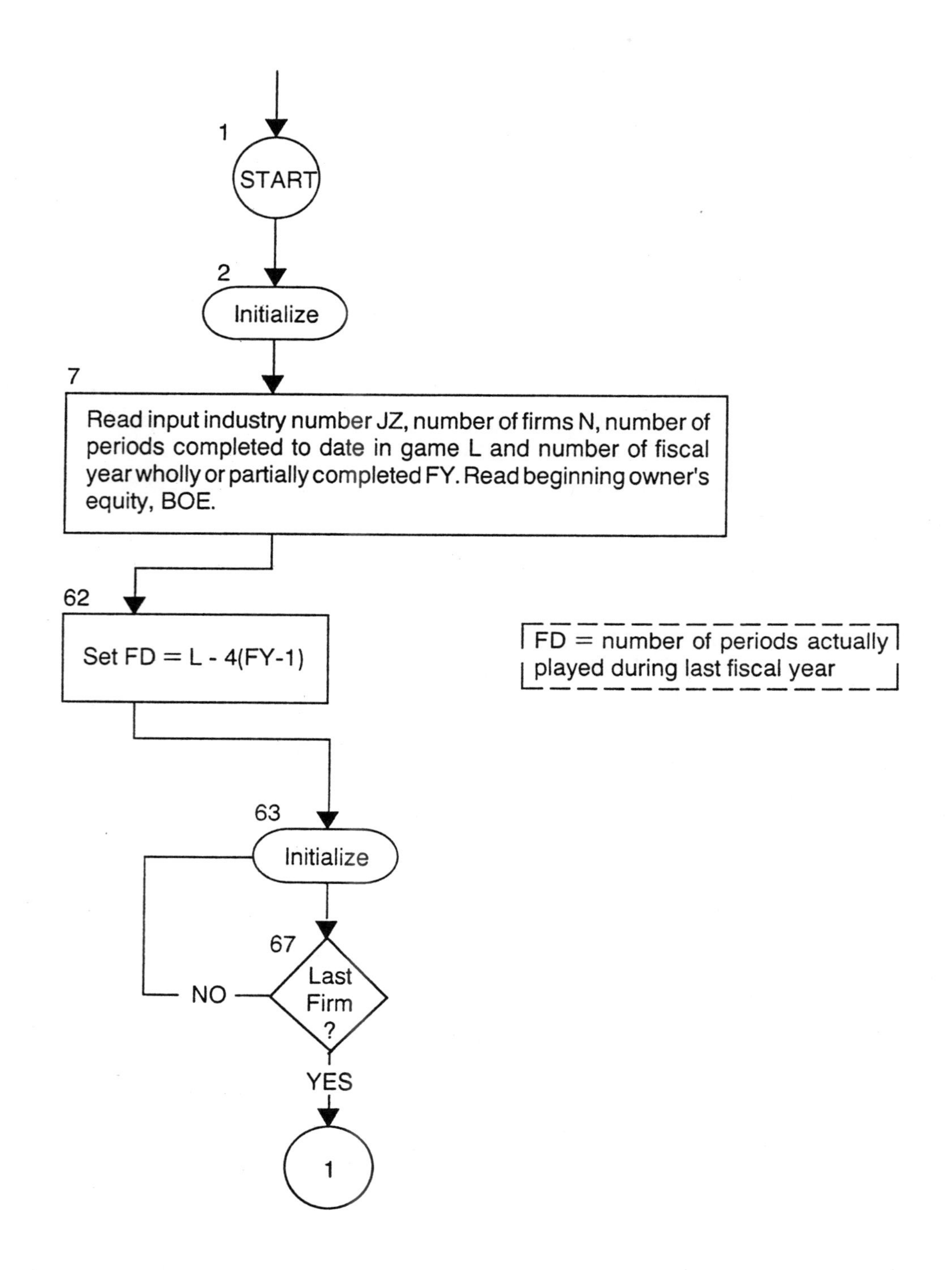

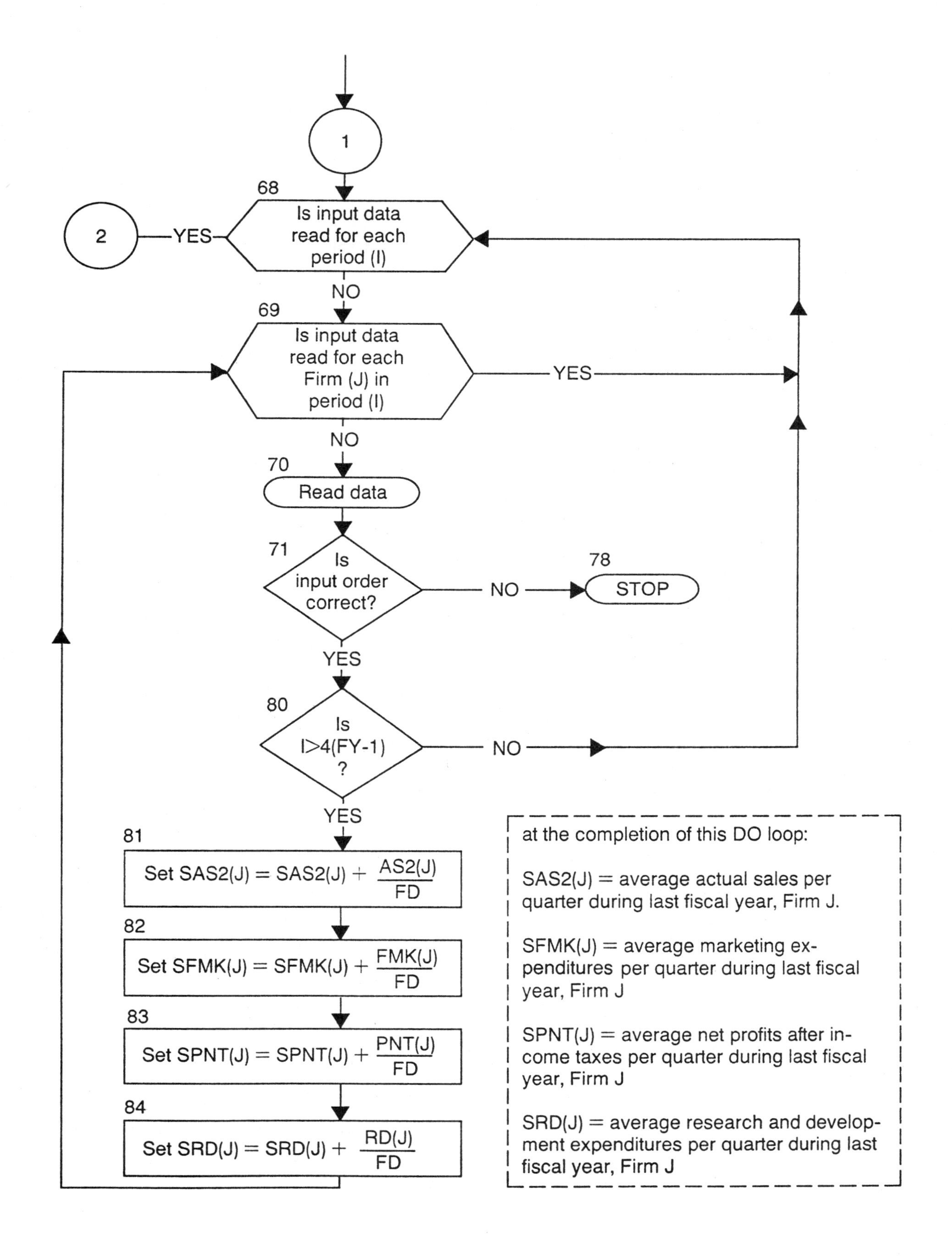
1
68
Is input data read for each period (I)
2
YES
NO
69
Is input data read for each Firm (J) in period (I)
YES
NO
70
Read data
71
Is input order correct?
NO
78
STOP
YES
80
Is I>4(FY-1) ?
NO
YES
81
Set SAS2(J) = SAS2(J) + AS2(J)/FD
82
Set SFMK(J) = SFMK(J) + FMK(J)/FD
83
Set SPNT(J) = SPNT(J) + PNT(J)/FD
84
Set SRD(J) = SRD(J) + RD(J)/FD
at the completion of this DO loop:
SAS2(J) = average actual sales per quarter during last fiscal year, Firm J.
SFMK(J) = average marketing expenditures per quarter during last fiscal year, Firm J
SPNT(J) = average net profits after income taxes per quarter during last fiscal year, Firm J
SRD(J) = average research and development expenditures per quarter during last fiscal year, Firm J

11. Calculation of rate of return earned on beginning owners' equity and ranks of firms based thereon

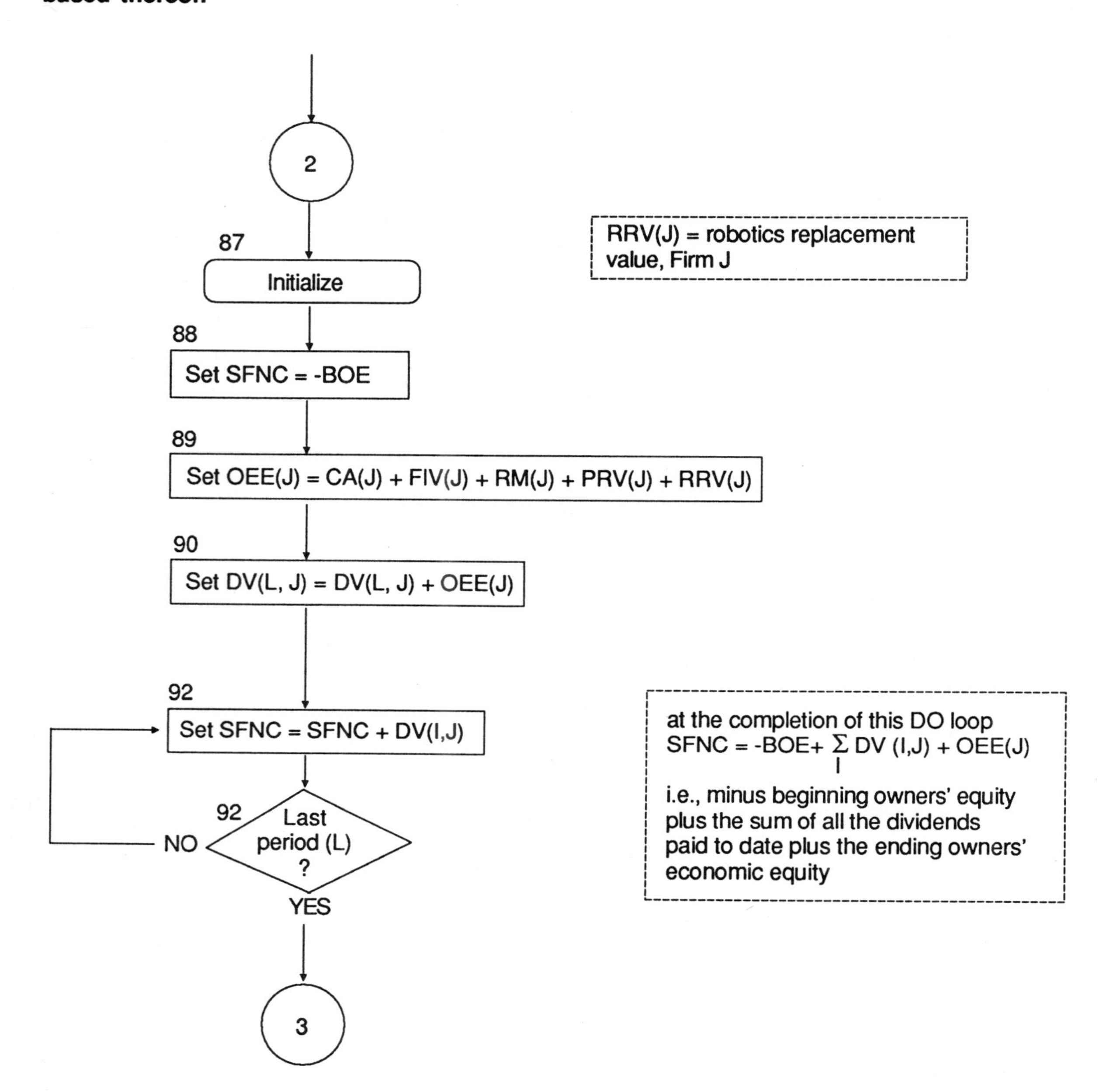

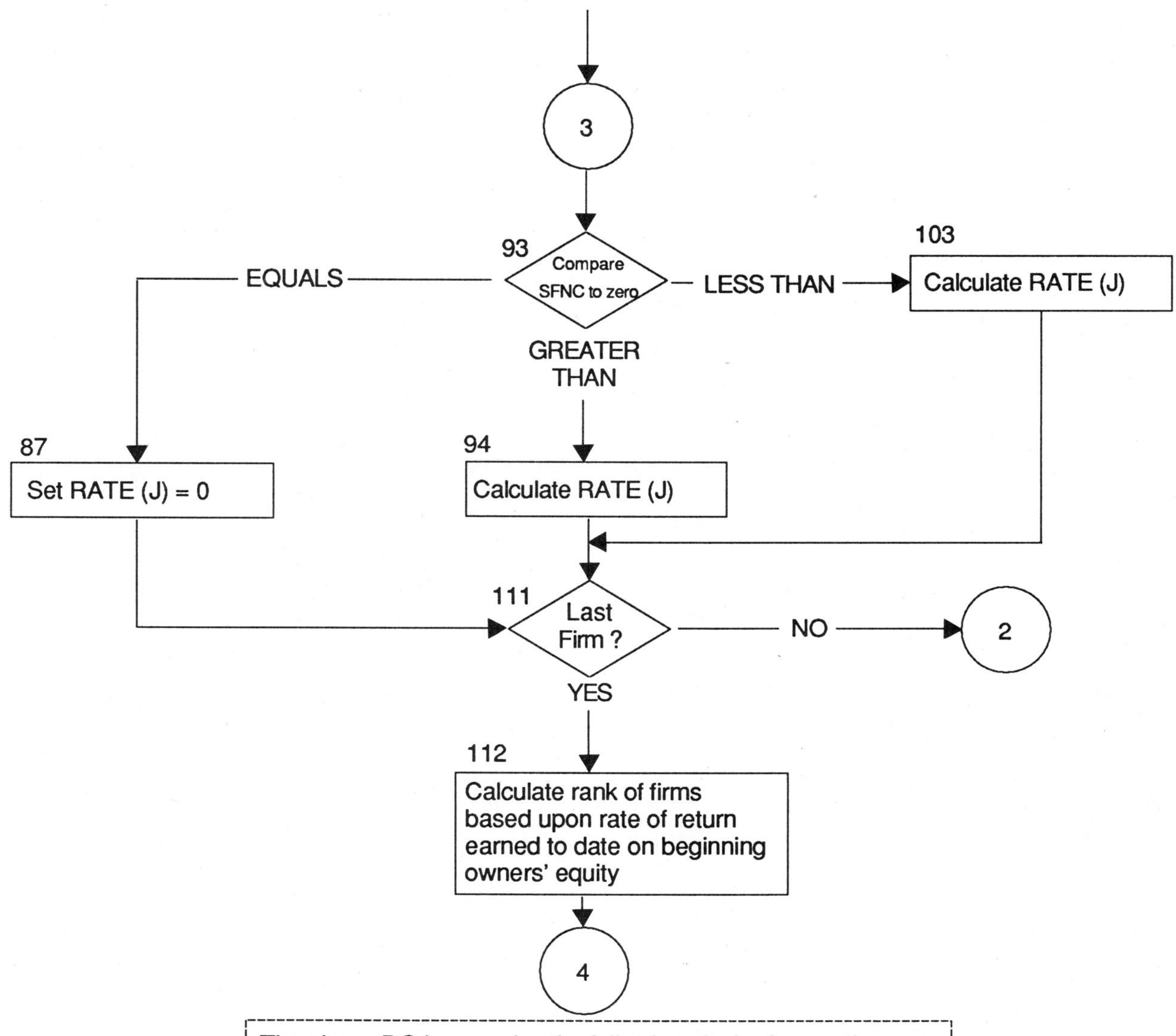

The above DO loops solve the following algebraic equation, one for each firm J, for the discounted rate of return earned on beginning owners' equity RATE (J), by iteration on the computer:

$$BOE = \frac{DV\,(1, J)}{(1+RATE(J))} + \frac{DV\,(2, J)}{(1 + RATE(J))^2} + \ldots + \frac{DV\,(L, J) + OEE(J)}{(1 + RATE(J)^L}$$

In the above equation RATE (J) represents the quarterly rate of return earned on beginning owners' equity. This is converted to an <u>annual basis</u> before being printed out.

12. Storing of output data

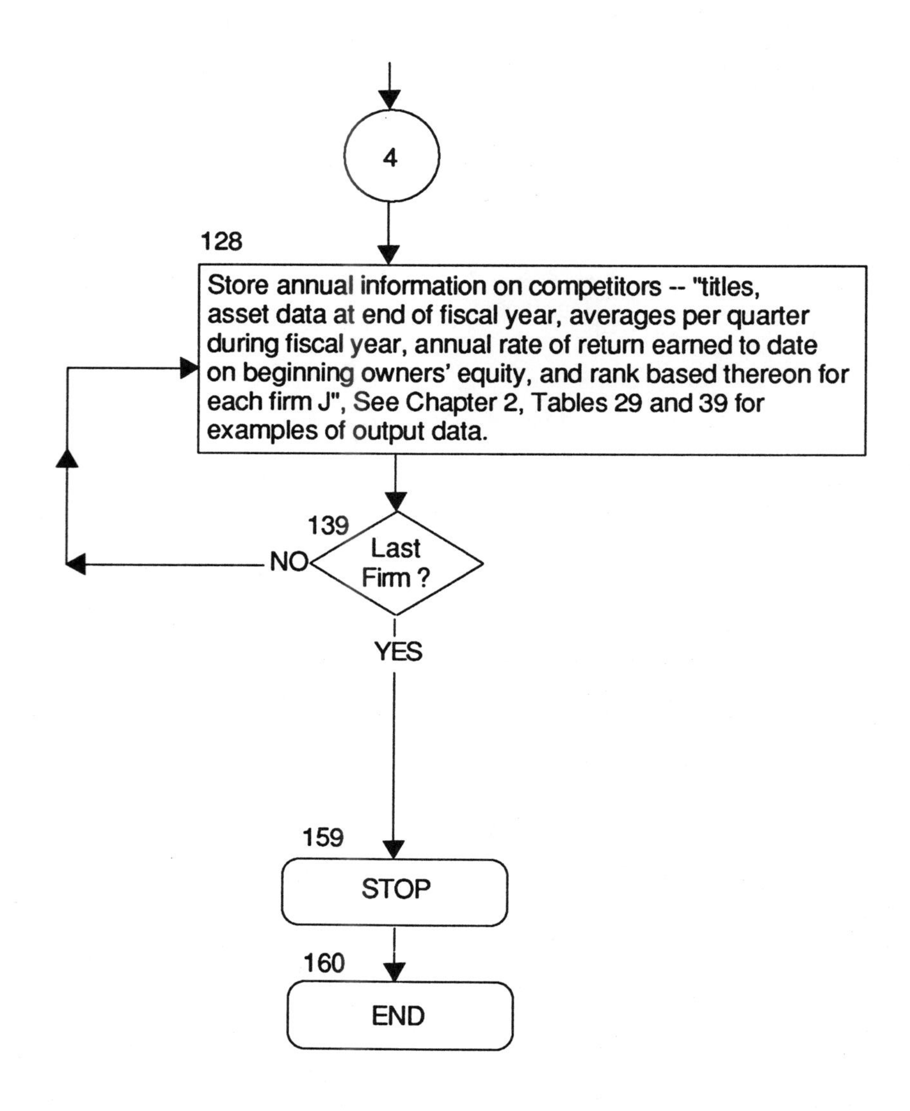

APPENDIX B

Alphabetical List of Variables and Their Definitions in Executive Game (XGAME) FORTRAN Program

ACA(J)	Addition to cash assets, Firm J, current period
AL(J)	Administration expense, includes CS(J), Firm J, current period
AOE(J)	Addition to owner's equity, Firm J, current period
AS1(J)	Actual sales first approximation, Firm J, current period
AS21(J)	Actual sales, Firm J, history (previous) period
AS22(J)	Actual sales, Firm J, current period
BT(J)	Net profit before income tax, Firm J, current period
C(J)	Cost of raw materials per unit of finished product, Firm J, current period. The first time C(J) is calculated, it represents the cost that would have occurred in the absence of inflation. Then it is recalculated a second time reflecting the effects of inflation.
CA1(J)	Cash assets, Firm J, history period
CA2(J)	Cash assets, Firm J, current period
CCFG(J)	Inventory carrying charges on finished goods, Firm J, current period
CCRM(J)	Inventory carrying charges on raw materials, Firm J, current period
CS(J)	This variable permits arbitrary addition or subtractions from the administration expense account for Firm J, current period. The statement on line 44 in Appendix C sets CS(J) = 0. In order to use this variable, change the statement to 45 CONTINUE
CX(J)	Cash expense, Firm J, current period
CY1(J)	Plant capacity this quarter, Firm J, independent of the effects of robotics
CY2(J)	Plant capacity next quarter, Firm J, including the effects of robotics
CY3(J)	Plant capacity at the end of the quarter, Firm J, independent of the effects of robotics

CY4(J)	Plant capacity next quarter, Firm J, including the effects of robotics
C1(J)	An intermediate calculation of C(J) (first approximation) Firm J, independent of the effects of robotics
DB(J)	Total cash disbursements, Firm J, current period
DCA	Cash deficit, Firm J, history period. This variable and various others that follow are not subscripted because they are used entirely within a single loop and thus do not have to be stored for further use
DFLAT	Deflation index, current period; reciprocal of price index P12.
DL(J)	Cost of direct labor per unit of finished product, Firm J, current period
DL1(J)	An intermediate calculation of DL(J), Firm J, independent of the effects of robotics
DP(J)	Dollar amount of depreciation of Plant and Equipment, Firm J, current period
DPR	Quarterly percentage rate of depreciation applicable to Plant and Equipment Book Value at the end of last quarter
DV(J)	Dividend, Firm J, current period
E	Actual economic index, current period
EL(J)	Direct labor expense, Firm J, current period
EN(K)	Error number, period K. The number is added to the forecast of the economic index to produce the actual economic index value.
ERR	A real variable defining the values of error statements
EX(J)	Total expenses, Firm J, current period
F(K)	Annual percentage rate of inflation, period K; i.e., annual percentage rate of change in the general price index during the quarter (period) K
FAC	Forecast of the annual percentage change in the general price index during the coming year; i.e., 4 quarters
FAS1	Total industry sales, first approximation, current period
FAS2	Actual total industry sales, current period
FC(J)	Financing charges and penalties related to a cash deficit, Firm J, current period
FCU	Total industry stockouts in units, first approximation
FE(K)	Forecasted economic index, period K
FFM	Industry marketing index, current period
FIV(J)	Inventory value of finished goods, Firm J, current period
FM1	Marketing index, deflated, Firm J, history period
FM2(J)	Marketing index, deflated, Firm J, current period
FMK(J)	Marketing budget, Firm J, current period

FN	Floating point representation of the number of firms N
FOC(J)	Ordering costs on raw materials, Firm J, current period
FP	Average industry price (of its product per unit) index, current period
FPS1	Total industry market potential, first approximation, current period
FPS2	Total industry market potential, current period
FR	Industry research and development index, current period
FUC(J)	Total industry orders not filled by firms other than Firm J which originally received the orders because of out-of-stock condition, current period
FW	Total of market share weighting factors, $\sum_J W(J)$, current period
G(J)	Available stock of finished goods, Firm J, current period
I	Dummy Index used in checking input order of history and decision data
II	Current period index
III	History (previous) period index
IPFN	Variable which defines permanent file name
IRT	An integer variable for detecting errors
IZ	Equals II + 2; it is used to terminate the loop used to calculate the general price indices.
J	Firm number index
JJ	Firm number index
JZ	Industry (or section) number index used to distinguish different groups who are playing the Game simultaneously
K	Period of the game index, past, present, future; K = 1,2, ..., III,II,II + 1, ..., 16, 17, ..., 19, 20
KI	Dummy index for entering input data
KKK	Dummy index for correcting typing input errors
L	Alternate firm number index
LL	Dummy index for entering input data
LLL	Dummy index for correcting typing input errors
M	Used to distinguish Model 1 and Model 2
MJZ	Dummy index used in checking order of histories input data
N	Number of firms
NC	Number of copies of results per firm to be output by computer and to be printed on printer
NJZ	Alternate industry (or section) number index used to check read in order of input data

NS1(J)	Number of shifts employed during history period, Firm J
NS2(J)	Number of shifts employed during current period, Firm J
NSD	Difference between the number of shifts employed in current period compared to history period, Firm J
OE(J)	Owners' equity, Firm J, current period
OEE(J)	Owners' economic equity, Firm J, current period
P(J)	Price (of product) index, Firm J, current period
PBV1(J)	Plant and Equipment net book value, Firm J, history period
PBV2(J)	Plant and Equipment net book value, Firm J, current period
PF	A real variable defining the permanent files
PFN	Permanent file name variable
PI0	General price index during the period prior to the history period
PI1	General price index, history period
PI2	General price index, current period; reciprocal of deflation index DFLAT
PI3	General price index during the period subsequent to the current period
PI4	General price index two periods subsequent to the current period
PM(J)	Purchase of materials, Firm J, current period
PNT(J)	Net profit after income tax, Firm J, current period
PR1(J)	Price of product per unit, deflated, Firm J, history period
PR2(J)	Price of product per unit, Firm J, current period
PRICEL	Price elasticity variable which is a function of FFM and FR
PRV(J)	Plant replacement value, Firm J, current period
PRV1(J)	Plant replacement values, Firm J, history period
PS1(J)	Market potential, first approximation, Firm J, current period
PS21(J)	Market potential, Firm J, history period
PS22(J)	Market potential, Firm J, current period
PV(J)	Production volume scheduled, Firm J, current period
PVA	Maximum production volume which raw materials inventory on hand will support, Firm J, current period
PVP(J)	Production volume produced, Firm J, current period
PV2	Production volume produced, an intermediate approximation, Firm J, current period
QTR(K)	Alphabetical variable for calendar quarter of year, i.e., JFM, AMJ, JAS, or OND, respectively, corresponding to period K
R1(J)	Research and development index, deflated, Firm J, history period

R2(J)	Research and development index, Firm J, current period
RBV1(J)	Robotics net book value, Firm J, history period
RBV2(J)	Robotics net book value, Firm J, current period
RD(J)	Research and development budget, Firm J, current period
RDP(J)	Dollar amount of depreciation applicable to robotics book value at the end of last quarter, Firm J
RDPR	Quarterly percentage rate of depreciation applicable to robotics book value at the end of history period
RINV(J)	Reduction in finished goods inventory value, Firm J, current period
RM1(J)	Raw materials inventory value, Firm J, history period
RM2(J)	Raw materials inventory value, Firm J, current period
RMD1(J)	Raw materials inventory value, deflated, Firm J, history period
RMD2(J)	Raw materials inventory value, deflated, Firm J, current period
RMDE(J)	Raw materials inventory value, deflated, Firm J, current period
RME(J)	Raw materials inventory value, current period
RRV(J)	Robotics replacement value, Firm J, current period
RRV1(J)	Robotics replacement value, Firm J, history period
RRV2	Arithmetic average of robotics replacement value for all firms during the history period
S(K)	Seasonal index, period K
SC1(J)	Standard cost of finished goods inventory per unit, Firm J, history period
SC2(J)	Standard cost of finished goods inventory per unit, Firm J, current period
SCC(J)	Shifts change costs, Firm J, current period
SP(J)	Percent share of industry sales, Firm J, current period
SR(J)	Sales revenue, Firm J, current period
ST1(J)	Remaining stock of finished goods, Firm J, history period
ST2(J)	Remaining stock of finished goods, Firm J, current period
SUN(J)	Sundry expenses dependent of plant size (fixed and semifixed; sundries), Firm J, current period
SURT	Percentage rate of surtax, current period
T1(J)	Maintenance index, deflated, Firm J, history period
T2(J)	Maintenance index, deflated, Firm J, current period
TC(J)	Maintenance budget, Firm J, current period
TCA	Maintenance adjustment factor for scheduled production rates at over or under capacity operations, Firm J, current period

TX(J)	Income tax, Firm J, current period
TXC	Investment tax credit variable
VP(J)	Investment in plant, Firm J, current period
VPE(J)	Expenses and penalties related to plant investment, Firm J, current period
VR(J)	Investment in robotics, Firm J, current period
W(J)	Market share weighting factor, Firm J, current period

APPENDIX C

Executive Game (XGAME) VS2 FORTRAN Program

```
LEVEL 2.2.0                              VS FORTRAN

OPTIONS IN EFFECT: NOLIST NOMAP NOXREF NOGOSTMT NODECK SOURCE TERM OBJECT FIXED TRMFLG
                   SDUMP(ISN) AUTODBL(NONE) NOSXM NOVECTOR IL NOTEST NODC NOICA NODIREC
                      OPT(0) LANGLVL(77) NOFIPS    FLAG(I)  NAME(MAIN)     LINECOUNT(60)

 IF DO    ISN    *....*...1.........2.........3.........4.........5.........6.........7.*

            1           PROGRAM XGAME
                 C      PROGRAM MODIFIED FOR USE ON IBM 3090
                 C      COPYRIGHT, 1988. RICHARD D. IRWIN, INC.
                 C      HOMEWOOD, ILLINOIS 60430
            2           DIMENSION ACA(9),AL(9),AOE(9),AS1(9),AS21(9),AS22(9),BT(9),C(9),
                       1CA1(9),CA2(9),CCFG(9),CCRM(9),CS(9),CX(9),CY1(9),CY2(9),DB(9),DL(9
                       2),DP(9),DV(9),EL(9),EN(16),EX(9),F(20),FC(9),FE(17),FIV(9),FM1(9),
                       3FM2(9),FMK(9),FOC(9),FUC(9),G(9),NS1(9),NS2(9),OE(9),OEE(9),P(9),
                       4PBV1(9),PBV2(9),PM(9),PNT(9),PR1(9),PR2(9),PRV(9),PS1(9),PS21(9)
            3           DIMENSION PS22(9),PV(9),PVP(9),QTR(16),R1(9),R2(9),RD(9),RINV(9),
                       1RM1(9),RM2(9),RMD1(9),RMD2(9),RMDE(9),RME(9),S(17),SC1(9),SC2(9),
                       2SCC(9),SP(9),SR(9),ST1(9),ST2(9),SUN(9),T1(9),T2(9),TC(9),TX(9),
                       3VP(9),VPE(9),W(9),RBV1(9),RRV1(9),C1(9),DL1(9),CY3(9),CY4(9),RRV
                       4(9),VR(9),RBV2(9),RDP(9),PRV1(9)
            4           INTEGER TAPE(22)
            5           CHARACTER PFN*40,QTR*3
            6           REAL PF,ERR
            7           CHARACTER*48 FILE
            8           CHARACTER*32 FILE2
            9           CHARACTER*2 UNITN
           10           INTEGER*4 IRT
           11           DATA QTR/'JAS','OND','JFM','AMJ','JAS','OND','JFM','AMJ','JAS',
                       +'OND','JFM','AMJ','JAS','OND','JFM','AMJ'/
           12           DATA S/95.,115.,90.,100.,95.,115.,90.,100.,95.,115.,90.,100.,95.,
                       +115.,90.,100.,95./
           13           DATA F/4.,5.,6.,5.,5.,4.,5.,6.,6.,7.,7.,8.,7.,6.,4.,4.,3.,2.,2.,2.
                       +/
           14           DATA FE/100.,95.,93.,90.,95.,97.,100.,100.,103.,105.,107.,107.,
                       +105.,104.,102.,102.,100./
           15           DATA EN/1.,-1.,2.,-1.,1.,-2.,1.,-1.,1.,-2.,1.,0.,-1.,2.,0.,-1./
           16           DATA FILE/'FILEDEF XX       DISK     XXXX     DAT                '/

                 C      CREATE TAPE 10
           17           FILE2='FILEDEF 10       TERMINAL
           18           CALL CMSCMD(FILE2,IRT)
           19           IF (IRT.NE.0) GOTO 5000
           20           OPEN (UNIT=10,STATUS='SCRATCH',IOSTAT=IRT,ERR=5000,
                       + ACCESS='SEQUENTIAL',FORM='  FORMATTED')
           21           DO 980 I=1,9
    1      22             TAPE(I)=I+10
    1      23    980      TAPE(I+10)=I+20
           24           TAPE(10)=10
           25           TAPE(20)=92
           26           TAPE(21)=94
           27           TAPE(22)=95
           28           PRINT 900
           29    900    FORMAT(80HOENTER INDUSTRY NO.,MODEL NO.,NUMBER OF FIRMS,AND PERIOD
                       + NO.,SEPARATED BY COMMAS/)
           30           READ(10,*) JZ,M,N,II
           31    2000   PRINT 2010, JZ,M,N,II
           32    2010   FORMAT(14HOYOUR INPUT IS/16HO1  INDUSTRY NO.,I3/13HO2  MODEL NO.,I
                       +3/19HO3  NUMBER OF FIRMS,I3/14HO4  PERIOD NO.,I4)
           33           PRINT 2020
           34    2020   FORMAT(35HOIF OK ENTER 0, IF IN ERROR ENTER 1 /)
           35           READ(10,*) LLL
           36           IF(LLL) 2000,2090,2030
```

```
IF DO    ISN    *....*...1.........2.........3.........4.........5.........6.........7.*

         37     2030   PRINT 3000
         38     3000   FORMAT(53HOENTER THE NUMBER OF THE DATA ITEM YOU WISH TO CHANGE/14
                      +HOENTER 0 IF OK /)
         39            READ(10,*) KKK
         40            IF (KKK) 2030,2000,2040
         41     2040   GO TO(6,9,7,8) KKK
         42     6      PRINT 2050
         43     2050   FORMAT(36HOENTER DATA ITEM 1, THE INDUSTRY NO. /)
         44            READ(10,*) JZ
         45            GO TO 2030
         46     9      PRINT 2060
         47     2060   FORMAT(33HOENTER DATA ITEM 2, THE MODEL NO. /)
         48            READ(10,*) M
         49            GO TO 2030
         50     7      PRINT 2070
         51     2070   FORMAT(39HOENTER DATA ITEM 3, THE NUMBER OF FIRMS /)
         52            READ(10,*) N
         53            GO TO 2030
         54     8      PRINT 2080
         55     2080   FORMAT(34HOENTER DATA ITEM 4, THE PERIOD NO. /)
         56            READ(10,*) II
         57            GO TO 2030
         58     2090   TXC=0.
         59            SURT=0.
         60            DPR=2.5
         61            RDPR=5.0
         62     1110   PRINT 1020,TXC,SURT,DPR,RDPR
         63     1020   FORMAT(36HOTHE CURRENT VALUES (IN PERCENT) ARE/24HO1 INVESTMENT TA
                      1X CREDIT,F6.1/9HO2 SURTAX,F6.1/24HO3 PLANT&EQ.DEPRECIATION,F8.3/24
                      2HO4 ROBOTICS DEPRECIATION,F8.3)
         64            PRINT 1030
         65     1030   FORMAT(35HOIF OK ENTER 0, IF IN ERROR ENTER 1 /)
         66            READ(10,*) KI
         67            IF(KI) 1040,1100,1040
         68     1040   PRINT 1050
         69     1050   FORMAT(53HOENTER THE NUMBER OF THE DATA ITEM YOU WISH TO CHANGE/
                      +16HO ENTER 0 IF OK./)
         70            READ(10,*) LL
         71            IF(LL) 1040,1110,1060
         72     1060   GO TO (1,2,3,4) LL
         73     1      PRINT 1070
         74     1070   FORMAT(45HOENTER DATA ITEM 1, THE INVESTMENT TAX CREDIT/)
         75            READ(10,*) TXC
         76            GO TO 1040
         77     2      PRINT 1080
         78     1080   FORMAT(30HOENTER DATA ITEM 2, THE SURTAX/)
         79            READ(10,*) SURT
         80            GO TO 1040
         81     3      PRINT 1090
         82     1090   FORMAT(41HOENTER DATA ITEM 3, PLANT&EQ.DEPRECIATION/)
         83            READ(10,*) DPR
         84            GO TO 1040
         85     4      PRINT 1095
         86     1095   FORMAT(41HOENTER DATA ITEM 4, ROBOTICS DEPRECIATION/)
         87            READ(10,*) RDPR
         88            GO TO 1040
         89     1100   IF(II-1) 1120,1120,1000
         90     1120   DO 990 J=1,N
     1   91            PR1(J)=25.6
     1   92            FM1(J)=240000.
```

```
 IF DO   ISN   *....*...1.........2.........3.........4.........5.........6.........7.*

    1     93            R1(J)=150000.
    1     94            T1(J)=75000.
    1     95            RM1(J)=1200000.
    1     96            CY1(J)=104643.
    1     97            RBV1(J)=0.
    1     98            RRV1(J)=0.
    1     99            ST1(J)=12750.
    1    100            PS21(J)=109720.
    1    101            AS21(J)=109720.
    1    102            CA1(J)=1022000.
    1    103            RMD1(J)=1200000.
    1    104            PBV1(J)=7325000.
    1    105            SC1(J)=12.
    1    106      990   NS1(J)=1
         107            GO TO 1010
               C        CREATE TAPE92
         108     1000   IPFN=
         109            WRITE(PFN,'(I6.6)') IPFN
         110            FILE(9:10)='92'
         111            FILE(25:31)=PFN
         112            CALL CMSCMD(FILE,IRT)
         113            IF (IRT.NE.0) GOTO 5010
         114            OPEN (UNIT=92,STATUS='OLD',IOSTAT=IRT,ERR=5010)
               C        CREATE TAPE01-0N
         115     1010   DO 912 J=1,N
    1    116            IPFN=
    1    117            WRITE(PFN,'(I4.4)') IPFN
    1    118            WRITE(UNITN,'(I2.2)') TAPE(J)
    1    119            FILE(9:10)=UNITN
    1    120            FILE(25:31)=PFN
    1    121            CALL CMSCMD(FILE,IRT)
    1    122            IF (IRT.NE.0) GOTO 5020
    1    123      912   OPEN (UNIT=TAPE(J),STATUS='OLD',IOSTAT=IRT,ERR=5020)
               C        CREATE TAPE94
         124            IPFN=
         125            WRITE(PFN,'(I6.6)') IPFN
         126            FILE(9:10)='94'
         127            FILE(25:31)=PFN
         128            CALL CMSCMD(FILE,IRT)
         129            IF (IRT.NE.0) GOTO 5030
         130            OPEN (UNIT=94,STATUS='NEW',IOSTAT=IRT,ERR=5030)
         131            IPFN=
         132            WRITE(PFN,'(I6.6)') IPFN
         133            FILE(9:10)='95'
         134            FILE(25:31)=PFN
         135            CALL CMSCMD(FILE,IRT)
         136            IF (IRT.NE.0) GOTO 5040
         137            OPEN (UNIT=95,STATUS='NEW',IOSTAT=IRT,ERR=5040)
         138      745   FORMAT(I2,I1,I2,F7.3,3F9.0,F10.0,3F9.0)
         139      755   FORMAT(I3,I1,I2,F9.0,2F8.0,F10.0,2F9.0,F11.7,I2/F8.0)
         140      765   FORMAT(I2,I1,I2,F6.2,2F9.0,4F8.0,2F9.0/F9.0)
         141        775 FORMAT(29H ERROR IN ORDER OF INPUT DATA)
         142            REWIND 92
         143            REWIND 94
         144            REWIND 95
         145            FN=N
         146            III=II-1
         147            I=III+1
         148            NJZ=JZ
         149            IF(II-1) 1140,1140,1130
```

```
 IF DO    ISN     *....*...1.........2.........3.........4.........5.........6.........7.*

          150     1130  DO 30 J=1,N
    1     151           READ(92,745)JZ,JJ,III,PR1(J),FM1(J),R1(J),T1(J),RM1(J),CY1(J),
    1                  1RBV1(J),RRV1(J)
    1     152           MJZ=JZ+JJ+III
    1     153           READ(92,755)JZ,JJ,III,ST1(J),PS21(J),AS21(J),CA1(J),RMD1(J),PBV1(J
    1                  1),SC1(J),NS1(J)
    1     154           IF(MJZ-JZ-JJ-III) 50,5,50
    1     155         5 IF(J-1)55,10,15
    1     156        10 NJZ=JZ
    1     157           I=III+1
    1     158        15 IF(NJZ-JZ)50,20,50
    1     159        20 IF(J-JJ)50,25,50
    1     160        25 IF(I-III-1)50,30,50
    1     161        30 CONTINUE
          162     1140  DO 45 J=1,N
    1     163           PRINT 965,J
    1     164           REWIND J
    1     165           READ(TAPE(J),765)JZ,JJ,II,PR2(J),FMK(J),RD(J),TC(J),PV(J),VR(J),
    1                  1VP(J),PM(J),DV(J),CS(J)
    1     166           IF(NJZ-JZ)50,35,50
    1     167        35 IF(J-JJ)50,40,50
    1     168        40 IF(II-I)50,45,50
    1     169        45 CS(J)=0.
          170           GO TO 60
          171        50 PRINT   775
          172        55 STOP
          173        60 FP=0.
          174           FFM=0.
          175           FR=0.
          176           FW=0.
          177           FPS2=0.
          178           FAS1=0.
          179           FAS2=0.
          180           RRV2=0.
          181           PI0=1.
          182           PI1=1.
          183           IZ=II+2
          184           DO 100 K=1,IZ
    1     185           IF(K-III)65,70,75
    1     186        65 PI0=PI0*(.01*F(K)+1.)
    1     187           GO TO 100
    1     188        70 PI1=PI0*(.01*F(II)+1.)
    1     189           GO TO 100
    1     190        75 IF(K-II)55,80,85
    1     191        80 PI2=PI1*(.01*F(K)+1.)
    1     192           GO TO 100
    1     193        85 IF(K-II-1)55,90,95
    1     194        90 PI3=PI2*(.01*F(K)+1.)
    1     195           GO TO 100
    1     196        95 PI4=PI3*(.01*F(K)+1.)
    1     197       100 CONTINUE
          198           PI0=PI0**.25
          199           PI1=PI1**.25
          200           PI2=PI2**.25
          201           PI3=PI3**.25
          202           PI4=PI4**.25
          203           DFLAT=1./PI2
          204           E=FE(II)+EN(II)
          205           FAC=(F(II+1)+F(II+2)+F(II+3)+F(II+4))*.25
          206           DO 125 J=1,N
```

```
 IF DO   ISN    *....*...1.........2.........3.........4.........5.........6.........7.*

     1   207          IF(PR2(J)-SC1(J))105,120,110
     1   208      105 PR2(J)=SC1(J)
     1   209          GO TO 120
     1   210      110 IF(PR2(J)-36.*PI0)120,120,115
     1   211      115 PR2(J)=36.*PI0
     1   212      120 P(J)=1.2*PR2(J)/PI0-0.2*PR1(J)
     1   213          FP=FP+1./P(J)
     1   214          FM2(J)=0.7*(FMK(J)+40000.)*DFLAT+0.3*FM1(J)
     1   215          FFM=FFM+FM2(J)/FN
     1   216          RRV2=RRV2+RRV1(J)/FN
     1   217          R2(J)=0.3*(RD(J)+50000.)*DFLAT+0.7*R1(J)
     1   218          FR=FR+R1(J)/FN
     1   219          CY2(J)=CY1(J)*(2.-2.718**(-RRV1(J)/.1E8))+1.
     1   220          PRV1(J)=70.*CY2(J)*PI1
     1   221          TCA=TC(J)/PI3*(CY2(J)+50000.)/(PV(J)+50000.)
     1   222      125 T2(J)=0.5*TCA+0.5*T1(J)
         223          FP=FN/FP
         224          PRICEL=6.*2.718**(-(FFM+FR+RRV2)/1.E6)
         225          DO 130 J=1,N
     1   226          W(J)=(40.-P(J))**PRICEL*((FM2(J)+150000.)*(R1(J)+400000.))**.7
     1   227          W(J)=W(J)*(2.-2.718**(-RRV1(J)/1.2E6))
     1   228      130 FW=FW+W(J)
         229          FPS1=(44.-FP)**2.*FN*E**1.4*S(II)*.01223645*(FFM+100000.)*(FR+RRV2
                     1/2.+50000.)/((FFM+300000.)*(FR+RRV2/2.+150000.))
         230          DO 190 J=1,N
     1   231          PS1(J)=FPS1*W(J)/FW+0.4*(PR1(J)*PI0/PR2(J))**3.*(PS21(J)-AS21(J))
     1   232          FPS2=FPS2+PS1(J)
     1   233          C1(J)=8.60-(8.*R1(J)+4.*T2(J)+650000.)/(2.*R1(J)+T2(J)+562500.)
     1   234          C(J)=C1(J)/(2.-2.718**(-RRV1(J)/0.6E7))
     1   235          IF(M-1)135,135,140
     1   236      135 IF(1.4*CY2(J)-PV(J))145,155,155
     1   237      140 IF(3.*CY2(J)-PV(J))150,155,155
     1   238      145 PV2=1.4*CY2(J)
     1   239          GO TO 160
     1   240      150 PV2=3.*CY2(J)
     1   241          GO TO 160
     1   242      155 PV2=PV(J)
     1   243      160 PVA=RMD1(J)/C(J)
     1   244          IF(PV2-PVA)165,165,170
     1   245      165 PVP(J)=PV2
     1   246          GO TO 175
     1   247      170 PVP(J)=PVA
     1   248      175 G(J)=ST1(J)+PVP(J)
     1   249          IF(PS1(J)-G(J))180,180,185
     1   250      180 AS1(J)=PS1(J)
     1   251          GO TO 190
     1   252      185 AS1(J)=G(J)
     1   253      190 FAS1=FAS1+AS1(J)
         254          FCU=FPS2-FAS1
         255          DO 210 J=1,N
     1   256          FUC(J)=(FCU-PS1(J)+AS1(J))*0.5
     1   257          PS22(J)=(FPS1+.5*FUC(J))*W(J)/FW+0.4*(PR1(J)*PI0/PR2(J))**3.
     1               1*(PS21(J)-AS21(J))-(PS1(J)-AS1(J))*0.5
     1   258          IF(PS22(J)-G(J)) 195,195,200
     1   259      195 AS22(J)=PS22(J)
     1   260          GO TO 205
     1   261      200 AS22(J)=G(J)
     1   262      205 FAS2=FAS2+AS22(J)
     1   263      210 ST2(J)=G(J)-AS22(J)
         264          DO 455 J=1,N
```

```
 IF DO   ISN    *....*...1.........2.........3.........4.........5.........6.........7.*

     1   265          SP(J)=100.*AS22(J)/FAS2
     1   266          DL1(J)=7.80*PI1-(2.*R1(J)+14.*T2(J)+350000.)/(.5*R1(J)+3.5*T2(J
     1               1)+487500.)
     1   267          SR(J)=AS22(J)*PR2(J)
     1   268          DL(J)=DL1(J)/(2.-2.718**(-RRV1(J)/.5E7))
     1   269          CY3(J)=0.980*CY1(J)+VP(J)/(PI2*70.)
     1   270          RRV(J)=RRV1(J)*.96875*PI2/PI1+VR(J)
     1   271          CY4(J)=CY3(J)*(2.-2.718**(-RRV(J)/.1E8))
     1   272          DP(J)=PBV1(J)*DPR*.01
     1   273          RDP(J)=RBV1(J)*RDPR*.01
     1   274          PRV(J)=70.*CY3(J)*PI2
     1   275          IF(PVP(J)-CY2(J))235,235,240
     1   276      235 EL(J)=DL(J)*PVP(J)
     1   277          AL(J)=(150000.+1.28*CY2(J))*PI1
     1   278          NS2(J)=1
     1   279          GO TO 285
     1   280      240 IF(PVP(J)-1.40*CY2(J))255,255,260
     1   281      255 EL(J)=DL(J)*CY2(J)+1.5*DL(J)*(PVP(J)-CY2(J))
     1   282          AL(J)=(200000.+1.28*CY2(J))*PI1
     1   283          NS2(J)=1
     1   284          GO TO 285
     1   285      260 IF(PVP(J)-2.*CY2(J))265,265,270
     1   286      265 EL(J)=DL(J)*PVP(J)
     1   287          AL(J)=(250000.+1.28*CY2(J))*PI1
     1   288          NS2(J)=2
     1   289          GO TO 285
     1   290      270 IF(PVP(J)-2.5*CY2(J))275,275,280
     1   291      275 EL(J)=DL(J)*2.*CY2(J)+1.5*DL(J)*(PVP(J)-2.*CY2(J))
     1   292          AL(J)=(300000.+1.28*CY2(J))*PI1
     1   293          NS2(J)=2
     1   294          GO TO 285
     1   295      280 EL(J)=DL(J)*PVP(J)
     1   296          AL(J)=(350000.+1.28*CY2(J))*PI1
     1   297          NS2(J)=3
     1   298      285 AL(J)=AL(J)/(2.-2.718**((-R1(J)-PRV1(J)/20.)/4.5E7))+ CS(J)
     1   299          NSD=NS2(J)-NS1(J)
     1   300          IF(NSD*NSD-1)290,295,300
     1   301      290 SCC(J)=0.
     1   302          GO TO 305
     1   303      295 SCC(J)=100000.*PI1
     1   304          GO TO 305
     1   305      300 SCC(J)=200000.*PI1
     1   306      305 RMDE(J)=C(J)*PVP(J)
     1   307          C(J)=C(J)*RM1(J)/(RMD1(J)+.001)
     1   308          RME(J)=C(J)*PVP(J)
     1   309          IF(AS22(J)-ST1(J))310,315,315
     1   310      310 RINV(J)=SC1(J)*AS22(J)-12.*PVP(J)*PI1
     1   311          SC2(J)=(SC1(J)*(ST1(J)-AS22(J))+12.*PVP(J)*PI1)/(ST1(J)-AS22(J)
     1               1+PVP(J))
     1   312          GO TO 320
     1   313      315 RINV(J)=SC1(J)*ST1(J)-12.*ST2(J)*PI1
     1   314          SC2(J)=12.*PI1
     1   315      320 IF(CA1(J))330,325,325
     1   316      325 DCA=0.
     1   317          GO TO 335
     1   318      330 DCA=CA1(J)
     1   319      335 CCRM(J)=0.05*RM1(J)
     1   320          VPE(J)=1.0E-7*(VP(J)+VR(J))**2.
     1   321          FC(J)=0.9E-7*DCA*DCA*PI4/PI0
     1   322          SUN(J)=(10000.+.72*CY2(J))*PI1
```

```
 IF DO    ISN    *....*...1.........2.........3.........4.........5.........6.........7.*

     1    323          SUN(J)=SUN(J)/(2.-2.718**((-R1(J)-PRV1(J)/20.)/4.9E7))
     1    324          CCFG(J)=2.*ST2(J)*SC2(J)/12.
     1    325          IF(PM(J))340,340,345
     1    326      340 FOC(J)=0.
     1    327          GO TO 350
     1    328      345 FOC(J)=50000.*PI1
     1    329      350 EX(J)=EL(J)+RME(J)+RINV(J)+AL(J)+FMK(J)+RD(J)+TC(J)+DP(J)+CCRM(J)+
     1                1CCFG(J)+VPE(J)+FC(J)+FOC(J)+SCC(J)+SUN(J)+RDP(J)
     1    330          BT(J)=SR(J)-EX(J)
     1    331          TX(J)=(.34*BT(J)-TXC*(VP(J)*.005+VR(J)*.01))*(1.+SURT*.01)
     1    332          PNT(J)=BT(J)-TX(J)
     1    333          IF(CA1(J)+SC1(J)*ST1(J)+RM1(J)+PBV1(J)+RBV1(J)-
     1                1.9E7)445,445,435
     1    334      435 IF(CA1(J)+SC1(J)*ST1(J)+RM1(J)+PBV1(J)+RBV1(J)-
     1                1.9E7)440,450,450
     1    335      440 DV(J)=CA1(J)+SC1(J)*ST1(J)+RM1(J)+PBV1(J)+RBV1(J)
     1                1-.9E7
     1    336          GO TO 450
     1    337      445 DV(J)=0.
     1    338      450 AOE(J)=PNT(J)-DV(J)
     1    339          CX(J)=EX(J)-RME(J)-RINV(J)-DP(J)-RDP(J)
     1    340          DB(J)=CX(J)+TX(J)+DV(J)+VP(J)+PM(J)+VR(J)
     1    341          ACA(J)=SR(J)-DB(J)
     1    342          CA2(J)=CA1(J)+ACA(J)
     1    343          FIV(J)=SC2(J)*ST2(J)
     1    344          RM2(J)=RM1(J)+PM(J)-RME(J)
     1    345          RMD2(J)=RMD1(J)+PM(J)/PI1-RMDE(J)
     1    346          PBV2(J)=PBV1(J)-DP(J)+VP(J)
     1    347          RBV2(J)=RBV1(J)-RDP(J)+VR(J)
     1    348          OE(J)=CA2(J)+FIV(J)+RM2(J)+PBV2(J)+RBV2(J)
     1    349      455 OEE(J)=OE(J)-PBV2(J)+PRV(J)-RBV2(J)+RRV(J)
          350          PI2=100.*PI2
          351          DO 465 J=1,N
     1    352          K=J+10
     1    353          IPFN=
     1    354          WRITE(PFN,'(I5.5)') IPFN
     1    355          WRITE(UNITN,'(I2.2)') TAPE(K)
     1    356          FILE(9:10)=UNITN
     1    357          FILE(25:31)=PFN
     1    358          CALL CMSCMD(FILE,IRT)
     1    359          IF (IRT.NE.0) GOTO 5050
     1    360          OPEN (UNIT=TAPE(K),STATUS='NEW',IOSTAT=IRT,ERR=5050)
     1    361          PRINT 965,K
     1    362          WRITE(TAPE(K),765)JZ,J,II,PR2(J),FMK(J),RD(J),TC(J),PV(J),VR(J),
     1                1VP(J),PM(J),DV(J)
     1    363          WRITE(TAPE(K),815)M,II,QTR(II),PI2,FAC,S(II),S(II+1),E,FE(II+1)
     1    364          DO 460 L=1,N
     2    365      460 WRITE(TAPE(K),825)L,PR2(L),DV(L),AS22(L),PNT(L)
     1    366          WRITE(TAPE(K),835)JZ,J,PS22(J),AS22(J),SP(J),PVP(J),ST2(J),CY4(J)
     1    367          WRITE(TAPE(K),845)SR(J),FMK(J),RD(J),AL(J),TC(J),DL(J),EL(J),C(J),
     1                + RME(J)
     1    368          WRITE(TAPE(K),855)RINV(J),DPR,DP(J),RDPR,RDP(J),CCFG(J),CCRM(J),
     1                + FOC(J)
     1    369          WRITE(TAPE(K),860)SCC(J),VPE(J)
     1    370          WRITE(TAPE(K),865)FC(J),SUN(J),EX(J),BT(J),TXC,SURT,TX(J),PNT(J),
     1                1DV(J),AOE(J)
     1    371          WRITE(TAPE(K),875)SR(J),CX(J),TX(J),DV(J),VR(J),VP(J),PM(J),DB(J),
     1                + ACA(J)
     1    372          WRITE(TAPE(K),880)
```

```
 IF DO   ISN    *....*...1.........2.........3.........4.........5.........6.........7.*

     1   373     465 WRITE(TAPE(K),885)CA2(J),FIV(J),RM2(J),RRV(J),RBV2(J),PRV(J),
     1              1PBV2(J),OEE(J),OE(J)
         374          PRINT 895
         375          DO 470 J=1,N
     1   376          PRINT   905,JZ,J,II,CA2(J),FIV(J),RM2(J),RRV(J),PRV(J),FMK(J),RD(J
     1              1),AS22(J),DV(J),PNT(J)
     1   377     470 WRITE(94,915)JZ,J,II,CA2(J),FIV(J),RM2(J),RRV(J),PRV(J),FMK(J),RD(
     1              1J),AS22(J),DV(J),PNT(J)
         378          PRINT 925
         379          DO 475 J=1,N
     1   380          PR2(J)=PR2(J)/PIO
     1   381          PRINT   935,JZ,J,II,PR2(J),FM2(J),R2(J),T2(J),RM2(J),CY3(J),
     1              1RBV2(J),RRV(J)
     1   382          PRINT   945,JZ,J,II,ST2(J),PS22(J),AS22(J),CA2(J),RMD2(J),PBV2(J),
     1              1SC2(J),NS2(J)
     1   383          WRITE(95,745)JZ,J,II,PR2(J),FM2(J),R2(J),T2(J),RM2(J),CY3(J),
     1              1RBV2(J),RRV(J)
     1   384     475 WRITE(95,755)JZ,J,II,ST2(J),PS22(J),AS22(J),CA2(J),RMD2(J),PBV2(J)
     1              +,SC2(J),NS2(J),RBV2(J)
         385     815 FORMAT(    30X,14HEXECUTIVE GAME/ 5HMODEL,I2,7H PERIOD,I3,1X,A3,12
                    1H PRICE INDEX,F6.1,23H FORECAST,ANNUAL CHANGE,F5.1,4H 0/0/ 10HSEAS
                    2.INDEX,F5.0,10H NEXT QTR.,F5.0,12H  ECON.INDEX,F5.0,19H FORECAST,N
                    3EXT QTR.,F5.0//18X,11HINFORMATION,10X,2HON,11X,11HCOMPETITORS/12X,
                    45HPRICE,11X,25HDIVIDEND      SALES VOLUME,8X,10HNET PROFIT)
         386     825 FORMAT( 6H  FIRM,I2,5H   $ ,F5.2,7X,1H$,F9.0,7X,F9.0,9X,1H$,F10.0)
         387     835 FORMAT(/36X,4HFIRM,I3,I2/28X,20HOPERATING STATEMENTS/5X,16HMARKET
                    1POTENTIAL,24X,F9.0/5X,12HSALES VOLUME,28X,F9.0/5X,31HPERCENT SHARE
                    2 OF INDUSTRY SALES,9X,F9.1/5X,23HPRODUCTION,THIS QUARTER,17X,F9.0/
                    35X,24HINVENTORY,FINISHED GOODS,16X,F9.0/5X,27HPLANT CAPACITY,NEXT
                    4QUARTER,13X,F9.0)
         388     845 FORMAT(32X,16HINCOME STATEMENT/5X,22HRECEIPTS,SALES REVENUE,33X,1H
                    1$,F10.0/5X,18HEXPENSES,MARKETING,22X,1H$,F9.0/7X,24HRESEARCH AND D
                    2EVELOPMENT,15X,F9.0/7X,14HADMINISTRATION,25X,F9.0/7X,11HMAINTENANC
                    3E,28X,F9.0/7X,29HLABOR(COST/UNIT EX.OVERTIME $,F5.2,5H)    ,F9.0/7
                    4X,29HMATERIALS CONSUMED(COST/UNIT ,F5.2,5H)     ,F9.0)
         389     855 FORMAT(7X,29HREDUCTION,FINISHED GOODS INV.,10X,F9.0/7X,22HPLANT&EQ
                    1.DEPRECIATION(,F5.3,5H 0/0),7X,F9.0/7X,22HROBOTICS DEPRECIATION(,F
                    25.3,5H 0/0),7X,F9.0/7X,29HFINISHED GOODS CARRYING COSTS,10X,F9.0/7
                    3X,28HRAW MATERIALS CARRYING COSTS,11X,F9.0/7X,14HORDERING COSTS,25
                    4X,F9.0)
         390    860   FORMAT(7X,19HSHIFTS CHANGE COSTS,20X,F9.0/7X,20HINVESTMENTS EXPENS
                    1ES,19X,F9.0)
         391     865 FORMAT(7X,31HFINANCING CHARGES AND PENALTIES,8X,F9.0/7X,8HSUNDRIES
                    1,31X,F9.0,7X,F9.0/5X,24HPROFIT BEFORE INCOME TAX,32X,F10.0/5X,20HI
                    2NCOME TAX(IN.TX.CR.,F4.0,11H 0/0,SURTAX,F4.0,5H 0/0),12X,F10.0/5X,
                    327HNET PROFIT AFTER INCOME TAX,29X,F10.0/5X,14HDIVIDENDS PAID,43X,
                    4F9.0/5X,25HADDITION TO OWNERS EQUITY,31X,F10.0/37X,9HCASH FLOW)
         392     875 FORMAT(5X,22HRECEIPTS,SALES REVENUE,33X,1H$,F10.0/5X,26HDISBURSEME
                    1NTS,CASH EXPENSE,10X,1H$,F10.0/7X,10HINCOME TAX,25X,F10.0/7X,14HDI
                    2VIDENDS PAID,22X,F9.0/7X,19HROBOTICS INVESTMENT,17X,F9.0/7X,19HPLA
                    3NT&EQ.INVESTMENT,17X,F9.0/7X,19HMATERIALS PURCHASED,17X,F9.0,9X,F1
                    40.0/5X,23HADDITION TO CASH ASSETS,33X,F10.0)
         393     880 FORMAT(32X,19HFINANCIAL STATEMENT)
         394     885 FORMAT(5X,15HNET ASSETS,CASH,40X,1H$,F10.0/7X,25HINV. VALUE,FINISH
                    1ED GOODS,30X ,F9.0/7X,25HINVENTORY VALUE,MATERIALS,30X,F9.0/7X,33H
                    2ROBOTICS BOOK VALUE(REPLACE.VAL.$,F10.0,1H),11X,F9.0/7X,33HPLANT&E
                    3Q.BOOK VALUE(REPLACE.VAL. ,F10.0,1H),11X,F9.0/5X,35HOWNERS EQUITY(
                    4ECONOMIC EQUITY       ,F10.0,1H),11X,F9.0)
         395    895   FORMAT(1H1,17HXRATE INPUT DATA.)
```

```
 IF DO    ISN    *....*...1.........2.........3.........4.........5.........6.........7.*

          396    905     FORMAT(1H0,I1,I1,I2,F9.0,2F8.0,3F9.0,2F8.0/F8.0,F9.0)
          397    915     FORMAT(I1,I1,I2,F9.0,2F8.0,3F9.0,2F8.0/F8.0,F9.0)
          398    925     FORMAT(1H0/33H XGAME HISTORIES FOR NEXT PERIOD.)
          399    935     FORMAT(1H0,I2,I1,I2,F7.3,3F9.0,F10.0,2F9.0/F9.0)
          400      945   FORMAT(1H0,I3,I1,I2,F9.0,2F8.0,F10.0,2F9.0,F11.7,I2)
          401      965   FORMAT(1H0,10H FILE NO.    ,I5)
          402            DO 922 J=1,19
      1   403    922     REWIND TAPE(J)
          404            REWIND 94
          405            REWIND 95
          406            CLOSE (UNIT=10,ERR=5000,IOSTAT=IRT,STATUS='DELETE')
          407            CLOSE (UNIT=92,ERR=5010,IOSTAT=IRT,STATUS='KEEP')
          408            DO 4998 J=1,N
      1   409            K=J+10
      1   410            CLOSE (UNIT=TAPE(K),ERR=5050,IOSTAT=IRT,STATUS='KEEP')
      1   411    4998    CLOSE (UNIT=TAPE(J),ERR=5020,IOSTAT=IRT,STATUS='KEEP')
          412            CLOSE (UNIT=94,ERR=5030,IOSTAT=IRT,STATUS='KEEP')
          413            CLOSE (UNIT=95,ERR=5040,IOSTAT=IRT,STATUS='KEEP')
          414            STOP
          415    5000    PRINT *,' I/O ERROR WITH TAPE 10',IRT
          416            STOP
          417    5010    PRINT *,' I/O ERROR WITH TAPE 92',IRT
          418            STOP
          419    5020    PRINT *,' I/O ERROR WITH TAPE ',J,IRT
          420            STOP
          421    5030    PRINT *,' I/O ERROR WITH TAPE 94',IRT
          422            STOP
          423    5040    PRINT *,' I/O ERROR WITH TAPE 95',IRT
          424            STOP
          425    5050    PRINT *,' I/O ERROR WITH TAPE ',K,IRT
          426            STOP
          427            END

*STATISTICS*   SOURCE STATEMENTS = 427, PROGRAM SIZE = 31124 BYTES, PROGRAM NAME = XGAME

*STATISTICS*   NO DIAGNOSTICS GENERATED.

**XGAME** END OF COMPILATION 1 ******
```

APPENDIX D

Alphabetical List of Variables and Their Definitions in Executive Game Year-End (XRATE) FORTRAN Program

AS2(J)	Actual sales, Firm J
BOE	Beginning owners' equity; note: the beginning owners' equity and the beginning owners' economic equity are equal in the Executive Game
CA(J)	Cash assets, Firm J
DV(I,J)	Dividends Paid, Firm J, period I
ERR	A real variable defining the values of error statements
FD	Number of periods actually played during the last fiscal year
FI	Floating point representation of the integer I
FIV(J)	Inventory value finished goods, Firm J
FL	Floating point representation of the integer L
FMK(J)	Marketing budget, Firm J
FY	Number of the fiscal year
I	Period number index
II	Period number index
IPFN	Variable that defines permanent file names
IRANK(J) or IRANK(K)	Rank of Firm J = K based upon rate of return earned on beginning owners' equity
IRT	An integer variable for detecting errors
J	Firm number index
JJ	Alternate firm number index
JZ	Industry (or section) number index

K	Dummy index used for various purposes in XRATE program
KKK	Dummy index for correcting typing input errors
L	Number of periods in the Game for which play has been completed
L1	Alternate firm number index used in ranking the firms based upon discounted rate of return earned on beginning owners' equity
LL	Special dummy index used in calculating the discounted rate of return earned on beginning owners' equity
LLL	A dummy branching index
N	Number of firms
NJZ	Firm number index used to check read in order of input data
OEE(J)	Owners' economic equity, Firm J
PF	A real variable defining the permanent files
PFN	Permanent file name variable
PNT(J)	Net profit after income tax, Firm J
PRV(J)	Plant Replacement Value, Firm J
RATE(J)	Discounted rate of return earned on beginnings owners' equity, Firm J
RD(J)	Research and development budget, Firm J
RM(J)	Raw materials inventory, Firm J
RRV(J)	Robotics replacement value, Firm J
SAS2(J)	Average actual sales per quarter, Firm J, during last fiscal year
SFMK(J)	Average marketing expenditure per quarter, Firm J, during last fiscal year
SFNC	A working variable used in calculating rate of return earned on beginning owners' equity, Firm J
SPNT(J)	Average net profit after income tax per quarter, Firm J, during last fiscal year
SRD(J)	Average research and development expenditure per quarter, Firm J, during last fiscal year

APPENDIX E

Executive Game Year-End (XRATE) VS2 FORTRAN Program

```
LEVEL 2.1.1                     VS FORTRAN

OPTIONS IN EFFECT: NOLIST NOMAP NOXREF NOGOSTMT NODECK SOURCE TERM OBJECT FIXED TRMFLG
                   SDUMP(ISN) AUTODBL(NONE) NOSXM NOVECTOR IL NOTEST NODC NODIRECTIVE
                     OPT(3) LANGLVL(77) NOFIPS   FLAG(I)  NAME(MAIN)    LINECOUNT(60)

 IF DO    ISN    *....*...1.........2.........3.........4.........5.........6.........7.*

           1            PROGRAM XRATE
                 C      PROGRAM MODIFIED FOR USE ON IBM 3090
                 C      COPYRIGHT 1988. RICHARD D. IRWIN, INC.
                 C      HOMEWOOD, ILLINOIS 60430
           2            DIMENSION AS2(9),CA(9),DV(16,9),FIV(9),FMK(9),IRANK(9),OEE(9),
                       1PNT(9),PRV(9),RATE(9),RD(9),RM(9),SAS2(9),SFMK(9),SPNT(9),SRD(9),
                       2RRV(9)
           3            INTEGER TAPE(19)
           4            CHARACTER PFN*40
           5            CHARACTER*2 UNITN
           6            CHARACTER*48 FILE
           7            CHARACTER*32 FILE2
           8            INTEGER*4 IRT
           9            REAL PF,ERR
          10            DATA FILE/'FILEDEF XX      DISK    XXXX    DAT              '/
          11            DO 980 I=1,16
     1    12     980    TAPE(I)=I+20
          13            TAPE(17)=17
          14            TAPE(19)=90

          15       747 FORMAT(I1,I1,I2,F9.0,2F8.0,3F9.0,2F8.0/F8.0,F9.0)
          16       767 FORMAT(29H ERROR IN ORDER OF INPUT DATA)
          17            PRINT 200
          18     200    FORMAT(74HOENTER INDUSTRY NO.,NUMBER OF FIRMS,NUMBER OF PERIODS,AN
                       +D FISCAL YEAR NO.,/20HOSEPARATED BY COMMAS/)

                 C      CREATE TAPE17
          19            FILE2='FILEDEF 17      TERMINAL         '
          20            CALL CMSCMD(FILE2,IRT)
          21            IF (IRT.NE.0) GOTO 500
          22            OPEN (UNIT=17,STATUS='SCRATCH',IOSTAT=IRT,ERR=500,
                       +ACCESS='SEQUENTIAL',FORM='  FORMATTED')
          23            READ(17,*) JZ,N,L,FY
          24     2000   PRINT 2010, JZ,N,L,FY
          25     2010   FORMAT(14HOYOUR INPUT IS/16HO1  INDUSTRY NO.,I3/19HO2  NUMBER OF F
                       +IRMS,I3/21HO3  NUMBER OF PERIODS,I4/19HO4  FISCAL YEAR NO.,F4.0)
          26            PRINT 2020
          27     2020   FORMAT(35HOIF OK ENTER 0, IF IN ERROR ENTER 1 /)
          28            READ(17,*) LLL
          29            IF(LLL) 2000,2090,2030
          30     2030   PRINT 3000
          31     3000   FORMAT(53HOENTER THE NUMBER OF THE DATA ITEM YOU WISH TO CHANGE/14
                       +HOENTER 0 IF OK /)
          32            READ(17,*) KKK
          33            IF(KKK) 2030,2000,2040
          34     2040   GO TO(1,2,3,4) KKK
          35     1      PRINT 2050
          36     2050   FORMAT(36HOENTER DATA ITEM 1, THE INDUSTRY NO. /)
          37            READ(17,*) JZ
          38            GO TO 2030
          39     2      PRINT 2060
```

```
 IF DO    ISN    *....*...1.........2.........3.........4.........5.........6.........7.*

           40    2060   FORMAT(35HOENTER DATA ITEM 2, NUMBER OF FIRMS  /)
           41           READ(17,*) N
           42           GO TO 2030
           43    3      PRINT 2070
           44    2070   FORMAT(37HOENTER DATA ITEM 3, NUMBER OF PERIODS /)
           45           READ(17,*) L
           46           GO TO 2030
           47    4      PRINT 2080
           48    2080   FORMAT(35HOENTER DATA ITEM 4, FISCAL YEAR NO. /)
           49           READ(17,*) FY
           50           GO TO 2030
           51    2090   BOE=9700000.
           52           DO 210 J=1,L
      1    53           IPFN=
      1    54           WRITE(PFN,'(I6.6)') IPFN
      1    55           WRITE(UNITN,'(I2.2)') TAPE(J)
      1    56           FILE(9:10)=UNITN
      1    57           FILE(25:31)=PFN
      1    58           CALL CMSCMD(FILE,IRT)
      1    59           IF (IRT.NE.0) GOTO 510
      1    60    210    OPEN (UNIT=TAPE(J),STATUS='OLD',IOSTAT=IRT,ERR=510)
           61           FL=L
           62           FD=FL-4.*(FY-1.)
           63           DO 7 J=1,N
      1    64           SAS2(J)=0.
      1    65           SFMK(J)=0.
      1    66           SPNT(J)=0.
      1    67         7 SRD(J)=0.
           68           DO 77 I=1,L
      1    69           DO 77 J=1,N
      2    70           READ(TAPE(I),747)JZ,JJ,II,CA(J),FIV(J),RM(J),RRV(J),PRV(J),FMK(J),
      2               1RD(J),AS2(J),DV(I,J),PNT(J)
      2    71           IF(I-1)56,14,28
      2    72        14 IF(J-1)56,21,28
      2    73        21 NJZ=JZ
      2    74        28 IF(NJZ-JZ)49,35,49
      2    75        35 IF(J-JJ)49,42,49
      2    76        42 IF(I-II)49,63,49
      2    77        49 PRINT   767
      2    78        56 STOP
      2    79        63 FI=I
      2    80           IF(FI-4.*(FY-1.))77,77,70
      2    81        70 SAS2(J)=SAS2(J)+AS2(J)/FD
      2    82           SFMK(J)=SFMK(J)+FMK(J)/FD
      2    83           SPNT(J)=SPNT(J)+PNT(J)/FD
      2    84           SRD(J)=SRD(J)+RD(J)/FD
      2    85        77 CONTINUE
           86           DO 147 J=1,N
      1    87           RATE(J)=0.
      1    88           SFNC=-BOE
      1    89           OEE(J)=CA(J)+FIV(J)+RM(J)+PRV(J)+RRV(J)
      1    90           DV(L,J)=DV(L,J)+OEE(J)
      1    91           DO 84  I=1,L
      2    92        84 SFNC=SFNC+DV(I,J)
      1    93           IF(SFNC)119,147,91
      1    94        91 DO 112 K=1,7
```

```
 IF DO   ISN   *....*...1.........2.........3.........4.........5.........6.........7.*

     2    95     98 RATE(J)=RATE(J)+0.1**K
     2    96        SFNC=-BOE*(1.0+RATE(J))**L
     2    97        DO 105 I=1,L
     3    98        LL=L-I
     3    99    105 SFNC=SFNC+DV(I,J)*(1.0+RATE(J))**LL
     2   100        IF(SFNC)112,98,98
     2   101    112 RATE(J)=RATE(J)-0.1**K
     1   102        GO TO 147
     1   103    119 DO 140 K=1,7
     2   104    126 RATE(J)=RATE(J)-0.1**K
     2   105        SFNC=-BOE*(1.0+RATE(J))**L
     2   106        DO 133 I=1,L
     3   107        LL=L-I
     3   108    133 SFNC=SFNC+DV(I,J)*(1.0+RATE(J))**LL
     2   109        IF(SFNC)126,126,140
     2   110    140 RATE(J)=RATE(J)+0.1**K
     1   111    147 CONTINUE
         112        DO 168 K=1,N
     1   113        J=0
     1   114        DO 161 L1=1,N
     2   115        IF(RATE(K)-RATE(L1))154,161,161
     2   116    154 J=J+1
     2   117    161 CONTINUE
     1   118    168 IRANK(K)=J+1

               C    CREATE TAPE90
         119        IPFN=
         120        WRITE(PFN,'(I6.6)') IPFN
         121        FILE(9:10)='90'
         122        FILE(25:31)=PFN
         123        CALL CMSCMD(FILE,IRT)
         124        IF (IRT.NE.0) GOTO 520
         125        OPEN (UNIT=90,STATUS='NEW',IOSTAT=IRT,ERR=520)
         126        DO 170 J=1,N
     1   127    170 RATE(J)=((1.+RATE(J))**4.-1.)*100.
         128        WRITE(90,907)FY
         129        PRINT   907,FY
         130        WRITE(90,917)
         131        PRINT   917
         132        DO 175 J=1,N
     1   133        WRITE(90,927)JZ,J,CA(J),FIV(J),RM(J),RRV(J),PRV(J),OEE(J)
     1   134    175 PRINT   927,JZ,J,CA(J),FIV(J),RM(J),RRV(J),PRV(J),OEE(J)
         135        WRITE(90,947)FY
         136        PRINT   947,FY
         137        DO 182 J=1,N
     1   138        WRITE(90,967)JZ,J,SFMK(J),SRD(J),SAS2(J),SPNT(J),RATE(J),IRANK(J)
     1   139    182 PRINT   967,JZ,J,SFMK(J),SRD(J),SAS2(J),SPNT(J),RATE(J),IRANK(J)
         140        WRITE(90,987)L,FY
         141        PRINT   987,L,FY
         142    907 FORMAT(1H ,27X,14HEXECUTIVE GAME//25X,18HEND OF FISCAL YEAR,F4.0//
                  172H FIRM    NET        INVENTORY    INVENTORY    ROBOTICS     PLANT&EQ.
                  2OWNERS    / 72H NO.     CASH           VALUE          VALUE         REPLACE.
                  3REPLACE.  ECONOMIC  /72H           ASSETS       FIN.GOODS     MATERIALS
                  4 VALUE        VALUE       EQUITY    )
         143    917 FORMAT(8X,3H($),9X,3H($),9X,3H($),8X,3H($),8X,3H($),8X,3H($))
         144    927 FORMAT(I2,I1,F10.0,4X,F9.0,2X,F10.0,1X,F10.0,2X,F10.0,F10.0/)
```

```
IF DO   ISN   *....*...1.........2.........3.........4.........5.........6.........7.*

        145      947 FORMAT(/40H    AVERAGES PER QUARTER FOR FISCAL YEAR,F3.0,5H ONLY//
                    158H  FIRM   MARKET-      R          SALES       NET     RATE OF/58H
                    2 NO.        ING          AND D    VOLUME    PROFIT    RETURN*/64H
                    3      ($)         ($)        (UNITS)      ($)         (0/0)  RANK*)
        146      967 FORMAT(I3,I1,2X,F9.0,F11.0,F11.0,F10.0,3X,F7.2,2X,I3/)
        147      987 FORMAT(63H  * RANK AND ANNUAL RATE OF RETURN ARE BASED UPON DIVIDE
                    1ND PAY-/13H  OUT FOR ALL,I3,46H PERIODS AND OWNERS ECONOMIC EQUITY
                    2 AT THE END/16H  OF FISCAL YEAR,F3.0)
        148             REWIND 90
        149             CLOSE (UNIT=17,ERR=500,IOSTAT=IRT,STATUS='DELETE')
        150             DO 499 J=1,L
     1  151      499    CLOSE (UNIT=TAPE(J),ERR=510,IOSTAT=IRT,STATUS='KEEP')
        152             CLOSE (UNIT=90,ERR=520,IOSTAT=IRT,STATUS='KEEP')
        153             STOP
        154      500    PRINT *,' I/O ERROR WITH TAPE 17',IRT
        155             STOP
        156      510    PRINT *,' I/O ERROR WITH TAPE ',TAPE(J),IRT
        157             STOP
        158      520    PRINT *,' I/O ERROR WITH TAPE 90',IRT
        159             STOP
        160             END

*STATISTICS*   SOURCE STATEMENTS = 160, PROGRAM SIZE = 8676 BYTES, PROGRAM NAME = XRATE

*STATISTICS*    NO DIAGNOSTICS GENERATED.

**XRATE** END OF COMPILATION 1 ******
```

APPENDIX F

Forms for Playing the Executive Game

TABLE 50

PARTICIPANT'S WORK SHEET

-to be detached and handed in at the end of Game.

Firm No. _________

Periods ____ - ____ Model No. ____

Periods ____ - ____ Model No. ____

Period of Year	Period No.	Price $	Marketing Budget $	R & D Budget $	Maintenance Budget $	Prod. Vol. Sch. Maximums: Model 1 1.4xCY1 Model 2 3.0xCY1 units	Investment in Robotics $	Investment in Plant & Equipment $	Purchase of Materials $	Dividend Declared (Max: owners' equity minus $9,000,000 $
AMJ	0	25.60	200,000	100,000	75,000	100,000	0	500,000	1,000,000	53,000
JAS	Trial 1	.	,	,	,	,	,	,	, ,	,
OND	Trial 2	.	,	,	,	,	,	,	, ,	,
AMJ	0	25.60	200,000	100,000	75,000	100,000	0	500,000	1,000,000	53,000
JAS	1	.	,	,	,	,	,	,	, ,	,
OND	2	.	,	,	,	,	,	,	, ,	,
JFM	3	.	,	,	,	,	,	,	, ,	,
AMJ	4	.	,	,	,	,	,	,	, ,	,
JAS	5	.	,	,	,	,	,	,	, ,	,
OND	6	.	,	,	,	,	,	,	, ,	,
JFM	7	.	,	,	,	,	,	,	, ,	,
AMJ	8	.	,	,	,	,	,	,	, ,	,
JAS	9	.	,	,	,	,	,	,	, ,	,
OND	10	.	,	,	,	,	,	,	, ,	,
JFM	11	.	,	,	,	,	,	,	, ,	,
AMJ	12	.	,	,	,	,	,	,	, ,	,

FORECASTS: ECONOMIC AND SEASONAL INDICES

Period of Year	AMJ	JAS	OND	AMJ	JAS	OND	JFM	AMJ	JAS	OND	JFM	AMJ	JAS	OND	JFM	AMJ
Period No.	0	T1	T2	0	1	2	3	4	5	6	7	8	9	10	11	12
Forecast, Econ. Index	100	100	95	100	100	95	93	90	95	97	100	100	103	105	107	107
Changes (if any)																
Seasonal Index	100	95	115	100	95	115	90	100	95	115	90	100	95	115	90	100
Changes (if any)																

* The individual team member should enter his/her own preferred decision values on this sheet.

TABLE 50 (continued)

PARTICIPANT'S WORK SHEET

-to be detached and handed in at the end of Game.

Firm No. _________

Periods ____ - ____ Model No. ____
Periods ____ - ____ Model No. ____

Period of Year	Period No.	Price $	Marketing Budget $	R & D Budget $	Maintenance Budget $	Prod. Vol. Sch. Maximums: Model 1 1.4xCY1 Model 2 3.0xCY1 units	Investment in Robotics $	Investment in Plant & Equipment $	Purchase of Materials $	Dividend Declared (Max: owners' equity minus $9,000,000 $
AMJ	12	.	,	,	,	,	,	,	, ,	,
JAS	13	.	,	,	,	,	,	,	, ,	,
OND	14	.	,	,	,	,	,	,	, ,	,
AMJ	15	.	,	,	,	,	,	,	, ,	,
JAS	16	.	,	,	,	,	,	,	, ,	,
		.	,	,	,	,	,	,	, ,	,
		.	,	,	,	,	,	,	, ,	,
		.	,	,	,	,	,	,	, ,	,
		.	,	,	,	,	,	,	, ,	,
		.	,	,	,	,	,	,	, ,	,
		.	,	,	,	,	,	,	, ,	,
		.	,	,	,	,	,	,	, ,	,
		.	,	,	,	,	,	,	, ,	,
		.	,	,	,	,	,	,	, ,	,
		.	,	,	,	,	,	,	, ,	,
		.	,	,	,	,	,	,	, ,	,

FORECASTS: ECONOMIC AND SEASONAL INDICES

Period of Year	AMJ	JAS	OND	JFM	AMJ	JAS										
Period No.	12	13	14	15	16	17										
Forecast, Econ. Index	107	105	104	102	102	100										
Changes (if any)																
Seasonal Index	100	95	115	90	100	95										
Changes (if any)																

* The individual team member should enter his/herown preferred decision values on this sheet.

Table 51
Executive Game Quarterly Statement, Period 0

```
    0 25.60   200000.  100000.  75000. 100000.      0. 500000. 1000000.    53000.

                                     EXECUTIVE GAME
MODEL 1 PERIOD  0 AMJ PRICE INDEX 100.0 FORECAST,ANNUAL CHANGE   .  0/0
SEAS.INDEX 100. NEXT QTR.  95.  ECON.INDEX 100. FORECAST,NEXT QTR. 100.

                  INFORMATION          ON          COMPETITORS
              PRICE           DIVIDEND      SALES VOLUME          NET PROFIT
  FIRM 1    $ 25.60        $    53000.         109720.          $    282104.
  FIRM 2    $ 25.60        $    53000.         109720.          $    282104.
  FIRM 3    $ 25.60        $    53000.         109720.          $    282104.
  FIRM 4    $ 25.60        $    53000.         109720.          $    282104.
  FIRM 5    $ 25.60        $    53000.         109720.          $    282104.
  FIRM 6    $ 25.60        $    53000.         109720.          $    282104.
  FIRM 7    $ 25.60        $    53000.         109720.          $    282104.
  FIRM 8    $ 25.60        $    53000.         109720.          $    282104.
  FIRM 9    $ 25.60        $    53000.         109720.          $    282104.

                                          FIRM
                                  OPERATING STATEMENTS
     MARKET POTENTIAL                                 109720.
     SALES VOLUME                                     109720.
     PERCENT SHARE OF INDUSTRY SALES                        .
     PRODUCTION,THIS QUARTER                          100000.
     INVENTORY,FINISHED GOODS                          12750.
     PLANT CAPACITY,NEXT QUARTER                      104643.
                                     INCOME STATEMENT
     RECEIPTS,SALES REVENUE                                            $  2808832.
     EXPENSES,MARKETING                             $  200000.
       RESEARCH AND DEVELOPMENT                        100000.
       ADMINISTRATION                                  278000.
       MAINTENANCE                                      75000.
       LABOR(COST/UNIT EX.OVERTIME $ 5.74)             573939.
       MATERIALS CONSUMED(COST/UNIT  6.31)             630667.
       REDUCTION,FINISHED GOODS INV.                   116638.
       PLANT&EQ.DEPRECIATION(2.500 0/0)                183125.
       ROBOTICS DEPRECIATION(5.000 0/0)                     0.
       FINISHED GOODS CARRYING COSTS                    25500.
       RAW MATERIALS CARRYING COSTS                     41533.
       ORDERING COSTS                                   50000.
       SHIFTS CHANGE COSTS                                  0.
       INVESTMENTS EXPENSES                             25000.
       FINANCING CHARGES AND PENALTIES                      0.
       SUNDRIES                                         82000.          2381402.
     PROFIT BEFORE INCOME TAX                                            427430.
     INCOME TAX(IN.TX.CR.  0. 0/0,SURTAX  0. 0/0)                        145326.
     NET PROFIT AFTER INCOME TAX                                         282104.
     DIVIDENDS PAID                                                       53000.
     ADDITION TO OWNERS EQUITY                                           229104.
                                          CASH FLOW
     RECEIPTS,SALES REVENUE                                            $  2808832.
     DISBURSEMENTS,CASH EXPENSE                 $  1450972.
       INCOME TAX                                   145320.
       DIVIDENDS PAID                                53000.
       ROBOTICS INVESTMENT                               0.
       PLANT&EQ.INVESTMENT                          500000.
       MATERIALS PURCHASED                         1000000.             3149298.
     ADDITION TO CASH ASSETS                                            -340466.
                                     FINANCIAL STATEMENT
     NET ASSETS,CASH                                                   $  1022000.
       INV. VALUE,FINISHED GOODS                                          153000.
       INVENTORY VALUE,MATERIALS                                         1200000.
       ROBOTICS BOOK VALUE(REPLACE.VAL.$          0.)                          0.
       PLANT&EQ.BOOK VALUE(REPLACE.VAL.     7325000.)                    7325000.
     OWNERS EQUITY(ECONOMIC EQUITY          9700000.)                    9700000.
```

TABLE 52
WORK SHEET FOR ANALYSIS OF OPERATIONS

-to be detached and handed in at the end of the Game-the individual team member should enter his/her decisions and forecasts on this sheet each quarter.

Firm No. ________ Periods ____ - ____ Model # ____
Periods ____ - ____ Model # ____

	Trial Period 2		Trial Period 1		Period 0
	Actual	Forecast	Actual	Forecast	Actual
I (a) Price Index (Period 0=100%)/(b) Forecast, Annual Change (%)	/	/	/	/	100.0/
II (a) Calendar Quarter/(b) Seasonal Index (Average Period=100%)	OND/	OND/	JAS/	JAS/	AMJ/100
III Economic Index (Period=100%)					100
IV (a) Inv. Tax Cr. %/(b) Surtax %/(c) PI & Eq. Depr. %/(d) Robotics Depr. %	/ / /	/ / /	/ / /	/ / /	/ / /
1 (a) Firm's Price/(b) Average Industry Price ($)	/	/	/	/	25.60 /25.60
2 Total Industry Sales - in units (not dollars)					
3 Market Potential (units)					109,720
4 Sales Volume (units)					109,720
5 Percent Share of Industry Sales (%)					
6 Production, This Quarter (units)					100,000
7 (a) Labor Cost per Unit/(b) Material Cost per Unit ($)	/	/	/	/	5.74/6.31
8 Inventory, Finished Goods (units)					12, 750
9 Plant Capacity, Next Quarter (units)					104,643
10 INCOME (and expense) STATEMENT ($)					
11 Receipts, Sales Revenue					2,808,832
12 Expenses, Marketing Expense					200,000
13 Research and Development Expense					100,000
14 Administration Expense					278,000
15 Maintenance Expense					75,000
16 Labor Expense					573,939
17 Materials Expense					630,667
18 Reduction, Finished Goods Inventory Value					116,638
19 Plant and Equipment Depreciation					183,125
20 Robotics Depreciation					0
21 Finished Goods Carrying Costs					25,500
22 Raw Materials Carrying Costs					41,533
23 Ordering Costs					50,000

24 Shifts Change Costs					0
25 Investment Expenses					25,000
26 Financing Charges and Penalties					0
27 Sundries Expenses					82,000
28 Total Expenses					2,381,402
29 Profit Before Income Taxes					427,430
30 Income Tax					145,326
31 Net Profit After Income Tax					282,104
32 Dividends Paid					53,000
33 Addition to Owners' Equity					229,104
34 CASH FLOW STATEMENT ($)					
35 Receipts, Sales Revenue					2,808,832
36 Disbursements, Cash Expense					1,450,972
37 Income Tax					145,326
38 Dividends Paid					53,000
39 Robotics Investments					0
40 Plant and Equipment Investments					500,000
41 Materials Purchased					1,000,000
42 Total Disbursements					3,149,298
43 Addition to Cash Assets					-340,466
44 FINANCIAL STATEMENT ($)					
45 Net Assets, Cash					1.022,000
46 Inventory Value, Finished Goods					153,000
47 Inventory Value, Materials					1,200,000
48 Robotics Book Value					0
49 Plant and Equipment Book Value					7,325,000
50 Owners' Equity					9,700,000
51 Plant and Equipment Replacement Value					7,325,000
52 Robotics Replacement Value					0
53 Owners' Economic Equity					9,700,000

TABLE 52 (continued)
WORK SHEET FOR ANALYSIS OF OPERATIONS

-to be detached and handed in at the end of the Game-the individual team member should enter his/her decisions and forecasts on this sheet each quarter.

Periods _____ - _____ Model # ____ Periods _____ - _____ Model # ____	Period 1 Forecast	Actual	Period 2 Forecast	Actual	Period 3 Forecast	Actual
I (a) Price Index (Period 0=100%)/(b) Forecast, Annual Change (%)	/	/	/	/	/	/
II (a) Calendar Quarter/(b) Seasonal Index (Average Period=100%)	JAS/	JAS/	OND/	OND/	JFM/	JFM/
III Economic Index (Period=100%)						
IV (a) Inv. Tax Cr. %/(b) Surtax %/(c) Pl & Eq. Depr. %/(d) Robotics Depr. %	/ / /	/ / /	/ / /	/ / /	/ / /	/ / /
1 (a) Firm's Price/(b) Average Industry Price ($)	/	/	/	/	/	/
2 Total Industry Sales - in units (not dollars)						
3 Market Potential (units)						
4 Sales Volume (units)						
5 Percent Share of Industry Sales (%)						
6 Production, This Quarter (units)						
7 (a) Labor Cost per Unit/(b) Material Cost per Unit ($)	/	/	/	/	/	/
8 Inventory, Finished Goods (units)						
9 Plant Capacity, Next Quarter (units)						
10 INCOME (and expense) STATEMENT ($)						
11 Receipts, Sales Revenue						
12 Expenses, Marketing Expense						
13 Research and Development Expense						
14 Administration Expense						
15 Maintenance Expense						
16 Labor Expense						
17 Materials Expense						
18 Reduction, Finished Goods Inventory Value						
19 Plant and Equipment Depreciation						
20 Robotics Depreciation						
21 Finished Goods Carrying Costs						
22 Raw Materials Carrying Costs						
23 Ordering Costs						

24 Shifts Change Costs						
25 Investment Expenses						
26 Financing Charges and Penalties						
27 Sundries Expenses						
28 Total Expenses						
29 Profit Before Income Taxes						
30 Income Tax						
31 Net Profit After Income Tax						
32 Dividends Paid						
33 Addition to Owners' Equity						
34 CASH FLOW STATEMENT ($)						
35 Receipts, Sales Revenue						
36 Disbursements, Cash Expense						
37 Income Tax						
38 Dividends Paid						
39 Robotics Investments						
40 Plant and Equipment Investments						
41 Materials Purchased						
42 Total Disbursements						
43 Addition to Cash Assets						
44 FINANCIAL STATEMENT ($)						
45 Net Assets, Cash						
46 Inventory Value, Finished Goods						
47 Inventory Value, Materials						
48 Robotics Book Value						
49 Plant and Equipment Book Value						
50 Owners' Equity						
51 Plant and Equipment Replacement Value						
52 Robotics Replacement Value						
53 Owners' Economic Equity						

TABLE 52 (continued)
WORK SHEET FOR ANALYSIS OF OPERATIONS

-to be detached and handed in at the end of the Game-the individual team member should enter his/her decisions and forecasts on this sheet each quarter.

Periods ____ - ____ Model # ____ Periods ____ - ____ Model # ____	Period 4		Period 5		Period 6	
	Forecast	Actual	Forecast	Actual	Forecast	Actual
I (a) Price Index (Period 0=100%)/(b) Forecast, Annual Change (%)	/	/	/	/	/	/
II (a) Calendar Quarter/(b) Seasonal Index (Average Period=100%)	AMJ/	AMJ/	JAS/	JAS/	OND/	OND/
III Economic Index (Period=100%)						
IV (a) Inv. Tax Cr. %/(b) Surtax %/(c) Pl & Eq. Depr. %/(d) Robotics Depr. %	/ / /	/ / /	/ / /	/ / /	/ / /	/ / /
1 (a) Firm's Price/(b) Average Industry Price ($)	/	/	/	/	/	/
2 Total Industry Sales - in units (not dollars)						
3 Market Potential (units)						
4 Sales Volume (units)						
5 Percent Share of Industry Sales (%)						
6 Production, This Quarter (units)						
7 (a) Labor Cost per Unit/(b) Material Cost per Unit ($)	/	/	/	/	/	/
8 Inventory, Finished Goods (units)						
9 Plant Capacity, Next Quarter (units)						
10 INCOME (and expense) STATEMENT ($)						
11 Receipts, Sales Revenue						
12 Expenses, Marketing Expense						
13 Research and Development Expense						
14 Administration Expense						
15 Maintenance Expense						
16 Labor Expense						
17 Materials Expense						
18 Reduction, Finished Goods Inventory Value						
19 Plant and Equipment Depreciation						
20 Robotics Depreciation						
21 Finished Goods Carrying Costs						
22 Raw Materials Carrying Costs						
23 Ordering Costs						

24 Shifts Change Costs						
25 Investment Expenses						
26 Financing Charges and Penalties						
27 Sundries Expenses						
28 Total Expenses						
29 Profit Before Income Taxes						
30 Income Tax						
31 Net Profit After Income Tax						
32 Dividends Paid						
33 Addition to Owners' Equity						
34 CASH FLOW STATEMENT ($)						
35 Receipts, Sales Revenue						
36 Disbursements, Cash Expense						
37 Income Tax						
38 Dividends Paid						
39 Robotics Investments						
40 Plant and Equipment Investments						
41 Materials Purchased						
42 Total Disbursements						
43 Addition to Cash Assets						
44 FINANCIAL STATEMENT ($)						
45 Net Assets, Cash						
46 Inventory Value, Finished Goods						
47 Inventory Value, Materials						
48 Robotics Book Value						
49 Plant and Equipment Book Value						
50 Owners' Equity						
51 Plant and Equipment Replacement Value						
52 Robotics Replacement Value						
53 Owners' Economic Equity						

TABLE 52 (continued)
WORK SHEET FOR ANALYSIS OF OPERATIONS

-to be detached and handed in at the end of the Game-the individual team member should enter his/her decisions and forecasts on this sheet each quarter.

Periods _____ - _____ Model # ____ Periods _____ - _____ Model # ____	Period 7 Forecast	Actual	Period 8 Forecast	Actual	Period 9 Forecast	Actual
I (a) Price Index (Period 0=100%)/(b) Forecast, Annual Change (%)	/	/	/	/	/	/
II (a) Calendar Quarter/(b) Seasonal Index (Average Period=100%)	JFM/	JFM/	AMJ/	AMJ/	JAS/	JAS/
III Economic Index (Period=100%)						
IV (a) Inv. Tax Cr. %/(b) Surtax %/(c) PI & Eq. Depr. %/(d) Robotics Depr. %	/ / /	/ / /	/ / /	/ / /	/ / /	/ / /
1 (a) Firm's Price/(b) Average Industry Price ($)	/	/	/	/	/	/
2 Total Industry Sales - in units (not dollars)						
3 Market Potential (units)						
4 Sales Volume (units)						
5 Percent Share of Industry Sales (%)						
6 Production, This Quarter (units)						
7 (a) Labor Cost per Unit/(b) Material Cost per Unit ($)	/	/	/	/	/	/
8 Inventory, Finished Goods (units)						
9 Plant Capacity, Next Quarter (units)						
10 INCOME (and expense) STATEMENT ($)						
11 Receipts, Sales Revenue						
12 Expenses, Marketing Expense						
13 Research and Development Expense						
14 Administration Expense						
15 Maintenance Expense						
16 Labor Expense						
17 Materials Expense						
18 Reduction, Finished Goods Inventory Value						
19 Plant and Equipment Depreciation						
20 Robotics Depreciation						
21 Finished Goods Carrying Costs						
22 Raw Materials Carrying Costs						
23 Ordering Costs						

24 Shifts Change Costs						
25 Investment Expenses						
26 Financing Charges and Penalties						
27 Sundries Expenses						
28 Total Expenses						
29 Profit Before Income Taxes						
30 Income Tax						
31 Net Profit After Income Tax						
32 Dividends Paid						
33 Addition to Owners' Equity						
34 CASH FLOW STATEMENT ($)						
35 Receipts, Sales Revenue						
36 Disbursements, Cash Expense						
37 Income Tax						
38 Dividends Paid						
39 Robotics Investments						
40 Plant and Equipment Investments						
41 Materials Purchased						
42 Total Disbursements						
43 Addition to Cash Assets						
44 FINANCIAL STATEMENT ($)						
45 Net Assets, Cash						
46 Inventory Value, Finished Goods						
47 Inventory Value, Materials						
48 Robotics Book Value						
49 Plant and Equipment Book Value						
50 Owners' Equity						
51 Plant and Equipment Replacement Value						
52 Robotics Replacement Value						
53 Owners' Economic Equity						

TABLE 52 (continued)
WORK SHEET FOR ANALYSIS OF OPERATIONS

-to be detached and handed in at the end of the Game-the individual team member should enter his/her decisions and forecasts on this sheet each quarter.

Periods _____ - _____ Model # ____ Periods _____ - _____ Model # ____	Period 10 Forecast	 Actual	Period 11 Forecast	 Actual	Period 12 Forecast	 Actual
I (a) Price Index (Period 0=100%)/(b) Forecast, Annual Change (%)	/	/	/	/	/	/
II (a) Calendar Quarter/(b) Seasonal Index (Average Period=100%)	OND/	OND/	JFM/	JFM/	AMJ/	AMJ/
III Economic Index (Period=100%)						
IV (a) Inv. Tax Cr. %/(b) Surtax %/(c) PI & Eq. Depr. %/(d) Robotics Depr. %	/ / /	/ / /	/ / /	/ / /	/ / /	/ / /
1 (a) Firm's Price/(b) Average Industry Price ($)	/	/	/	/	/	/
2 Total Industry Sales - in units (not dollars)						
3 Market Potential (units)						
4 Sales Volume (units)						
5 Percent Share of Industry Sales (%)						
6 Production, This Quarter (units)						
7 (a) Labor Cost per Unit/(b) Material Cost per Unit ($)	/	/	/	/	/	/
8 Inventory, Finished Goods (units)						
9 Plant Capacity, Next Quarter (units)						
10 INCOME (and expense) STATEMENT ($)						
11 Receipts, Sales Revenue						
12 Expenses, Marketing Expense						
13 Research and Development Expense						
14 Administration Expense						
15 Maintenance Expense						
16 Labor Expense						
17 Materials Expense						
18 Reduction, Finished Goods Inventory Value						
19 Plant and Equipment Depreciation						
20 Robotics Depreciation						
21 Finished Goods Carrying Costs						
22 Raw Materials Carrying Costs						
23 Ordering Costs						

24 Shifts Change Costs						
25 Investment Expenses						
26 Financing Charges and Penalties						
27 Sundries Expenses						
28 Total Expenses						
29 Profit Before Income Taxes						
30 Income Tax						
31 Net Profit After Income Tax						
32 Dividends Paid						
33 Addition to Owners' Equity						
34 CASH FLOW STATEMENT ($)						
35 Receipts, Sales Revenue						
36 Disbursements, Cash Expense						
37 Income Tax						
38 Dividends Paid						
39 Robotics Investments						
40 Plant and Equipment Investments						
41 Materials Purchased						
42 Total Disbursements						
43 Addition to Cash Assets						
44 FINANCIAL STATEMENT ($)						
45 Net Assets, Cash						
46 Inventory Value, Finished Goods						
47 Inventory Value, Materials						
48 Robotics Book Value						
49 Plant and Equipment Book Value						
50 Owners' Equity						
51 Plant and Equipment Replacement Value						
52 Robotics Replacement Value						
53 Owners' Economic Equity						

TABLE 52 (continued)
WORK SHEET FOR ANALYSIS OF OPERATIONS

-to be detached and handed in at the end of the Game-the individual team member should enter his/her decisions and forecasts on this sheet each quarter.

Periods _____ - _____ Model # ____ Periods _____ - _____ Model # ____	Period 13 Forecast	Actual	Period 14 Forecast	Actual	Period 15 Forecast	Actual
I (a) Price Index (Period 0=100%)/(b) Forecast, Annual Change (%)	/	/	/	/	/	/
II (a) Calendar Quarter/(b) Seasonal Index (Average Period=100%)	JAS/	JAS/	OND/	OND/	JFM/	JFM/
III Economic Index (Period=100%)						
IV (a) Inv. Tax Cr. %/(b) Surtax %/(c) Pl & Eq. Depr. %/(d) Robotics Depr. %	/ / /	/ / /	/ / /	/ / /	/ / /	/ / /
1 (a) Firm's Price/(b) Average Industry Price ($)	/	/	/	/	/	/
2 Total Industry Sales - in units (not dollars)						
3 Market Potential (units)						
4 Sales Volume (units)						
5 Percent Share of Industry Sales (%)						
6 Production, This Quarter (units)						
7 (a) Labor Cost per Unit/(b) Material Cost per Unit ($)	/	/	/	/	/	/
8 Inventory, Finished Goods (units)						
9 Plant Capacity, Next Quarter (units)						
10 INCOME (and expense) STATEMENT ($)						
11 Receipts, Sales Revenue						
12 Expenses, Marketing Expense						
13 Research and Development Expense						
14 Administration Expense						
15 Maintenance Expense						
16 Labor Expense						
17 Materials Expense						
18 Reduction, Finished Goods Inventory Value						
19 Plant and Equipment Depreciation						
20 Robotics Depreciation						
21 Finished Goods Carrying Costs						
22 Raw Materials Carrying Costs						
23 Ordering Costs						

24 Shifts Change Costs						
25 Investment Expenses						
26 Financing Charges and Penalties						
27 Sundries Expenses						
28 Total Expenses						
29 Profit Before Income Taxes						
30 Income Tax						
31 Net Profit After Income Tax						
32 Dividends Paid						
33 Addition to Owners' Equity						
34 CASH FLOW STATEMENT ($)						
35 Receipts, Sales Revenue						
36 Disbursements, Cash Expense						
37 Income Tax						
38 Dividends Paid						
39 Robotics Investments						
40 Plant and Equipment Investments						
41 Materials Purchased						
42 Total Disbursements						
43 Addition to Cash Assets						
44 FINANCIAL STATEMENT ($)						
45 Net Assets, Cash						
46 Inventory Value, Finished Goods						
47 Inventory Value, Materials						
48 Robotics Book Value						
49 Plant and Equipment Book Value						
50 Owners' Equity						
51 Plant and Equipment Replacement Value						
52 Robotics Replacement Value						
53 Owners' Economic Equity						

TABLE 52 (continued)
WORK SHEET FOR ANALYSIS OF OPERATIONS

-to be detached and handed in at the end of the Game-the individual team member should enter his/her decisions and forecasts on this sheet each quarter.

Periods _____ - _____ Model # ____
Periods _____ - _____ Model # ____

	Period 16 Forecast	Period 16 Actual				
I (a) Price Index (Period 0=100%)/(b) Forecast, Annual Change (%)	/	/				
II (a) Calendar Quarter/(b) Seasonal Index (Average Period=100%)	AMJ/	AMJ/				
III Economic Index (Period=100%)						
IV (a) Inv. Tax Cr. %/(b) Surtax %/(c) Pl & Eq. Depr. %/(d) Robotics Depr. %	/ / /	/ / /				
1 (a) Firm's Price/(b) Average Industry Price ($)	/	/				
2 Total Industry Sales - in units (not dollars)						
3 Market Potential (units)						
4 Sales Volume (units)						
5 Percent Share of Industry Sales (%)						
6 Production, This Quarter (units)						
7 (a) Labor Cost per Unit/(b) Material Cost per Unit ($)	/	/				
8 Inventory, Finished Goods (units)						
9 Plant Capacity, Next Quarter (units)						
10 INCOME (and expense) STATEMENT ($)						
11 Receipts, Sales Revenue						
12 Expenses, Marketing Expense						
13 Research and Development Expense						
14 Administration Expense						
15 Maintenance Expense						
16 Labor Expense						
17 Materials Expense						
18 Reduction, Finished Goods Inventory Value						
19 Plant and Equipment Depreciation						
20 Robotics Depreciation						
21 Finished Goods Carrying Costs						
22 Raw Materials Carrying Costs						
23 Ordering Costs						

24 Shifts Change Costs						
25 Investment Expenses						
26 Financing Charges and Penalties						
27 Sundries Expenses						
28 Total Expenses						
29 Profit Before Income Taxes						
30 Income Tax						
31 Net Profit After Income Tax						
32 Dividends Paid						
33 Addition to Owners' Equity						
34 CASH FLOW STATEMENT ($)						
35 Receipts, Sales Revenue						
36 Disbursements, Cash Expense						
37 Income Tax						
38 Dividends Paid						
39 Robotics Investments						
40 Plant and Equipment Investments						
41 Materials Purchased						
42 Total Disbursements						
43 Addition to Cash Assets						
44 FINANCIAL STATEMENT ($)						
45 Net Assets, Cash						
46 Inventory Value, Finished Goods						
47 Inventory Value, Materials						
48 Robotics Book Value						
49 Plant and Equipment Book Value						
50 Owners' Equity						
51 Plant and Equipment Replacement Value						
52 Robotics Replacement Value						
53 Owners' Economic Equity						

TABLE 53

MASTER COPY–to be detached and handed in at end of Game

EXECUTIVE GAME–DECISION SHEET*

Firm No. __________ Periods _____ - _____ Model No. _____ Periods _____ - _____ Model No. _____

Period of Year	Period No.	Price $	Marketing Budget $	R & D Budget $	Maintenance Budget $	Prod. Vol. Sch. Maximums: Model 1 1.4xCY1 Model 2 3.0xCY1 units	Investment in Robotics $	Investment in Plant & Equipment $	Purchase of Materials $	Dividend Declared (Max: owners' equity minus $9,000,000 $
AMJ	0	25.60	200,000	100,000	75,000	100,000	0	500,000	1,000,000	53,000
JAS	Trial 1	.	,	,	,	,	,	,	, ,	,
OND	Trial 2	.	,	,	,	,	,	,	, ,	,
AMJ	0	25.60	200,000	100,000	75,000	100,000	0	500,000	1,000,000	53,000
JAS	1	.	,	,	,	,	,	,	, ,	,
OND	2	.	,	,	,	,	,	,	, ,	,
JFM	3	.	,	,	,	,	,	,	, ,	,
AMJ	4	.	,	,	,	,	,	,	, ,	,
JAS	5	.	,	,	,	,	,	,	, ,	,
OND	6	.	,	,	,	,	,	,	, ,	,
JFM	7	.	,	,	,	,	,	,	, ,	,
AMJ	8	.	,	,	,	,	,	,	, ,	,
JAS	9	.	,	,	,	,	,	,	, ,	,
OND	10	.	,	,	,	,	,	,	, ,	,
JFM	11	.	,	,	,	,	,	,	, ,	,
AMJ	12	.	,	,	,	,	,	,	, ,	,

FORECASTS: ECONOMIC AND SEASONAL INDICES

Period of Year	AMJ	JAS	OND	AMJ	JAS	OND	JFM	AMJ	JAS	OND	JFM	AMJ	JAS	OND	JFM	AMJ
Period No.	0	T1	T2	0	1	2	3	4	5	6	7	8	9	10	11	12
Forecast, Econ. Index	100	100	95	100	100	95	93	90	95	97	100	100	103	105	107	107
Changes (if any)																
Seasonal Index	100	95	115	100	95	115	90	100	95	115	90	100	95	115	90	100
Changes (if any)																

* The individual team member should enter his/her team's consolidated decisions for each quarter on this sheet.

TABLE 53 (continued)

MASTER COPY–to be detached and handed in at end of Game

EXECUTIVE GAME–DECISION SHEET*

Firm No. __________

Periods _____ - _____ Model No. _____
Periods _____ - _____ Model No. _____

Period of Year	Period No.	Price $	Marketing Budget $	R & D Budget $	Maintenance Budget $	Prod. Vol. Sch. Maximums: Model 1 1.4xCY1 Model 2 3.0xCY1 units	Investment in Robotics $	Investment in Plant & Equipment $	Purchase of Materials $	Dividend Declared (Max: owners' equity minus $9,000,000 $
AMJ	12	.	,	,	,	,	,	,	, ,	,
JAS	13	.	,	,	,	,	,	,	, ,	,
OND	14	.	,	,	,	,	,	,	, ,	,
AMJ	15	.	,	,	,	,	,	,	, ,	,
JAS	16	.	,	,	,	,	,	,	, ,	,
		.	,	,	,	,	,	,	, ,	,
		.	,	,	,	,	,	,	, ,	,
		.	,	,	,	,	,	,	, ,	,
		.	,	,	,	,	,	,	, ,	,
		.	,	,	,	,	,	,	, ,	,
		.	,	,	,	,	,	,	, ,	,
		.	,	,	,	,	,	,	, ,	,
		.	,	,	,	,	,	,	, ,	,
		.	,	,	,	,	,	,	, ,	,
		.	,	,	,	,	,	,	, ,	,
		.	,	,	,	,	,	,	, ,	,

FORECASTS: ECONOMIC AND SEASONAL INDICES

Period of Year	AMJ	JAS	OND	JFM	AMJ	JAS										
Period No.	12	13	14	15	16	17										
Forecast, Econ. Index	107	105	104	102	102	100										
Changes (if any)																
Seasonal Index	100	95	115	90	100	95										
Changes (if any)																

* The individual team member should enter his/her team's consolidated decisions for each quarter on this sheet.

TABLE 54
WORK SHEET FOR ANALYSIS OF OPERATIONS

-to be detached and handed in at the end of the Game-the individual team member should enter his/her team's consolidated decision and forecasts on this sheet each quarter.

Firm No. _________ Periods _____ - _____ Model # ____ Periods _____ - _____ Model # ____

	Trial Period 2		Trial Period 1		Period 0
	Actual	Forecast	Actual	Forecast	Actual
I (a) Price Index (Period 0=100%)/(b) Forecast, Annual Change (%)	/	/	/	/	100.0/
II (a) Calendar Quarter/(b) Seasonal Index (Average Period=100%)	OND/	OND/	JAS/	JAS/	AMJ/100
III Economic Index (Period=100%)					100
IV (a) Inv. Tax Cr. %/(b) Surtax %/(c) PI & Eq. Depr. %/(d) Robotics Depr. %	/ / /	/ / /	/ / /	/ / /	/ / /
1 (a) Firm's Price/(b) Average Industry Price ($)	/	/	/	/	25.60 /25.60
2 Total Industry Sales - in units (not dollars)					
3 Market Potential (units)					109,720
4 Sales Volume (units)					109,720
5 Percent Share of Industry Sales (%)					
6 Production, This Quarter (units)					100,000
7 (a) Labor Cost per Unit/(b) Material Cost per Unit ($)	/	/	/	/	5.74/6.31
8 Inventory, Finished Goods (units)					12, 750
9 Plant Capacity, Next Quarter (units)					104,643
10 INCOME (and expense) STATEMENT ($)					
11 Receipts, Sales Revenue					2,808,832
12 Expenses, Marketing Expense					200,000
13 Research and Development Expense					100,000
14 Administration Expense					278,000
15 Maintenance Expense					75,000
16 Labor Expense					573,939
17 Materials Expense					630,667
18 Reduction, Finished Goods Inventory Value					116,638
19 Plant and Equipment Depreciation					183,125
20 Robotics Depreciation					0
21 Finished Goods Carrying Costs					25,500
22 Raw Materials Carrying Costs					41,533
23 Ordering Costs					50,000

24 Shifts Change Costs					0
25 Investment Expenses					25,000
26 Financing Charges and Penalties					0
27 Sundries Expenses					82,000
28 Total Expenses					2,381,402
29 Profit Before Income Taxes					427,430
30 Income Tax					145,326
31 Net Profit After Income Tax					282,104
32 Dividends Paid					53,000
33 Addition to Owners' Equity					229,104
34 CASH FLOW STATEMENT ($)					
35 Receipts, Sales Revenue					2,808,832
36 Disbursements, Cash Expense					1,450,972
37 Income Tax					145,326
38 Dividends Paid					53,000
39 Robotics Investments					0
40 Plant and Equipment Investments					500,000
41 Materials Purchased					1,000,000
42 Total Disbursements					3,149,298
43 Addition to Cash Assets					-340,466
44 FINANCIAL STATEMENT ($)					
45 Net Assets, Cash					1.022,000
46 Inventory Value, Finished Goods					153,000
47 Inventory Value, Materials					1,200,000
48 Robotics Book Value					0
49 Plant and Equipment Book Value					7,325,000
50 Owners' Equity					9,700,000
51 Plant and Equipment Replacement Value					7,325,000
52 Robotics Replacement Value					0
53 Owners' Economic Equity					9,700,000

TABLE 54 (continued)
WORK SHEET FOR ANALYSIS OF OPERATIONS

-to be detached and handed in at the end of the Game-the individual team member should enter his/her team's consolidated decision and forecasts on this sheet each quarter.

Periods _____ - _____ Model # ____ Periods _____ - _____ Model # ____	Period 1 Forecast	Actual	Period 2 Forecast	Actual	Period 3 Forecast	Actual
I (a) Price Index (Period 0=100%)/(b) Forecast, Annual Change (%)	/	/	/	/	/	/
II (a) Calendar Quarter/(b) Seasonal Index (Average Period=100%)	JAS/	JAS/	OND/	OND/	JFM/	JFM/
III Economic Index (Period=100%)						
IV (a) Inv. Tax Cr. %/(b) Surtax %/(c) PI & Eq. Depr. %/(d) Robotics Depr. %	/ / /	/ / /	/ / /	/ / /	/ / /	/ / /
1 (a) Firm's Price/(b) Average Industry Price ($)	/	/	/	/	/	/
2 Total Industry Sales - in units (not dollars)						
3 Market Potential (units)						
4 Sales Volume (units)						
5 Percent Share of Industry Sales (%)						
6 Production, This Quarter (units)						
7 (a) Labor Cost per Unit/(b) Material Cost per Unit ($)	/	/	/	/	/	/
8 Inventory, Finished Goods (units)						
9 Plant Capacity, Next Quarter (units)						
10 INCOME (and expense) STATEMENT ($)						
11 Receipts, Sales Revenue						
12 Expenses, Marketing Expense						
13 Research and Development Expense						
14 Administration Expense						
15 Maintenance Expense						
16 Labor Expense						
17 Materials Expense						
18 Reduction, Finished Goods Inventory Value						
19 Plant and Equipment Depreciation						
20 Robotics Depreciation						
21 Finished Goods Carrying Costs						
22 Raw Materials Carrying Costs						
23 Ordering Costs						

24 Shifts Change Costs						
25 Investment Expenses						
26 Financing Charges and Penalties						
27 Sundries Expenses						
28 Total Expenses						
29 Profit Before Income Taxes						
30 Income Tax						
31 Net Profit After Income Tax						
32 Dividends Paid						
33 Addition to Owners' Equity						
34 CASH FLOW STATEMENT ($)						
35 Receipts, Sales Revenue						
36 Disbursements, Cash Expense						
37 Income Tax						
38 Dividends Paid						
39 Robotics Investments						
40 Plant and Equipment Investments						
41 Materials Purchased						
42 Total Disbursements						
43 Addition to Cash Assets						
44 FINANCIAL STATEMENT ($)						
45 Net Assets, Cash						
46 Inventory Value, Finished Goods						
47 Inventory Value, Materials						
48 Robotics Book Value						
49 Plant and Equipment Book Value						
50 Owners' Equity						
51 Plant and Equipment Replacement Value						
52 Robotics Replacement Value						
53 Owners' Economic Equity						

TABLE 54 (continued)
WORK SHEET FOR ANALYSIS OF OPERATIONS

-to be detached and handed in at the end of the Game-the individual team member should enter his/her team's consolidated decision and forecasts on this sheet each quarter.

Periods _____ - _____ Model # ____ Periods _____ - _____ Model # ____	Period 4		Period 5		Period 6	
	Forecast	Actual	Forecast	Actual	Forecast	Actual
I (a) Price Index (Period 0=100%)/(b) Forecast, Annual Change (%)	/	/	/	/	/	/
II (a) Calendar Quarter/(b) Seasonal Index (Average Period=100%)	AMJ/	AMJ/	JAS/	JAS/	OND/	OND/
III Economic Index (Period=100%)						
IV (a) Inv. Tax Cr. %/(b) Surtax %/(c) PI & Eq. Depr. %/(d) Robotics Depr. %	/ / /	/ / /	/ / /	/ / /	/ / /	/ / /
1 (a) Firm's Price/(b) Average Industry Price ($)	/	/	/	/	/	/
2 Total Industry Sales - in units (not dollars)						
3 Market Potential (units)						
4 Sales Volume (units)						
5 Percent Share of Industry Sales (%)						
6 Production, This Quarter (units)						
7 (a) Labor Cost per Unit/(b) Material Cost per Unit ($)	/	/	/	/	/	/
8 Inventory, Finished Goods (units)						
9 Plant Capacity, Next Quarter (units)						
10 INCOME (and expense) STATEMENT ($)						
11 Receipts, Sales Revenue						
12 Expenses, Marketing Expense						
13 Research and Development Expense						
14 Administration Expense						
15 Maintenance Expense						
16 Labor Expense						
17 Materials Expense						
18 Reduction, Finished Goods Inventory Value						
19 Plant and Equipment Depreciation						
20 Robotics Depreciation						
21 Finished Goods Carrying Costs						
22 Raw Materials Carrying Costs						
23 Ordering Costs						

24 Shifts Change Costs						
25 Investment Expenses						
26 Financing Charges and Penalties						
27 Sundries Expenses						
28 Total Expenses						
29 Profit Before Income Taxes						
30 Income Tax						
31 Net Profit After Income Tax						
32 Dividends Paid						
33 Addition to Owners' Equity						
34 CASH FLOW STATEMENT ($)						
35 Receipts, Sales Revenue						
36 Disbursements, Cash Expense						
37 Income Tax						
38 Dividends Paid						
39 Robotics Investments						
40 Plant and Equipment Investments						
41 Materials Purchased						
42 Total Disbursements						
43 Addition to Cash Assets						
44 FINANCIAL STATEMENT ($)						
45 Net Assets, Cash						
46 Inventory Value, Finished Goods						
47 Inventory Value, Materials						
48 Robotics Book Value						
49 Plant and Equipment Book Value						
50 Owners' Equity						
51 Plant and Equipment Replacement Value						
52 Robotics Replacement Value						
53 Owners' Economic Equity						

TABLE 54 (continued)
WORK SHEET FOR ANALYSIS OF OPERATIONS

-to be detached and handed in at the end of the Game-the individual team member should enter his/her team's consolidated decision and forecasts on this sheet each quarter.

Periods _____ - _____ Model # ____ Periods _____ - _____ Model # ____	Period 7 Forecast	Period 7 Actual	Period 8 Forecast	Period 8 Actual	Period 9 Forecast	Period 9 Actual
I (a) Price Index (Period 0=100%)/(b) Forecast, Annual Change (%)	/	/	/	/	/	/
II (a) Calendar Quarter/(b) Seasonal Index (Average Period=100%)	JFM/	JFM/	AMJ/	AMJ/	JAS/	JAS/
III Economic Index (Period=100%)						
IV (a) Inv. Tax Cr. %/(b) Surtax %/(c) PI & Eq. Depr. %/(d) Robotics Depr. %	/ / /	/ / /	/ / /	/ / /	/ / /	/ / /
1 (a) Firm's Price/(b) Average Industry Price ($)	/	/	/	/	/	/
2 Total Industry Sales - in units (not dollars)						
3 Market Potential (units)						
4 Sales Volume (units)						
5 Percent Share of Industry Sales (%)						
6 Production, This Quarter (units)						
7 (a) Labor Cost per Unit/(b) Material Cost per Unit ($)	/	/	/	/	/	/
8 Inventory, Finished Goods (units)						
9 Plant Capacity, Next Quarter (units)						
10 INCOME (and expense) STATEMENT ($)						
11 Receipts, Sales Revenue						
12 Expenses, Marketing Expense						
13 Research and Development Expense						
14 Administration Expense						
15 Maintenance Expense						
16 Labor Expense						
17 Materials Expense						
18 Reduction, Finished Goods Inventory Value						
19 Plant and Equipment Depreciation						
20 Robotics Depreciation						
21 Finished Goods Carrying Costs						
22 Raw Materials Carrying Costs						
23 Ordering Costs						

24 Shifts Change Costs						
25 Investment Expenses						
26 Financing Charges and Penalties						
27 Sundries Expenses						
28 Total Expenses						
29 Profit Before Income Taxes						
30 Income Tax						
31 Net Profit After Income Tax						
32 Dividends Paid						
33 Addition to Owners' Equity						
34 CASH FLOW STATEMENT ($)						
35 Receipts, Sales Revenue						
36 Disbursements, Cash Expense						
37 Income Tax						
38 Dividends Paid						
39 Robotics Investments						
40 Plant and Equipment Investments						
41 Materials Purchased						
42 Total Disbursements						
43 Addition to Cash Assets						
44 FINANCIAL STATEMENT ($)						
45 Net Assets, Cash						
46 Inventory Value, Finished Goods						
47 Inventory Value, Materials						
48 Robotics Book Value						
49 Plant and Equipment Book Value						
50 Owners' Equity						
51 Plant and Equipment Replacement Value						
52 Robotics Replacement Value						
53 Owners' Economic Equity						

TABLE 54 (continued)
WORK SHEET FOR ANALYSIS OF OPERATIONS

-to be detached and handed in at the end of the Game-the individual team member should enter his/her team's consolidated decision and forecasts on this sheet each quarter.

Periods _____ - _____ Model # ____ Periods _____ - _____ Model # ____	Period 10 Forecast	Actual	Period 11 Forecast	Actual	Period 12 Forecast	Actual
I (a) Price Index (Period 0=100%)/(b) Forecast, Annual Change (%)	/	/	/	/	/	/
II (a) Calendar Quarter/(b) Seasonal Index (Average Period=100%)	OND/	OND/	JFM/	JFM/	AMJ/	AMJ/
III Economic Index (Period=100%)						
IV (a) Inv. Tax Cr. %/(b) Surtax %/(c) PI & Eq. Depr. %/(d) Robotics Depr. %	/ / /	/ / /	/ / /	/ / /	/ / /	/ / /
1 (a) Firm's Price/(b) Average Industry Price ($)	/	/	/	/	/	/
2 Total Industry Sales - in units (not dollars)						
3 Market Potential (units)						
4 Sales Volume (units)						
5 Percent Share of Industry Sales (%)						
6 Production, This Quarter (units)						
7 (a) Labor Cost per Unit/(b) Material Cost per Unit ($)	/	/	/	/	/	/
8 Inventory, Finished Goods (units)						
9 Plant Capacity, Next Quarter (units)						
10 INCOME (and expense) STATEMENT ($)						
11 Receipts, Sales Revenue						
12 Expenses, Marketing Expense						
13 Research and Development Expense						
14 Administration Expense						
15 Maintenance Expense						
16 Labor Expense						
17 Materials Expense						
18 Reduction, Finished Goods Inventory Value						
19 Plant and Equipment Depreciation						
20 Robotics Depreciation						
21 Finished Goods Carrying Costs						
22 Raw Materials Carrying Costs						
23 Ordering Costs						

24 Shifts Change Costs						
25 Investment Expenses						
26 Financing Charges and Penalties						
27 Sundries Expenses						
28 Total Expenses						
29 Profit Before Income Taxes						
30 Income Tax						
31 Net Profit After Income Tax						
32 Dividends Paid						
33 Addition to Owners' Equity						
34 CASH FLOW STATEMENT ($)						
35 Receipts, Sales Revenue						
36 Disbursements, Cash Expense						
37 Income Tax						
38 Dividends Paid						
39 Robotics Investments						
40 Plant and Equipment Investments						
41 Materials Purchased						
42 Total Disbursements						
43 Addition to Cash Assets						
44 FINANCIAL STATEMENT ($)						
45 Net Assets, Cash						
46 Inventory Value, Finished Goods						
47 Inventory Value, Materials						
48 Robotics Book Value						
49 Plant and Equipment Book Value						
50 Owners' Equity						
51 Plant and Equipment Replacement Value						
52 Robotics Replacement Value						
53 Owners' Economic Equity						

TABLE 54 (continued)
WORK SHEET FOR ANALYSIS OF OPERATIONS

-to be detached and handed in at the end of the Game-the individual team member should enter his/her team's consolidated decision and forecasts on this sheet each quarter.

Periods _____ - _____ Model # ____ Periods _____ - _____ Model # ____	Period 13		Period 14		Period 15	
	Forecast	Actual	Forecast	Actual	Forecast	Actual
I (a) Price Index (Period 0=100%)/(b) Forecast, Annual Change (%)	/	/	/	/	/	/
II (a) Calendar Quarter/(b) Seasonal Index (Average Period=100%)	JAS/	JAS/	OND/	OND/	JFM/	JFM/
III Economic Index (Period=100%)						
IV (a) Inv. Tax Cr. %/(b) Surtax %/(c) PI & Eq. Depr. %/(d) Robotics Depr. %	/ / /	/ / /	/ / /	/ / /	/ / /	/ / /
1 (a) Firm's Price/(b) Average Industry Price ($)	/	/	/	/	/	/
2 Total Industry Sales - in units (not dollars)						
3 Market Potential (units)						
4 Sales Volume (units)						
5 Percent Share of Industry Sales (%)						
6 Production, This Quarter (units)						
7 (a) Labor Cost per Unit/(b) Material Cost per Unit ($)	/	/	/	/	/	/
8 Inventory, Finished Goods (units)						
9 Plant Capacity, Next Quarter (units)						
10 INCOME (and expense) STATEMENT ($)						
11 Receipts, Sales Revenue						
12 Expenses, Marketing Expense						
13 Research and Development Expense						
14 Administration Expense						
15 Maintenance Expense						
16 Labor Expense						
17 Materials Expense						
18 Reduction, Finished Goods Inventory Value						
19 Plant and Equipment Depreciation						
20 Robotics Depreciation						
21 Finished Goods Carrying Costs						
22 Raw Materials Carrying Costs						
23 Ordering Costs						

24 Shifts Change Costs						
25 Investment Expenses						
26 Financing Charges and Penalties						
27 Sundries Expenses						
28 Total Expenses						
29 Profit Before Income Taxes						
30 Income Tax						
31 Net Profit After Income Tax						
32 Dividends Paid						
33 Addition to Owners' Equity						
34 CASH FLOW STATEMENT ($)						
35 Receipts, Sales Revenue						
36 Disbursements, Cash Expense						
37 Income Tax						
38 Dividends Paid						
39 Robotics Investments						
40 Plant and Equipment Investments						
41 Materials Purchased						
42 Total Disbursements						
43 Addition to Cash Assets						
44 FINANCIAL STATEMENT ($)						
45 Net Assets, Cash						
46 Inventory Value, Finished Goods						
47 Inventory Value, Materials						
48 Robotics Book Value						
49 Plant and Equipment Book Value						
50 Owners' Equity						
51 Plant and Equipment Replacement Value						
52 Robotics Replacement Value						
53 Owners' Economic Equity						

TABLE 54 (continued)
WORK SHEET FOR ANALYSIS OF OPERATIONS

-to be detached and handed in at the end of the Game-the individual team member should enter his/her team's consolidated decision and forecasts on this sheet each quarter.

Periods _____ - _____ Model # ____
Periods _____ - _____ Model # ____

	Period 16 Forecast	Actual				
I (a) Price Index (Period 0=100%)/(b) Forecast, Annual Change (%)	/	/				
II (a) Calendar Quarter/(b) Seasonal Index (Average Period=100%)	AMJ/	AMJ/				
III Economic Index (Period=100%)						
IV (a) Inv. Tax Cr. %/(b) Surtax %/(c) PI & Eq. Depr. %/(d) Robotics Depr. %	/ / /	/ / /				
1 (a) Firm's Price/(b) Average Industry Price ($)	/	/				
2 Total Industry Sales - in units (not dollars)						
3 Market Potential (units)						
4 Sales Volume (units)						
5 Percent Share of Industry Sales (%)						
6 Production, This Quarter (units)						
7 (a) Labor Cost per Unit/(b) Material Cost per Unit ($)	/	/				
8 Inventory, Finished Goods (units)						
9 Plant Capacity, Next Quarter (units)						
10 INCOME (and expense) STATEMENT ($)						
11 Receipts, Sales Revenue						
12 Expenses, Marketing Expense						
13 Research and Development Expense						
14 Administration Expense						
15 Maintenance Expense						
16 Labor Expense						
17 Materials Expense						
18 Reduction, Finished Goods Inventory Value						
19 Plant and Equipment Depreciation						
20 Robotics Depreciation						
21 Finished Goods Carrying Costs						
22 Raw Materials Carrying Costs						
23 Ordering Costs						

24 Shifts Change Costs						
25 Investment Expenses						
26 Financing Charges and Penalties						
27 Sundries Expenses						
28 Total Expenses						
29 Profit Before Income Taxes						
30 Income Tax						
31 Net Profit After Income Tax						
32 Dividends Paid						
33 Addition to Owners' Equity						
34 CASH FLOW STATEMENT ($)						
35 Receipts, Sales Revenue						
36 Disbursements, Cash Expense						
37 Income Tax						
38 Dividends Paid						
39 Robotics Investments						
40 Plant and Equipment Investments						
41 Materials Purchased						
42 Total Disbursements						
43 Addition to Cash Assets						
44 FINANCIAL STATEMENT ($)						
45 Net Assets, Cash						
46 Inventory Value, Finished Goods						
47 Inventory Value, Materials						
48 Robotics Book Value						
49 Plant and Equipment Book Value						
50 Owners' Equity						
51 Plant and Equipment Replacement Value						
52 Robotics Replacement Value						
53 Owners' Economic Equity						

Index

J-K

L

M

N

O

P

Q

R

S

T

U

V

W

X-Z